A TOUCHSTONE BOOK
PUBLISHED BY SIMON & SCHUSTER INC.
NEW YORK LONDON TORONTO SYDNEY TOKYO SINGAPORE

THE PULITZER PRIZES

1990

EDITED BY

KENDALL J. WILLS

TOUCHSTONE
Simon & Schuster Building
Rockefeller Center
1230 Avenue of the Americas
New York, New York 10020

TOUCHSTONE and colophon are
registered trademarks of Simon & Schuster Inc.

Designed by Bonni Leon
Manufactured in the United States of America

10   9   8   7   6   5   4   3   2   1

Library of Congress Cataloging-in-Publication Data
The Pulitzer prizes 1990/edited by Kendall J. Wills.
      p.   cm.
   "A Touchstone book."
   1. Journalism—United States.   2. Pulitzer prizes.   I. Wills,
Kendall J.
PN4726.P825   1990
071'.3—dc20   90-10255
                                                  CIP

ISBN 0-671-72584-X

(continued on page 491)

CONTENTS

INTRODUCTION

If the news of the year could be compressed into one newspaper, with the top writers, photographers and editorial cartoonists from papers all over the country contributing their best work, what a treasure that paper would be. In a sense, *The Pulitzer Prizes, 1990* is that newspaper.

With datelines from Beijing, China, to Buffalo, New York; from Washington, D.C., to Washington, North Carolina; from Eastern Europe to Albuquerque, New Mexico; from Philadelphia and Pottstown, Pennsylvania, to Colorado Springs, Colorado; from St. Paul, Minnesota, to Valdez, Alaska, and San Jose, Los Angeles, San Francisco and Oakland, California, here are all the 1990 Pulitzer Prize–winning news and feature stories, commentary, editorials, photographs and political cartoons.

The past year unleashed a torrent of dramatic news. Revolutionary changes disrupted decades-old political alignments in Eastern Europe; a tragic oil spill by the *Exxon Valdez* supertanker dealt enormous environmental damage to huge areas of the Alaska coast; Californians were rocked by the destructive force of the earth when a major quake struck the Bay Area; and shock waves were felt around the world as soldiers opened fire on pro-democracy demonstrators in China.

These stories are told here by some of the country's best journalists.

There are also less dramatic but equally important stories that helped shape the way we look at the country and ourselves. Revelations by Tamar Stieber of *The Albuquerque Journal,* for instance, about the health dangers of the over-the-counter dietary supplement L-Tryptophan helped bring about a federal ban on the sale of the product.

Also in this collection, two reporters, Lou Kilzer and Chris Ison of the *Minneapolis–St. Paul Star Tribune,* uncover a network of businessmen with close ties to members of the St. Paul Fire Department, which allegedly gained financially from a series of suspicious fires.

Thomas J. Hylton, editorial writer for *The Pottstown* (Pa.) *Mercury*, leads a crusade for the successful passage of a bond issue that would help protect farmland from the encroachment of developers and preserve a way of life.

The *Washington* (N.C.) *Daily News*, with its staff of only eight people, reveals the breach of public trust that residents of the small community had placed in their elected officials, who kept from them the important information that their water was contaminated.

Dave Curtin of the *Colorado Springs Gazette Telegraph* spent six months trailing burn victims and sensitively tells how two disfigured children and their community got reacquainted.

Los Angeles Times sports columnist Jim Murray, from the unique vantage point of some 30 years on the job, offers commentary on sports, yes, but on human nature, too.

From the corridors of power in Washington to the interiors of monied institutions in New York, *The Washington Post* reporters Steve Coll and David A. Vise profile John S. R. Shad, the son of a launderer who rose to become Wall Street's "top cop."

Putting his critic's stamp of approval or rejection on the architecture of the Bay Area, *San Francisco Chronicle* critic Allan Temko calls for a new brand of thinking, with national and international input, on plans for the Presidio, "the finest urban site in the world."

No newspaper is complete, and this special volume is no exception, without editorial cartoons. The caricatures drawn by Tom Toles of *The Buffalo News* help deflate the images of would-be environmentalists, educators and other "public servants."

This anthology—the "Extra!" edition newspaper—offers something that cannot be found in any of the newspapers that contributed prize-winning material. Here, in essays that introduce each chapter, readers can go behind the scenes and hear in the words of the journalists how they made their stories, photographs or cartoons prize-winners.

What is evident from these essays is that instinct, a hunch, tenacity, plain hard work and maybe even a little luck at being in the right place at the right time played a part—small comfort to the teams of editors at some papers who try to cook up potential Pulitzer Prize—winning stories.

Readers will learn what makes journalists pursue certain leads and not let go until they have the answers for which they are looking. In the case of the *Washington* (N.C.) *Daily News,* for example, the editor noticed a simple statement on the back of his water bill that made him wonder about the quality of water he and other residents were drinking. He assigned a reporter to follow up.

Gilbert M. Gaul, a reporter with *The Philadelphia Inquirer* who regularly volunteered to donate blood, started asking himself a few basic questions about what happened to the blood he and others donated. Those questions led to an 18-month search that identified a multibillion-dollar business in which blood was traded like any other commodity.

"Time and time again," Gaul writes, "blood banks did not tell donors that their blood might be sold to another center hundreds or thousands of miles away. Nor were donors told of the bidding process for blood on the spot market, which is not unlike the oil or soybean commodities market."

Similarly, Lou Kilzer and Chris Ison didn't have any secret sources or tip-offs to instigate their articles on arson in St. Paul. Instead, while poring over an official report that had been sealed by court order for 10 years, the reporters noticed something strange.

"Buried in those hundreds of pages were several mentions of arson," they write, "and evidence of a curious loan from the city's fire chief that helped launch a local public insurance adjusting firm years before." Some of their painstaking investigation turned up pay dirt. Other times, hours of effort revealed nothing, such as when they decided to canoe across a lake to avoid guard dogs at the home of one of the story's subjects.

"All the glamour was gone three sweaty hours later when we paddled back after negotiating a half-dozen thickly wooded tributaries with nary a glimpse of the house," they relate.

Nicholas D. Kristof and Sheryl WuDunn tried to write objectively in their dispatches for *The New York Times* about the standoff between Chinese government troops and pro-democracy protesters in Tiananmen Square. The deadlock was broken when the troops started firing on the crowds of protesters. "It is quite difficult," the husband-wife team writes, "to feel neutral about people who are shooting at you."

Despite the firing, Kristof headed toward Tiananmen Square on a bicycle. "It was a crazy bicycle ride," he recalls, "swerving madly around tank traps, bullets overhead, the road lit by burning tanks, and this inescapable feeling that any sensible person would be rushing just as madly in the opposite direction."

Many of the writers recall pursuing their stories relentlessly, despite danger to their own safety or criticism from some of those they had to interview. Tamar Stieber recalls that when people hung up the phone on her or called her a "pit bull," it only made her commitment to pursue the story greater. One doctor she interviewed even said publication of her findings of a possible connection between L-Tryptophan and a spate of illnesses would be "unethical."

Other subjects of stories tried unsuccessfully to use their influence with publishers or editors to "kill" a story or have the reporters called off. The Pulitzer awards are a tribute to the resolve of the press to let the facts guide the investigations.

Some of the prize-winning articles stand out because the reporters left the "pack" of national and international journalists who were covering a story and sought a perspective the others had missed. David Boardman, assistant city editor at *The Seattle Times,* describes how his team of reporters beat the competition when the *Exxon Valdez* started leaking oil in what would become the worst oil spill in the country's history.

"They were among the first to portray the magnitude of the disaster, to cut through Exxon's public-relations pablum and Alaska state officials' hysteria," Boardman writes. "They found their truth by leaving the pack of journalists in Valdez—which itself was unscarred by the spill—and finding their way to islands stained purple-black with the viscous oil."

These and other "stories behind the story" offer rare glimpses into the journalists' thinking that went into the articles before they could be published. They describe the pitfalls, the dead ends, the false starts, the deadline pressures and finally the successful pulling together of information into gripping news stories that shape our perception of the world.

This book is a permanent record of some of the best achievements of the journalism profession in the last year. It also stands as a tribute to the winners, who, collectively, make this volume a lasting treasury of great reporting and writing.

Michael Macor, a photographer for *The Tribune* of Oakland, Ca., who found himself reacting to the chaos and devastation caused by the California earthquake, voiced what many of these journalists must have felt about their historical role.

"There was no way to set the stuff up," Macor said of the rapid sequence of events. "I was recording history as best I could."

Indeed, here is the most recent chapter in our nation's—and the world's—history.

Kendall J. Wills
Plain, Wisconsin
1990

THE PULITZER PRIZES

PULITZER PRIZE BOARD

ONE

NOT A DROP TO DRINK
and
THE BLOOD BROKERS

1990 WINNERS IN THE PUBLIC SERVICE CATEGORY

"For a distinguished example of meritorious public service by a newspaper through the use of its journalistic resources . . . a gold medal."

Washington (N.C.) Daily News
Staff

The Philadelphia Inquirer
Gilbert M. Gaul

For eight years, public officials kept silent about a potential cancer-causing substance that had contaminated the drinking water in Washington, North Carolina. The *Washington Daily News* decided it was time someone told the public the truth.

In the summer of 1989, Bill Coughlin, the editor of the *Washington* (N.C) *Daily News,* was paying his home water bill in person at city hall. As he did, he noticed a new statement on the back of the bill: The town had been testing for chemicals in its water system.

When he got back to the office, Coughlin called the notice to the attention of Betty Gray, one of four reporters on the small afternoon daily, circulation 10,500.

Gray, digging intermittently as her other duties permitted, obtained a list of the 42 chemicals in the water and began checking it with private and state toxicologists. She was told that one of the chemicals was carcinogenic and that it was in the water far in excess of the level the U.S. Environmental Protection Agency considered safe.

She learned that the local office of the state environmental agency had been using city water as a control in checking other water throughout the region. She obtained copies of memos showing that the agency had been advised by its home office in Raleigh that its control water over a period of months appeared to be contaminated.

None of this had been made public.

Gray also learned that residents of Washington, like those in many small towns in the United States, were unprotected by the federal Safe Drinking Water Act, which exempts communities of less than 10,000. Just under 10,000 were hooked up to the city system.

Because of that same exemption, Gray discovered, 56,000 water treatment plants serving millions of people across the United States were not protected by the Environmental Protection Agency. Of those plants, 104 were in North Carolina.

When she felt she had enough information to confront city officials, Gray met with City Manager Bruce Radford in his office on Wednesday, September 13. The interview was at 10:30 a.m., with press time less than two hours away. Radford broke off their talk but promised to see her again before noon.

At 11 a.m., the city manager appeared in the newspaper office with a legal notice that he said he wanted to run in the classified advertising section. Told that those pages already were on the press, he asked that it be run that day as a display ad. It also was too late for that.

He left the notice on the editor's desk and returned to his office for the interview with Gray. The notice admitted publicly for the first time the presence of "levels of certain chemicals which exceeded EPA recommendations" in the city's water supply.

The front page was made over to lead the paper with Gray's interview. She returned to the office at noon. The press was held for half an hour while she sent out her story in takes.

Reporter Mike Voss was assigned to join Gray on the story.

In an interview with Voss published the following day, Radford, the city manager, said the city had known for three years of excessive levels of the cancer-causing chemical in its water supply, although it had not made the information public.

But Mayor J. Stancil Lilley, in an interview with Voss, said he and the city council had known of the problem for only "a week . . . or a little over."

Radford, declaring that the water was safe, appeared on television drinking a glass of city water to refute what the TV newscast called unconfirmed reports of contamination.

That was before the city released test results showing levels of carcinogens in the water that averaged nine times the EPA's safety limit at 10 locations around the city, including a drinking fountain on the second floor of city hall.

On Monday, following a telephone tip, the *Daily News* again hit pay dirt. The president of the local Coca-Cola Bottling Company said his firm had been alerted by the home office in Atlanta three or four years earlier that testing showed Washington water was contaminated. The company had alerted the city and started carbon filtering of its own supply.

The former city manager, reached by telephone in another city, confirmed the Coca-Cola report and said he had told the city council at the time of the problem.

Gray later obtained memos showing that the city had, in fact, known for eight years about the presence of carcinogens in the water. Three mayors, three city managers, the state and the EPA had known about the problem without advising the public because there were no regulations requiring them to do so.

On Wednesday, the *Daily News* obtained and published exclusively a state report that a second carcinogenic chemical had been found in city water that was combining with the first to produce such deadly concentrations that the water plant might have to be shut down.

Mayor Lilley complained that the newspaper's coverage was throwing the city into "turmoil" and appeared at its office to protest to the owner, a friend for many years. The coverage continued.

On Thursday, the state summoned city officials to a meeting to inform them that the combination of chemicals in the water was so dangerous that the cancer risk was an astounding one-in-250, not the one-in-10,000 that city officials had been citing or the one-in-1,000,000 that the EPA and the state considered safe.

"Our citizens are ready to hang us," the mayor said, again complaining about the information published in the *Daily News*.

"This is the biggest story to come out of your town," he was told by a state official. The official added: "The state was responding to direct questions from a reporter who knows what questions to ask . . . the state is not going to lie when questioned by a reporter."

On Friday, the state government told residents of the city of Washington not to drink the water, not to clean or cook fruits or vegetables with it, not to drink tea, coffee or lemonade made with it and not to take showers in it.

City schools turned off their drinking fountains and switched to paper plates and throwaway plastic forks and knives. The hospital announced that if other measures failed, it would sink its own well.

On Saturday, September 23, just 10 days after the *Washington Daily News* broke a story that city officials had been covering up for eight years, a U.S. Marine convoy rolled across the Pamlico River bridge into Washington and set up water wagons throughout the city to provide its residents with uncontaminated drinking water.

The scene was like conditions in some third world country.

On October 10, in an election that both winners and losers agreed turned on the water issue, the mayor and the majority of the city council were swept out of office to be replaced by newcomers pledged to do something about the water.

The city, after failing to act for eight years, took emergency measures that by November 22 enabled the state health director to announce that the drinking water was safe and to lift the water ban— just two months after it was issued.

The exclusive *Daily News* report that carcinogens were tainting the water supplies of 13 other North Carolina communities was disseminated throughout the state by The Associated Press. At this writing, seven of those communities have reduced the contaminants to safe levels. The state is working with the others to eliminate the hazards.

In addition, both state and federal officials have announced that as a result of the situation uncovered in Washington, N.C., they are changing their regulations to assure that it cannot happen again.

Dr. Ron Levine, the state health director, said he will recommend to the North Carolina Health Commission that the state require testing of water in all North Carolina towns, even where it is not required by the EPA.

Michael Leonard, chief of the drinking water section of the EPA office in Atlanta, told the *Daily News* that the U.S. Environmental Protection Agency is reviewing its requirements for the water supplies of all smaller U.S. communities in light of Washington's water problems.

New regulations could be in place in 1991 or 1992 that extend environmental safeguards to millions of Americans served by the 56,000 water treatment plants not now covered, he said.

—The Editors
Washington (N.C.) *Daily News*

CITY WATER SUPPLY SAID TO BE HAZARDOUS

WEDNESDAY, SEPTEMBER 13, 1989

BY BETTY GRAY

Scientists with the state Division of Environmental Health are in Washington today investigating a cancer-causing chemical that has made its way into the city's drinking water supply source, the Daily News has learned.

But a spokesman for the N.C. Department of Environment, Health and Natural Resources said no one is in danger from drinking the water.

"The consistency of the water is the same," City Manager Bruce Radford said in an interview today. "We have been drinking water from the same source for 40 years and we don't have any cancer-related deaths so far."

If individuals are concerned they can supplement city water with water from an alternative source or they can boil their water to eliminate the chemical, said Fred Hill, water quality consultant with the state health division.

Hill will be in Washington today sampling water throughout the city. He will take the samples back to Raleigh where they will be tested.

Results of the tests should be announced by the city Friday, Radford said.

The state has found increased levels of trihalomethanes in the city's water source at Tranter's Creek. Water from a city-owned well on Slatestone Road is apparently not contaminated, Hill said.

The amount of trihalomethanes in the water has been about 937 parts per billion since April. The EPA sets limits of 100 parts per billion for cities of more than 10,000 people. A spokesman for the N.C. Environmental Defense Fund today said limits of 300 parts per billion are "of concern."

"Recent investigation of unregulated organic compounds in the

Washington city water supply have shown levels of certain chemicals which exceeded EPA recommendations," a statement from the city said.

"The U.S. Environmental Protection Agency . . . requires that certain water suppliers serving 10,000 people or more control the concentration of trihalomethanes in the water served to consumers," it said. "Trihalomethanes are a group of organic compounds, including chloroform and bromoform that are formed by the reaction of chlorine used in the water treatment process with certain organic compounds."

The organic compounds are naturally occurring substances in the water formed by the decay of plant and animal material, the report said.

EPA still is studying the health effects of trihalomethanes, but one test found that high doses of chloroform can cause cancer in rats and mice, the city said.

Therefore, EPA considers chloroform itself a potential carcinogen, the statement said. The agency also believes that the other trihalomethanes are implicated, by association, as potential carcinogens.

"The limit for total trihalomethane concentration is 100 parts per billion," the city said. "Samples taken from Washington's system during the past year have exceeded that level."

The city and its water department is "committed to providing the highest quality drinking water possible to its customers."

Eliminating chlorine, and so trihalomethanes, from water treatment is not a simple procedure, the city said. It reported that the water department has undertaken "an extensive treatability study of different disinfectants and treatments to determine how the trihalomethanes can be lowered to acceptable levels at the least possible cost to consumers."

STATE OFFICE INSTALLS BOTTLED WATER DISPENSERS

THURSDAY, SEPTEMBER 14, 1989

BY BETTY GRAY

While Washington officials were assuring residents city water was safe to drink, staff members of the state's Department of Environment, Health and Natural Resources were installing bottled water dispensers in their Carolina Avenue office.

Elevated amounts of trihalomethanes, a cancer-causing chemical, were known to be in the Washington water supply as long as three years ago, and the city was officially warned by test results in March.

Nothing was said in public about that report until inquiries about the city water supply were made yesterday by the Daily News.

But in a memo early last week, the supervisor of the state's environmental office here, Jim Mulligan, advised Raleigh that "as a preliminary precaution, while awaiting further advice from the Division of Health Services, bottled water dispensers are to be installed for the regional office."

His memo went to R. Paul Wilms, director of the state Division of Environmental Management.

Another memo written by Mulligan that same Monday, Sept. 11, by Rudy Smithwick, regional DEM hydrologist, said the staff at the division office had collected water samples from the water fountain and lavatory sink for several months.

The concentrations of trihalomethanes in the tap water at the Washington office exceeded limits suggested by the U.S. Environmental Protection Agency by 4 to 16 times, the memo said.

Dr. Kenneth Rudo, epidemiologist with the Division of Health Service, advised the Washington staff that "due to extremely high concentrations of chloroform . . . consumption of this supply should cease immediately," the memo said.

Smithwick's recommendation in his memo was "to advise all employees in this office not to consume the water until adequate treatment is provided to remove contaminants or until an alternative supply is provided such as bottled water."

Mulligan, when contacted by the Daily News yesterday, would not comment on the memos or recommendations.

COKE BOTTLER WARNED CITY OF POLLUTION

TUESDAY, SEPTEMBER 19, 1989

BY BETTY GRAY

Coca-Cola Bottling Co. of Washington has been filtering city water since its parent company several years ago alerted the local distributor of contamination in the water supply, a company official told the Daily News yesterday.

Officials with the local company met with then city manager Ralph Clark about trichloromethane after it came to the attention of the parent company three or four years ago, said Braxton B. Dawson, president of Coca-Cola Bottling of Washington, yesterday.

Coca-Cola does not bottle its product here but uses local water in making ice.

Clark, now city manager in Smithfield, told the Daily News he had spoken with Dawson about trichloromethanes in the city water supply and said he had brought this to the attention of the city council.

This is only one item in a growing chain of evidence indicating the city and the city council has known about trihalomethanes in its water supply for several years without telling the public about it.

The Washington City Council will hold a special meeting at 5 p.m. today in the city council chamber of the municipal building to discuss the city water supply. City Manager Bruce Radford, hospitalized for treatment of stomach troubles, will not attend.

Washington Mayor J. Stancil Lilley told the Daily News last week that the city council became aware of the problem "about a week ago or a little over," but it wanted more information before going public with it.

"We've known we had trichloromethanes," said city councilman Ursula F. Loy today.

The city council has been working toward building a new water treatment plant for several years and trichloromethanes are "one of the factors that was pushing us to do so," she said.

"We were concerned," Mrs. Loy said.

Mrs. Loy said the city council has met with Russell Waters, director of public works, and Jerry Cutler, supervisor of the water treatment plant, in open session on the city water supply.

"We have made no effort to hide this," Mrs. Loy said.

A search of city council minutes from 1985–87 revealed no discussion of trihalomethanes, a cancer-causing chemical, although plans for a larger water treatment plant were discussed in open session. Reporters who have covered council meetings recall no discussion of that problem.

Dawson said his company has "treated its water for several years." Coca-Cola uses a carbon filter to strain city water, and samples that are sent to the Atlanta office have shown no signs of trihalomethanes.

Carbon filters take the chemical out of the water. Dawson said the filters are expensive and are probably impractical for large uses such as a municipal water supply.

The information about trihalomethanes was not made public "because the City of Washington serves less than 10,000 water customers and the U.S. Environmental Protection Agency does not require that municipalities under 10,000 test or report levels of trihalomethanes," Radford, city manager, told the Daily News earlier this week.

Scientists with the state Division of Environmental Health were in Washington last week investigating the high amounts of trihalomethanes in the city's drinking water supply, including chloroform and carbon tetrachloride.

"Trihalomethanes" are a group of organic compounds, including chloroform and bromoform. They are formed when chlorine, used in the water treatment process, reacts with certain organic compounds. The organic compounds are naturally occurring substances in the water formed when plants and animals decay.

Chloroform has been linked to colon, liver, kidney and urological cancers, scientists believe.

Increased nutrients in the upper portions of Tranters Creek may have caused an increase in trihalomethanes in the city water, water plant supervisor Cutler told the Daily News today.

The main intake for the municipal surface water supply is on Tranters Creek near the Clarks Neck Road bridge, Cutler said. During the summer, however, when salt in the water increases, the city cannot use that intake.

It then begins taking water from its pumps at Latham Station on Tranters Creek near U.S. 264 east of Washington near the Pitt County line. The river upstream in Tranters Creek has more organic material, which reacts with the chlorine, forming trihalomethanes, Cutler said.

The county health director cautioned city residents about overreacting to the test results.

"We're a lot better at making a chemical test that sorts out parts per billion than we are at interpreting what they mean," said Beaufort County Health Director Gary Taylor.

Employees in the Washington office of the Department of Environment, Health and Natural Resources on Carolina Avenue are still using bottled water, said Lorraine Shinn, regional director.

"The situation is fairly serious," Ms. Shinn said. "I want to know why scientists around here have turned their coffee-makers off, but the city has not cautioned other people about drinking the waters."

Beaufort County Hospital is still using city water, a spokesman there said today.

Water samples taken by the state showed trihalomethane concentrations of 1,367 parts per billion at the state environmental office here and at the hospital of about 805 parts per billion. The Environmental Protection Agency's maximum limit for cities over 10,000 is 100 parts per billion.

ANOTHER TOXIC CHEMICAL FOUND IN HIGH QUANTITY

WEDNESDAY, SEPTEMBER 20, 1989

BY BETTY GRAY

Another toxic chemical has been found in Washington drinking water in concentrations considered so deadly that shutdown of the city's water treatment plant may be imminent, the Daily News has learned.

Scientists found the chemical, carbon tetrachloride, in city water in amounts up to seven times higher than the maximum allowed by the U.S. Environmental Protection Agency, said Dr. Kenneth Rudo, state toxicologist for the environmental epidemiology section of the N.C. Division of Health Services.

While chemicals in the water may be reduced by boiling, they are so toxic that inhaling the steam may be hazardous, it was learned.

"Boil the water, but don't inhale the stuff," Rudo said.

Carbon tetrachloride is one of eight substances regulated by the federal Safe Drinking Water Act. By exceeding EPA maximum limits for this chemical, the city could be subject to action ranging from fines to a shutdown of the city water system, said Michael Leonard, chief of the drinking water section for the EPA regional office in Atlanta.

Carbon tetrachloride is a "very toxic and deadly compound," one state environmental source said. "This is much more serious than trihalomethanes (found earlier)." Both are believed to cause cancer, and carbon tetrachloride is suspected of producing birth defects.

Tests revealed that drinking water on the second floor of city hall is seven times higher in carbon tetrachloride than the maximum allowable level and water at Beaufort County Hospital nearly three times that level.

The compliance order from the state will force the city to take early action, possibly by shutting down the water treatment plant and drilling groundwells for the entire city water supply, state officials said.

"We don't intend to wait a year," Rudo said. "We want to get you guys down there off that water."

Groundwater in the area is ample for the purpose and free of pollution, he said. Enough wells to replace the city's surface water supply could be drilled within two months, he estimated.

State scientists tested the city's water for a variety of chemicals at 10 sites last week. The increased carbon tetrachloride and trihalomethane was discovered during these tests, Rudo said.

Only drinking water supplied by the city's surface water plant, which draws water from Tranters Creek, a tributary of the Tar River west of the city, is contaminated by the two substances. The chemicals were not found in the city's groundwater well on Slatestone Road, Rudo said.

"Carbon tetrachloride" is an organic compound similar to trihalomethanes. It is known to cause cancer in laboratory animals and has been linked to cancer and birth, developmental and neurological disorders in humans.

"Trihalomethanes" are a group of organic compounds, including chloroform and bromoform. They are formed when chlorine, used in the water treatment process, reacts with certain organic material. The organic material occurs naturally in the water when plants and animals decay. Chloroform has been linked to colon, liver, kidney and urological cancers.

"Something's wrong with the chlorination process or with the source of organics," said Douglas N. Rader, senior scientist with the N.C. Environmental Defense Fund.

"Exposure to two cancer-causing chemicals will increase the risk," Rader said. "People ought to be upset about it."

Test results, made public by the state environmental epidemiology section yesterday, are to be sent to the state public water supply section today.

The city and its water treatment department should receive the test results along with a compliance order from the water section this week, Rudo said. The compliance order will ask the city to outline how it plans to eliminate carbon tetrachloride from its water system and how long it will take to do it.

The Safe Drinking Water Act is a federal law that addresses specific public health issues of two groups of chemicals—eight regulated and 36 unregulated—in drinking water, EPA's Leonard said. The Safe Drinking Water Act is enforced in North Carolina by the state health service.

Carbon tetrachloride is one of the eight regulated chemicals with a maximum allowable concentration of 5 parts per billion. Under federal law, this chemical must be reported by all cities over 3,000 population.

The EPA sets limits of 100 parts per billion for trihalomethanes, including chloroform, for cities of more than 10,000 people. The EPA does not require cities under 10,000 people to meet this limit.

Concentrations of carbon tetrachloride above the legal allowable limits were found in seven out of 10 samples taken by state scientists last week, Rudo said.

Water samples taken from Beaufort County Community College had carbon tetrachlorides of 0.8 parts per billion; Beaufort County Hospital, 12th Street, 13.8; Oakdale Cemetery, 7.3; Third and Bridge streets, 17.2 parts per billion; the Department of Environment, Health and Natural Resources, 20.2; Slatestone Road water well, undetectable; city hall, Market and Second streets, 36; elevated water tank, Third Street, 17.3; Third and Hudnell streets near Havens Gardens, less than 1; water treatment plant, 11.

Tests from the same 10 locations for trihalomethanes last week showed an average of about 964 parts per billion in tap water throughout the city.

The Slatestone Road well, which pumps water from the groundwater supply, showed "a safe level" of all chemicals tested, Rudo said.

"The well contained nothing that should cause any health problems to anybody," Rudo said.

EPA considers concentrations of twice the maximum limit as an "unreasonable risk of health," Leonard said. Because of this, when concentrations this high are found in public water supplies, the EPA usually requires cities to modify their water treatment process, increase their monitoring and "consider an alternate water supply."

This could include shutting the city's affected water supply system down and offering bottled water as a substitute, Leonard said.

As part of last week's tests, water from the city surface water plant was boiled for five minutes. This reduced chloroform and carbon tetrachloride to acceptable concentrations. However, vapors from the boiling water also present a serious health hazard, Rudo said.

"Until other solutions to the problems are implemented, the results of this test show that boiling the water for five minutes will remove the chloroform to a level that should not pose any health problems whatsoever and will eliminate the other contaminants," Rudo said.

"However, inhaling these chemicals could be as hazardous as drinking the water," he said. "So if you're going to boil the water, do it where you have some kind of exhaust system."

State officials should meet with city officials soon to work out a schedule of compliance with EPA limits. This schedule could range from one month to two years depending on the severity of the problem, said Wallace Venrick, chief of the public water supply section.

The state recently completed a compliance action against Elizabeth City which was notified about one year ago that it exceeded trihalomethane restrictions, Venrick said.

"Skewed results" from water samples taken by Division of Environmental Management staff in Washington first alerted state officials to the contamination of the city's water supply, a spokesman for the agency said last week.

When local staff members of the DEM tested for water quality in the Pamlico River and other waterways, they used Washington tap water as a "control" for the tests. The Washington water was intended to serve as an example of normal water.

But eight samples examined by DEM scientists in Raleigh taken over a six-month period turned up abnormal results for city water. At that point, when most results showed dramatically increased concentrations of trihalomethanes, the state stepped in.

STATE: CITY CANCER RISK COULD BE 1-IN-250

FRIDAY, SEPTEMBER 22, 1989

BY BETTY GRAY

GREENVILLE—The cancer risk from two toxic chemicals in Washington's contaminated water supply could be as high as one-in-250, not the much-quoted one-in-10,000, the state informed city officials in a dramatic confrontation here yesterday.

That means if 250 residents drank two litres of the water a day for 70 years, one person from that group would contract cancer from drinking the water—or 40 cases of cancer over the 70-year period in a city the size of Washington. No city in the state has ever been told its water supply contained such deadly amounts, state scientists said.

"You have a cancer risk way above what we consider a safe level," Dr. Kenneth Rudo, state toxicologist for the environmental epidemiology section of the N.C. Division of Health Services, said.

"We've never seen levels this high anywhere," said Wallace Vendrick, chief of the public water section, of the trihalomethanes found last week in the city's water supply.

"We've got to bring these levels down and we can't wait until January to do it," Venrick said.

The city is expected to have test results in January from a pilot water treatment study of using chemicals other than chlorine in treating water.

"If we go back and notify the schools and hospitals not to use our drinking water, then we set the community in a spin," said Washington Mayor Stancil Lilley. "The only thing we've been trying to do is calm our people."

No statistically accurate information on the level of cancer deaths in the city has been available either locally or from the state in response to queries over the past week. Compiling of those figures locally may be completed by next week, one source said.

The one-in-250 chance of contracting cancer stems from the combination of high levels of both trihalomethanes and carbon tetrachlorides believed to be in the city water supply, Rudo said yesterday.

From long-term exposure to just the trihalomethane chloroform in the water supply, residents have a one-in-2,000 chance of contracting the disease, Rudo said.

Rudo was one of 17 state and local officials meeting yesterday afternoon in the boardroom of the Greenville Utilities Commission to discuss what to do about dangerous chemicals found in the Washington water system in concentrations higher than state scientists have ever seen.

Scientists consider a one-in-1,000,000 chance an acceptable cancer risk, Rudo said. City Manager Bruce Radford has quoted the 1-in-10,000 figure several times in the past week.

Engineers for Rivers & Associates and Environmental Engineering and Technology, working with the city to design a new water treatment plant, are not sure anything can be done to the city's water plant within the next few months to bring the trihalomethanes down to a safe concentration.

State Health Director Ronald Levine planned to issue a report today on the health risks of drinking city water for the 30 days while a short-term solution to the excess trihalomethanes in the city water supply is being developed.

One recommendation may be that the city be supplied with bottled water until the problem is remedied.

In a heated exchange with state officials, Mayor Lilley said he was concerned that the state told the Daily News about carbon tetrachloride test results before it told the city.

"Somebody owes the City of Washington an apology," Lilley declared.

"This is the biggest story to come out of your town," Debbie Crane, public relations officer with the state Division of Environmental Management in Raleigh, responded.

"The state was responding to direct questions from a reporter who knows what questions to ask," she said. "As soon as information is written down on a piece of paper, it becomes part of the public record, and the state is not going to lie when questioned by a reporter."

"Our citizens are ready to hang us," Lilley said.

"Mr. Mayor, you have a major cancer risk in your water supply," Rudo said. "It's real, it's in there and in all probability they've been drinking water of this quality for 40 years."

The state will retest the 10 sites for carbon tetrachloride contamination it found last week, said Richard Rowe, director of the state Division of Environmental Health.

State scientists found concentrations of the chemical in the city water supply up to seven times the amount considered safe by the U.S. Environmental Protection Agency.

Previous and subsequent tests by Oxford Laboratories of Wilmington, a private laboratory contracted to sample and analyze city water, did not report increased carbon tetrachlorides at the city's surface water plant.

The carbon tetrachlorides could have entered the system as a contaminant of the chlorine used that day to purify the water, state officials said.

There would be no long- or short-term health risks from a one-time exposure to carbon tetrachloride, Rudo said.

The state also asked the two engineering firms to study how much trihalomethanes could be removed from the city's water by changing chemicals used to purify it and to study how much these changes would cost the city. It asked the state toxicologist to study what the long- and short-term health effects would be of making these short-term changes.

The state is to receive the results of these studies in one month, Rowe said.

Tests last week from 10 locations throughout the city showed an average of about 964 parts per billion of trihalomethanes in tap water. The samples ranged from about 57 parts per billion at Beaufort County Community College to about 1,367 at the regional Department of Environmental, Health and Natural Resources office, which has switched to drinking bottled water.

Similar concentrations were found by a Division of Environmental Management laboratory in Cary and by Oxford Labs.

The EPA considers concentrations of 100 parts per billion a safe amount.

The high levels of chemicals were found in treated water drawn from Tranters Creek. None of the chemicals was found in threatening levels at the city's groundwell on Slatestone Road. Engineers are building a pilot water treatment plant to treat water with various chemicals to help them decide how to design a larger plant that will meet proposed new clean water regulations being imposed by the EPA.

Groundwells were dismissed as an alternate source of drinking water because they would be too costly and could not supply an adequate amount of drinking water, representatives of EET and Rivers & Associates said.

DEM hydrogeologist Rudy Smithwick took issue with the statements, saying that areas of the Castle Hayne aquifer east of the city are deep enough and contain enough water to supply the city's water needs.

"Trihalomethanes" are a group of organic compounds, including chloroform. They are formed when chlorine, used in the water treatment process, reacts with certain organic material. The organic material occurs naturally in the water when plants and animals decay. Chloroform has been linked to colon, liver, kidney and urological cancers.

"Carbon tetrachloride" is an organic compound similar to trihalomethanes. It is known to cause cancer in laboratory animals and has been linked to cancer and birth, developmental and neurological disorders in humans.

WATER DANGERS KNOWN IN 1981

THURSDAY, OCTOBER 19, 1989

BY BETTY GRAY

City officials knew about possible contamination of Washington's water supply by cancer-causing chemicals as early as 1981, newly obtained documents reveal.

Alerted by warnings in state and federal government publications, Jerry Cutler, Washington superintendent of water resources, sent samples of city tap water off for testing that year.

On Aug. 14, 1981, an Ashboro laboratory, Moore, Gardner & Associates, informed Cutler that the tests showed carcinogenic trihalomethanes at 908 parts per billion, more than nine times the maximum amount regarded as safe by the U.S. Environmental Protection Agency.

This was the first record of trihalomethanes in city water, five years earlier than officials have yet acknowledged.

About two weeks later, Sept. 2, 1981, Cutler wrote a memorandum to Gilbert R. Alligood, then director of public works for the city, recommending the city pay for an engineering study of water treatment problems. Alligood is now an engineer with Rivers & Associates, consultant to the city on its proposed new water treatment plant.

One of the major problems identified by Cutler was trihalomethanes in the water.

"At the present, they are nine times higher than the maximum contaminant level," his memo said.

The alarming news was not made public.

Since that information became available, at least three city managers, three mayors, the state and the EPA have known of the problem, Cutler told the Daily News recently.

But there were no federal and state regulations forcing the city to act on the information, he said. What appeared to be more pressing problems and a scarcity of funds may also have played a role, he said.

State and federal regulators have known for nearly a decade that trihalomethanes have been linked to cancer, Cutler pointed out.

"They knew we had a problem by the potential of trihalomethanes," he said. "Knowing how our system operated, they knew we had a problem."

But towns between 3,300 and 10,000 population were only required to begin quarterly monitoring in January of this year.

The U.S. Environmental Protection Agency first issued regulations for trihalomethanes in 1979 as part of the Safe Drinking Water Act. The law required phased-in monitoring and reporting for municipalities based on population size.

In passing the federal Water Pollution Control Act and the Clean Water Act, both meant to protect the American public from hazards in surface water, Congress made provision for financial aid to communities to upgrade their sewage treatment facilities.

Not so with the Safe Drinking Water Act.

The cost of improving drinking water is borne mainly by the utility and, eventually, the consuming public.

Cutler's 1981 memo to Alligood put forward suggestions for upgrading and replacing equipment at the surface water plant or for replacing the surface water treatment plant with four wells and a groundwater treatment plant.

During this time, the city was beleaguered by a wastewater treatment plant that did not meet federal requirements and budget overruns in construction of a new electrical substation.

A lack of money combined with the lack of federal and state requirements governing drinking water apparently combined to give top priority to the other problems.

"The city's drinking water plant was operating within the law," Cutler said. "But our wastewater treatment plant was out of compliance so we had to take action on it."

An engineering study, completed Aug. 12, 1983, by Moore, Gardner & Associates and presented to Alligood, gave the city five alternatives in upgrading its surface water supply.

Among them: drilling a well system north of Washington, moving the plant from Tranters Creek to the Tar River or blending water from the city groundwater well with water from Tranters Creek before the treatment process to lower the amount of organics in the water.

Subsequent efforts to blend the water failed, Cutler said.

On May 23, 1986, Cutler sent a memorandum to Russell Waters, city director of public works, which identified three contaminants in the city drinking water at or above concentrations allowed under the amended Safe Drinking Water Act.

Turbidity and aluminum were two of the contaminants. Trihalomethanes were the third.

During a long-range planning meeting in February 1987, the Public Works Department requested $2,500,000 for water projects.

The planning report said the projects were needed "to reduce the high levels of trihalomethanes in the finished water."

It said EPA and the state government required this in systems which served more than 10,000 people.

"The City of Washington is near this population level," it said, noting that EPA was in the process of lowering the limit and had recently proposed new regulations for 83 specific chemical contaminants in drinking water which might have to be met over the next five years.

Chloroform, one of the trihalomethanes in the water, was a known carcinogen, the report said.

Quarterly tests by Oxford Laboratories of Wilmington began this past January as required by the Environmental Protection Agency. The tests showed concentrations of about 338 parts per billion in tap water on Jan. 6, 1989, and 934 parts per billion in tap water April 3, 1989, far above the EPA limit.

Oxford Labs sent written copies of the results to the state public water supply section and to the city.

As required under the Safe Drinking Water Act amended in 1986, the city sent written notices of the testing, but not the results, to its water customers.

About 20 people asked for copies of the test results, Cutler said.

Contamination of the city water supply became public knowledge after the Daily News obtained a copy of the report, and on Sept. 22 the state health director, Dr. Ronald Levine, told city residents they should not drink the water, wash or cook fruits and vegetables in it, or take showers in it because they might inhale the steam.

The following day, a U.S. Marine Corps convoy set up water wagons around the city to provide its residents with clean water.

In the past three weeks, city officials have taken emergency measures which reduced trihalomethane levels to a point where the advisory has been lifted except for the warning against drinking the water, using it in vaporizers or in preparing hot and cold drinks such as coffee or tea and juice from concentrates.

VOTERS SAY WATER PROBLEMS AFFECTING BALLOTING

TUESDAY, OCTOBER 10, 1989

BY MIKE VOSS

While people waited in line inside to vote today at the P.S. Jones precinct, another group lined up outside to fill jugs with safe water from a U.S. Marine Corps water wagon.

That clearly defined the major issue of the city elections, according to an informal exit poll of voters conducted by the Daily News today.

Polls, which opened at 6:30 a.m., will remain open until 7:30 p.m.

Registrars reported moderate to heavy turnout this morning, with one ward running 40 to 50 percent ahead of the 1987 election.

At 9 a.m., 140 people had voted at the Fourth Ward, 65 had voted by 9:15 a.m. at the Third Ward, 31 had voted at P.S. Jones by 9:25 a.m., 47 had voted at the Second Ward by 9:40 a.m. and 55 had voted at the First Ward by 9:50 a.m.

Slightly over 4,000 are registered to vote.

Terry Sneed, who voted at P.S. Jones, said his vote reflected his desire for a new look in the makeup of the city council.

"It's time for a change," he said.

"It was one of the most important considerations," said Sneed of how the water issue affected his vote. "The public is not being informed and they should be informed." He said he was upset his parents have been drinking city water and were not told until recently about the potential health problems.

"I am pretty sure the water issue will affect votes," said Thomas Green Jr., who also voted at P.S. Jones.

Green said the water issue caused him to vote for "at least one change" on the makeup of the council.

Jack Cherry, who voted in the Fourth Ward, said he also expected the water issue to determine the outcome.

Cherry said the water issue and fiscal management were issues he considered in deciding how he would vote.

"I'm just glad to see a healthy slate of candidates," said Cherry. Although he would not reveal who got his vote for mayor, he did say it was not the write-in candidate.

At the First Ward, Charles Berry said he expected today's vote to result in a change. "Yes, sir. I think so," he responded when asked if his vote would reflect a change in the current makeup of the council.

"I think that's going to be the whole thing. They lied to us," said Berry when asked if he thought the water issue was at the forefront of the election.

Fourth Ward Registrar Julie Koepnick characterized turnout as "moderate." Tom Blount, registrar at the Third Ward, said turnout was "about 40 to 50 percent ahead" of the turnout in the 1987 city election.

P.S. Jones Registrar Dorothy Edwards called turnout "very slow," but she expected it to pick up at noon and after 4 p.m.

"This is pretty good," said Second Ward Registrar Alice Pfeiffer of the turnout. Warren Lane, registrar of the First Ward, termed turnout moderate "but from this precinct that's the pattern."

Most of the registrars said they expected the turnout to be heavier than usual.

One voter, who asked not to be identified, said she voted her conscience and hoped others would vote that way. She called the water issue a "disgrace" and said the current city council did not act responsibly in handling the issue.

"I've got a jug out in my car. I'll be 80 years old next spring and I'm having to carry water around," she said.

She said the election will give voters a "chance to do something about taking care of the problem." She declined to say who she voted for, but said her vote would show her desire for a change in leadership.

OFFICIALS WANT DRINKING WATER RULES CHANGED

SATURDAY, OCTOBER 21, 1989

BY BETTY GRAY

State and federal officials said this week they will revise drinking water regulations to prevent another situation like that in Washington, where authorities failed to act for eight years on information that the tap water contained dangerous levels of cancer-causing chemicals.

The U.S. Environmental Protection Agency is reviewing its requirements for the water supplies of all smaller U.S. communities in light of Washington's water problems, Michael Leonard, chief of the drinking water section of EPA's regional office in Atlanta, told the Daily News.

"We are trying to review all regulations of contaminates, lowering the limits for some and lowering the populations to which these limits apply," Leonard said.

The new regulations could be in place in 1991 or 1992, he said.

Such action could extend environmental safeguards to 56,000 U.S. water treatment plants serving millions of people across the nation in communities of less than 10,000 population, which are not now regulated by EPA.

Just under 10,000 residents are connected to Washington's water system, according to authorities.

Drinking water for an estimated 195 million residents in U.S. cities above 10,000 already is protected by the federal Safe Drinking Water Act.

In North Carolina, 104 water treatment plants serve at least half a million residents in the under-10,000 category, according to estimates.

"I am concerned that people who live in small communities are not protected by U.S. Environmental Protection Agency requirements," said state health director Dr. Ronald Levine. "This clearly needs to be addressed."

The state already has found that the drinking water of 13 of those communities may contain carcinogens like those in Washington's water.

According to documents obtained by the Daily News, tests of the city's tap water in 1981 showed levels of carcinogenic trihalomethanes of 908 parts per billion, nine times the maximum safe level set by EPA. In April of this year, testing showed the city level to be 934 parts per billion.

Although state and federal regulators have known for nearly a decade that trihalomethanes have been linked to cancer, communities under 10,000 population have not been required to take action to remove the deadly chemicals from their water supplies.

Not until January of this year did EPA even require towns of between 3,300 and 10,000 population to test their drinking water. Not until 1990 will communities under 3,300 be required to do so.

In North Carolina, neither state nor federal regulations enforce safe water standards at those population levels. The state is allowed to establish standards higher than those set by the federal government but has not done so.

As a result of the disclosure of the problems in Washington's tap water, the N.C. Commission for Health Services will be asked to consider new drinking water regulations, health director Levine said. The earliest that could be done is February, he said, with new regulations in place by April 1.

The state's health department staff is to work in coming weeks to develop standards for chemicals such as trihalomethanes in city water supplies, he said. After that and consideration by the commission, public hearings will be held.

"The problem is not confined to Washington," Levine said.

Contamination of the city water supply became public knowledge after the Daily News obtained and published a copy of test reports in mid-September. On Sept. 22, state health director Levine told city residents they should not drink the water, wash or cook fruits and vegetables in it, or take showers in it because they might inhale the steam.

The following day, a U.S. Marine Corps convoy set up water wagons around the city to provide its residents with clean water.

In the past three weeks, city officials have taken emergency measures which reduced trihalomethane levels to a point where the advisory has been lifted except for the warning against drinking the water, using it in vaporizers or using it to prepare hot and cold drinks such as coffee, tea or juice from concentrates.

THE BLOOD BROKERS

Once blood leaves a donor's vein, the "gift of life" becomes the life source of a multibillion-dollar industry that buys, sells and even exports the valuable commodity. Gilbert M. Gaul traces the blood and the money trails.

Sometimes the best stories get started with a few simple questions.

Questions such as the ones that popped into my head one afternoon two years ago while donating blood here at *The Inquirer.*

Where does the blood go? I wondered. How is it processed? What does it cost the hospital patient who receives it? Who controls the blood supply in the United States?

Even though I was a regular donor, giving blood three or four times a year, I couldn't answer these basic questions. At first, that disturbed me. Then it got me to thinking. As a reporter specializing in medical economics, it might make an interesting story to examine the business side of blood, I reasoned.

I mentioned my interest to Craig Stock, my editor and like me a blood donor, and he agreed. I would poke around while continuing to cover my beat.

Little did we realize that it would be 18 months before I had answers to my original questions, not to mention a story.

My immersion into the business of blood began with a promise to myself: Everything I wrote would be documented and there would be no blind quotes. If someone wanted to go on background, I would listen, but I wouldn't use his comments. Due to the sensitivity of the subject, it absolutely had to be this way. And it was.

About the time I was beginning my research, the local Red Cross declared an emergency appeal for blood in the Philadelphia area. In hindsight, this event would prove to be a significant break in the series. It opened my eyes to issues I almost certainly would have overlooked: the link between management and blood shortages, the widescale trading of blood and the ethics of blood-bank administrators.

A local Red Cross doctor blamed the shortage on donors not showing up in sufficient numbers. It happened every year following the Christmas—New Year's holiday, he added. Donors just didn't keep their appointments.

As a donor, that didn't sit too well with me. I was ready and willing to give blood. Yet no one from the Red Cross had bothered to call or send me a postcard. When I pressed, the doctor acknowledged he didn't know why donors weren't coming. Management had never fully investigated the issue. It occurred to me that were this any other business, the blood bank would be down in the federal bankruptcy court. Instead, management turned to the media and declared an "Emergency Appeal" for blood, which cost them nothing.

In a subsequent interview, officials disclosed that Philadelphia was a "net importer" of blood. In other words, the blood center was unable to collect enough blood locally to meet the needs of hospitals, so it bought blood from other blood centers. The cost of buying this blood —more than $1 million in 1987—had pushed the blood center into the red. Management decided to eliminate the imports. Then the holiday crunch hit, and they had no imported blood as a buffer. That was another reason there was a blood shortage, albeit it wasn't one management publicized.

My interest aroused, I decided to take a look at the business of buying and selling blood, and quickly ran into a roadblock. The federal government didn't require blood banks to report sales and had no idea how much blood moved around the country—or in and out of the country, for that matter. Only one state, New York, required such reports.

After first agreeing to provide the data, the Red Cross' national headquarters in Washington later rejected my request, asserting it would be too much trouble. The American Association of Blood Banks provided me with aggregate numbers but declined to disclose specific transactions.

I then set out to create my own data base of blood sales. I did this by interviewing administrators at approximately 100 blood banks around the country and cataloging which centers were buying blood and which centers were selling blood, and then crossmatching the responses. Eventually, I was able to track a half-million pints of blood around the country, in some cases watching them change hands several times.

These interviews also enabled me to gain an understanding of the economics of these transactions, especially how blood is priced. Despite the rhetoric about saving lives and doing community good, some centers were clearly brokering blood to build up revenues. In one case, the profits were being used to finance a battle for market share with a rival blood bank.

One of the more disturbing aspects of this blood brokering was that donors were being kept in the dark. Time and time again, I found, blood banks did not tell donors that their blood might be sold to another center hundreds or thousands of miles away. Nor were donors told of the bidding process for blood on the spot market, which is not unlike the oil or soybean commodities market.

To understand the finances of nonprofit blood banks, I submitted approximately 100 requests to regional Internal Revenue Service centers for the most recent tax returns filed by the blood centers. I obtained about 75 returns, filling in the gaps with letters requesting audited financial statements from other centers.

By this juncture—about six months into the project—I was relieved of most of my usual duties and allowed to pursue the story on nearly a full-time basis.

The series also took a turn at this point when several large blood centers were forced to recall hundreds of pints of blood that had tested positive for AIDS or hepatitis but had been released anyway. I hadn't intended to look at safety issues, but I now found myself unable to avoid them. It was pretty clear that management in some centers wasn't getting the job done and it was costing these centers (and the public) substantial money—not to mention putting lives at risk.

I submitted the first of what would be 40 Freedom of Information Act requests for federal inspection reports of troubled blood banks—eventually gathering approximately 20,000 pages that documented a long-standing pattern of mismanagement, safety errors and bureaucratic malaise. In effect, these documents revealed, the Food and Drug Administration had turned regulation of the blood industry over to the industry itself.

During this process, I discovered quite by accident that the FDA was faxing some of my requests to lawyers at the Red Cross for their comments and suggestions. When I quizzed FDA officials about this, an official replied that it was a common practice. The Red Cross declined comment.

The Inquirer printed a single story in March 1989, based on FDA inspection reports and hundreds of pages of internal Red Cross documents I had obtained from sources. The story showed that computer problems and testing errors were putting the nation's blood supply at risk. Three weeks later, the president of the Red Cross and three top officials, including the individual in charge of its computer systems, resigned.

The "Blood Brokers" series ran six months later in September 1989, prompting widespread response from around the country. A committee in Congress that had been investigating the FDA expanded its probe to include the agency's regulation of the blood industry. Another federal agency began its own review. And the FDA changed the way it monitors imports of foreign blood.

More recently, Congress has moved to provide the agency with money for an additional 150 blood-bank inspectors. And some blood banks have begun to share additional information with their donors about finances and blood brokering.

I am often asked, "Given the abuses you uncovered, do you still donate blood?" The answer is an unequivocal "yes." The point of this series wasn't to harm blood donations, but to explore an area of medicine that is at best little understood. To the extent that *The Inquirer* helped shed some light in this area, and fostered positive changes, I am proud of this series.

—Gilbert M. Gaul
The Philadelphia Inquirer

HOW BLOOD, THE 'GIFT OF LIFE,' BECAME A BILLION-DOLLAR BUSINESS

SUNDAY, SEPTEMBER 24, 1989

BY GILBERT M. GAUL

Last December, the Community Blood Center in Appleton, Wis., made a public appeal for blood. Residents were asked to "dig farther, wider and deeper" than ever before to keep local blood supplies at desired levels.

"We've never had it quite this tough," Alan W. Cable, executive director of the nonprofit blood bank, told the local newspaper.

The citizens did dig deep; last year, 15,000 pints of blood were donated by Appleton residents to help save the lives of their friends and neighbors.

What they didn't know, though—don't know to this day—was that the same month the blood bank was appealing for blood, it sold 650 pints—half its monthly blood collection—at a profit to other blood banks around the country.

Or that last year the blood center in Appleton contracted to sell 200 pints a month to a blood bank 528 miles away in Lexington, Ky.

Or that Lexington sold half the blood it bought from Appleton to yet a third blood bank near Fort Lauderdale, Fla. Which in turn sold thousands of pints it bought from Lexington and other blood banks to four hospitals in New York City.

What began as a generous "gift of life" from people in Appleton to their neighbors ended up as part of a chain of blood brokered to hospitals in Manhattan, where patients were charged $120 a pint. Along that 2,777-mile route, human blood became just another commodity.

The buying and selling of blood has become big business in America —a multibillion-dollar industry that is largely unregulated by the government.

Each year, unknown to the people who give the blood, blood banks buy and sell more than a million pints from one another, shifting blood all over the country and generating an estimated $50 million in revenues.

It is not uncommon for some blood banks to broker between 20 percent and 40 percent of what they collect. In Appleton, nearly half the blood collected from donors in the last two years was sold outside the area. In Waterloo, Iowa, the American Red Cross sold six of every 10 pints collected last year to other blood banks.

They do it, blood bank officials say, to share a limited resource. Although they have a monopoly, blood banks in dozens of cities— Philadelphia among them—are unable to collect as much blood as they need. To cover their shortfalls, they buy blood from centers, such as Appleton, that collect more than they need.

Nobody disputes the value of sharing blood. But in the last 15 years, this trading in blood has become a huge, virtually unregulated market—with no ceiling on prices, with nonprofit blood banks vying with one another for control of the blood supply, with decisions often driven by profits and corporate politics, not medical concerns.

In this marketplace, blood, a vital resource, gets less government protection than grapes or poultry or pretzels. Dog kennels in Pennsylvania are inspected more frequently than blood banks.

And donors are rarely told what happens to their blood.

"People are being fooled," said Dr. Aaron Kellner, recently retired president of the New York Blood Center, which buys 300,000 pints of blood a year. "Nobody is telling them that their blood is going to us. They would be furious if they knew about it."

"I didn't give blood so someone else can make money from my blood. I gave it to be used at the least expense by anyone who would need it," Lynne Nelson, 24, of Appleton, said when told by a reporter recently that some blood collected there is sold elsewhere.

It is not just a question of candor. As more and more blood is traded around the country—changing hands two, three or four times—it becomes much more difficult to keep track of which blood came from where, or from whom. As the collection and distribution network becomes more complex, chances of errors multiply.

In fact, errors at blood banks have increased dramatically in the last two years as overworked technicians struggle to keep up with more and more tests for detecting viruses in the blood, including those for hepatitis and AIDS.

The potential for fatal mistakes is "a ticking time bomb," said Frank E. Young, commissioner of the Food and Drug Administration.

Most blood sales take place through clearinghouses operated by the American Red Cross and other nonprofit blood-collecting groups. But there is also a spot market—not unlike the one for oil—where hundreds, possibly thousands, of sales occur each year.

"It functions rather like the NASDAQ," a national system for trading over-the-counter stocks, said Dr. Charles L. Rouault, president of the Broward Community Blood Center near Fort Lauderdale. "You pick up the phone and call somebody you know."

No one—not the federal government, not the blood banks themselves—knows for sure how much blood is bought and sold on the open market. There are no requirements that sales be reported; no government agency keeps track.

All of which should be of grave concern to Americans, for the very safety of the nation's blood supply is at stake.

A FLAWED SYSTEM

A yearlong examination of the American blood system by The Inquirer has uncovered major flaws in the way blood is collected, distributed and regulated. Among the findings:

• The federal government has failed to adequately police the blood business, in essence allowing the industry to regulate itself.

• With no one overseeing prices, blood banks are free to charge hospitals whatever the market will bear. Hospitals add their own markups, often unrelated to their actual costs. And blood centers facing shortages are left to scramble to find blood.

• Prices vary widely from region to region, and sometimes within a region. Patients are charged by hospitals up to $300 a unit for blood that was given *free* by donors.

• Nonprofit blood banks compete directly with commercial companies in some lucrative areas of the blood business. Their commercial competitors say the blood banks enjoy an unfair business advantage because they are exempt from paying taxes.

• At least 40,000 people a year contract hepatitis through blood transfusions. Yet until the AIDS epidemic, doctors routinely ordered transfusions for patients undergoing surgery, often unnecessarily exposing them to risks of blood-borne infections.

• Blood collectors say they have done everything possible to ensure the safety of the blood supply. Yet confidential documents show the industry ignored or delayed using readily available tests and procedures to make blood and transfusions safer.

• At a time when AIDS was showing up in the blood supply in the early 1980s, the FDA reduced its inspections of blood-collecting facilities from once a year to once every two years.

• Thousands of pints of suspect blood and other blood components have been released by blood banks and commercial plasma centers as a result of testing errors, computer problems and other mistakes.

This haphazard system exists because the United States has failed to develop a comprehensive blood program that ensures adequate, safe supplies to all regions of the country at fair prices.

The United States is one of only a handful of Western nations that leave the collection and distribution of blood scattered among a patchwork of private and quasi-public groups.

"What we have is not so much a system as a non-system," said Norman R. Kear, administrator of the Red Cross' blood center in Los Angeles. "Blood-collecting groups like the Red Cross cooperate when it is in their interest to cooperate, and when it's not in their interest, they fail to cooperate."

□ □ □

The blood industry is in the spotlight today as never before because of AIDS.

A total of 2,668 patients have contracted the disease through transfusion of infected blood since June 1981, when the federal Centers for Disease Control began tracking AIDS cases. That is a small percentage of the 4 million transfusions each year but enough to have caused widespread concern about the safety of blood.

Spokesmen for the industry, while conceding past problems, contend that the blood supply today is safe. They say the period of greatest risk was from 1978 when AIDS was first recognized, to 1985, when testing of blood for the virus began. The tests have virtually eliminated the risk of getting AIDS from blood transfusions, blood industry spokesmen say.

And they say a new test for hepatitis, expected to be available in 1990, should help reduce the risk of contracting that disease.

But recent research on AIDS and blood has brought new concerns. A study by University of California, Los Angeles, researchers published in July found that some infected people may carry the AIDS virus for up to three years before they begin to produce antibodies, which are what the AIDS screening tests detect. The research raised the possibility that the screening methods used by blood banks may be less reliable than thought.

In addition, the sheer volume of tests performed by blood banks—each unit of blood undergoes six tests for infectious diseases—and the need for massive record keeping have led to overload at many blood centers.

From March 1988 to March 1989, blood banks and commercial plasma centers had to recall nearly 100,000 blood components and medicines made from blood that had been erroneously released, FDA records show.

"Blood banks can keep telling the public that the blood supply is as safe as it can be, but the public isn't buying that anymore because they sense it isn't true," said Dr. Cory SerVass, a member of the Presidential Commission on AIDS, which issued its final report in June 1988.

While questions of blood safety are paramount, The Inquirer's examination of the system by which blood is collected and distributed revealed other causes for concern.

The blood business has grown so large and complex, with so much emphasis on sales and profits, that many "nonprofit" blood banks have become virtually indistinguishable from other big businesses, critics inside and outside the industry say.

"The pathetic thing is that the idea of blood as a resource being shipped around the country strikes me as perfectly reasonable. The problem is it has gotten too commercial. There's too much dollars and cents about it," said Norman Selby, a consultant hired in 1987 to help deal with a financial crisis at the New York Blood Center, the nation's biggest buyer of blood.

A judge in Florida who was brought in to arbitrate a dispute between two blood banks wrote much the same thing in his ruling: *"Serving your fellow man and supporting your community* makes nice-sounding verbiage, but the bottom line is that both groups sell this blood to these hospitals," he wrote. "They will tell you that it is at cost, that this is nonprofit, but between cost and nonprofit is a lot of 'expense,' including many jobs and many salaries."

HOW THE BLOOD BUSINESS WORKS

Nonprofit blood banks generate at least $1 billion a year in revenues, tax returns examined by The Inquirer show. Exact figures are impossible to obtain; there are no comprehensive government or industry estimates.

Blood is processed into a number of finished products. Whole blood, collected by nonprofit blood banks, is separated into red blood cells, platelets and plasma. Plasma collected by for-profit centers is used to make a variety of medicines, such as Factor VIII clotting concentrate and hepatitis vaccines.

Three organizations—the American Red Cross, the American Association of Blood Banks and the Council of Community Blood Centers—make up the blood-banking business in the United States. All are incorporated as nonprofit organizations.

The Red Cross is by far the largest. With 56 regional blood centers, it accounts for at least half the estimated 13.5 million pints of blood collected each year.

The Red Cross blood program had revenues of more than $500 million last year. Operating profits for its blood program, which the Red Cross calls "excesses over expenses," totaled more than $300 million from 1980 through 1987, according to the organization's tax returns.

Other "nonprofits" also make substantial profits from the sale of blood. Some blood banks have built up large reserves of cash and investments, and pay their officers salaries of $150,000 a year or more, plus expensive company cars and other perks.

Blood-bank officials say the proceeds are put back into their operations and are used for such things as construction and equipment.

These "excesses" also help build up financial reserves, a cushion against future losses.

But the distinction between nonprofit and for-profit sometimes gets blurred.

In one case, a nonprofit blood bank in Oklahoma City has begun to sell donated blood to a for-profit company in Los Angeles, which marks up the price and sells it to hospitals. The director of the nonprofit blood bank is one of three owners of the for-profit company.

These are the nonprofit organizations—2,024 facilities—that collect the blood used by hospitals for transfusions.

There is also a thriving commercial business in plasma, the protein-rich liquid part of blood from which many medicines are made. Unlike blood banks, the multibillion-dollar for-profit plasma industry pays donors for the plasma collected at 400 centers—from $8 to $25 for each donation.

At one time blood banks paid donors, too. As recently as the late 1960s, about 15 percent of the blood supply came from paid donors. They received about $10 for a unit of whole blood, which contains oxygen-carrying red cells (used in transfusions and to combat anemia), platelets (used to promote clotting) and plasma.

Paid donors were driven from the system in the early 1970s because of fears that vagrants, alcoholics and other unhealthy donors who sold their blood were spreading hepatitis through the blood supply.

So today, the blood banks depend almost exclusively on volunteer donors. And blood banks are extremely sensitive about doing anything that could upset these donors.

"There is a tendency to tell donors . . . the least amount they need to know," said Nancy R. Holland, former executive director of the American Blood Commission, an advisory group made up of industry, consumer and government representatives.

In Appleton, for instance, donors were not told that their blood was being sold until July, after an Inquirer reporter had raised questions. The blood center then began to give donors a written statement saying that "only leftover blood and blood components that would otherwise be lost" are sold.

"The needs of our local hospitals and their patients have, and always will, come first; they are why the Community Blood Center exists," the statement said.

Interviews with more than a dozen Appleton donors found that they interpreted the two-page statement to mean that only a small amount of blood was being sold outside the area.

"As I understand it, the only way it would be sold is if they have an overabundance at the blood bank here and instead of throwing it out . . . they would sell it," said Steve Hermsen, 30, a sales representative for an Appleton paper company.

"It's used locally and sold to people at cost or close to cost," said donor Randy Jones, 33.

In fact, nearly half of all blood collected by the Appleton Community Blood Center is sold outside the area—information left out of the blood center's statement. In 1988, the blood center sold 6,800 pints to other centers, or 46 percent of the 14,700 pints it distributed that year. In 1987, it sold 6,900 out of 14,600 pints—47 percent.

The blood center earned $10 for each pint it sold, according to executive director Alan Cable. That was in addition to the standard charge to hospitals of $33 a pint in 1988—a fee that since has been raised to $38.

Cable said the money from outside sales helps keep Appleton's blood charges among the lowest in the nation. By collecting more blood than is needed locally, Appleton also has a buffer against emergencies, Cable said.

Moreover, he said, Appleton's medical community would never stand for blood imported from outside. "They don't want blood coming in from anyplace else because of AIDS and the hepatitis risk," he said.

WHAT DONORS ARE NOT TOLD

Cable was asked about his appeal for donors last December. If his center had excess blood to sell, why did he tell the local newspaper, "We've never had it quite this tough"?

His recruiters were having to work harder to get donors, Cable said. "When my staff has to make twice as many phone calls to get in that number of donors, that becomes a real concern," he said.

"I confess there's a lot about any blood program the donors are probably not aware of. It's not as a result of not wanting to tell somebody. It's a matter of [their] not asking the right questions," Cable said in an earlier interview.

Appleton isn't the only blood center that has kept donors in the dark. Interviews in the last year with 70 blood-bank officials found that none told donors explicitly that their blood might be sold for a profit.

In Waterloo, where 60 percent of the blood collected is sold to hospitals in other areas, Red Cross administrator Michael Liesch said recruiters work with donor groups "to make it very clear up front that blood is a national resource." But Liesch acknowledged "we don't tell the individual donors as they come in" that their blood may be sold elsewhere.

The Red Cross and many other blood banks recruit donors by appealing to their sense of community responsibility. "This joining of individual action in the interest of maintaining a reliable community blood supply is what the Red Cross means by community responsibility in blood service," one Red Cross document notes.

"Blood bankers have for years fooled the American public. They have built up their regional centers on the idea of community pride, and to change that now would be very difficult and would probably cost them blood," said Kear, the Red Cross official in Los Angeles.

Kear's boss at Red Cross national headquarters in Washington, Dr. Lewellys F. Barker, said: "As far as we're concerned . . . your neighbor is someone who is in need. It is not necessarily someone in the nearest hospital or even in the same town or county or municipality."

Why doesn't the Red Cross tell donors that their blood may be sold outside the area?

"I guess if we thought that it was of great interest or concern, we would deal with it more aggressively. Maybe it is," Barker said. "I don't think we know that this is of great interest or concern to donors. In fact, when we talk to donors, what they want to know is that the patient who needs blood is going to benefit from their donation."

"If you're going to do it, you have to tell people up front, publicize the fact," said Kellner of the New York Blood Center. "People are being fooled now. They don't know. It's unethical."

Donors in Oklahoma City do not know, for example, that some of their blood is being sold by their blood bank directly to a for-profit company.

Under an agreement made in July, the Oklahoma Blood Institute, a nonprofit blood center, is selling 300 pints of blood and blood products a week to the American Blood Institute, a for-profit company in Los Angeles.

Dr. Ronald O. Gilcher, who in 1987 earned $159,000 as director of the nonprofit blood center, is a medical director-consultant and part-owner of the for-profit company that is buying blood from his center, according to licensing records filed with the California Department of Health. The company sells the blood to hospitals in the Los Angeles area at a profit.

In an interview, Gilcher said his Oklahoma blood center charges the American Blood Institute the same price it charges nonprofit blood banks. Gilcher declined to say what that price was.

Gilcher's blood bank sells a pint of red cells to Oklahoma City hospitals for $58. Blood from the same blood bank is sold to Los Angeles–area hospitals for $67 to $69 by the for-profit American Blood Institute.

Asked about his dual roles, Gilcher said, "They have given me a very small amount of stock in ABI." He said his "relationship with American Blood Institute was cleared by the executive committee [of his board of directors] so I can act as medical consultant" to the company.

Dr. Joseph J. Stone, one of Gilcher's co-owners in American Blood Institute, said the company was receiving no unfair advantage because of Gilcher's dual roles. "There has been no compromise of integrity or ethics. I quite frankly think it is a smoke screen. The argument just doesn't hold at all."

REGIONAL MONOPOLIES

Most Americans think of blood banks as struggling community agencies that provide an essential service to local residents at cost. That is the image the blood banks have worked hard to foster through their regular media appeals.

In fact, they are regional monopolies, granted exclusive rights to collect blood through a government-industry pact worked out in the early 1970s with the goal of ensuring an adequate blood supply.

With only a few exceptions, blood banks have geographic franchises over the blood supply. In this respect, they are like utility companies that are allowed a monopoly because it is the most efficient way to provide an important service.

But while government regulators limit how much electric and telephone companies may charge and monitor their business activities through public utility commissions, no comparable public agency oversees blood banks.

If a blood bank's officials choose to raise their prices, increase their profits or build up their cash reserves and investments, they are free to do so. The government, which does regulate safety matters, rarely involves itself in blood banks' business decisions.

If they decide to collect more blood than they need and sell it elsewhere at a profit, no outsider questions that.

"They're local monopolies providing a vital public service without the regulation," said Harvey M. Sapolsky, a political scientist at Massachusetts Institute of Technology and co-author of a 1982 book on blood banks. "When there is competition, in the couple of instances where that has occurred, the price falls. That's good evidence that there is monopoly pricing."

In general, regions that sell blood tend to be near small cities, with few hospitals or indigents. Many are in the Midwest, which some in the industry refer to as the nation's "blood basket."

"The people have a tendency to be very altruistic in nature," said Liesch, the blood-bank administrator in Waterloo.

That contrasts sharply with the situation in a big city like Chicago, where blood banks have a long history of being unable to collect enough blood. In 1987, one of every four pints of blood transfused in metropolitan Chicago came from outside the area.

In New York City, need for blood so outstripped collections that nearly one of every three pints of blood supplied to hospitals by the New York Blood Center in 1988 was purchased from other blood centers, including Red Cross centers in Europe.

The economics of blood-bank sales are a closely guarded secret. While it is impossible to say with certainty how many centers buy and sell blood, this much is clear: The number of transactions has grown dramatically since the early 1970s, when fewer than 200,000 pints of blood changed hands, industry documents show.

As part of its examination of the blood industry, The Inquirer was able to track the movement of nearly 500,000 pints of blood last year —about half the amount believed to be brokered.

It found a brisk business in the demand for blood. Centers with blood to spare can charge whatever they want and centers facing shortages have to ante up. When supplies tighten, as they have for the last year, prices go up. And when demand for a particular type of blood is great, such as it now is for O Positive, bidding wars can occur.

"I've heard of some centers asking $100 for a unit [pint] of O Positive," said Rouault of the Broward Community Blood Center in Lauderhill, Fla.

On a smaller scale, the Community Blood Bank of Southern New Jersey in Cherry Hill has purchased several hundred pints of blood on the spot market for several years, marked it up and resold it to local hospitals.

"We can make a business deal with it and still make a slight profit on it," said the center's director, Emilio Louis Fanjul.

Even without shortages, there are big differences in what blood centers charge. Prices for some services varied as much as 400 percent in The Inquirer survey.

For example, people who set aside their own blood before surgery at a blood bank in Grand Rapids, Mich., last year were assessed a surcharge of $40. In Springfield, Ill., and a dozen other cities, there was no surcharge. In Philadelphia, there was a $25 charge until last October, when the fee was dropped.

In Waco, Texas, a pint of red blood cells cost hospitals $33 as of June 30, 1988. In San Jose, Calif., the same pint of red cells sold for $79—a 139 percent difference. In Philadelphia, it was $46.80; it has since been raised to $53.40.

The price for cryoprecipitate, a blood component used to treat bleeding disorders, varied nationwide from $10 a unit to $39 a unit —a difference of 290 percent. In Philadelphia, it was $15.90.

These prices are what the blood banks charge hospitals, not what the public pays. The prices that hospitals charge patients also vary dramatically.

One hospital may charge as little as $15 to "crossmatch" blood against a patient's antibodies to ensure that the blood to be transfused is compatible. Another may charge more than $100 for the same procedure.

When the cost of administering the blood and the hospital's profit are tacked on, those charges can soar.

For example, in 1988 a patient at Crozer-Chester Medical Center in Delaware County receiving two units of blood during surgery would have been charged $497, according to the hospital's former blood-bank director. A patient at Abington Memorial Hospital in Montgomery County would have been charged $439.60. And a patient at Temple University Hospital would have been charged $591.60.

Hospital officials are often at a loss to explain such variations or even how they set their charges for blood and blood products.

"Do you want the sensible answer or the honest answer?" asked Elizabeth Borowski, the former director of the blood bank at Crozer-Chester who now works for the Red Cross. "The truthful answer is the way hospitals do their cost analysis is not very standardized. In fact . . . hospitals often don't know their costs."

The decisions frequently are made by hospitals' financial departments, which may apply a uniform markup without considering the actual costs.

Some critics are outraged at prices of up to $300 a pint for something that was *donated* to begin with.

Blood-bank officials say that they charge hospitals fees for processing blood, not for the blood itself. These fees include the costs of recruiting donors, collecting blood, separating the components of whole blood, testing for viruses, distributing the blood to hospitals, administration, overhead, and any "excess," or profit.

Some blood-bank officials say price variations exist because it costs more to operate in some areas of the country than others. Salaries differ. Real estate costs vary. Workers at some centers are unionized, while those at other centers are not.

Others say the differences can't be explained that easily, especially where price fluctuations exist within a single state.

In California, for instance, the price that hospitals paid for a pint of red cells in 1988 ranged from $50 to $79, a variation of nearly 60 percent. And prices for some specialized blood products and services varied by 200 percent.

"That has always mystified me," said Dr. Edgar Engleman, director of the Stanford University Medical Center blood bank. "One of the reasons we formed our own blood bank here was that we thought the charges of the local [San Jose Red Cross] blood bank were too high."

What few blood-bank officials say publicly is that there are also huge variations in the productivity of their centers. Some blood banks are more efficient than others at collecting blood. Some are more productive in making components from whole blood.

In Appleton, for example, the center collected an average of nearly 3,000 pints of blood for each full-time employee. By comparison, the blood bank in Tampa, Fla., collected just 377 pints per worker per year.

The average, according to The Inquirer's review of 70 blood banks, was 821 pints of blood per worker. In Philadelphia, the Red Cross collected 600 pints per worker.

"The implication is that there is a great deal of opportunity for improvements in productivity in blood services," Edward Wallace, a professor of management at the State University of New York at Buffalo and an adviser to the Red Cross' blood program, told a group of blood-bank administrators in 1986.

But because blood banks rarely face competition or outside scrutiny, they are not always pressured to operate in the most efficient manner. And hospitals, stuck with a single supplier of blood, have rarely pressured blood banks to keep their prices low.

PASSING COSTS ALONG

"For years and years, there was no impetus to be efficient. You just passed costs along to the hospitals. Those bad habits die hard. That's what you're looking at," said John H. Flynn, executive director of the Palm Beach Blood Bank in Florida.

Until recently, hospitals were able to pass along any price increases to patients' insurance companies with few challenges.

Nonprofit blood centers often base their prices on what the local market will bear—not their actual costs in processing the blood.

An advisory from Red Cross national headquarters to regional blood centers on "cost-accounting guidance" noted that the prices set by its blood centers "must be primarily market-based. For example, the product cost of platelets [a blood component that causes clotting] might be $15, but market forces permit a price of $27.50 to be charged. In this case, platelets would be making a contribution to joint (total blood center) costs of $12.50 per unit," the advisory, dated December 1984, said.

In other words, if a center could make platelets for $15 but sell them for $27.50, it should do so and use the profits to cover other expenses and build up financial reserves. Such cost-accounting continues to be practiced by the Red Cross.

There is one other key element in the determination of blood prices: competition. In the few cases where blood banks do not have monopolies, the results are revealing.

In South Florida, for instance, where rival blood banks are engaged in fierce competition, prices are among the lowest in the nation. The Miami Red Cross charged hospitals $38 a pint at the time of The Inquirer survey last year; the Broward Community Blood Center charged $39.

"It's all very obvious," said Rouault, president of the Broward Community Blood Center. "The centers with $39 prices have competition. Those with $67 prices [and higher] are those without competition."

When the Red Cross' monopoly in Tucson, Ariz., was broken by the arrival in 1985 of another nonprofit blood bank that offered blood for lower prices, the Red Cross cut its price of $53.35 a pint by nearly $20 to meet the challenge from United Blood Services.

By lowering its price, the Red Cross succeeded in protecting its lock on Tucson. Several years later, United Blood Services left Tucson, after it had trouble persuading enough hospitals to buy its blood.

"It didn't matter what we put our price at. They [the Red Cross] would have put their price at $20 if we had," said Joseph Dockery, former director of United Blood Service's Tucson operation. Dockery now works for the Red Cross.

The results were predictable, said Sapolsky, the MIT political scientist. "The voluntary sector can't be expected to provide [its own] regulatory control. They have a financial interest. You can't expect them to do it. There has to be some governmental oversight."

□ □ □

Ten years ago, in June 1979, a congressional subcommittee questioned why prices for blood varied so widely from region to region.

"I am . . . distressed by the impact of inflated blood-product charges on health-care costs," said Richard S. Schweiker, then a Republican senator from Pennsylvania. "What is the advisability of allowing unregulated public and nonprofit agencies to exercise monopoly power?"

In 1979, Schweiker introduced a bill that would have required government officials to collect and analyze data on the cost of blood and to determine "fair and reasonable exchange rates" for blood.

It was never enacted. Today, the blood industry remains without any such regulatory oversight on pricing.

And a group that was supposed to represent consumers and help shape national policies related to blood has fallen on hard times.

The American Blood Commission, an advisory group, was formed in 1975 amid concerns about the safety, supply and cost of blood. As part of its mission, the commission was to collect and analyze data on prices and blood use. It did for a while.

But by 1981 those efforts had collapsed, in part because of problems getting blood banks to disclose their financial data, former commission officials say. And so the database intended to be used to monitor prices never materialized.

"Nothing much was ever really done about that . . . and so we've been operating on data that really goes back to the surveys done in 1979 and 1980," said Douglas MacN Surgenor, chairman of the Center for Blood Research in Boston, which is affiliated with Harvard University. "I think that's been a critical shortcoming."

It is because of the American Blood Commission that most blood banks today may set prices without pressure from competitors.

"When the ABC was first established, it was considered sacred and the right and proper thing to do to have one blood center serve an area. It espoused monopolies," said Nancy Holland, former executive director of the commission.

But while the commission encouraged the development of large regional blood centers, it failed to monitor how those blood centers set prices or conducted their business.

The reason may have had something to do with the makeup of the commission, which came to be dominated by representatives from the blood-banking industry, according to Holland and others. And they were reluctant to address controversial issues that could hurt blood sales—such as AIDS or methods for reducing blood use.

"I think the blood bankers came to believe that our role was to help them achieve their goals. The blood-banking organizations do not want the ABC shaping their policies," Holland said.

The commission played virtually no role in formulating critical public policies on AIDS and the blood supply. The one conference on AIDS that it sponsored in 1985 received little publicity; blood-bank representatives feared bad publicity would hurt their blood collections, Holland said.

In early 1988, the American Association of Blood Banks withdrew from the commission, saying it no longer played an important role in policy issues and was competing with the association by sponsoring seminars and conferences.

Other members criticized the commission for failing to adequately represent consumers or develop safe standards for using blood.

A consultant's study made public this year was critical of the commission's failure to take a leadership role during the AIDS crisis. It recommended the commission assume a consumer-advocacy role or shut down.

The government's track record is not much better. The Food and Drug Administration, the agency charged with ensuring blood safety, does not even know how much blood is collected or how it is used and must rely on the industry for such data.

"We tried to get funds allocated for collecting this type of data but without much success. The attitude [under the Reagan and Bush administrations] has not been to add regulation, but one of deregulation," said Dr. Kathleen Sazama of the FDA's Division of Blood and Blood Products.

While the government *does* track AIDS cases contracted through blood, it still keeps no records of hepatitis-linked deaths from blood —even though hepatitis is the most common infection contracted from blood.

A reporter calling the hepatitis division at the federal Centers for Disease Control in Atlanta was told no figures were kept for hepatitis deaths attributable to blood transfusions. "Try calling the Red Cross," a CDC physician suggested.

Staff cuts have hurt the FDA's inspection ability at a time when problems in blood banks have been mounting. Even with recent hires, the agency still suffers from a serious shortage of inspectors.

The FDA estimates that approximately 130 inspectors spend some time during the year inspecting the 2,424 blood banks and commercial plasma centers nationwide. All told, the agency has the equivalent of 28 full-time employees who work on blood issues.

Compare that with the U.S. Department of Agriculture, which has 7,200 agents conducting daily inspections of the nation's 6,300 meat and poultry processing plants.

"We can't have a cop on every corner," said Young, the FDA commissioner. Without additional money, the FDA will be forced to juggle inspectors from emergency to emergency, Young said. "That's the most efficient way to use our limited resources."

The government's lackadaisical oversight of the blood industry can be seen in one recent action:

In July, the FDA published a proposed rule that would change the way blood banks label blood. It came seven years and one month after the issue was first recommended by an FDA advisory panel.

THE LOOSE WAY THE FDA REGULATES BLOOD INDUSTRY

MONDAY, SEPTEMBER 25, 1989

BY GILBERT M. GAUL

For at least a year, people who had tested positive for the deadly AIDS virus were allowed to walk the streets of Philadelphia without knowing it.

They had sold their blood plasma to the Community Blood and Plasma Center at 1201 Race St., a commercial facility that collects plasma for a manufacturer of plasma medicines based in Vienna, Austria.

The center tested the blood for the AIDS virus and until 1987 notified in writing anyone who tested positive, according to a company executive. But that year, the center stopped mailing these notifications after a city-funded AIDS group objected to the way it was being done.

Eugene A. Timm, head of U.S. operations for the Austrian manufacturer, Immuno AG, said the center "bowed to the request from the local {city} health office not to send out such letters."

"We never suggested that they stop informing donors, only that they do so in a humane and compassionate way," said Dr. Louis van de Beek, medical director of Philadelphia's AIDS Activities Coordinating Office. "This is a terribly unfortunate choice they made. A choice of tremendous health consequences."

It was also a choice the center could make because there is no federal regulation requiring blood banks to notify donors who test positive for AIDS.

The Food and Drug Administration, the federal agency responsible for the safety of the American blood supply, recommends notifying donors but leaves the decision up to the blood banks and plasma centers.

That kind of hands-off attitude is not uncommon at the FDA. When Timm informed the agency in May 1988 that the Race Street center had resumed mailing AIDS test results, FDA officials accepted his word for it. An inspector did not return to the plasma center to verify the statement until half a year later.

Even that was an improvement, though: The FDA did not inspect the center at all between May 1986 and April 1988.

What was discovered at the Philadelphia plasma center is typical of the loose government supervision under which the blood industry operates. A yearlong Inquirer investigation found time and again that, even in matters of safety, government regulators have dragged their feet or turned over important decisions to the blood industry.

Item. The FDA did not require an AIDS test on donated blood until Jan. 5, 1988, almost three years after the first test for detecting AIDS antibodies in blood came into use in March 1985. In the interim, the FDA recommended its use. But some blood banks delayed using it and others did not test thousands of pints of blood already in their inventories.

Item. The FDA is only now developing proposed quality assurance standards for the required tests for AIDS, more than four years after the tests were put into use. Even so, the proposed standards fail to cover four tests now used by blood banks, including one used to confirm that a person has AIDS.

Item. The FDA's workforce was cut sharply during the early 1980s, at precisely the time AIDS was threatening the blood supply. Inspections of blood-collection facilities were reduced in 1983 from once a year to once every two years (annual inspections have since been restored). In Pennsylvania, large dog kennels are inspected three times a year.

Item. The FDA now has 900 inspectors to keep track of 2,424 blood banks and plasma centers. By comparison, the U.S. Agriculture Department has 7,200 agents conducting on-site inspections of the nation's 6,300 meat and poultry plants.

Item. The FDA is a paper tiger. It has no authority to fine blood banks that violate federal safety standards. And while it can suspend or revoke operating licenses, in the last four years the FDA has imposed those sanctions only 33 times—an average of eight times a year.

Item. Many FDA inspectors are ill-trained to detect problems in computerized, high-tech facilities. Some inspectors still have not been trained to interpret results of AIDS tests, four years after blood banks started using them.

Item. The FDA has relied heavily on the blood industry in setting safety standards. In 1984, the agency rejected use of a test that some experts said could have identified nearly 90 percent of the blood donors at high risk for AIDS. The agency based its decision on recommendations from two industry-dominated advisory groups.

Item. Critics say there is a revolving door between the FDA and the blood industry. Regulators leave the agency and go to work for blood banks, plasma manufacturers and trade groups. Once there, they can use their access to influence government policy decisions and protect their new interests, critics say.

"The FDA has over-relied on the blood bankers to set the minimum standards it has, and that has resulted in a trade-off between the health interests of consumers and the interests of the blood banks," said Ross D. Eckert, a professor at Claremont McKenna College in California and a member of an FDA advisory panel on blood.

LIFE-THREATENING ERRORS

Those health interests are increasingly at risk. A growing number of potentially life-threatening errors has been occurring within blood banks and commercial plasma centers.

The plasma facilities collect and process blood plasma into a number of finished products, such as Factor VIII blood-clotting concentrate and hepatitis vaccines. In addition, nonprofit blood banks collect whole blood and separate it into its various components—red blood cells, platelets and plasma.

Between 1987 and 1988, the number of recalls of suspect blood products more than tripled—to 101 recalls.

Thousands of pages of blood-bank inspection reports, FDA documents and confidential industry records obtained by The Inquirer depict an industry bordering on overload as it tries to collect, test and track more than 20 million blood products a year.

The records show that centers have released blood products that repeatedly failed tests for AIDS and hepatitis, have failed to follow their own requirements for testing and handling blood, and have relied on poorly designed computer systems that failed to meet federal standards.

In the last two years:

• In Los Angeles, a Red Cross blood center recalled 1,400 suspect blood products following what FDA investigators called a "systemic failure" to follow safe testing procedures.

• In Columbus, Ohio, a Red Cross blood center recalled 376 blood products that had been shipped to New York, Georgia, Florida and Switzerland. The suspect blood was distributed even though it had repeatedly tested reactive for the AIDS virus or had come from donors who had previously tested positive for AIDS.

• In Tyler, Texas, the W. E. & Lela I. Stewart Blood Center recalled 315 suspect blood components that repeatedly tested positive for hepatitis but were nonetheless labeled safe and distributed throughout Texas and Florida.

• In Charlotte, N.C., a Red Cross blood center recalled 1,617 blood products that tested positive for AIDS or hepatitis but had been distributed anyway. The blood center also failed to enter the names of suspect donors into a special computer registry of dangerous donors.

• In New York City, the New York Blood Center recalled nearly 12,000 vials of Factor VIII blood-clotting concentrate and other blood plasma products after they were manufactured from hepatitis-contaminated blood.

• And in Lincoln, Neb., the operating license of the Community Blood Bank was suspended in July for "numerous deviations" from federal safety standards, including release of blood "unsuitable for distribution" and failure to monitor "the reliability, accuracy, precision and performance of test procedures."

Industry officials point out that, to date, no one is known to have contracted AIDS from the suspect blood products released as a result of these errors.

Yet "the fact is there were a lot of units of blood that got out that shouldn't have," FDA official P. Ann Hoppe told a gathering of more than 200 blood-industry managers in San Francisco in April.

BLOOD-BANK INSPECTIONS

As a result of the growing number of errors, FDA Commissioner Frank E. Young announced in March 1988 that his agents would begin inspecting blood banks every year.

"Seeing a problem in an area we were concerned, I said, 'Wait a minute. We're not going to do an inspection every two years. That's

inadequate. I want a profile . . . of all blood banks in a single year,' "
Young said in an interview with an Inquirer reporter last fall.

He gave a similar explanation at a Senate hearing on April 21,
1988: "I do believe the blood supply is safe as it can be at this time. I
would, however, like to be sure that a safe blood supply is made even
safer by reducing human errors and making sure that the laboratory
tests are done in a correct fashion under visual inspection of an inspector."

What Young did not say on either occasion was that until July
1983, it *had* been FDA policy to inspect blood banks at least once a
year.

That policy was scrapped as part of the Reagan administration's
sweeping deregulation efforts of the early 1980s—with the blessing
of the blood industry and with Young's own tacit approval.

That information is buried among thousands of pages of government announcements of forthcoming hearings and changes in federal
rules published daily in the Federal Register. On July 30, 1982, FDA
officials published a proposed rule change to cut back blood-bank
inspections from "at least once every year to at least once every two
years."

"This action will provide flexibility for the agency to reduce the
inspection burden on a specific portion of the regulated industry," the
announcement in the Federal Register said.

The blood industry supported the cutback, which took effect July
7, 1983. "The American Red Cross Blood Services supports the proposed rule . . . which would reduce the frequency of inspections,"
wrote Dr. Joseph P. O'Malley of the Red Cross.

Anyone who was not aware of the change could easily be left with
the impression that the FDA was embarking on a tough new regulatory path in March 1988—when, in fact, it was merely returning to
an inspection schedule it had followed until July 1983.

Young acknowledged in the interview that had there been more
frequent inspections, the problems in blood banks would have been
detected sooner.

"What we're really doing is ferreting out problems that were probably there for some time," he said. "I'm not sure what 'some time'
was."

Government records show that after inspections were cut in half in 1983, the number of recalls dropped for three years, then increased sharply in 1986, the year after testing for AIDS began.

The records also show that testing errors were occurring in blood banks and plasma centers even before testing for AIDS began in 1985. Those errors involved the release of products that repeatedly tested positive for hepatitis.

The government's slowness in responding to the AIDS threat to the blood supply is evident from a review of events:

At a July 1982 conference in Washington, it was disclosed that three hemophiliacs had contracted AIDS and dozens of other hemophiliacs had symptoms of the deadly disease that destroys the body's immune system. The hemophiliacs had no apparent risk factors except that they used large amounts of Factor VIII, the clotting concentrate made from plasma.

By December of that year, the number of infected hemophiliacs had risen to seven and the first case had been reported of a person—a 20-month-old infant—apparently contracting AIDS through a transfusion.

Less than a year later, the number of transfusion-associated cases of AIDS had risen to 31 and the number of infected hemophiliacs had reached 19.

Yet in June 1983, the FDA announced it was cutting the frequency of its blood-bank inspections.

By then, it had become evident that AIDS could be transmitted through blood transfusion or by using medicines made from plasma.

"By 1983, everything epidemiologically was pointing to a contagious agent that was probably blood-borne," said Dr. Bruce Evatt of the federal Centers for Disease Control and an expert on blood diseases.

Yet it would be five more years before the FDA required any testing of blood for the AIDS virus. By then, 60 percent of America's 20,000 hemophiliacs—12,000 people—had been infected through contaminated blood-clotting medicine.

And as of July 31 of this year, 1,044 adults and children with hemophilia had developed the full-blown disease from clotting factor. In addition, 2,668 people had contracted AIDS from transfusions of tainted blood, according to the Centers for Disease Control.

Young provided several explanations for why the agency didn't move sooner. He said he moved quickly when he saw the number of errors committed by blood banks double between 1987 and 1988. "At that point, I said to myself . . . that it could not be business as usual."

In fact, the number of errors had been increasing for some time, government documents show. In 1985, there were 21 recalls by blood centers. In 1986, there were 51—an increase of 143 percent.

Young also said the agency was forced to adopt a crisis-management style due to its limited cadre of inspectors and overall cutbacks at the agency dating to the Carter administration.

"We can't work with smoke and mirrors," Young said. "We've got an agency here that is responsible for $570 billion worth of industry a year—25 cents on every dollar that is spent in the U.S."

The FDA, in addition to monitoring the blood supply, is responsible for assuring the safety of prescription drugs, imported fish and produce, medical devices, vaccines and cosmetics.

Young said that when a crisis develops in one area, he "shifts the agency's resources toward that problem. What we are constantly doing is moving resources around. But we only have [900] inspectors."

As a result of this strategy, the FDA is forced sometimes to disregard problems, Young said. For example, the agency stopped all inspections of medical-manufacturing facilities in Texas between 1986 and 1988 in order to examine problems in blood banks in that state, Young said.

And in March of this year, the FDA poured unprecedented resources into pinpointing two cyanide-laced grapes that were among 364,000 boxes of Chilean red seedless grapes unloaded at the port of Philadelphia. FDA inspectors found those two grapes in less than 48 hours.

When Ronald Reagan became president in January 1981, the FDA had 7,799 full-time employees. By 1987, the agency's workforce had been cut nearly 11 percent, to 6,963 full-time employees, government records show.

Figures were not available for inspectors. However, Young said that the agency corps of inspectors was "downsized" 22 percent between 1977 and 1984 and that the FDA was unable to hire needed specialists due to the overall cutbacks.

At present, the FDA has just six computer experts nationwide who can be called on when the agency uncovers an industry problem linked to computers. Most FDA inspectors are considered "generalists" and are responsible for many different industries.

Most generalists go through a one-week training course in blood banks. During training they are taught how to use a checklist when they inspect a blood bank or plasma center. About 2½ hours of training are spent on what to look for when blood banks are computerized.

"It's not a lot. I admit that. But we give them a checklist for them to follow," said Mary Ann Tourault, a top FDA consumer-safety officer. "We haven't quite gotten there, but we're pedaling as fast as we can."

Tourault said FDA officials recently began going into the field to train inspectors how to interpret tests for AIDS—four years after blood banks started using the test.

"I did have a job before AIDS," Tourault said. "I don't know what it is anymore. We're trying to keep up with everything and get it out into the field as soon as we can. It's been a very, very difficult job. We're drowning."

Young supported the use of generalists as inspectors. "I would strongly defend that an inspector of a blood bank should be a generalist. And there is a lack of understanding on the part of some blood-bank people as to what to anticipate in this. If they are expecting the level of a resident of hematology to walk in there, that's not going to happen at all.

"Would we like to have more people who are trained in laboratory medicine who could do inspections? Absolutely. We're moving more and more to specialists."

FDA officials are currently preparing what they call a "unified memo" on AIDS that will consolidate all the agency's previous recommendations. Among them is a new recommendation that blood banks and plasma centers notify donors who test positive for AIDS.

The notification recommendation comes more than four years after the blood industry began to test donors for the disease.

"That's true. We are adding it in the informed consent. You should be told when you give blood now and test positive," said Joel Solomon, who became director of the FDA's Division of Blood and Blood Products in 1988.

"I don't know why it wasn't done before. I wasn't here then. What happened before I can't speak to," Solomon said.

But the recommendation is just that. It will not carry the force of law, as a regulation does. If a blood bank or plasma center chooses to ignore it, it can do so with immunity.

In May 1986, an FDA agent spent three days inspecting the Community Blood and Plasma Center on Race Street. According to a report the inspector later prepared, he found several deficiencies, none of which appeared to be life-threatening.

They were serious enough, however, that a report was written and given to officials at the center pointing out what needed to be corrected.

An inspector did not return to the facility until two years later, on April 5, 1988. That was when FDA investigator Richard E. Harrison found that donors with positive test results for AIDS were not being notified, as required by the center's own standard operating procedures.

"The SOP calls for letter notification to all donors found reactive," Harrison's report notes. "I found that this facility has not sent notification letters to such HIV [Human Immuno-deficiency Virus, the AIDS virus] positive donors . . . since as far back as 5/21/87."

Documents describing the inspection do not indicate how many plasma donors tested positive for AIDS in the period examined by Harrison. A company official said it was "only a few." However, during the three days Harrison spent at the center, he reported seeing at least two such blood donations being destroyed by workers.

During a discussion with the FDA agent following his inspection, center officials conceded they "should have been sending out the letters as required," according to Harrison's report.

"I pointed out . . . that waiting for all donors to come in and then notifying them was not the best way to do it as, given the inconsistent attendance of donors and the high dropout rate, some positive HIV test donors might not come in again for a long while or even ever again and would thus remain uninformed," Harrison's report says.

The Race Street center is one of 16 that collect plasma from paid donors for Immuno-US Inc., a subsidiary of Immuno AG, a large, for-profit plasma manufacturer in Vienna.

On April 25, 1988, FDA officials asked a representative of Immuno-US what the company was doing to correct the problem at its Race Street operation.

On May 6, the company's president, Eugene A. Timm, responded: "Letters are now being mailed after verification of lab results."

In explaining why the center stopped mailing notices, Timm wrote, "This is because our local center management bowed to the request from the local Health Office not to send out such letters."

Richard Dice, executive director of Community Blood and Plasma Inc., said in an interview earlier this year that the Race Street center was contacted by an official from the Philadelphia Health Department "in mid-1985. My recall is the Health Department called us and frankly told us not to report positive test results to the donors. I thought it was some doctor with the Health Department. I can't recall his name."

Former and current administrators at the city Health Department could not recall contacting the plasma center in 1985. However, Dr. van de Beek, director of the city's AIDS Activities Coordinating Office, said a representative of his office did contact the plasma center in 1987.

CONTACTING DONORS

Dr. van de Beek said at least one donor who had received a letter from the plasma center and "was considering suicide" turned out, after additional testing, not to have AIDS.

"It became apparent to us there was an incredible threat to the health of individuals receiving information in this fashion," he said.

"We basically told them [plasma center officials] that there was a much more compassionate way to do this. What these people really need at a time like this is a hug. They need medical care. This is not something you learn about by mail," van de Beek said.

He also insisted his group did not tell the plasma collection center to stop notifying donors by letter—only that it be done after proper testing and that those who tested positive for AIDS should be brought in for counseling.

"That [the decision to stop sending letters] is the first I've heard of that," van de Beek said. "[With proper notification] those individuals who are infected could get life-saving therapies and get information that could save the lives of other people."

FDA officials, meanwhile, accepted Timm's April 1988 explanation that letters were again being sent to donors testing positive for AIDS and filed it away.

"We have placed this material in this facility's file and its contents will be verified at the time of the next inspection," a compliance officer informed Timm in a letter dated May 17, 1988.

And while a subsequent inspection found that letters were indeed being mailed, the inspection did not take place until November 1988 —six months later.

The FDA has never told blood banks and plasma centers that they must inform donors who test positive for AIDS. In October 1985, the U.S. Public Health Service recommended notifying donors and referring them to doctors for an evaluation. But these recommendations were never made into law.

□ □ □

The FDA has been slow to formulate requirements covering the use of computers by blood banks—in part, due to its own lack of expertise —or to develop proficiency standards covering tests used for AIDS and hepatitis.

While blood banks have used computers for years, it was not until this month that specific FDA requirements governing computers were issued. They mandate that blood banks must be able to show that their systems perform consistently and accurately. And while the agency has drawn up a proposed rule requiring blood banks to have independent outside auditors review the accuracy of their testing, a top FDA official conceded she "didn't know what we will do if someone fails the program."

The FDA recently provided an answer. Officials announced in June that they "would work closely" with any blood center that fails the testing program "to improve the quality of its performance."

In March, the FDA published a notice in the Federal Register indicating that its inspectors would not even ask to see "reports of any internal audits conducted by an [outside] firm to determine compliance with its own quality assurance program when the quality assurance program is required by regulation."

"FDA will not review or copy reports and records that result from audits and inspections of a written quality assurance program," the agency said in a June notice in the Federal Register clarifying its position.

In other words, an independent audit might find potentially dangerous problems in a blood bank. But unless the FDA knew about the problems beforehand, agency officials would not ask to see the audit records.

That approach reflects the extraordinary trust the agency places in the industry's willingness to regulate itself.

Indeed, the FDA often relies on the industry for advice.

The close relationship between the agency and the industry is reflected in many of the actions taken by the FDA's Blood Products Advisory Committee.

Formed in 1980, the committee's charter calls for it to advise the "commissioner in discharging his responsibilities as they relate to assuring safe and effective biological products and related medical devices."

Until recently, committee members were almost exclusively blood-bank officials and medical researchers. As of May, 10 of the committee's 11 voting members came from the blood industry or were physicians and/or researchers. The chairwoman, Dr. Louise J. Keating, is the director of the Red Cross blood bank in Cleveland.

The committee includes a consumer representative and an official from the commercial plasma industry, but neither is allowed to vote.

"Even today, it remains what I call an Old Boys' Club," complained Thomas Asher, chairman of a California company that sells specialized blood products. "It's insular to a fault and it's very protective of its own self-interests."

In its June 1988 final report, the Presidential Commission on AIDS warned against this close government-industry relationship, saying it fostered "a relationship that presents a significant opportunity for conflicts of interest."

In April 1988, Eckert, the Claremont McKenna College economist, was appointed to the committee. "Clearly, there hasn't been enough diversity," he said in an interview. "My appointment is a step in the right direction, but there needs to be a lot more done."

While the committee's character directs it to offer advice, in practice it does much more. It helps shape policies affecting the collection, distribution and testing of blood. Moreover, a review of more than a dozen hearings since 1982 shows that its recommendations are rarely rejected by FDA officials.

For instance, the FDA turned to the committee in 1983, when it was trying to decide whether blood banks should be required to use a test for identifying high-risk donors for AIDS.

Studies at the Centers for Disease Control, made public at a widely attended meeting in Atlanta in January 1983, had showed that nearly 90 percent of AIDS patients and others considered at risk of developing AIDS had antibodies in their blood indicating a history of hepatitis. Thus, CDC officials reasoned, in the absence of a specific test for AIDS, a test for hepatitis—known as the hepatitis B-core antibody test—could be used to identify those at high risk for AIDS.

In other words, by using a laboratory test that detects the hepatitis B-core antibodies, blood banks and plasma centers could identify and exclude blood donors who also were at risk of having or developing AIDS.

"To some of us [at CDC], what should have been done was relatively clear," Evatt said. "We were recommending using the test."

While CDC officials could recommend it, they did not have the regulatory power to require the test. That authority belonged to the FDA. And there, officials turned to the industry for direction.

In December 1983, the Blood Products Advisory Committee met on the campus of the National Institutes of Health near Washington to debate the issue. During the long and sometimes heated session, it became apparent that even though the antibody test could identify donors at high risk for AIDS, not to mention hepatitis, many representatives from the blood industry objected to its use.

Because it was not a specific test for AIDS, they argued, its use would result in the exclusion of some safe donors and of many homosexual donors who had a history of hepatitis but not of AIDS. It was argued that in cities that depended heavily on gay blood donors, such as San Francisco and New York, use of the test could seriously reduce local supplies.

Another argument was that it would be too costly. In addition to an estimated $3 for the test itself, there would be added expenses to recruit new replacement donors, several blood-bank officials said.

Near the end of the meeting, Michael Rodell, a representative of the plasma industry, suggested that a task force be formed to further study using the antibody test. The advisory committee unanimously agreed with the suggestion, a transcript of the December hearing says.

It is notable that, at a meeting the evening before the Dec. 15 meeting, the plasma manufacturers decided to request that a task force be formed.

According to a memorandum prepared a few days later by an official of Cutter Biologicals Inc., the largest U.S.-based plasma manufacturer: "This proposal was one that had been agreed upon by all the fractionators (plasma manufacturers) the previous evening. The general thrust of the task force is to provide a delaying tactic. It was generally agreed that core testing would eventually become a requirement."

"I never heard of that [meeting]," said Dr. Dennis Donahue, who was director of the FDA's Division of Blood and Blood Products from 1980 to 1986 and played a key role in many of the agency's decisions.

Donahue was one of two non-industry members of the task force that was formed to study the hepatitis B-core antibody test. Six of the other nine members were from the plasma industry and three were from blood banks.

In May 1984, the task force issued its findings, saying it could not reach a consensus. Citing many of the same arguments made five months earlier, a majority of the task force opposed requiring the test. Three members, including Donahue, favored requiring it.

The minority position paper drafted by Donahue's group noted that AIDS cases were doubling every six months and that voluntary steps to exclude high-risk donors were not working in all cases.

"In the absence of a test for the presence of the causative agent of AIDS, the only means of reversing this trend is to more effectively identify plasma donors who are members of high-risk groups," the position paper argued.

Donahue said recently that while he believed his approach was logical, "The fact of the matter is, there are two sides to every argument."

The FDA accepted the view of the industry-dominated task force and did not require the test.

While the FDA declined to take action, some blood banks and plasma centers started to use the hepatitis antibody test on their own. The reasons: public pressure and competition. Among them was Cutter.

In the same memo that described the task force's delaying tactic, the Cutter official privately wrote his colleagues that "the anti-core testing would add a further measure of confidence in product safety at a relatively low cost for the products involved."

Even before the December 1983 meeting of the Blood Products Advisory Committee, Cutter officials began implementing the test at their collection sites.

"We recommend that the implementation of core testing be accelerated to the maximum degree possible to obtain a competitive advantage in the marketplace," says a Dec. 19, 1983, internal company memo. "We made no mention of our plans to the others."

By June 1984, three of the five largest blood banks in northern California were using the test, usually in response to pressure from patients, hospitals and doctors.

The FDA seemed to go to unusual lengths to downplay these developments. In April 1984, the agency released a statement reading in part:

"On the basis of the information available to date, it is possible that screening tests other than anti-core may ultimately prove to be more predictive and generally useful in improving the safety of blood and blood products. It would therefore be unwise to adopt anti-core testing to the exclusion of other screening tests."

In other words, until there's a better test, don't do anything.

In February 1986, the Blood Products Advisory Committee finally recommended using the hepatitis B-core antibody test—but only for screening out donors with a history of hepatitis.

The FDA accepted the recommendation. Even though the test is now used by almost all blood banks, the regulatory agency still does not legally require it and has no standards governing its use.

FEAR OF AIDS SPURS CHANGE

TUESDAY, SEPTEMBER 26, 1989

BY GILBERT M. GAUL

William Polikoff survived the Bataan Death March and was a POW in the Pacific for 3½ years during World War II. But he could not survive AIDS.

Three years after receiving three pints of tainted blood while undergoing cardiac bypass surgery in San Diego, Polikoff died at age 70 on Dec. 9, 1987, of complications from AIDS.

"He went through hell and back, and then to have this happen was just so unfair," Polikoff's widow, Dorothy, said.

In May 1988, Dorothy Polikoff told the Presidential Commission on AIDS that her husband had never been advised that there were alternatives to being transfused with blood from the hospital's blood bank.

"If we had known the risk, his family could have given blood. His golf buddies would have given blood. His {four} children could have given blood," Polikoff said in an interview. "The fact is, they never told us."

Dorothy Polikoff is herself now infected with AIDS, which she contracted through sexual relations with her husband. Had doctors warned them, they would have abstained from sex, she said.

"It's very hard coping," she said. "I spend each day just waiting to see what happens. The same thing my husband went through I know I will have to go through. I'll be 65 next October and each day is precious.

"I ask myself, 'Where was the government to prevent this from happening?'" Polikoff said. "Someone has to try to make sure this devastation doesn't ever happen. It should never happen again."

□ □ □

Until AIDS, doctors routinely ordered blood transfusions for their surgery patients.

They did it relying on a medical standard promulgated half a century ago—one that said if the hemoglobin in a patient's blood was below a certain level, a transfusion should be ordered. That dictum, it turns out, had never been clinically tested and, in fact, is now under challenge.

But in the medical schools and hospitals of America it was passed along as dogma, so that generation after generation of doctors-in-training learned to do it, unquestioningly.

"For years, doctors have given blood like it was aspirin. And many solutions that would have allowed patients to do without blood were ignored, neglected or overlooked," said Theresa L. Crenshaw, a physician and member of the Presidential Commission on AIDS.

As a result, experts now say that over the years millions of patients have received blood transfusions unnecessarily, exposing them to risks ranging from fever and chills to life-threatening diseases such as AIDS. The number who have died is unknown.

That is because no one—not the government, not the blood banks—has kept track of these deaths. But the number is easily in the thousands, transfusion experts say, and hundreds of thousands of other patients have been infected with hepatitis, a potentially virulent disease that attacks the liver.

It is estimated that each year between 40,000 and 200,000 Americans—or up to 5 percent of all transfusion recipients—contract a form of the disease called Non-A, Non-B hepatitis from blood. An estimated 60 percent of these patients develop chronic hepatitis. And approximately 20 percent develop cirrhosis of the liver within five to 10 years.

Because cirrhosis is often fatal, most of these patients eventually die from their post-transfusion hepatitis. Again, no one knows the precise number. But it may be more than 1,000 patients a year. In May 1988 testimony before the Presidential Commission on AIDS, one speaker estimated it could be as high as 4,000 patients a year.

"This is a staggering statistic when put into perspective. Assuming transfusion cirrhosis is fatal, losing 4,000 people per year is roughly like losing the passengers on one fully loaded DC-10 every month," said Ross Eckert, an economist at Claremont McKenna College in California and a member of a federal advisory panel on blood.

But there has been no outcry, in large part because most Americans have little idea about the risk of contracting hepatitis from blood transfusions. Even though it affects many more transfusion recipients, hepatitis has received far less publicity than AIDS. Even those who understood the risk have downplayed it.

"Physicians were well aware of the risks, but they chose to ignore it or said it wasn't as great as the risk of not getting blood," said Dr. Bruce A. Friedman of the University of Michigan Medical Center, one of the few researchers to study in detail how blood is used.

The blood industry also failed to promote several basic steps to protect patients getting blood.

Equipment for recycling a patient's blood during surgery, available since the mid-1970s, was generally ignored until recently. And few blood banks encouraged patients to pre-deposit their own blood before surgery—the safest form of transfusion possible.

The Presidential Commission on AIDS said in a June 1988 report that some blood centers "have been hesitant" to promote these steps, "since their operating income is derived from the sale of blood." The report also concluded that many physicians and hospitals had not "adequately informed their patient population about the availability of alternatives [to transfusions]."

Now, after years of neglect, things are beginning to change.

The reason, in a word, is AIDS—and the widespread fears it has generated about the safety of the blood supply.

Since June 1981, when the federal Centers for Disease Control began tracking AIDS cases, 2,668 patients have gotten the deadly disease from transfusions of infected blood, including 196 children.

These victims, who account for 2.5 percent of all AIDS cases, are just the first of a wave to come. CDC researchers estimate that there are 12,000 people still living who were infected with AIDS from blood transfusions given between 1978 and 1984, before testing for AIDS started in 1985.

"AIDS is driving everything we do today. Patients have picked up that fear and are demanding that we do things differently," said Dr. William J. Ledger of New York Hospital, where women undergoing obstetrical and gynecological procedures are now routinely pre-depositing their own blood.

The dreaded disease has forced unprecedented changes upon the medical community and the blood industry, changes they had been reluctant to make on their own:
• In record numbers, patients are refusing blood, second-guessing their physicians and donating their own blood before surgery.
• Blood banks that once resisted efforts to conserve blood are now

buying machines that recycle blood during surgery and are marketing these services to hospitals.

• For the first time in decades, doctors and researchers are questioning the standards they use for ordering blood and attempting to conserve blood wherever possible.

• In some places, sales of blood have slowed or actually decreased, causing financial problems for some blood banks and prompting others to diversify into new areas. They include storing a patient's frozen blood for a fee, offering cholesterol testing, and expanding into the growing market for bone and tissue transplants.

• The recent development of a test to detect Non-A, Non-B hepatitis has raised new hopes for a safer blood supply. Studies to date indicate that the test, developed by Chiron Corp. of California, successfully identified the virus in medical trials.

• Patients infected with AIDS through transfusions are suing blood banks and hospitals in increasing numbers—in a few cases winning multimillion-dollar verdicts, despite state laws that grant blood banks virtual immunity from tort awards.

Says James L. MacPherson of the Council of Community Blood Centers in Washington, "Today, many in blood banking feel like they have been taking a beating."

The victims have their own views on who's taking the beating.

□ □ □

Shortly after their only child, Michael, was born in February 1983, Mary and Paul Osborn learned he would have to undergo open-heart surgery to repair a congenital defect. The two arteries carrying blood from Michael's heart to his lungs were transposed.

Without corrective surgery, he would be starved of oxygen-rich blood, would not develop normally and might even die.

When the Osborns were advised that Michael would need transfusions during surgery, they asked to have family and friends donate blood—a practice known as a directed or designated donation.

The parents' request was rejected by officials of the Irwin Memorial Blood Bank in San Francisco, according to court records and interviews. Irwin supplies most of the hospitals in San Francisco, including the University of California at San Francisco Medical Center, where Michael Osborn underwent surgery at four weeks of age.

Irwin, like many other blood banks at the time, discouraged directed dona-
tions.

"We wanted our blood designated for Michael. But when we went down
there they told us, 'You don't direct blood from Irwin, you donate for the
pool,' " Michael's mother, Mary, said in an interview.

The Osborns did not learn that the blood Michael had received during
surgery was tainted with AIDS until he was 4½ years old. They received a
letter from hospital officials at that point suggesting that Michael be tested.
The reason: Infected donors had given blood to Irwin.

"We called our pediatrician and he said there was nothing to be concerned
about; it was a routine thing for everyone who had gotten blood during this
period," Mary Osborn said. "So we had Michael tested and he was positive.
We got tested ourselves and we were both negative. Then we had Michael tested
again and he was positive again.

"For a time we kept hoping and believing that Michael would be someone
who had the disease but didn't get sick. But that just isn't so."

Michael turned 6 in January. He suffers from a brain tumor that distorts
the size of his head. His speech is severely impaired. He is only now learning
to walk. And the right side of his face and body are partially paralyzed.

"He's got high spirits and he keeps us going that way," Mary Osborn said.
"Sometimes even I have a difficult time understanding him. But then he'll
point and he'll indicate to me, 'Never mind.' "

Michael attends a special school program for seriously ill children two days
a week near his home in Sacramento. "He enjoys seeing his friends there,"
Mary Osborn said. "And sometimes someone close will come over and he plays.
He just loves to play."

In December, a Superior Court jury in San Francisco found Irwin Memorial
negligent in handling the blood it provided for Michael and awarded his
family $750,000.

Michael Moriarty, an attorney representing the Osborns, told the court that
Irwin disallowed a directed donation because it would have cut into its profits,
a charge denied by the blood bank.

Attorneys for Irwin have appealed the decision—the first jury verdict in
which a blood center was found negligent for providing blood that carried the
AIDS virus. And that appeal is continuing.

"We don't expect to see anything," Mary Osborn said. "We just hope at
this point not to lose any money."

Michael's mother recently quit her part-time job as a telephone operator so she could spend more time with her son. "If Michael's not feeling well, I just couldn't go to work," she said. "Every day is different. Some days I don't know how we're going to make it. But we'll make it somehow."

□ □ □

In 1941, Dr. John S. Lundy, an anesthesiologist at the Mayo Clinic in Rochester, Minn., wrote in a medical journal that patients with less than 10 grams of hemoglobin, an oxygen-carrying protein, in a deciliter of their blood should receive a transfusion before surgery.

For unknown reasons, Lundy's 10-gram standard was never subjected at the time to the rigorous scientific scrutiny that most medical advances face.

"The gods who walked the earth in the '20s, '30s, and '40s said on essentially no clinical data that 10 grams is necessary . . . and it's been self-perpetuated," said Dr. Richard K. Spence of the Robert Wood Johnson Medical School in Camden. Spence performs surgery on Jehovah's Witnesses, who decline transfusions for religious reasons.

Today, nearly 50 years later, there is still a gaping hole in scientific literature on when to give blood.

"We never have been able to come up with good scientific data to substantiate the 10-gram requirement," said Dr. Margot S. Kruskall, medical director of the blood bank at Beth Israel Hospital in Boston and one of the nation's leading experts on the use of blood. "People have used a series of crutches along the way. Now we are learning that they are just that—crutches—and we know we have tended to overuse blood.

"Why, in 1988, don't we have good standards?" Kruskall asked. "It seems like a basic question that we ought to have the answer to. But nobody knows."

"Many physicians still use blood inappropriately and very frequently it is for unexplained reasons," said Dr. James W. Mosley, a professor at the University of Southern California and director of a federally funded study on transfusion safety.

In the mid-1970s, government and industry officials adopted a national blood policy that included among its goals the development of standards for blood use. "But nothing was ever done about the [developing standards]," said Douglas MacN Surgenor, chairman of the Center for Blood Research, a nonprofit research center in Boston that is affiliated with Harvard University.

The federal government, which has primary responsibility for overseeing the blood supply, has been slow to fill the gap.

Other than sponsoring some conferences and a small amount of research on blood use, federal officials have left it to the medical community to develop standards—the same medical community that has been content to use a 50-year-old, unproven one.

"This is not necessarily a federal solution," said Frank E. Young, commissioner of the Food and Drug Administration. "In our pluralistic society we really do best when we identify a problem . . . and then the medical profession takes over." Nevertheless, Young said that there is "an enormous overuse of blood around the country."

Even today, doctors-in-training spend a lot of time learning about the basic science of blood and "too little time" learning when it is necessary to transfuse a patient, said Dr. Richard S. Eisenstaedt of Temple University Hospital, an expert on the use of blood.

"That's mainly because transfusion medicine doesn't have the image or weight that many other disciplines have," he said.

Young doctors learn what they know about transfusing patients largely by "osmosis," said Dr. Jerome Avorn of the Harvard Medical School. "One's decision to transfuse is shaped by watching people around you."

For the last half-century, that has meant relying on the 10-gram standard developed by Lundy—a standard Dr. Howard L. Zauder of the State University of New York Health Science Center at Syracuse describes as "cloaked in tradition, shrouded in obscurity and unsubstantiated by clinical or experimental evidence."

Indeed, Spence says that he and other doctors have operated on Jehovah's Witnesses with hemoglobin levels as low as five grams without transfusing any blood.

"What I've found with the Witnesses is that the lower hemoglobin does not relate to [higher] mortality at all," Spence said. "The 10-gram standard is a myth."

□ □ □

In April 1985, John Carroll, an insurance agent from Brookfield, Wis., entered a hospital near his home to have heart-bypass surgery. Following the procedure, he was transfused with cryoprecipitate, a blood-clotting concentrate used to stop bleeding. It was provided by the Blood Center of Southeastern Wisconsin in Milwaukee.

According to a lawsuit Carroll later filed, he rejected a nurse's attempts to give him the blood-clotting agent three days after surgery when she could not guarantee it had been screened for AIDS. The next day, a second nurse attempted to give him cryoprecipitate, this time assuring Carroll that it had been tested. He then agreed to the transfusion.

Ten months after the operation, Carroll learned from a doctor that he had been infected with AIDS as a result of the transfusion.

The blood center had started testing its blood supply on March 7, 1985. But the test could not be used on cryoprecipitate already in its inventory, according to Carroll's attorney, Robert Habush. The cryoprecipitate Carroll got in April that year came from this inventory.

"It should have been recalled," Habush said.

On Dece. 9, 1988, a jury found the Blood Center of Southeastern Wisconsin negligent and awarded Carroll $3.9 million, the largest such award to date. A spokeswoman said the blood center does not intend to appeal.

Habush described Carroll's condition today as "perilous. He has been given anywhere from six months to a year and a half to live."

Said Carroll, who is 63: "I'm going to spend the rest of my short life trying to help other people who are less fortunate than me and also help victims of AIDS, no matter how they caught it."

□ □ □

Dr. Anita Ali of the Canadian Red Cross is one of the few researchers who have attempted to calculate how often blood is used unnecessarily.

Last summer, Ali made public the results of a study showing that 15 percent of the patients given blood in a group of Canadian hospitals were transfused for no sound medical reason.

"If 15 percent of surgical patients are receiving a treatment that is of doubtful benefit and not without risk, further investigation . . . appears justified," Ali concluded.

Applying Ali's 15 percent finding to transfusions in the United States would mean that 600,000 of the four million transfusions given annually are done unnecessarily.

Saving that blood would help ease spot shortages and lead to a savings of more than $100 million a year.

But blood banks would lose millions of dollars in sales. And that may explain why the blood industry has been so slow to adopt procedures to conserve blood.

"I remember when I ran the blood program for the Red Cross in New England," Surgenor said. "I proposed to the board that we hold a scientific meeting and talk about blood conservation. They really didn't want to hear anything about it."

The Presidential Commission on AIDS concluded in its June 1988 report: "Some regional blood centers have been hesitant to promote strategies that minimize the use of transfusion . . . since their operating income is derived from the sale of blood and blood products."

Where blood banks do question the use of blood, less blood ends up being transfused. And money is saved. For example:

• In Seattle, the Puget Sound Blood Center is one of the few centers in the country that scrutinize how hospitals use blood. A study last year by Surgenor and his colleagues found that of every 1,000 patients admitted to Seattle hospitals, 451 pints of blood were transfused, compared with 755 pints of blood for every 1,000 patients admitted to Massachusetts hospitals.

• In Houston, by requiring that all transfusion orders be reviewed, doctors at the M. D. Anderson Hospital blood bank reduced transfusions of blood by nearly 19 percent and of some other blood components by 57 percent. Writing in the journal Laboratory Medicine in April 1988, they estimated savings to patients of nearly $800,000 a year.

• In Boston, similar efforts at Massachusetts General Hospital resulted in a reduction of blood use by 25 percent between 1982 and 1987, said Dr. Charles Huggins, director of the hospital's blood-transfusion service. Huggins monitors the amount of blood used at the hospital on a daily basis.

"I try to do it in as nice and unthreatening a way as I can," he said, "but yet get the point across that the director of transfusion services is out looking over their shoulders.

"We like to talk about how the blood supply is safe. But each time a doctor transfuses a patient, there's some risk," Huggins said. "The best approach is to minimize transfusion wherever possible."

□ □ □

On Feb. 5, 1985, Carol Marcella of Parkersburg, Chester County, sustained serious injuries in a car accident and was hospitalized at Brandywine Hospital in Caln Township.

During her 51-day hospital stay, she received blood transfusions, according to a lawsuit filed late last year by attorneys for Marcella, her husband, Timothy, and their two sons. The lawsuit named Brandywine Hospital, the local Red Cross and five doctors as defendants.

According to the lawsuit, Timothy Marcella questioned whether the blood his wife was to get had been tested for the AIDS virus "and was informed by Defendants that it had been so tested. The information was false."

The lawsuit also says that the family of Carol Marcella was not offered a chance to donate blood for her.

"As a direct result of the negligent, careless and reckless acts and omissions of defendants, Carol Marcella was given blood transfusions that resulted in her contracting the Acquired Immune Deficiency Syndrome (AIDS) virus," the suit contends.

Susan White, a Philadelphia attorney representing the Marcella family, said that one of the units of blood that Marcella was given came from an inventory of blood that had been collected by the Red Cross' Penn-Jersey Regional Blood Services in February 1985. She said that Red Cross officials received test kits for detecting the AIDS virus in mid-March 1985 and began to use them about that time.

In its response to the suit, the Red Cross asked that the charges be dropped, contending that such claims are barred by state law. In this case, the plaintiffs contend that there was an implied warranty that the blood given to Marcella would be safe. The state's blood-shield law bars suits for breach of "implied warranty." To successfully sue a blood bank, a person must prove negligence.

A spokeswoman for Red Cross' Penn-Jersey Regional Blood Services referred questions about the Marcella case to a Red Cross attorney in Washington. The attorney did not return telephone calls from The Inquirer.

□ □ □

When Dr. Howard F. Taswell first walked into a surgical suite more than 25 years ago, he was appalled by the amount of blood being wasted.

"There was all of this blood just going down the drain," Taswell, the medical director of the Mayo Clinic Blood Bank, recalled in an interview. "It was appalling."

In 1962, Taswell wrote that recycling the blood lost by patients during surgery was possible, thereby reducing waste and the risk of infection from transfused blood. "But nobody paid attention."

These days, nearly everybody in blood banking is paying attention —because of AIDS and the risk of lawsuits.

Failing to offer patients alternatives to transfusions could constitute grounds for a lawsuit, Dr. Lester Sauvage of the Hope International Heart Research Institute in Seattle told the Presidential Commission on AIDS last year.

Sales of equipment for recycling blood have more than doubled, to 2,500 machines nationwide, according to one industry estimate. More than 200,000 such procedures are now performed in hospitals each year.

Haemonetics Corp., a manufacturer near Boston, reports that its sales have increased from less than $40 million in 1986 to nearly $100 million last year. It has been selling machines for recycling blood since the early 1970s, spokesman Stephen P. Oliver said.

The technology is deceptively simple. Blood is sucked up by a vacuum tube during surgery, cleansed of any impurities inside a portable unit, then transfused back into the patient, either during surgery or later.

Hospitals that use recycling equipment say they can break even if they salvage an average of two units of blood from each patient. More than that and they save money by reducing the amount of blood they have to buy. The cost of recycling equipment ranges from about $15,000 to more than $40,000.

At the Mayo Clinic, Taswell said about 20 percent of all blood used during surgery in 1987 came from the patient. "It has been going up very rapidly here. A large percent of major surgeries, we now salvage [save and recycle blood]. We can return it almost as fast as the patient is bleeded," Taswell said.

At the Cleveland Clinic Foundation, the percentage of patients undergoing bypass surgery who receive blood has been reduced from nearly 100 percent in the early 1980s to 30 percent today, according to Dr. Delos M. Cosgrove, director of cardiovascular surgery. Surgeons have been able to accomplish this change with "no adverse influence on hospital mortality," Cosgrove said.

Many blood centers that previously ignored the recycling technology are now using it. In some instances, it is viewed as a new money-making service, in others as a way to fend off competitors, such as PSICOR Inc., a California firm now marketing the service nationally. For others, it is an added layer of protection against blood-related lawsuits.

For example, the Red Cross blood program in Miami started marketing the recycling procedure last year with the promise "it can lower your hospital's potential liability for adverse effects of transfusion."

In Philadelphia, the Red Cross started marketing the recycling equipment last fall as part of what was called "a new effort" to promote alternatives to blood transfusion. And in December, the University of Pennsylvania Medical Center introduced a "new system" for recycling a patient's blood following orthopedic surgery.

AIDS also has prompted blood banks and doctors to rediscover another overlooked procedure: patients setting aside their own blood before surgery.

Termed an *autologous donation,* this procedure has been cited in medical literature for years as the safest form of transfusion because it eliminates the risk of disease.

Despite that recommendation, doctors and blood banks did little to promote autologous donations until AIDS raised patients' fears and lawsuits galvanized the industry to offer an alternative to transfusion.

Dr. William C. Sherwood, administrator of the Red Cross' Philadelphia-area blood program, said he did not promote a pre-deposit program until 1986 because he thought it would be inconvenient for patients.

Asked how he came to that conclusion, Sherwood said, "It's just a feeling, a gut feeling I had, that given the inconvenience [patients wouldn't want to do it]."

When the Red Cross finally promoted its program, the response was strong. In three years—1986 through 1988—the number of patients setting aside their own blood grew by more than 600 percent —and it's still growing. Sherwood said he now encourages autologous donations.

Interviews with dozens of blood-bank directors around the country turned up similar responses.

"Our blood center has always had an autologous program, but it wasn't used much and it wasn't promoted much by us or the medical community," said David W. Parker, administrator of the Red Cross blood program in San Jose, Calif. "We really got into it with promotional materials around 1984–1985. Now we do a couple thousand autologous procedures a year," he said.

"Fear of AIDS is what has prompted this [growth]," said Joan Norberg, director of the Blood Bank of the Redwoods in Santa Rosa, Calif. Nearly 25 percent of her center's activities now involve patients setting aside their blood before surgery, she said.

"If I had to undergo surgery, I'd go with my own blood as much as I could," said Dr. Morton Spivack, director of Mount Sinai Medical Center's blood bank in New York. "I wish I had a freezer-full of autologous blood here."

At the same time, Spivack and other blood-bank directors said they think patients need to be reasonable in their concerns about the blood supply. "For example, I don't think it's a good idea for somebody with a GI [gastrointestinal] bleed waiting around for his friends to donate blood for him while he's bleeding to death," Spivack said.

At present, autologous donations account for about 5 percent of the blood used nationwide. But Norberg and other officials said they believe that figure could grow to as high as 50 percent if such donations were promoted aggressively by blood banks.

One hospital that has already benefited financially is Underwood-Memorial Hospital in Woodbury, N.J., which has a thriving autologous program. In 1987, the hospital saved more than $12,000 by using about 400 units of blood pre-deposited by its patients.

"The savings are the difference between what it would have cost us to buy that blood from the local Red Cross and what it cost the hospital to collect it itself," said David G. Schoenleber, the hospital's transfusion service supervisor.

Meanwhile, several dozen private blood services have formed recently in response to the growing demand for autologous donations.

One, the Idant Division of the publicly traded Daxor Corp., will store pre-deposited frozen blood at a center in Memphis and ship it wherever the patient requires it, a spokesman said.

Another, Merus Personal Blood Banks in San Diego, will draw

blood in a patient's home, using a portable collection unit, and store it at their facilities. These services often cost several hundred dollars.

Some experts question whether freezing one's blood is really a necessary or practical way to prepare for surgery. Right now, the fledgling industry accounts for only a minuscule amount of the blood that is transfused.

Nevertheless, a growing number of blood banks have begun to offer similar services in an effort to respond to these competitive challenges. In Oklahoma City, the regional blood bank has embarked on a six-point program to "do everything possible to limit a person's potential exposure" to risk—from stressing autologous donations to using blood from repeat donors who have a proven record of safe blood.

At least some officials think the pressures brought by patients and private vendors have had a positive effect.

"I think what AIDS has brought to blood banking is change, and I'm not sure that's bad," said Connie P. O'Neill, former director of the Champaign (Ill.) Blood Bank.

"It's forced us to be a lot more sensitive to donors, to [promote] education and to do things differently than we did 10 years ago. And that's good."

RED CROSS: FROM DISASTER RELIEF TO BLOOD

WEDNESDAY, SEPTEMBER 27, 1989

BY GILBERT M. GAUL

When the American Association of the Red Cross was formed by Clara Barton on May 21, 1881, it was with a clear mission.

A charter later approved by Congress spelled out its purpose as a voluntary relief agency providing medical aid to victims of wars and other great "national calamities," including pestilence, famine, fire and floods.

That is still the image the Red Cross portrays in its advertising and solicitations. "When people are in trouble, the American Red Cross gets down to business—the emergency-services business. It's what we do best," the Red Cross said in its 1986 annual report.

But tax records and financial statements show that, a century after its founding, the Red Cross' main business is no longer disaster relief.

Its main business is selling blood.

Consider these facts:

• Fifty-nine cents out of every dollar that the Red Cross spent in the fiscal year ended June 30, 1988, went to operate its blood program. Less than a dime out of every dollar went to disaster services.

• The majority of the Red Cross' revenues—nearly 53 percent—now comes from blood, up from 19 percent in 1971.

• From 1980 through 1987, the blood program generated average operating profits of $38 million a year. Last year, profits fell to $4 million as a result of safety problems that increased costs. The blood program's total profits, which the Red Cross calls "excesses over expenses," were nearly $307 million for the 1980–88 period.

• From 1980 through 1988, the blood program's net worth grew 161 percent, to $188 million. Overall, the Red Cross had a net worth of nearly $1 billion in 1988, with cash and investments of $559 million listed on its balance sheets. (Net worth is the amount by which an organization's assets exceed its liabilities.)

In short, the Red Cross has undergone a major transformation in the last 15 years—from predominantly a relief agency to a giant in the blood business.

Today, the Red Cross controls at least half of all the blood collected and sold to hospitals in the United States.

The Red Cross' blood operations are so big that if the blood program alone were a public company, its 1988 revenues of $535.5 million would have ranked 477th on the Fortune 500, just ahead of Affiliated Publications Inc., owner of the Boston Globe.

And the Red Cross' total 1988 revenues of $985 million from all sources would have ranked 339th on the Fortune 500, ahead of Bausch & Lomb Inc., the lens and eye-care company.

Before its financial problems last year, the Red Cross' profit margin would have been the envy of many companies. Its overall 8.7 percent profit margin in 1987, for instance, would have ranked 98th on the Fortune 500, ahead of such giants as General Electric Co., Mobil Corp. and Chrysler Corp.

Another advantage those corporations could only wish for: the services of nearly 1.4 million volunteers, who donate their time for Red Cross blood drives, First Aid classes and disaster aid. That's in addition to the organization's 23,357 paid workers.

Over the years, the Red Cross has built a vast network that now includes 56 regional blood centers, a Washington headquarters, 2,817 Red Cross chapters, a multimillion-dollar research lab, a closed-circuit television network and production studio, and its own offshore insurance company—Boardman Indemnity Ltd. in Bermuda—to cover losses from AIDS lawsuits and other claims.

And as a nonprofit charitable organization, the Red Cross benefits from $90 million worth of free television, radio and print advertising a year, at least one-third of which is devoted to its blood program.

In recent years the Red Cross has become a major player in the largely commercial plasma business, where the Red Cross now has about a 15 percent share of the U.S. market, with sales of about $75 million a year.

The Red Cross' rise to dominance of the blood business has not been without controversy. Officials of other nonprofit blood banks criticize it for aggressive tactics and say the Red Cross is trying to take over the blood business. And its commercial competitors contend that the Red Cross has an unfair competitive advantage because of its tax-exempt status, which they say the blood portion of its operations does not deserve.

"Red Cross is in business—both in the blood business and in the finished plasma business—and building up a Taj Mahal," said Thomas Hecht, chairman of Continental Pharma Cryosan Inc., a plasma business in Montreal.

"The American Red Cross is perceived by the public as a benevolent group of volunteers, who make the donation of blood as painless and socially significant as possible," H. Edward Matveld of Alpha Therapeutics Inc. said in testimony in June 1987 before a U.S. House subcommittee that was examining the question of taxing nonprofit groups. "The public is not generally aware of . . . its incredible wealth.

" . . . The plasma services division [of the Red Cross] has grown disproportionately so that its revenues are not substantially related to the performance of the original tax-exempt purpose," Matveld said. "It therefore appears appropriate for Congress to review the American Red Cross charter and mission as they pertain to competitive, for-profit activities."

Red Cross officials have fended off suggestions the organization should pay taxes on its blood business, arguing that no one benefits personally from its profits, which are used to further the organization's work. Red Cross officials also say they act as stewards of the blood they collect from unpaid donors.

"We have no stockholders," Dr. Lewellys F. Barker, the Red Cross' senior vice president for blood services, said in an interview. "To me, that's probably the most fundamental difference between nonprofit and commercial entities. We both need to have substantial finances to be able to provide our services.

"Our objective is to meet patients' needs," Barker said. "I think it's pretty traditional in this country for business objectives to make a profit. I don't object to that. That's their primary purpose, as I see it. But that's not our primary purpose."

In earlier testimony before the congressional subcommittee examining nonprofits, Barker said: "We operate [the blood services] on a cost-recovery basis. That is to say, obviously, the total revenue with an excess that we require for working capital and equipment and buildings and so forth basically balances the total expenses. It is a wash."

Its critics contend that the Red Cross has used its "excesses"— profits—over the years to build an ever-expanding empire, paying executive salaries of $150,000 or more and amassing larger-than-necessary financial reserves.

In the interview with The Inquirer, Barker was asked about a 15 percent profit margin budgeted for the Red Cross' plasma business this year. He said that the Red Cross needs to maintain adequate reserves. "This is a service which has some cycles, ups and downs, for which we need [financial] reserves."

It is Red Cross policy that each of its 56 blood centers should maintain financial reserves sufficient to cover a minimum of 45 days' worth of operations, and up to a maximum of 180 days. However, an internal Red Cross financial document obtained by The Inquirer notes that "some regions have liquidity levels above what can reasonably be considered necessary to operate their blood centers.

"In a few cases, liquidity levels exceed one year. As a nonprofit organization, it is difficult for the Red Cross to explain the need for excessive amounts of liquidity," the Feb. 17, 1989, internal report said.

While the blood business has been a major revenue source for the Red Cross, profits from blood are not used to pay for disaster relief. The two programs are operated separately.

The blood program is self-supporting; other Red Cross services, such as disaster relief and water-safety programs, are financed through contributions from the public—$315 million in 1988. Most of those contributions come through the United Way.

One reason the Red Cross is sensitive about its profits from blood sales is fear that public knowledge about them might affect charitable contributions, some industry officials say.

"Red Cross doesn't want the American public to know it is a big blood business," said James Holland, former president of Blood Centers of America Inc., which represents eight nonprofit blood banks. Holland said that the Red Cross promotes its disaster-relief activities and plays down its blood program "to keep the [charitable] donations coming in."

In Philadelphia, the Southeastern Pennsylvania Chapter of Red Cross received 52 percent—or $3,173,506—of its funding in 1988 from United Way contributions. The chapter had total revenues of $6.1 million last year and spent $885,036 on disaster services. Its largest expenditures were nearly $1.6 million contributed to national headquarters in Washington and $1.1 million for management and chapter activities.

In 1971, contributions from all sources accounted for 78 percent of the national organization's total revenues of $174 million. By 1988, contributions had tumbled to 32 percent of revenues—$315 million out of nearly $985 million.

That trend has caused concern. The Philadelphia chapter lists as one of its current management goals: "To stabilize United Way funding relationship while expanding supplemental fund-raising efforts."

When the Red Cross was formed in 1881, the charter spelling out its mission contained no references to collecting or selling blood. It still doesn't.

The organization began distributing blood during World War II, at the request of the U.S. government. The Red Cross and a group called the National Resource Council supplied the armed forces with 13 million pints throughout the war.

After the war, Red Cross officials wrestled for two years with the question of whether to resume collecting blood, according to two official histories of the organization.

In 1947, they decided to embark on a nationwide blood program to supply hospitals, in order to keep the Red Cross' name before the public and to generate new revenue, according to the histories.

"The new program marked a major departure for Red Cross—away from the strictures of its traditional and Charter-mandated activities and into the realm of civilian medical service," says a background paper written by Norman R. Kear, administrator of the Red Cross' blood center in Los Angeles.

Kear's paper lists five general purposes for the 1947 decision, one of which was "to develop an activity that would be constant and thus keep the American Red Cross continuously in the midst of the people on whom it depends for support."

Although it had the backing of several national groups, the Red Cross' initial efforts ran into opposition from other blood suppliers, including hospitals and community blood banks. These two groups formed the American Association of Blood Banks to act as a counterforce to the Red Cross.

It was not until the 1970s that the Red Cross' blood program really began to mushroom. From a loss of $15 million in 1971, the program turned in a profit of more than $9 million by 1977. And between 1980 and 1987, the program's operating profits never dropped below $20 million a year, reaching as high as $56.6. million in 1983.

The Red Cross benefited from a federal policy, developed in 1972, that encouraged the formation of large regional blood centers to ensure an adequate national blood supply.

The transformation of the Red Cross may be seen in two sets of figures: Between 1971 and 1987, spending on disaster relief rose from $25.5 million to $89.4 million, an increase of 250 percent. Spending on the blood program went from $48 million to $488.2 million, an increase of 917 percent.

By the early 1980s, the Red Cross controlled half of all blood collections and was a serious competitor in the plasma business. More recently, the Red Cross has expanded into the growing market in bone and bone marrow for transplant, operating a nationwide network of bone banks. It is now the largest supplier in the United States of bones and tissue for transplant.

In the blood business, the Red Cross now accounts for slightly more than half the estimated 13.5 million pints of blood collected each year. From that blood, it makes nearly 10 million separate blood products and sells them to 3,300 hospitals.

For its supply, the Red Cross depends on volunteers to donate blood each year at thousands of businesses, churches and other sites. An estimated 4.3 million people donated blood last year.

According to Red Cross statements, the blood program is operated on the premise that "healthy members of the community have a responsibility to donate adequate amounts of blood to meet the needs of their sick and injured neighbors."

"Someone you love needs life-giving blood," says the Red Cross' 1988 annual report.

The Red Cross does not pay donors for their blood. In 1976, Red

Cross president George M. Elsey wrote that paying for blood was "medically and morally unjustifiable."

"We of the American National Red Cross have never paid any donor at any time for her or his blood and most certainly never shall," Elsey wrote to Elmer B. Staats, then-comptroller general of the United States.

Red Cross officials also say they do not charge hospitals for the blood they purchase. Rather, hospitals are billed a "processing fee" that covers the cost of collection and production, the Red Cross says.

That distinction has worn a little thin on some operators of other blood banks.

"It drives me crazy when the Red Cross says it doesn't sell blood. That's like the supermarket saying they're only charging you for the carton, not the milk," said Richard D. Crowley, executive director of the Central Illinois Blood Bank in Springfield. "What else do you call it? We're in the blood-selling business."

The "processing fees" are the prices that hospitals are charged by Red Cross blood centers. And those prices vary dramatically from region to region.

In its plasma business, some Red Cross blood centers are instructed by national headquarters to mark up their products by fixed amounts, known inside the organization as "overrides." In other cases, the centers are free to charge hospitals whatever the local market will bear, internal Red Cross documents show.

And, while the Red Cross doesn't pay donors for their blood, it does use money as an incentive for the collection of more blood.

In 1988, the Red Cross began a pilot project in which blood centers were paid a $15-a-pint bonus for collecting more blood than they need —blood to be sold to other centers. Known as National Premium Contracts, the bonus program yielded an extra 26,000 pints last year, according to a Red Cross planning document.

Red Cross officials hope to collect up to 104,000 extra pints annually, according to the document. At $15 a pint, that would mean a payout of $1,560,000 in bonuses to blood banks.

Some Red Cross blood centers also offer cash bonuses to workers who solicit blood donors by telephone. The workers earn the bonuses, tacked on to their salaries, by exceeding goals set by the blood centers.

Telephone solicitors for the Red Cross blood program in Philadelphia can earn bonuses of $80 to $200 a year by exceeding recruitment goals.

To earn a $200 bonus, a solicitor must average three donor appointments per hour during the year, according to spokeswoman Christie Phillips. Recruiters are required to make at least 1.75 donor appointments an hour, Phillips said.

Supervisors are eligible for bonuses—up to $600 a year—based on the performance of the recruiters they oversee, Phillips said.

Barker said the practice of offering financial incentives to tele-recruiters was consistent with the volunteer philosophy the Red Cross always has espoused.

"We draw a very clear line between paying donors and paying fees . . . whether they are a cost-plus incentive or whatever. We see those as totally different issues. At least I do."

□ □ □

In the last 18 months, problems in the Red Cross' blood program have shaken the organization and had a severe impact on finances.

Nearly two-thirds of the 56 regional blood centers were identified as having deficiencies following the discovery in March 1988 of problems at blood centers in Washington and Nashville.

Most of the safety problems involved inadequate testing of blood before it was released or failures involving the computerized records systems used to log results of blood tests and to keep track of dangerous donors.

Between March 1988 and March 1989, the Red Cross recalled 5,700 units of blood and blood components that had not been properly tested for AIDS and hepatitis. (The Philadelphia blood bank was not among those with safety problems.) And the Red Cross had to shut down its $75 million-a-year plasma business for six months because of concerns about blood safety.

In late February, the Red Cross' board of directors named a special committee to examine the operation of its blood program. The committee was expected to report its findings in October.

The problems led to a shakeup of top management at national headquarters in Washington and in the field. President Richard F. Schubert and three other senior staff members, including the head of computer operations, announced their resignations in April. Several top administrators of regional blood centers were demoted or replaced, and top blood-program staff at national headquarters has been reorganized.

A Red Cross internal investigation and FDA inspection reports traced the release of some suspect blood to vaguely worded instructions from national headquarters on testing for AIDS—with different blood centers interpreting the test instructions in various ways.

"This was the single biggest cause of erroneous releases [of suspect blood]. . . . Thus our own [directives] were the principal cause of our current plasma financial crisis and the attendant media attention about erroneous releases," the November 1988 internal report said.

Another internal report was highly critical of the computerized system for recording results of AIDS and other tests on blood and for keeping track of dangerous donors.

"Efforts in automation are dismal failures; poor system design has contributed to [the] erroneous release problem; FDA and independent consultants indicate that systems do not comply with [federal] requirements," the report said.

The problems also affected morale and exacerbated tensions between the regional blood centers and national Red Cross officials at headquarters in Washington. The relationship between national headquarters and the regions was characterized as one of "intensely mutual lack of trust" in a Dec. 7, 1988, analysis prepared by directors of a number of regional blood centers.

"NHQ staff are not accountable. . . . Lack of stable knowledgeable staff. . . . Organization is slow to change in a rapidly changing environment . . . and is inwardly focused. . . . Too much time spent doing business within the organization," were some of the criticisms made in the analysis.

In a national teleconference in February to introduce members of the newly appointed study commission and to calm employees' concerns, Schubert, then president, noted that the Red Cross was suffering from "unfortunate divisiveness and hostility."

Dr Fred Katz, a vice president of the Red Cross, said during the teleconference that the safety problems had resulted "in decreased confidence in our ability to release only safe products. The public and our customers had opportunity to question our claims of safety." And because of the quarantine of Red Cross plasma, and of the cost of dealing with safety problems, "Red Cross was financially damaged," Katz said.

"We have just got to operate in such a way . . . we don't have a repetition of what has happened over this last year," Schubert said during the two-hour teleconference. The Inquirer obtained a videotape of the meeting.

As a result of the shutdown of the plasma program and other problems, operating profits for fiscal year 1988 dropped to about $4 million from nearly $34 million the previous year. The Red Cross borrowed $20.7 million from the blood program's reserves of $209 million for capital improvements.

Barker said that most of the problems were compliance issues, which did not directly affect public safety.

Since January, the FDA has released most of the quarantined plasma medicines and Red Cross officials have launched a wide-ranging offensive to get their $75 million plasma program back on track. Regional blood centers have been instructed by national headquarters to collect as much plasma as possible, internal documents show.

"Red Cross ability to maintain or increase our market share . . . is a key organizational goal," a Feb. 17 budget-planning document states. It also noted that the Red Cross anticipated recovering a "substantial increase" in revenues from the blood-clotting medicine it sells to hospitals and hemophiliacs.

In another step aimed at shoring up the Red Cross' overall financial position, chairman George Moody late last year informed 5,700 retirees of the board of governors' plans to terminate the Red Cross' $730 million pension plan and to replace it with a different system.

Contending that the pension plan was overfunded, the board proposed to tap $100 million of an estimated $400 million surplus for operating expenses.

The plan angered many Red Cross retirees. Moody defended the action in a letter to one retiree who had objected. As a nonprofit organization, he wrote, "we believe that a portion of the excess funds . . . should be used to meet humanitarian and organizational needs."

In an interview, pensioner James B. Foley described the plan as a "ripoff" and said that the average Red Cross pensioner receives a monthly check of $422—about $5,000 a year.

Virginia Mankin, manager and secretary of the retirement fund, said the number of pensioners receiving benefits as of July 26 was 5,757. The average monthly check was $436—or $5,232 a year.

She said that pensions are based on the number of years a person worked at Red Cross—the more years, the higher the pension. "There's quite a few people who would leave at age 65 with very low service," she said. "It also covers part-time and per diem people."

As the blood portion of its operations has grown, officials of the Red Cross in Washington have become increasingly secretive, apparently for competitive reasons, regional Red Cross managers and others say.

The organization used to publish annually a report on its operations that contained information about each of its 56 blood centers, with data ranging from amount of blood collected to prices charged.

"Now you practically have to go underground to get one," said Nancy R. Holland, former executive director of the American Blood Commission, an organization that once helped shape public policies on blood.

Many reports containing routine data on Red Cross operations are now stamped "confidential," "secret" or "For Internal Use Only." Key officials within the Red Cross' regional blood banks are required to sign confidentiality statements, promising not to disclose financial and operational data.

"There is a genuine fear of outsiders, which is unfortunate because it makes it appear we have something to hide," said Kear, administrator of the Red Cross blood center in Los Angeles.

Most Red Cross officials are truly interested in doing a good job, Kear said. But he said the organization has become "unnecessarily bureaucratic" and "paranoid."

Others use even stronger language.

"They actually have a mind-set that on the day of creation, when the Earth was just one big steaming molten mass and hot sulfur clouds were churning around, the hand of God reached through with a bag of blood and handed it to them and said, 'Here, take this exclusively and spread it among all mankind,' " said Thomas M. Asher, chairman of a publicly traded company in Sherman Oaks, Calif., that competes with the Red Cross.

"The Red Cross in my mind is the evil empire," said Leslie Vogt, president of a nonprofit blood bank in Richmond, Va., that is not affiliated with the Red Cross. "They want to be the only blood supplier nationally. It's run like a big business. And it's more political than most people think."

For nearly a decade, between 1977 and 1987, the Richmond center bought several thousand pints of blood a year from the Red Cross' regional blood program in Roanoke, 165 miles away. Vogt needed the blood to cover shortages in her city.

"It was a good, friendly relationship. They had a surplus of blood and we needed blood," Vogt said.

Then, in 1986, she was told by Roanoke officials that she would have to buy blood through the Red Cross' new national clearinghouse. That meant paying more for the blood, and Vogt said she was afraid Richmond would be cut off if there was a shortage in the Red Cross system somewhere.

"They took a relationship that worked for 10 years and wrecked it," Vogt said.

Vogt opted to buy her blood from several other blood banks.

"It's crazy. You have two blood banks 165 miles apart that can't share, while the blood drawn in Roanoke is probably being shipped all over the country," Vogt said.

AMERICA: THE OPEC OF THE GLOBAL PLASMA INDUSTRY

THURSDAY, SEPTEMBER 28, 1989

BY GILBERT M. GAUL

In the spring of 1988, Dr. Carol Kasper began to have problems purchasing Factor VIII, the lifesaving blood-clotting concentrate she uses to treat hemophiliacs.

With it, hemophiliacs can lead relatively normal lives; without it, they can bleed to death from a minor cut.

By fall, as a nationwide shortage of Factor VIII deepened, the supply at the hemophilia clinic that Kasper runs in Los Angeles had dwindled to one-third of usual levels, and she faced a wrenching choice:

Should she save her limited supply of a new, safer Factor VIII for the children, or share it among all 500 hemophiliacs she treats— including many adults already suffering from AIDS?

The children had not yet been exposed to the AIDS virus. But by that time, 60 percent of all adult hemophiliacs in America had become infected, as a result of using clotting factor made from blood plasma contaminated with AIDS.

While the doctor wrestled with her life-and-death decision, U.S.-based manufacturers of Factor VIII were making decisions of their own.

Several companies stopped making Factor VIII as long as three months before introducing their new, safer clotting concentrate; one company raised prices nearly 20 percent at the height of the shortage, and three manufacturers continued to export large amounts to Japan and Europe, where they could charge higher prices.

As a result, America's 20,000 hemophiliacs faced not only a health crisis but a financial one as well—a crisis that continues today, even though the shortage has eased.

The average cost to hemophiliacs soared from about $8,000 a year in 1987 to more than $50,000 a year today. Hemophiliacs who must use large amounts of the clotting medicine pay as much as $80,000 a year.

Manufacturers denied they were profiteering. They cited higher production costs and said that profits from the worldwide sale of clotting factor helped underwrite lower prices paid by Americans.

In many ways, though, their justifications underscored a fundamental tenet of business: Companies will try to sell their products wherever the most profit can be made. That is as true in the blood business as it is in the oil or steel industries.

The buying and selling of blood is a multibillion-dollar business. And plasma, from which many medicines are made, is the most commercial part of the blood business. The plasma industry had sales of more than $2 billion in 1988.

Unlike blood banks, the plasma industry operates on a global scale, is highly competitive and experiences dramatic swings in the availability and price of its products—as with Factor VIII last year.

Plasma and the medicines made from it are bought and sold like other commodities, with decisions made in one country often causing sharp price changes or shortages in other countries.

"It's like selling hog bellies or wheat or beef. It gets sold all over," said Thomas M. Asher, chairman of Hemacare Co., a for-profit company in Sherman Oaks, Calif., that trades in plasma and other blood products.

And if U.S.-based manufacturers choose to sell plasma medicines such as Factor VIII to other countries while there's a shortage here, they are free to do so. The U.S. government makes no attempt to restrict exports of such medicines during shortages to ensure an adequate domestic supply.

When it comes to selling blood, the United States has the most liberal standards in the world for how often a person may sell his own plasma.

Federal regulations allow individuals to sell up to 60 liters a year (nearly 127 pints) of their own plasma—a maximum of two donations a week. That is twice the amount allowed by the next country, Canada. And it is four times the amount—15 liters a year—recommended by the World Health Organization. (A liter is a little more than a quart.)

Result: More than half the estimated 12 million liters of plasma used in medicines worldwide comes from the United States.

"The U.S. is the OPEC of the plasma business," said Thomas O. Hecht, chairman and chief executive officer of Continental Pharma Cryosan Inc., a Montreal-based distributor of plasma products. "You know what that stands for: the Organization of Plasma Exporting Countries."

To put the 60-liter figure in human terms, the average American male could each year sell the equivalent of 21 times the amount of plasma in his veins at any given time.

Most of this plasma is collected at the nearly 400 commercial centers that operate nationwide. The centers pay between $8 and $25 for a donation of plasma, which is extracted as whole blood and then put into a centrifuge, which spins out and separates the plasma. The oxygen-carrying red blood cells are then transfused back into the donor.

Many plasma centers offer bonuses to encourage frequent donations. Some advertise special Christmas deals, with the message that selling your plasma is a good way to earn money for Christmas gifts.

While U.S. donors are the source of more than 60 percent of the world's plasma, foreign owners dominate the business. Four of the six largest plasma companies in the United States are owned or controlled by foreign corporations based in Japan, West Germany, Austria and Canada.

JAPAN BUYS THE MOST

These companies collect and buy more than three million liters of plasma in America annually and sell them overseas to other companies, brokers or foreign governments.

They also sell the majority of their plasma medicines abroad. Japan in the single biggest customer, each year importing more than $300 million worth of plasma and plasma medicines. In 1988, 90 percent of plasma products used in Japan were made from blood collected in the United States.

On a per-capita basis, the Japanese use about three times more plasma medicine than either the French or English, according to a World Health Organization report. But Japan collects only about 10 percent from its own donors.

In this international market, it is not uncommon for plasma to change hands several times. Sometimes plasma brokers—middlemen who profit by bringing together those who have plasma with those who need it—are involved.

Even in industry circles, brokers are considered a secretive lot. There are no lists of brokers and finding one is no small task. Locating one willing to talk is even harder.

Asked to describe his business during a brief telephone conversation, one of them, Eric Jarrett, a Woodland Hills, Calif., broker, said: "We sell plasma to whoever wants to buy it."

"No one knows how much they control," said Joseph Rosen, vice president of SeraTech Biologicals Inc., a New Jersey company. "One broker may sell to another broker, who again may sell it to me or to a company in Europe."

Tracking this plasma once it leaves the country is difficult at best, industry officials and government regulators say.

Besides a registration requirement, the federal Food and Drug Administration does not regulate the activities of brokers and does not inspect their operations.

"Whether or not sterility is ever a problem, we do not really know," P. Ann Hoppe, assistant director of the FDA's Division of Blood and Blood Products, told an industry meeting last November. "The storage conditions often are such that bacterial contamination could proliferate if there were any present. So sterility may be less than 100 percent."

□ □ □

This volatile worldwide system for buying and selling plasma generally works well, industry leaders say.

"It's a very dynamic, interrelated business that has served many persons well," said Robert W. Reilly, president of the American Blood Resources Association, a trade group in Annapolis, Md. "Thousands of hemophiliacs have lived longer and better lives and thousands of other patients worldwide have benefited from products made by the commercial plasma industry."

Reilly and others also stress that the plasma industry has worked hard in the last decade to clean up its tawdry image by moving many of its collection centers out of inner-city sites into college towns and suburbs.

An increasing number of the newer centers have invested in automated equipment for collecting plasma that is quicker and safer, they say. Some of these centers even have video movies for donors to watch.

"We have intentionally designed the location of our centers to avoid the higher-risk groups," said Jack Luchese, who until recently was an executive of Armour Pharmaceutical Co. in Blue Bell, Pa., a large plasma manufacturer. "It's all prevention. You start with the right location. You get the right crowd to walk in. You . . . turn down the people who don't fit," Luchese said.

"There is a good side to this industry," said Ralph E. Eacret, president of Associated Bioscience Inc., which operates automated centers in Phoenix and half a dozen college towns. "This is it."

Not all commercial plasma centers are in college towns or suburbs, though. And not all the clients are as well off as Luchese and others would like.

In Philadelphia, for example, after inspecting the Community Blood and Plasma Center at 1201 Race St., a federal inspector filed a report in April 1988 observing that "there was no soap, hand towels or toilet tissue in the male donor restroom."

When the inspector asked an official of the plasma center why that was so, the official, M. Dempsey Dudley, said that "given the type of clientele at the facility, it was hard to keep these items in the restroom due to theft," the inspector's report says.

And, along the U.S.-Mexican border, a string of plasma centers attracts thousands of poor Mexicans. Each week they walk, wade or pay a dollar or two to be ferried across the Rio Grande to sell their blood.

There were 22 plasma centers operating along the border in 1988 —more than the number in Chicago, New York and Philadelphia combined.

Depending on your point of view, the centers are either preying upon poor Mexicans or boosting the cross-border economy.

"We are providing a valuable source of income to Mexicans, and it is probably a significant amount of money compared to what they might have gotten elsewhere," said David J. Gury, president of North American Biologicals Inc., a Miami-based company that owns two plasma centers in El Paso.

"It's a throwback to a time when maybe the industry didn't have such a good image," said Anita Bessler, vice president of sales and marketing for Baxter-Hyland Co., a plasma distributor that does not operate a border center. Some critics call this plasma "vampire blood."

In El Paso alone, there were eight commercial plasma centers operating this summer—one for every 53,125 residents. By comparison, Philadelphia has two—one for every 844,105 residents.

A visit in June to one of Gury's centers found that a majority of the donors were from Juarez, right across the border.

"I don't think it's important that they are coming across the border," Gury said. "The important thing is that the donor meets all of the qualifications as to health and suitability."

□ □ □

During the early 1980s, many commercial plasma centers were placed in so-called "hot spots"—cities such as San Francisco and Los Angeles that had large populations of gay men. This played a critical, if inadvertent, role in the spread of AIDS into the hemophilic population.

Federal records show that in 1981—before it was known that AIDS was spread through blood—there were eight plasma collection centers in the San Francisco area and 10 in the Los Angeles area. Some of these centers actively recruited homosexuals because they were considered steady, reliable donors.

In addition, some centers recruited homosexuals who had been exposed to hepatitis because their blood contained hepatitis antibodies, used to make vaccines. Spokesmen for the plasma companies say the plasma from these homosexuals was used only to make the vaccines and did not get into the larger plasma pool used to make Factor VIII.

But at least one expert, Dr. James W. Mosley, believes that by recruiting homosexuals as paid donors, these plasma centers may have contaminated the Factor VIII supply. For, unknown to the plasma collectors, some of these homosexual donors had AIDS and their plasma was used to make Factor VIII, spreading the infection among hemophiliacs who used the clotting factor.

In making Factor VIII, the natural clotting proteins in blood plasma are extracted and concentrated in strength. Clotting proteins from as many as 20,000 plasma donors may be mixed together to form a single batch of the concentrate, increasing the risk that only a few infected donors could contaminate the batch.

While it is not known how many infected donors actually sold their plasma, "it does not seem unreasonable . . . to suggest that homosexual men became disproportionately represented among paid donors," Mosley told a gathering of experts on hemophilia in March. Mosley is a professor of medicine at the University of Southern California and an expert on blood.

"Under the circumstances described, one would expect that introduction of HIV [human immunodeficiency virus, the AIDS virus] into the homosexual community would be quickly followed by introduction among hemophiliacs treated with [blood-clotting] concentrates," Mosley said.

And that is exactly what happened, data collected by federal officials show.

AIDS was introduced into the hemophilic population around 1979 —shortly after it started to appear among homosexuals. By 1982, an estimated half of all American hemophiliacs had been infected with the virus, although only a small percentage had symptoms of the disease, according to the Centers for Disease Control.

People with AIDS antibodies—that is, those who are infected—do not always exhibit symptoms, though it is now believed that all will eventually come down with the fatal disease.

That same year, an FDA official told the major plasma collectors they should close their centers in high-risk areas. By late 1983, most had been closed.

But by then it was too late. Federal records show that by December 1983, two dozen hemophiliacs had developed AIDS symptoms as a result of injecting tainted clotting concentrate, and thousands of others had been infected with the virus.

Today, at least 60 percent of American hemophiliacs—12,000 people—are infected with AIDS, according to Alan P. Brownstein, executive director of the National Hemophilia Foundation. And among those suffering from the severest form of hemophilia—those who need the greatest amount of clotting factor—nearly nine of every 10 are infected with AIDS.

Company documents made public in AIDS-related lawsuits show

the industry fought the introduction of a test for detecting hepatitis in blood that also was thought to be effective in identifying groups at risk for AIDS. It is known as the hepatitis B anti-core test.

One study at the time, January 1983, showed that nearly 90 percent of people judged to be at high risk of developing AIDS also tested positive for the hepatitis B-core antibodies. Thus, proponents argued, in the absence of a specific test for AIDS, the B-core test should be used.

But most plasma manufacturers didn't agree. And on Dec. 14, 1983, the evening before an important meeting with FDA officials, they gathered in a hotel room in suburban Washington to devise a strategy to delay requirement of the test, an internal memorandum written by an official of Cutter Biologicals Inc. shows.

"This proposal was one that had been agreed upon by all the fractionators [manufacturers] the previous evening," the Cutter company memorandum summarizing the meeting said. "The general thrust . . . is to provide a delaying tactic for the implementation of further testing."

The memorandum was written by Steven J. Ojala and was widely circulated throughout Cutter Biologicals, the largest U.S.-based plasma manufacturer, with headquarters in Berkeley, Calif. At the time, Ojala was director for regulatory affairs at Cutter. He now works for a different company in Kansas. He did not respond to telephone messages left with his wife.

The day after the manufacturers' discussion, federal officials agreed to an industry representative's request to form a task force to "study" the test.

Four months later, an industry-dominated advisory panel that included no consumer representatives reported to the FDA that its members were divided on whether the test should be used. The FDA subsequently accepted the position of those who opposed the test.

The anti-core test was rejected despite government and industry data available at the time showing that as few as four infected donors could contaminate an entire year's worth of Factor VIII.

By that time, epidemiologists from the Centers for Disease Control had linked AIDS to 30 cases involving blood transfusions.

Why were the companies opposed to the test?

Testimony before an FDA panel, Cutter internal records and interviews show that there were several concerns. One was that the hepatitis B-core antibody test was not a specific test for AIDS and would eliminate some donors who did not have the disease.

Another reason was the cost of the test—estimated to be $3—plus the expense of recruiting new donors to replace the blood that would have to be discarded. One plasma manufacturer, not specifically identified in the documents, estimated that implementing the test would cost his company between $350,000 and $2 million a year.

While most of the industry opposed the hepatitis B-core test, at least one company, Cutter Biologicals, was quietly moving ahead to use it, company records show. Cutter is owned by Bayer AG, a German pharmaceutical and chemical company.

"We recommend that the implementation of core testing be accelerated to the maximum degree possible to gain a competitive advantage in the marketplace," a Cutter memorandum says. "We made no mention of our plans to the others [plasma companies]."

The U.S.-based manufacturers also were slow to implement a process for making Factor VIII safer, one in which viruses are inactivated by heating the concentrate for 10 hours or more, FDA and industry documents and interviews show.

A PASTEURIZED VERSION

Behringwerke AG, a German manufacturer, developed a pasteurized version of Factor VIII in 1978 and began to market it in Germany. Behringwerke filed a U.S. patent application in 1980 describing its pasteurization process in detail and obtained a patent a year later.

During this time, most of the U.S.-based manufacturers were experimenting with heat-treated products in their laboratories. But none of these products was introduced until late 1983—after the majority of hemophiliacs had been infected with AIDS.

"I don't know why we didn't have a product sooner," Luchese said. "All I can say, from what I can see, the knowledge base wasn't at a stage that was considered something to be done."

Lawyers for hemophiliacs suing manufacturers for negligence contend that once the AIDS crisis had created public pressure for safer clotting factor, the manufacturers were able to develop a heat-treated concentrate within six months.

"There is no reason . . . to not have had pasteurized product on the market by 1980, had reasonable and prudent research and development been used," Thomas Drees, former head of Alpha Therapeutics Inc., said in 1988 in a sworn affidavit filed in a lawsuit in Hawaii. Los Angeles–based Alpha, one of the largest manufacturers in the United States, is a wholly owned subsidiary of Green Cross, a large Japanese drug company.

Documents show that, once introduced, the heat-treated concentrates came close to eliminating new cases of AIDS among American hemophiliacs. The National Hemophilia Foundation and the FDA have identified only 18 new infections since 1985 linked to heat-treated Factor VIII, FDA records obtained under the Freedom of Information Act show.

That compares with 1,044 hemophiliacs who had developed full-blown AIDS as of July 31 from Factor VIII made before heat-treated products became available. Because AIDS has a latency period of up to 10 years, that figure is expected to grow substantially as increasing numbers of infected hemophiliacs develop the disease.

"We really blew it on this," said Brownstein, executive director of the National Hemophilia Foundation, which was slow to encourage the use of heat-treated Factor VIII.

"We didn't have a consensus and we approached this from the view that we needed more definite scientific data. Then, when we saw later what it could do . . . it was stunning. We don't ever want to get burned like we did in 1983 again."

□ □ □

Hemophiliacs have been both victims and beneficiaries of the plasma business.

Some are living longer, more productive lives as a result of new generations of Factor VIII concentrates. But AIDS has taken a heavy toll. And the cost of these new medicines now threatens to impoverish thousands of them. Some are beginning to run out of insurance coverage.

"This has placed an untenable burden on a group that has already been traumatized by AIDS. It has been devastating," said Dr. Louis

M. Aledort, director of the hemophilia program at Mount Sinai Medical Center in New York City.

The price of Factor VIII last year increased between 600 percent and 900 percent after manufacturers switched from the heat-treated process to new technologies. Some manufacturers now use a mix of heat and detergents to kill viruses in the plasma, while others make a monoclonal version of Factor VIII—made by cloning the natural clotting proteins in plasma.

Hospital markups, added to the manufacturers' higher prices, have pushed costs even higher.

Last year, the Robert Wood Johnson Medical Center in New Brunswick, N.J., charged $1.50 a unit for concentrate it bought for 65 cents, according to FDA records. When a doctor complained, the medical center lowered the price to $1.15 a unit, the FDA records show.

A hemophiliac suffering from the severest form of the disease may use 50,000 or more units of Factor VIII a year, depending on how active he is. The annual price tag for the monoclonal version: $50,000 to $80,000.

By comparison, a patient with AIDS pays about $8,000 annually for AZT, a drug that helps slow the virus' growth. Following months of protests and lobbying by advocates for AIDS victims, the company that makes AZT agreed recently to cut its price by 20 percent.

There have been no such price cutbacks for hemophiliacs. And Factor VIII remains one of the most expensive medicines ever marketed.

Manufacturers attribute their higher prices to the expense of developing the safer monoclonal product and to lower yields; the new process initially produced only about half as much clotting factor per liter of plasma as the old method, the manufacturers say.

"It's an entirely different process and it's just more expensive to make," Luchese of Armour Pharmaceutical said when asked about it last fall.

Though yields have improved substantially since then, prices remain high.

"If your yields improve, then economics say the price should come down. That hasn't happened," said Brownstein of the National Hemophilia Foundation.

Manufacturers say that's because they are still recovering research and development costs. The higher prices also reflect cost-shifting that commonly occurs in the volatile plasma business—making up the losses in one product by raising the price of another.

For example, when revenues from albumin —a plasma protein used to treat burn victims and surgery patients—fell sharply three years ago after Japan's government cut its purchases by 25 percent, manufacturers moved to make up for that by increasing their prices for Factor VIII. Albumin was their largest-selling product, totaling more than $200 million in the United States alone.

"I'm not going to deny that reallocation goes on—it's how the economics of this business works. Everything is tied to what we get from a liter of plasma," said Anita Bessler, vice president for marketing for Baxter-Hyland Inc., the plasma division of Baxter Healthcare Corp.

"For purchasers of Factor VIII, I don't know that they are going to see any great change in price," she said. "And part of the reason for that is you are seeing manufacturers trying to recapture those lost albumin revenues."

Some doctors who work with hemophiliacs say they believe the manufacturers took advantage of the Factor VIII shortage to reap windfall profits—or at least to recover their development costs as quickly as possible.

Mount Sinai's Aledort questioned the timing of the decisions by Armour and Baxter-Hyland Inc. to stop selling heat-treated Factor VIII more than three months before the companies started marketing their new products last year.

Spokesmen for Armour Pharmaceutical and Baxter-Hyland said they removed their heat-treated Factor VIII from the market because there was still a small, but real, possibility that AIDS might be transmitted through the product.

Spokesmen for both companies said they believed at the time that their inventories would be adequate to cover demand during the three-month gap before a new cloned version of Factor VIII was available.

"In hindsight, it could have [had an impact on the shortage] but it shouldn't have had," said Bessler of Baxter-Hyland. "There was a three-month lead time. . . . We anticipated the yield swings, and we thought there would be enough inventory. . . . But a number of other things were happening."

Among them: An estimated 50 million vials of Factor VIII made by the Red Cross—about 8 percent of the total U.S. supply—were quarantined by the FDA for six months because of safety concerns.

Manufacturers say that, by producing a purer concentrate in which extraneous proteins are eliminated, they are reducing the risk of transmitting viruses, making the product safer.

"If we have a very safe concentrate—whatever safe turns out to be—and it is so scarce and expensive that it is not readily available, where are we?" Dr. Carol Kasper asked at the March meeting.

Industry officials don't dispute that the higher prices have put a heavy financial burden on hemophiliacs. But they were under heavy pressure to make a safer product, they say.

"The same treaters who are complaining now about the cost are the ones who encouraged the industry to develop products that were viral-free, requiring substantial investments in new technology," said Reilly, president of the industry trade association.

"To the extent that we encouraged these companies to develop safer products, we are responsible," Brownstein acknowledged. "We are super-pleased with what appears to be a safe product. But we are very displeased with the financial consequences this has wrought."

Last fall, as the Factor VIII shortage deepened, Luchese of Armour Pharmaceutical was asked about prices.

"Too often people make the mistake of saying we're gouging the public. And I can tell you nothing is further from the truth," Luchese said.

Five weeks later, Armour raised the price of its Factor VIII.

On Oct. 31, the company notified its customers that it was raising the price from 55 cents a unit to 65 cents, an increased of nearly 20 percent. The suggested list price for wholesale distributors and state and federal agencies was increased to 90 cents.

Jeff Richardson, a spokesman for Armour's parent corporation, Rorer Group Inc., said the increase was needed to pay for improvements at Armour's manufacturing plant in Kankakee, Ill., and to cover a $3 increase in fees paid to plasma donors—from $15 to $18.

According to the National Hemophilia Foundation, three organizations—Alpha Therapeutics Inc., Cutter Biologicals Inc. and the New York Blood Center—raised the prices of their older heat-treated Factor VIII following the introduction of the monoclonal products last year.

"The increases averaged from 52 percent to 122 percent and they all occurred after the newer products [were introduced]," Brownstein said. "I don't understand that. The costs of making *these products* didn't change."

Spokesmen for Alpha declined to respond. The vast majority of Alpha's products are sold in Japan.

Spokesmen for the other two companies said the increased costs reflected higher plasma collection and manufacturing costs. They declined to provide more specific details, saying the information was proprietary.

Manufacturers who continued to ship substantial amounts of Factor VIII to Japan and European countries during the shortage were asked about that.

"We developed an allocation program during the shortage, both in the U.S. and countries outside the U.S.," said Bessler of Baxter-Hyland. She declined to disclose either the percentage or the amount of Factor VIII that Baxter-Hyland shipped overseas. In addition to the United States, Baxter-Hyland sells concentrate in Japan, Holland and Canada.

Cutter Biologicals also continued selling Factor VIII overseas during the shortage.

"We continue to supply all of the markets we sold in before, which is basically West Germany, Japan and the U.S.," said Sunil Bhonsle, director of plasma procurement for Cutter. "I know we've had to face shortages in all of these markets. So we've not supplied one and not the other." He, too, declined to say what percentage of the company's Factor VIII is shipped overseas.

Luchese said Armour had sold "a small amount" of its new Factor VIII product in Europe. "But this is the truth: I could ship out five million units tomorrow to Europe, and I could get a significantly higher price. The reason we're not doing that is there is a tight supply in this country, and we're respecting that," Luchese said.

Brownstein said the National Hemophilia Foundation had difficulty monitoring how much Factor VIII was shipped out of the United States during the crisis. What data officials were able to gather indicated "we were being disproportionately burdened," he said. "We thought they were playing a shell game with us."

Foundation officials attempted to "jawbone" manufacturers to increase U.S. supplies but without much success, Brownstein said.

"That's why we originally asked the government to step in, to create the specter of government involvement. We also touched base with several people in Congress and had them make inquiries," Brownstein said.

The industry's response?

"The companies came back and threatened us and said they don't have to stay in the market. They can drop it [making Factor VIII]. It was kind of a classic threat," Brownstein said.

Government officials weren't much help, either. National Hemophilia Foundation representatives met with officials in the U.S. Department of Health and Human Services and appealed to them to take steps to protect hemophiliacs in the United States.

"We went to HHS, held several meetings, wrote letters, begging the government to either mandate no exportation or to grant the industry immunity for malpractice [so companies could sell potentially less safe Factor VIII without fear of being sued]. They were all very sympathetic and nobody did a thing," said Aledort of Mount Sinai Medical Center in New York.

□ □ □

When the shortage reached a critical level last fall, doctors in the United States stopped performing all but emergency surgery on hemophiliacs. And they cut back the amount of Factor VIII given to hemophiliacs to administer to themselves at home.

That forced many hemophiliacs to curtail their lifestyles and increased their dependence on special treatment centers in hospitals. There are eight such centers in Pennsylvania and two in New Jersey.

The center at Thomas Jefferson University Hospital in Philadelphia had to temporarily suspend its home therapy program for hemophiliacs in June 1988, when supplies of Factor VIII reached low levels.

"We set aside enough to make sure we could cover any emergencies. But in June we realized we didn't have enough to continue home therapy," said Joan Tannenbaum, coordinator of the hemophilia center at Thomas Jefferson.

"Normally we would distribute two cases of Factor VIII at a time for patients on home care, enough to cover two months' worth of infusions. By May, we were down to distributing one month. By July, we were giving out two vials per patient, enough for two infusions," Tannenbaum said.

As a result, hemophiliacs had to cut back on activities that might put them in danger of injuries, forgo dental work and elective surgery and come into the center more frequently for treatment and supplies, she said.

At Orthopedic Hospital in Los Angeles, which has one of the largest programs for hemophiliacs in the country, Kasper made her decision at the height of the shortage.

She asked her adult patients to remain on the heat-treated Factor VIII so the children could get the limited supply of monoclonal clotting factor.

Most of the adults agreed with her decision to help the children.

"It was a very emotional time for us and a very painful thing to do," Kasper said.

The supply situation at Jefferson and Orthopedic Hospital has improved greatly in recent months. But prices are still high.

Said Brownstein: "If you've got the money you can get monoclonal products, but there's still a real shortage of less expensive alternatives."

TWO

EARTHQUAKE!

1990 WINNER IN THE GENERAL NEWS REPORTING CATEGORY

"For a distinguished example of reporting within a newspaper's area of circulation that meets the daily challenges of journalism such as spot news reporting or consistent beat coverage . . ."

San Jose Mercury News
Staff

The devastation was widespread and swift—the result of a natural and inevitable geological shift in the planet's crust. The *San Jose Mercury News* skillfully recorded the physical and the psychological damage from the Bay Area earthquake.

On October 17, 1989, we became afraid of where we lived. One of the most powerful earthquakes to strike the United States in the 20th century—20 seconds of terror that we describe in shorthand as "a 7.1"—consumed our staff and our readers like no other story in our memory.

Some readers and *Mercury News* staffers still haven't been able to return to their homes—and some of us never will. Every aftershock made hearts race and brought a new rush of fear: "When are these going to stop?"

The *Mercury News* was at the heart of this event: The quake's epicenter was less than 25 miles south of our newsroom, far from the Oakland–San Francisco area that first flashed across the nation's television screens. Whole sections of our primary readership area—Los Gatos, Santa Cruz, Watsonville and miles of rugged mountain areas—were devastated.

In a scant five hours after the earthquake—and despite near-complete failure of telephone and freeway systems in some areas—we pulled together 12 full pages of stories, color photographs, scientific explanation and advice.

For thousands of readers throughout the Bay Area, the *Mercury News* became a lifeline of information in a time of uncertainty, an element of stability in a time of chaos—even a place to share emotions when so many nerves were frayed.

Consider the breadth, the depth and the tenor of our coverage of the events of October 17, 1989, and the extraordinary week that followed. Here's what you'll see:
• A lifeline of information: We performed our most basic function with a strong, clear voice and offered the most comprehensive, well-

rounded coverage in the Bay Area. Our readers desperately wanted information. Of our first-day newspaper at her door, Eulalia Atkinson wrote from Aptos: "Here was living proof that life was still going on out there somewhere and it was going to be all right. It was our first real news of what happened elsewhere, and the realization of how lucky we were."

• Vivid, compelling writing: You may need to read only one story, titled, "We Will Not Forget," to understand how it felt to live through this earthquake. We also set up a special phone line and invited readers to share their earthquake experiences.

• The human touch: We spoke to readers' emotions in our color stories about the need all of us had to share our experiences and fears.

• Investigative reporting: We were the first paper to report that state officials knew for more than a decade that Oakland's Cypress Street Viaduct was vulnerable to shock waves.

• Thoughtful explanatory journalism: Our stories made clear and comprehensible the powerful forces at work deep in the earth.

• A dire warning: In a special section, "We Are Not Prepared," we advanced this story to a logical and frightening conclusion: The real Big One will kill 10,000 of us and cause damage that will make the October 17 quake look like a fire drill. The lead story paints the most comprehensive picture that any paper has offered of which buildings are at risk.

There are few times in their lives when readers actually *need* a newspaper. At those times, we have the responsibility and privilege of touching, informing and comforting them.

—Robert D. Ingle,
Executive Editor
San Jose Mercury News

MASSIVE QUAKE

76 DIE IN SECONDS OF HORROR

WEDNESDAY,   OCTOBER   18,   1989

BY   DAVID   SCHRIEBERG

The biggest earthquake since 1906—7 on the Richter scale and possibly higher—hit the Bay Area at 5:04 p.m. Tuesday, killing at least 76 people, injuring more than 460, setting off fires in San Francisco and sending buildings, highways and bridges crashing down on people and cars across the region.

The quake, centered in the Santa Cruz Mountains, lasted from 20 to 40 seconds and frightened millions from Ukiah to San Diego. It was as strong as the quake that ravaged much of Soviet Armenia in December.

Damage throughout the Bay Area was staggering, as death and injury reports poured in to disaster centers and rose by the hour. Lt. Gov. Leo McCarthy said the damage could reach $1 billion.

In Oakland, officials feared that up to 200 people may have died when an elevated section of Interstate 880 toppled onto another part of the road. And the Alameda County coroner said the toll was expected to grow.

Victims from the freeway collapse were taken to a makeshift morgue at the Ralph Bunche Elementary School in Oakland.

An Oakland police spokeswoman said violence erupted in the city, much of which remained darkened by power outages.

"There's been a lot of shootings, stabbings and lootings," the spokeswoman said.

In addition to that area, hardest hit appeared to be: San Francisco, Los Gatos and Santa Cruz—where the historic downtown sustained major damage.

The California Office of Emergency Services declared emergencies in four Bay Area counties—Santa Clara, San Mateo, Santa Cruz and Monterey. San Francisco County officials said they did not need to declare a state of emergency.

State National Guardsmen were activated Tuesday night at bases statewide to help police and medical teams.

The impact of the earthquake was scattered and fickle. Isolated plumes of smoke rose above fires in San Francisco. Broad areas grappled with blackouts, water shortages and household damage ranging from minor to total.

Cars in San Francisco were crushed by huge chunks of concrete that fell from a building next to the Interstate 280 off-ramp near Sixth and Townsend streets. Firefighters pulled pieces of bodies from the twisted wreckage of the cars.

The Bay Bridge, which partially collapsed, was closed, as were numerous highways and roads throughout the region—leaving commuters with trips that could take them 50 miles off their normal routes.

But Caltrans pleaded with Bay Area residents not to drive today, even if it meant skipping work and school.

Long stretches of Highway 17 into the Santa Cruz Mountains and five miles of Interstate 280 in western Santa Clara County were closed because of landslides and buckling pavement.

Both San Francisco and Oakland international airports were to remain closed today.

Three hours after the quake, San Jose International reopened for some flights and was expected to stay that way.

San Francisco and Alameda counties appeared to have the heaviest death and damage tolls. At least six people were killed in San Francisco when a building south of Market Street collapsed on cars. At least one person died when a 30-foot section of the upper deck of the Bay Bridge fell onto the lower deck.

In San Jose, Ed Kawazoe, a prominent leader of the Japanese-American community and Democratic Party activist, died of a heart attack during the quake. His was the only reported death in San Jose on Tuesday night. A 77-year-old Cupertino man died when he fell and hit his head, and two men died in Capitola and Mountain View.

Between 40,000 and 50,000 baseball fans calmly evacuated Candlestick Park, about a half-hour before Game 3 of the World Series—even taking with them souvenir chunks of concrete that had fallen from the stadium. The series was delayed indefinitely while officials tried to assess the damage to Candlestick and the Oakland Coliseum.

As many as a million people from Hollister to San Francisco were without power in the hours after the quake and well into the night as Pacific Gas & Electric Co. crews scrambled to repair lines. Much of San Francisco remained enveloped in darkness at midnight.

Gas and water lines in a widespread area were also ruptured.

Phone lines were also heavily affected as hundreds of thousands of calls were reported flooding into the area. American Telephone & Telegraph Corp. appealed to customers across the country not to try phoning the Bay Area. The company said it blocked part of a deluge of calls into the area so that local residents could call out.

Phone service was so bad that at 9 p.m., San Francisco Mayor Art Agnos asked San Jose Mayor Tom McEnery to phone him—an appeal he issued via television news broadcasters.

Seismologists set the quake's epicenter about 10 miles northeast of Santa Cruz, near Lake Elsman—the third time in 16 months that an earthquake had radiated from that spot. A final figure on the magnitude of the quake could be days away.

"Much of our equipment went off the scale," said Ann Becker, a research assistant at the University of California Seismographic Station at Berkeley. "It's still just crazy here trying to figure it out."

"The 1906 earthquake was the last quake of this magnitude," said Arthur Lomax, a seismologist at the Berkeley station.

In the hours after the main temblor, seismologists measured three quakes of 4.5 or greater on the Richter scale, and many other aftershocks too numerous to count, Lomax said.

'WE ALWAYS KNEW IT WAS COMING, BUT WE NEVER REALLY EXPECTED IT'

WEDNESDAY, OCTOBER 18, 1989

BY PAMELA KRAMER

Buildings disintegrated. Fire and smoke stained the sky. Highways and bridges crumbled. Broken power lines left many neighborhoods and intersections dark and dangerous as night fell. There was some heroism, and there was some looting. Hospitals filled up. People died.

And many of the living were more afraid than they ever could have imagined they'd be in an earthquake.

"My reaction was, 'My God, this is it,' " said Greg Terry, 28, of Oakland, who saw some of the death caused by the quake in a collapsed section of the Nimitz Freeway between 12th and 30th streets. "We always knew it was coming, but we never really expected it."

Employees of Jorgensen Steel near Interstate 880 had watched in horror as the section fell.

Ray Guajardo, a salesman at Jorgensen, ran to the rubble and groped to pull a man from a car.

"He was really bad," Guajardo said. "His face was lacerated. He was in a seizure. Most of his clothing was torn off."

Rick Andreotti, a spokesman for the Oakland Police Department, estimated authorities would be at their grim task of prying bodies from the wreckage all night.

At Candlestick Park, Game 3 of the World Series was delayed.

San Jose attorney Patrick McMahon and his father-in-law, 80-year-old Howard Diebel, were sitting in the upper deck of the stadium. "It was absolutely hair-raising, the scariest experience I've ever had," said McMahon. "We thought that if it shook for another 10 seconds, we were a goner. It felt like the entire deck was going to fall down onto the field."

McMahon still was sitting in the parking lot three hours later with thousands of others. Speaking over a cellular phone in his car, he relayed messages from strangers to his wife and daughter, who attempted to call various families around the Bay Area to let them know their loved ones were safe.

But while the baseball fans apparently escaped without serious injury, the death toll throughout the Bay Area continued to rise as emergency workers continued their searches.

In San Francisco, city workers turned off all the gas mains in a three- to four-square block area around the main area of a huge fire, at Divisadero and Beach, and all residents of that area were evacuated.

Several three-story buildings burned to the ground. Several other three- and four-story buildings collapsed.

Pointing to one of them, Sgt. Roger Battaglia said: "That was a three-story building. It just went down like an accordion."

According to Battaglia, all the most severely damaged buildings were wood frame corner buildings.

The main fire was brought under control around 7:30 p.m., but damage was so great that one three-story building had become a one-story pile of rubble. People huddled around portable radios and car radios, exchanging information. On some blocks there was a strong odor of gas and fire.

Charles Clark, 35, a professional photographer on assignment in San Francisco, was in the Marina District when the earthquake hit. "I was standing on the street. I turned around and the whole building was down." After the building collapsed, people crawled desperately from the wreckage. "There was mass panic. It was a really bad scene. People running and screaming."

In San Jose, parts of another old building threatened to fall at the corner of First and Santa Clara streets. At the old Bank of America building, city workers Steve Corchero and Manuel QuiÑonez cordoned off the sidewalk because the building was shedding chunks of marble. Two lanes of Third Street near San Fernando were also closed after the roof of a burned-out building scheduled for demolition pitched into the street.

Throughout the Santa Cruz Mountains, people were evacuated from their homes—if they still had homes to leave.

Ryan Moore, 20, didn't even have time to get out. He was sleeping in one of the bedrooms of his family's Hutchinson Road house in the mountains when the house started sliding downhill, disassembling as it went. The roof of the structure passed over him while he was in bed.

Moore, who was alone in the house, escaped with cuts and bruises. The house was a pile of lumber.

At the foot of the mountains in Los Gatos, old buildings along Main Street collapsed, and store owners stood guard outside their crumpled businesses.

Paul Tumason, who operates Tumason Portraits on East Main Street, said he would be spending the night in front of his store. The facade had collapsed, covering the sidewalk with bricks, and the building buckled.

"Those of us in these old buildings won't be able to get in them because they're going to be condemned," Tumason predicted.

But physical damage was not all the earthquake wreaked. Hours later, its victims were still shaking and marveling over what they had been through.

In the first few seconds of the quake, Richard De Vitto, 42, sat in his Watsonville office and reacted as he had to other earthquakes, the same as millions of others around the Bay Area: "You're used to earthquakes, so you kind of look at the person next to you and roll your eyes.

"But the next thing, I was grabbing something to try to stand up."

STATE IGNORED NIMITZ WARNING

275 FEARED DEAD AS DAMAGE COSTS SOAR INTO BILLIONS

THURSDAY, OCTOBER 19, 1989

BY PETE CAREY
AND GARY WEBB

State officials have known for more than a decade that Oakland's Cypress Street Viaduct, which collapsed in Tuesday's earthquake, had an outdated design that made it vulnerable to such shock waves.

But Caltrans officials said they doubted that the bridge's concrete support columns would collapse as they did—and they offered a variety of explanations about why the columns were not reinforced.

As the dust settled from Tuesday's murderous earthquake, it quickly became apparent that the collapse of the Oakland highway was the single deadliest event of the quake.

Investigators are focusing their attention on the failure of dozens of support columns separating the upper and lower decks of the viaduct.

And Gov. George Deukmejian called for an investigation of the collapse.

"I had assumed that the freeways were . . . constructed with adequate standards so that they would be able to withstand a quake of this severity," he said.

In 1977, the viaduct was retrofitted with a cable linking its road decks together. But it was the four-foot-thick concrete columns—and not the road decks—that gave way Tuesday.

Officials acknowledged that a 1987 quake in Whittier clearly showed the need for reinforcing the columns, which were built without the spiral steel reinforcements used in current bridges.

J. David Rogers, a Pleasant Hill engineer who studied the viaduct in 1975, said it was clear that the structure could not make it through an earthquake like Tuesday's—a north-south temblor shaking the structure along its entire length.

When those supports snapped, more than a mile of concrete roadway collapsed onto the lower deck of the bridge, crushing as many as 250 homeward-bound commuters.

State and federal highway officials Wednesday gave a variety of explanations why the columns on the 32-year-old structure—one of California's first double-decker freeways and a known earthquake hazard—hadn't been reinforced.

Dean Carlson, a top Federal Highway Administration official, said reinforcement work was imminent. After an Alameda press conference, state highway department structures chief James Roberts said research was under way and work was slated for 1991.

But several other top Caltrans officials told the California Transportation Commission Wednesday afternoon that the agency was nowhere near starting such work, since the technology to do it hasn't been developed yet.

"We hadn't started because we don't have the technical knowledge, nor does it exist in the world, to tell us how to retrofit," said William Schaefer, chief engineer for the Department of Transportation. Schaefer said the only elevated highway bridges in the state scheduled for column reinforcement are of a different construction than the Cypress Viaduct.

VIADUCT NOT ON RETROFIT LIST

Records of the Transportation Department's 1988–89 bridge reinforcement project schedule show that the Cypress Viaduct isn't on the list. However, the Embarcadero Viaduct in San Francisco—which is similar in construction to the Cypress and is a few years newer—is. It is scheduled to receive $75,000 worth of support column reinforcement this year.

The Embarcadero sustained heavy damage, but did not collapse. When asked why that bridge was on the bridge reinforcement project list if the technology doesn't exist to fix it, Caltrans officials said they thought experimental work was under way there.

It was clear that the state's top bridge and highway engineers were caught flat-footed by the Cypress Street Viaduct disaster.

"If you asked me two days ago, I would have told you that our best conclusion is that an earthquake involving the Cypress Viaduct wouldn't have resulted in the catastrophe that it did," said Caltrans spokesman Jim Drago.

Top Caltrans officials said the department's earthquake-proofing plans were based on the results of the 1971 quake in Silmar, during which bridges built like the Cypress Street Viaduct suffered the least amount of damage. The most damage resulted from road decks tearing apart.

As a result, the only retrofitting that had been done to the Cypress bridge involved lashing the roadway together with steel cables to prevent the road pieces from separating. That work was done in 1977, the last time the bridge had undergone a detailed seismic safety analysis, said James Gates, a senior structural engineer at Caltrans.

ONCE AN ENGINEERING SHOWPIECE

The highway, opened in July 1957, "went from being a showpiece of engineering to being a different kind of showpiece where we took classes of engineers out there" to study its problems and weak points, Pleasant Hill engineer Rogers said.

Rogers said his 1975 study found that the worst problems with the bridge were the support columns, which taper from top to bottom and lack spiral steel reinforcement now commonly used in column construction.

The Pleasant Hill engineer said his engineering professor in reinforced concrete design, Jerome Raphael, took the earthquake safety issue up with Caltrans officials.

"I remember at the time talking to Raphael. He talked with them directly. (He said) that they realized this viaduct had serious possibilities of problems in a major quake, of 6.5 and up lasting more than 25 seconds, because the structure is so long and the north end is built on old estuary deposits, bay muds and gravels."

In 1956–57, when the Cypress Street Viaduct was built, engineering knowledge did not include the use of spiral steel in support columns.

Rogers, after inspecting the bridge on Wednesday, said the viaduct collapsed under the quake in a sort of "zipper failure from south to the north."

The Bay Bridge, which saw a 50-foot section of its upper deck drop onto the lower deck, also received deck reinforcement under Phase I of the highway department's earthquake project. But Gates confirmed that the section of bridge that collapsed had not been strengthened with steel cables.

NO NEED WAS 'APPARENT'

"It wasn't apparent that there was a need (for deck strengthening) at that point," Gates said. "We're still looking at why that decision was made."

Chief Caltrans engineer Schaefer said he suspects the soil upon which the north end of the bridge rests will wind up being the culprit, as it is old fill dirt that is notoriously unstable in earthquakes.

"The Cypress bridge, I hate to say the word anomaly, but it does stick out as strange. There's something that's not right there. Bad soils. Liquefaction, maybe," he said.

Mercury News staff writer Neil Chethik contributed to this report.

A HARD-DRIVEN HERO

BUS DRIVER BRINGS COMFORT, COURAGE TO CYPRESS STREET

FRIDAY, OCTOBER 20, 1989

BY JOHN HUBNER

Mikki Redding's trip to hell began at 4:50 Tuesday afternoon, when she eased an AC Transit bus out of the Transbay Terminal in San Francisco. Five hours later, she was picking up bodies under the Cypress Street Viaduct in Oakland.

Packed with a standing-room-only crowd, Redding's bus had cleared the Bay Bridge and was on the ramp leading to Interstate 580. Suddenly the bus felt like it was hitting a series of very rough bumps.

"I looked in the rear-view mirror and saw 880 collapsing," Redding says. "Everything was dropping beneath the rear end of the bus. The bus would clear a section and the section would fall."

Redding floored it and drove like a stock-car racer, weaving around cars, aiming the big, top-heavy bus at the smallest openings in traffic.

"A guy standing near me yelled. 'Are you crazy?' " Redding said Thursday afternoon on a big yellow couch in her Oakland house. "I said, 'You better look what's happening behind you!' He looked and saw what was happening and screamed, 'Get us the hell out of here!' "

Redding got the bus off I-580 and into Oakland and dropped her passengers off on Oakland Avenue, a mile or two from the Cypress Viaduct. It may have been shock or simply an inability to comprehend the magnitude of what had just happened, but most passengers had no idea how close death had come to catching the bus.

"The lights were out, there were sirens and burglar alarms going off, and a lady getting off said to me, 'We must have had a power outage. And only 20 minutes before the first pitch of the World Series!' "

CHANGE OF CAREER

Redding, 44, is a registered nurse who practiced in New York but decided not to re-register when she came to California in 1976 with her twin daughter and son. For a while she worked as a home-care nurse. Tiring of that, she became a flight attendant and after 10 years in the air, took a higher-paying job as a bus driver in June 1986.

On Tuesday, Redding's nursing career came back to her. She turned the bus around and went to the Cypress Viaduct "to see if I could help and to see if what I thought had happened really had."

It had.

"There was a lot of fires, a lot of black smoke, a lot of fumes," Redding says, her voice quiet and methodical. "People covered with blood were crawling out from between where the roadway had sand-wiched. The police hadn't arrived yet. Neighbors were running up with ladders and blankets and flashlights. Bloody people were coming up to me. They were dazed, in shock. We wrapped them in blankets and put them in cars and taxicabs that took off for emergency rooms. I saw one man load two people in the back of a pickup and take off.

"People from the neighborhood, the people who survived, they were wonderful, just wonderful," Redding says, struggling to find words and hold back tears at the same time. "There was one guy who was up on the viaduct. He got out but his leg was broken. He kept climbing in between the sandwiched part of the roadway and bringing people out. One time, he came back with a woman whose arm was split down the middle."

EXPLOSION OF ACTIVITY

Police, ambulances and medical personnel quickly descended on the scene. Amtrak sent a truck full of blankets. The regional water company sent a load of first-aid kits. Redding kept giving survivors first aid and wrapping them in blankets. A police officer handed her a bunch of identification tags. She got victims' names and ages, printed them on the large tags and hung them around people's necks, and then guided them toward ambulances.

The Oakland Police Department had established an emergency medical center near the viaduct. When Redding told a sergeant she was a nurse as well as a bus driver, the sergeant told her there were dead bodies on the streets that had to be picked up.

"He told me to get a bus, they needed a mobile morgue," Redding says.

Redding and Thurman Washington, another Alameda County Transit driver, located the shortest bus at the scene and drove it under the viaduct. The Oakland police loaded body boards, blankets, identification tags and rubber gloves, and the grim search began.

"We found five bodies," Redding says. "I don't know if the quake pitched them out of their cars or if it knocked their cars off the viaduct. Two bodies were just laying there in the rubble, the other three were laying near cars.

"Their heads were split wide open," Redding continues, her voice trembling. "They'd hit so hard, their eyes had come out of their heads."

Redding wrapped the bodies in blankets and police officers placed them on body boards and loaded them on the bus.

"It was really difficult, getting them over the fare box," Redding says.

The bus took the bodies to a temporary morgue at the Ralph Bunche Elementary School on 18th Street, near the Cypress Street Viaduct. By the time Redding returned to the viaduct, the survivors had all been taken to hospitals. The Oakland police told Redding to go home, there was nothing more she could do.

"She's a hero, a real hero," Oakland police Lt. Larry Eade said of Redding the day after the quake. Eade was in charge of the Oakland police operation at the Cypress Viaduct and rode in the "mobile morgue" when it was collecting bodies. "She helped an awful lot of people and never batted an eye when we were out there picking up bodies. It made us all feel better to know a civilian could come through like that."

Redding's heroism is not without its price.

"When I got back to the (bus) yard, I realized that I didn't know where my purse was. Then I realized I didn't know where I was," Redding says.

Redding did not sleep Tuesday night. On Wednesday morning, she called her supervisor to request time off. She spent the day on the couch, watching earthquake coverage on television. She managed to fall asleep Wednesday night, but had nightmares and kept waking up screaming. Thursday morning, she was back in front of the television, watching the earthquake coverage.

"I didn't realize what I'd seen until I laid here yesterday watching it on TV," Redding says. "It's going to be a long time before the reality of what I saw becomes reality."

COMING TO GRIPS WITH TRAGEDY

BY FRAN SMITH

The first calls came from heroes who needed to talk about horror.

The phone started ringing minutes after the Northern California Psychiatric Society opened its counseling line late Thursday. A taxi driver who'd pulled people from rubble. A man who had clawed through a collapsed building, searching for survivors. Others who had been propelled by the crisis to courage—and now feel knocked down by stomachaches, diarrhea, a sense that they can't go on.

Just days after the Bay Area's devastating quake, shock is giving way to something deeper, something longer-lasting.

Grief, anxiety, guilt, hope, relief are palpable, as people take stock of their losses and luck. You can hear the emotions on the radio call-ins, from the woman who sobs because of aftershocks, to the callers who fume at their insurance companies. You can measure the emotions by the thousands of calls to crisis centers, mental health clinics, doctors' offices—anywhere that people can get through and be heard.

"I think this is a life-changing event," said Dr. Alan Brauer, director of the Brauer Medical Center in Palo Alto. "I don't think anybody is ever going to be quite the same."

The number of calls to the Brauer center, hospitals and suicide prevention lines have jumped 20 percent above normal and continue to climb as phone service is restored. In communities where people are too busy calculating the physical ruin to seek help with emotional rubble, counselors are going to them.

Laura Manning, a social worker who worked with victims of the 1982 San Lorenzo River floods and the 1985 Lexington fire, camped out at the Red Cross shelter on Summit Road on Friday afternoon. She said people keep replaying what happened to them Tuesday. In Santa Cruz, impromptu group therapy sessions reportedly took place on lawns. Leaflets appeared in Los Gatos with tips on common reactions and ways to cope.

Any moderate earthquake frays some nerves and leaves an anxious aftertaste. But a quake that kills people, levels houses and collapses familiar chunks of roads has a different emotional punch. "We count on Mother Earth to be stable," said Dr. Mark Antonucci, clinical director of Santa Clara County's Suicide and Crisis Service. "When she's pitching and tossing, it throws us into chaos."

DEEP EMOTIONAL WOUNDS

Not surprisingly, the people closest to death and destruction are vulnerable to the deepest emotional wounds. Some psychologists believe that as many as 80 percent of those who survived the collapse of the Cypress Street Viaduct, Bay Bridge or their homes will show symptoms of post-traumatic stress disorder. For a while at least, they may be depressed, guilty, distracted or physically sick. Already, psychologists know of children who refuse to eat or leave their parents' side.

But even people who got through Tuesday relatively well—the vast majority that was rattled but uninjured—may feel irritable and jumpy. And those who pride themselves on toughness, those who laughed at quakes and people who took cover, may be hardest hit, psychologists said.

"This quake has really been a great leveler both physically and emotionally," Brauer said.

Every therapy client Brauer has worked with since Wednesday morning spent the hour on the earthquake. Hot lines are teaching volunteers what to say to people who've suffered through trauma. And this weekend, the state Psychological Association will hold free training workshops for therapists who aren't sure how to deal with post-traumatic stress.

CALLS TAKE EMOTIONAL TURN

That nearly everybody needs to talk is obvious. Watch the knots of people on street corners. Listen to the litany on radio talk shows.

"For every call that's on the air, there must be a thousand calls, literally, that are coming into the newsroom," said Jerry Kay of KCBS radio.

To listen to Kay's all-night program this week was to hear the pulse of the Bay Area. Early in the week, the calls sounded practical. Calm, if disoriented, people described what they did when the earth rocked.

They asked how to check homes for structural damage, what to tell the kids.

But before dawn Thursday, the calls took an emotional turn. A frightened woman cried on the phone: "Why do I keep feeling these aftershocks?" People who lost only a favorite lamp or a few windows begged to know why bodies were still trapped beneath the Cypress structure. For the first time, callers vented anger.

People from the Santa Cruz Mountains demanded to know why the media kept calling the catastrophe the San Francisco, not the Loma Prieta, quake. People from San Francisco dialed by candlelight to rage at Pacific Gas & Electric Co. Baseball fans from all over made passionate pleas for or against next week's continuation of the World Series.

"I asked, 'Do you play or not play?' " Kay said Friday. "It really touched a nerve. It brought out something that's important."

Something that had nothing to do with the Giants or the A's.

To play, as psychologists see it, is a signal that life goes on. A sign —on national television—that we're OK.

To skip the game would be a tribute to the dead: like a moment of silence, the least you can do. But it also might be a collective act of penance—a symbolic sacrifice from people who feel guilty about their luck.

The games, of course, will be played. But they will not be the contest the Bay Area was primed to watch Tuesday night.

Before the Quake of '89, the series was a rivalry of neighboring cities as much as a sports championship. Now, there is talk of using it as a fund-raiser for disaster victims. Life goes on, altered.

WE WILL NEVER FORGET

SUNDAY, OCTOBER 22, 1989

BY GARY BLONSTON

In the geological life of the planet, the earthquake that struck the San Francisco Bay Area on Oct. 17 was no more than a passing snap of the fingers. In human scale, it was an event more jarring and costly than this generation of Northern Californians might ever experience again.

It began 11 miles beneath the surface of a nearly anonymous hump in the Santa Cruz Mountains, at 5:04 p.m. on a bright Tuesday afternoon. It happened as the Bay Area's workday was coming to an end, as people across the nation were tuning in for the third game of the World Series at Candlestick Park, as traffic was mounting on Interstate 880 in Oakland and life on Santa Cruz's Pacific Garden Mall was easing into evening. It happened just as the experts said it would, give or take a few decades.

It lasted a long time, 20 seconds in some places, 30 in others, and during its relentless lurch and roll, 5 million lives stopped. When the earthquake was over, scores of those lives were not to start again.

The Loma Prieta California Earthquake, named for that dark hill 10 miles northeast of Santa Cruz, changed the physical and psychological facts of life in Northern California in ways that can't yet be fully sensed. Four days after the quake, the earth was still moving, buildings were still collapsing, people were still missing—and, incredibly, rescuers were digging out a trapped survivor.

But its largest dimensions are clear. At worst, the death and personal loss it delivered will resonate for a generation. At best, the anxiety it planted like a malign seed will linger in the backs of minds for months and years.

It was not the devastating, ultimate seismic horror that will be visited on California some other day. It was 6.9, a number only medium-high on the exponentially ascending scale of such things. Furthermore, it surged beneath a region that had been preparing for decades to withstand just such an assault.

The cities by the bay survived. Though damage estimates climbed into the billions, destruction was the exception across the region, and even the death toll might have seemed relatively small, had it not been for the murderous collapse of Interstate 880's top deck onto more than a mile of rush-hour traffic.

But cumulative statistics mean little. Those who escaped the quake unscathed embraced one specific fact: The sad, climbing totals of damage and death didn't include them. And those who lost loved ones or property or their sense of place and peace had no need to check the numbers to know whether, in their lives, this had been the Big One.

□ □ □

The earth didn't move very much along the San Andreas Fault, maybe a yard or two, but the energy of that incidental shrug shot through the continent with speed and power that numbers only make more difficult to comprehend: Shock waves emanated at 7,000 mph, propelled by energy 100 times greater than the 20-kiloton atomic bomb that destroyed Hiroshima. Though it was not the Big One in scientific terms, it was a stupendous event.

In numbingly rapid succession during the earthquake's duration, the people around the epicenter, then the people of the Bay Area, the state and the nation came to know of the earthquake of 1989:

A 1,000-foot-long, five-foot-deep crack tore through the front yard of John and Freda Tranbarger a few miles from the hill called Loma Prieta and shook their house so thoroughly that they dived out a window to escape.

Due south in Aptos, orchards shuddered, and thousands of apples simultaneously thumped to the ground.

Southeast in Watsonville, the 86-year-old St. Patrick's Church, veteran of dozens of earthquakes, was rocked by this quake so severely that its brick steeple twisted like taffy.

Southwest in Santa Cruz, a high wall next to Ford's department store disassembled and fell through the store ceiling, killing a 75-year-old shopper named Catherine Treiman.

Just west of the summit on Highway 17, the shifting land ripped a deep gash across the pavement and broke the thick, 4-foot-high concrete median like a stick.

Near Big Basin State Park, Mike Kelley of the state forestry department stopped backing his truckload of firefighters into their station when the redwoods began to sway crazily, then watched through his rearview mirror as the station disintegrated behind him.

Employees of a Los Gatos bicycle shop called Velomeister scrambled to save themselves and their customers as the brick front wall of the building gave way in a roar and sent a river of rubble into the street.

Marble peeled away from the old Bank of America building in downtown San Jose and smashed onto the sidewalk without striking anyone.

In a Saratoga cat hospital, water lines blew and live wires fell, endangering the people who waded in to save the caged animals from drowning.

Up the Peninsula, Candlestick Park began to rumble as if fans in the rapidly filling stadium were stomping in unison. Several players dashed to the safest place available—the middle of the field. The stadium took only minor damage.

In San Francisco, a wall of the four-story office building near Sixth and Townsend collapsed on parked cars below, killing at least five people.

In the wharf area, the historic Ferry Building groaned with stress and the flagpole atop the dome bent to one side, whipped out of vertical by the lunge of the land below.

Over the San Francisco Bay, one end of a highway span broke loose on the double-deck Bay Bridge and fell to the roadway below.

In Oakland, the concrete supports of the two-level Cypress Street Viaduct of Interstate 880 began to fail, and the upper roadbed went into wild undulation before falling onto the cars beneath it.

People north in Ukiah, east in Reno, south in the San Fernando Valley sucked a quick breath and looked to their own walls and ceilings as the shake arrived underfoot.

Seismograph needles across America began to sketch quick, nervous peaks and valleys on the rolling graphs, charting the dimensions of force and fear.

What came next were hours of numbing realization and days of search, rescue and repair. They inevitably will be followed by weeks, months, years of reconstruction and rethinking, by chilling recollection and willful forgetting, by lingering loss and the gnawing irrationality of survivor guilt.

There will be public investigations and private therapy sessions, broad campaigns for aid to the homeless, quiet family talks about feeling safe and going forward.

And the force and the images of those first minutes will endure:

The china cabinet on its face, the house on its side, the refrigerator across the kitchen from where it belonged, the chimney lying on the car.

The apartment building fires lighting the San Francisco night.

The woman who didn't come out of the Santa Cruz coffee house with the rest; the trapped little boy who lay waiting in a crushed car while rescuers power-sawed through his dead mother's body to reach him.

The anxiety that rode home alongside thousands of people who didn't know if they would arrive to find a home or not.

The darkness and the dead phone and the distant, worried, unreachable relatives and the cowering dog and the movement, the damnable refusal of the earth to simply hold still.

The aftershocks came by the thousands. Less than three minutes after the initial 6.9 quake came a 5.9 aftershock, then 35 minutes later a 5.2, in the next 15 hours eight more jolts larger than 4.0 and countless other smaller ones, chewing away at the foundations, chewing away at the nerves. For the vast majority who experienced little or no loss of material things, the earthquake nonetheless strummed primitive chords of fear, testing the psychic footing of us all.

At Candlestick Park, many in the crowd at first treated the quake almost as a joke, a rattling of bats in the netherworld. It was a few minutes later, when portable television sets in the stands began to display pictures of devastation, that the true import of the moment began to sink in. People headed for the exits, pale and frightened.

Outside, motorists, too, misunderstood what was happening when they felt the sudden tug at their hands.

John and Dana Bowen, on their way to the ballgame, thought they had had a blowout and pulled to the side of the Bayshore Freeway. So did everyone else they saw. "Everyone was looking at their tires," said John Bowen, 36. "It was very weird."

At the same instant, John Canepa, 41, was riding his motorcycle to his home on Scott Street in the Marina District of San Francisco.

"It felt like I had two flat tires," he said later. "I knew it was an earthquake when I saw the building collapse." He pointed to a structure just a couple of doors from his own, an erstwhile four-floor building, now only one story high.

For the people at Candlestick, the Bowens, Canepa, for millions of others, the earthquake was an unnerving episode of near-misses and might-have-beens.

But across the bay in Oakland, the horror was real. The worst structural failure of the earthquake was occurring, the awesome fall of the upper deck of Interstate 880's Cypress Street Viaduct—more than a mile of pavement, 44 slabs of concrete roadbed each weighing 600 tons, descending to land at random angles and chillingly flat planes on the highway below.

Chris Miller of San Anselmo, traveling on the lower, northbound level, also thought his tires had blown. Then a piece of the freeway descended like a sledgehammer on his car. He frantically kicked out the back window and clambered free to find himself in a dark hell beneath the highway.

"There was nothing but the smell of gas and body parts all over the place, and there was nobody alive to come with me," he said. "I didn't know there was an earthquake. All I knew was there was a freeway on me. There was blood all over the ground. In front of me there was the brain of a person quivering on the ground."

Miller survived. At least 34 others didn't. At first, authorities thought 200 people might have died, but in the days after the quake, as their machines lifted the concrete away, they found fewer cars than they expected, and more cars whose occupants had escaped.

They theorized that the impending World Series game had drawn people to television sets who might otherwise have been driving north at 5:04 p.m. That knowledge made their task no easier, though, for the fatalities on the freeway were still a daunting number that promised to climb relentlessly as search and cleanup work continued.

Those laboring amid the wreckage actually found someone still alive Saturday—a 57-year-old survivor named Buck Helm—and new energy swept through the crews.

But one of the early rescue workers, Richard Riddle, 33, of San Leandro, came away from his time on the highway personally shattered, tears streaming. "This is the saddest damn thing I've ever seen," he said. "It looks like hell in there. We saw this Camaro, and it was only 10 inches high.

The Cypress structure is a 1.25-mile-long tombstone whose image will last long after it is dismantled or repaired. It is the signature of the Loma Prieta quake, a long wavering line whose message, from the first moment, was legible in any language.

□ □ □

The fallen freeway filled television screens around the world, sharing time with the Marina fires and the wreckage of downtown Santa Cruz and leaving some distant viewers with the sense that much of the Bay Area had either collapsed or burst into flames.

It seemed to confirm expectations that have grown with each passing year that a big earthquake hasn't come: One day California would fall into the sea. San Francisco would burn again, as it did in 1906. People who choose to live with earthquakes must someday pay the price.

When this quake did come, the message traveled quickly and graphically because the cameras, microphones, technicians and reporters already were in place, waiting at Candlestick Park for quite another event. It was a cable sports station, ESPN, that broadcast the first pictures of the earthquake, its first aftershock and some of its effect, and it was a sportscaster, Al Michaels of ABC, who provided some of the early network narrative.

By the end of the evening, the rest of the world's communications apparatus was aimed at the Bay Area, but no longer to cover games. Anchormen prepared to fly in. Baseball writers gave way to news reporters from across the country. Vice President Dan Quayle was on his way from Southern California. The White House was flying Gov. George Deukmejian back from Germany. President Bush would arrive a few days later, on Friday, for a personal inspection.

Appropriately, the focus of this global attention was on death and devastation, but what was noted only in passing was the widespread *lack* of damage.

That Northern California wasn't ruined—that more pervasive damage didn't occur amid such examples of intense destruction—was a matter of chance and soil structure and drought-compacted ground and angles of incidence and building codes and sheer mystery.

Generally, while buildings were falling in clouds of dust from the hills of Boulder Creek to the urban flats of Oakland, most Bay Area residents might have lacked electricity, water, or at first much sense of how bad things were for others, but their homes held firm.

New construction, and most dramatically the towers of the city skylines, swayed according to design and in the end prevailed. Homes and buildings on dry, compacted ground such as much of Santa Clara County survived because of the stable base beneath them.

The casualties were most common among the structures that might have been judged vulnerable well in advance, when seismologists forecast an earthquake centered in the Santa Cruz Mountains stretch of the San Andreas Fault. They were aging buildings in foothill towns near the epicenter, mountain houses close to the fault line or on steep, unstable ground, apartment buildings and expensive San Francisco homes built on sandy, watery landfill that literally was liquefied by the shock waves.

Even the double-decked stretch of I-880 in Oakland was mounted on concrete columns acknowledged to need modification because they fell short of state-of-the-art anti-earthquake design.

The only major damage that truly surprised engineers and seismologists was a structural failure that directly affected more people than any other—the break in the Bay Bridge, the only direct route by car between San Francisco and Oakland.

Until it is fixed, hundreds of thousands of commuters will have to find other, longer, slower, more expensive ways by car, train and boat to traverse the bay.

But if that was the most widely felt problem, it at least was a condition with a clear solution, however time-consuming.

There is no easy solution for a house off its foundations, uncovered by earthquake insurance, too precious to abandon and too expensive to repair.

There is no simple response when cherished personal possessions are smashed or soaked or burned.

There is no expedient way to replace a historic downtown, a stately church, a Victorian neighborhood.

And there is no way at all to patch up the personal voids, the through-and-through holes in hearts and souls.

Ruth Rabinowitz, 21, bears one of those. She was the longtime friend and roommate of Robin Ortiz, 22, and when Ortiz was trapped inside a ruined Santa Cruz coffee house, she refused to give up hope that Ortiz could be saved.

Rabinowitz and Ortiz had talked just before the earthquake struck. "She told me she'd missed me all day and gave me a big hug," Rabinowitz said. "The last thing I saw was a big smile on her face."

Ortiz's body was dug from the rubble two days later.

Multiply Rabinowitz's feelings by all the people who lost loved ones and friends, and the debt of sorrow forms an imposing entry on the ledger of this catastrophe, right beside the multibillion-dollar cost.

From the first moments after the quake, people outdid themselves, from donations of food and money and space to homeless people on the streets of San Francisco, volunteering to direct traffic in a blacked-out city illuminated only by headlights, stars and the eerie light of the reddish moon.

Helicopter pilots hauled equipment through the night so power could be restored around the bay, volunteers climbed through rubble on the chance that life still pulsed beneath it, and countless other people worked in a thousand ways, without sense of clock or calendar, at the vital humdrum of putting civilization back in order.

There was good news, and much of it came because of that phenomenon called disaster-community, the remarkable sharing of crisis that comes when storms or shipwrecks, wars or earthquakes, throw victims together.

Anyone with a knowledge of propane tanks and mountain houses was an instant friend to less-informed people who feared the potential of leaks and explosions. Strangers with cars became vital sources of transportation and comfort when disaster left its victims on foot and far from home.

People in Los Gatos opened their houses so newly homeless people from Santa Cruz Mountain neighborhoods could shower, heat food and share the warmth of someone else's sanctuary.

A supermarket employee in San Jose climbed through the chaos of his store's fallen merchandise to bag up baby formula, diapers and a loaf of bread for the distraught grandmother of a milk-allergic infant, then give it to her, free.

A San Francisco fire rescue team found four caged parakeets, alive, in the wreck of a building at Jefferson and Divisadero and delivered them gently to safety.

In all this, there was the catharsis of action, of making some sort of difference, if only by sympathizing, listening, talking and sharing the worst.

It felt good, to exchange stories, to offer help and take it, to hug a near-stranger who understood.

A San Jose 13-year-old named Jason Collamer learned about helping during the night he spent in an evacuation shelter. He helped direct traffic, watched a baby being born. "It was neat and scary at the same time," he said afterward. "I felt real good helping. I wish I could still do things."

It felt good even to share anger.

People raged together in San Francisco because Mayor Art Agnos showed up late to tell hundreds of displaced Marina residents they needed passes before they could take possessions from their shattered homes.

People raged together in Watsonville and Aptos and Pajaro because neither the authorities nor the media seemed to be paying enough attention to the considerable problems of their shaken little towns.

People all over the Bay Area raged together about why the World Series shouldn't be played, or why it should. It helped to rage, to throw things, to cry and then stop.

It helped, too, later in the week when the vice president, then the president, came to see the loss, and when the governor promised money, even if it takes a special tax.

But years will pass before there has been help enough. The difficulties immediately ahead are raw, fresh and widespread—getting to work, staying warm and dry, confronting the costs, searching for ways to confront the loneliness and loss.

Over the long term, others will be searching, too, for the explanations behind fallen freeways and bridge spans, for ways to rebuild the ambience that once defined old, comfortable California, for money to house and feed and succor thousands of people whose lives went from order to anguish in an instant.

There is no way to measure sadness and stress. There is no way to measure when it ends. A cosmic snap of the fingers might have started all this. It will take far, far more to end it.

This story was prepared with contributions from Miranda Ewell, Alan Gathright, Lisa Lapin, Philip J. Trounstine and Susan Yoachum.

WE ARE NOT PREPARED

SUNDAY, DECEMBER 31, 1989

**BY PETE CAREY
AND GLENNDA CHUI**

Someday, the earth along the East Bay or the San Francisco Peninsula will rupture and the Bay Area will shake more violently than it has in nearly a century. Only the exact date is uncertain.

In seconds, old buildings from San Jose to San Francisco will crumble, killing or injuring their occupants. There will be ruined hospitals, schools, small businesses, factories, apartments, bridges and freeways.

Much of that devastation is a certainty, mapped out in geologists' scenarios and government reports.

But much of it could be reduced or avoided.

For reasons ranging from the huge cost of some safety measures and conflicting social priorities to downright complacency and ignorance, the region remains vulnerable to devastation far greater than that brought by the earthquake of Oct. 17. In many ways, the cost of preparing now has been exchanged for the much higher cost of rebuilding later.

"We got off easy on this thing," Milpitas Fire Chief Michael Harwood says. "What I'm fearful of is that it's hard to get people motivated to be prepared. It almost takes something catastrophic to get people moving in the right direction."

PLAYING WITH FIRE

This blindness to danger is evident everywhere:

• Many schools, corporations and homeowners have not planned well for a major quake.

• Old hospital buildings will be reduced to rubble just when they're needed to help treat victims. Hospital officials say there's no money to strengthen them. "The cost would put some of these poor hospitals under," says Lori Aldrete, spokeswoman for the California Association of Hospitals and Health Systems.

• Technology exists to build better, safer buildings and to retrofit existing buildings, but is used more in Japan than in California.

• Utility planners don't design quake-proof systems because of the staggering costs, even though in a major quake, crews will be no match for power failures, telephone overloads and thousands of ruptures in natural gas, water and sewage lines.

• Engineers know how to make structures safe. Yet poorly trained designers have filled the region with buildings poorly designed to resist earthquakes, the California Seismic Safety Commission warned four years ago.

• Industry is unprepared for a severe earthquake. "It's almost like the ostrich with his head in the sand—it's not going to happen to us," says the corporate security manager of a large Silicon Valley semiconductor firm. "It's scary sometimes when I look around."

Not that there hasn't been progress. For instance, legislation passed before the Loma Prieta quake requires cities and counties to identify their hazardous buildings and to use up-to-date building codes; both laws take effect Monday.

And it's unreasonable to think the whole Bay Area can be earthquake-proofed. The cost would bankrupt society. Aaron Wildavsky, professor of public policy and political science at the University of California, Berkeley, says the "insane idea" that society can eliminate all its risks "would kill you on the spot."

COMPLACENCY

But progress has been slow and intermittent, punctuated by long periods of complacency between major earthquakes. And many reasonable steps aren't being taken.

For example, some homeowners could save their homes for less than $1,000 by bolting them to foundations, adding bracing and reinforcing chimneys. As the memory of the quake fades, the chance fades that many will do it.

The fact that many people fail to protect their single biggest asset shows widespread ignorance of what lies ahead, says Allan Lindh of the U.S. Geological Survey.

"There are a lot of people out there who just don't understand," he said. If an earthquake destroys their home for lack of $200 in bolting, "they may not get to buy a motor home and clog up the roads at

Yosemite when they get old. They may have to work until they drop dead. Their kids may not be able to go to college."

POLITICAL PROBLEMS

Yet politicians are unlikely to force the issue, says Raymond Seed, associate professor of geotechnical engineering at UC-Berkeley.

"If there were a mandate to do that, you would have a heck of a time getting legislation—because every voter would be affected, and the earthquake might not come," he says. "I think the problem very simply goes right to people's pocketbooks."

Earthquake safety also competes with other social and economic priorities.

Chinatown's brick buildings are clear dangers. But a forced seismic upgrading would cast poor people into the street by forcing destruction of some buildings and increasing rents in others, says Tom Chin, a structural engineer in San Francisco.

PROHIBITIVE SOCIAL COSTS

"You get a typical apartment (there) that's a little 10-by-10 room and an old lady has everything she owns in the apartment. . . . When you consider economic and social impacts, you think twice" about upgrading old buildings, he says.

"Sometimes you have to take a chance. That sounds awful. It's something I have a problem with myself. . . . I don't envy the politician."

When people hear that it would cost $5 billion to strengthen every old masonry and state-owned building in the state, they "just laugh," says Lloyd Cluff, manager of geosciences for Pacific Gas & Electric Co. and chairman of the California Seismic Safety Commission. "They say, 'God, we're not going to spend that kind of money.' "

The knowledge that total safety would cost billions of dollars has delayed setting priorities and taking smaller, less expensive steps that could save lives and property.

'YOU JUST WALK AWAY FROM IT'

"When you perceive the problem as being too big, you just walk away from it," says Peter Ward, a scientist who has spent his career studying earthquakes for the U.S. Geological Survey in Menlo Park. "But we know what we have to do."

Even Loma Prieta's warning jolt has sometimes backfired, lulling people into thinking they have faced the Big One and survived.

Devastating though Loma Prieta was, it was mild compared to big earthquakes to come. It was a flare compared to a 500-pound bomb— a "diagnostic quake, a service quake" to warn indifferent citizens, says Vitelmo Bertero, director of the Earthquake Engineering Research Center at UC-Berkeley.

And because of a geological quirk, the Oct. 17 quake lasted only half as long as it might have, producing a mere 15 seconds of intense shaking. This was barely enough to start liquefying sandy soil—the process that damaged airport runways and destroyed Marina District homes.

NO REPEAT OF '06

The Big One that planners are preparing for will not be a repeat of the 1906 San Francisco earthquake; that's unlikely to happen for decades, forecasters say.

Instead, it likely will be on the Hayward Fault, which runs 62 miles along the East Bay foothills from San Pablo Bay to near Mount Misery, east of San Jose.

True, the part of the San Andreas Fault that runs through the Peninsula also is considered ripe for a major earthquake. In a report last year, scientists gave it a 20 percent chance of a magnitude 7 quake within 30 years; those odds may have increased slightly because of stress added by the Loma Prieta quake.

FOCUS ON THE HAYWARD

But scientists and emergency planners worry much more about the Hayward. Scientists last year identified the Hayward as the most likely in the Bay Area to erupt in a major earthquake, with a 40 percent chance of producing a magnitude 7.

More troubling, it's also capable of a 7.5-magnitude quake—and that one would be the most devastating ever to hit California.

Unlike the San Andreas, much of which runs offshore and through rural areas, the Hayward slices through the thickly populated East

Bay; schools, hospitals, fire stations and other public buildings dot its length.

The fault also crosses lifelines that feed the entire Bay Area.

Such a quake on the Hayward Fault would "make this last event look like a picnic," says Christopher Rojahn, executive director of the Applied Technology Council, a non-profit Redwood City seismic engineering group.

TWICE AS LONG AS LOMA PRIETA

The quake would rumble for 25 to 35 gut-wrenching seconds—about twice as long as Loma Prieta.

It would be strong enough to severely damage buildings from Napa and Petaluma to south of San Jose.

In the heart of this danger zone—a swath five miles wide from San Pablo to San Jose—it would throw houses from their foundations and wreck earthquake-resistant buildings.

Violent shaking could kill up to 4,400 people and injure up to 145,000. More than 13,000 could require hospitalization.

But there would be little help for the hurt, the hungry or the homeless.

A 1987 report by the state Division of Mines and Geology describes this nightmarish aftermath:

Freeways would be impassable, blocked by accidents, fallen overpasses and hundreds of abandoned vehicles. The Richmond–San Rafael, Bay, San Mateo and Dumbarton bridges would close. Bay Area Rapid Transit District trains would stop; passengers would be forced to get out and walk along elevated tracks or through tunnels.

STUCK IN THE HORROR

Horrified survivors would find they couldn't get anywhere—not home to check on their families, not to work, not to the hospital for treatment of their injuries.

Neighborhoods would be isolated for days, cut off from food, water, power and emergency help. Volunteers would quickly organize to rescue people trapped in crushed cars or crumpled buildings—only to watch many die for lack of medical care.

The quake would bare two of the region's most glaring vulnerabilities:

• Most major rail, water and utility lines come into the Bay Area from the east—across the Hayward Fault. As the fault lurched 10 feet, it would snap some in two and severely damage others.

• The highly unstable land around the edge of the bay holds most of the area's vital transportation facilities. Airports. Docks. Railroad terminals. All the major bridge approaches. They would sustain major damage as the land quaked and liquefied, crippling the region's ability to recover.

DRY FOR MONTHS

As the shaking subsided, the flow of water from the Hetch Hetchy and South Bay aqueducts would slow to a trickle. Meanwhile, the quake would have broken local water pipes; many neighborhoods would have to rely on water from tanker trucks for weeks or even months.

The fault would break natural gas pipelines, cutting off gas to an area from San Pablo to Milpitas. Some places would be out of gas for weeks. The Peninsula might also suffer; with its regular lines cut, it would rely on flows from the Milpitas gas terminal, which sits on ground that liquefied in the 1906 earthquake.

Thousands of smaller gas lines would break throughout the East Bay, triggering fires in streets and buildings.

But with little water available, quenching those fires would be difficult. In any case, firefighters would have trouble reaching their stations, and some of those stations and their equipment would be damaged.

Sewage lines also would rupture. Emergency workers eventually would set up portable toilets in many neighborhoods; in some cases, sewage would flow through open trenches until repairs could be made.

RIVERS OF SEWAGE

Damaged sewage treatment plants would pour filth into the bay for up to a month. It "can be expected to pollute most waterways, channels, harbors and beaches, posing a public health risk," the state report says.

But in the urgent crush of problems following the earthquake, this problem, and the accompanying environmental degradation, would not head the list.

As shipments of food and emergency supplies flowed in from across the nation and the world, there would be few undamaged terminals to receive them.

The San Francisco and Oakland airports would close because their runways, built on fill, would be cracked and ruined. Only San Jose airport, and possibly Moffett Field, would remain open to large aircraft.

Many docks and railroad stations also sit on bad ground and would be unusable.

Once shipments came in, it would be difficult to route them over clogged and damaged roadways to people who desperately needed help.

Jammed phone lines and a general lack of communication would further delay relief efforts, costing some people their lives.

"You can move all the resources in," says Richard Eisner, director of the state government's Bay Area Regional Preparedness Project, "but if you don't know where they are needed, you can't get them to the local government level."

COMPOUNDED PROBLEMS

Each of these problems would be compounded as it interacted with others.

For instance, widespread power failures would limit the electricity available to pump water, treat sewage and run BART trains.

Without water and power, refineries in Contra Costa County could not manufacture gasoline. But it may be a moot point: Even if gasoline were available, tank trucks couldn't get to gas stations over the ruined freeways, and stations couldn't pump gas without electrical power.

Some of this damage and agony can be prevented, experts say, if people take a lesson from Loma Prieta and start preparing now.

Or they can wait for the next big quake to convince them.

"If you kill several thousand people, then you might get something done," said Cluff, the Seismic Safety Commission chairman. "That's probably what it will take."

THREE

ARSON FOR PROFIT

1990 WINNER IN THE INVESTIGATIVE REPORTING CATEGORY

"For a distinguished example of investigative reporting within a newspaper's area of circulation by an individual or team, presented as a single article or series . . ."

Minneapolis–St. Paul Star Tribune
Lou Kilzer and Chris Ison

When fire bells ring, some people stand to lose their homes and all of their possessions. Lou Kilzer and Chris Ison uncovered a network of businessmen with close ties to members of the St. Paul Fire Department, which allegedly profited from some suspicious fires.

The reporting for our articles has been described as "a combination of the old-fashioned, gumshoe detective work with modern, computerized, data-base reporting."

It was an apt description, if not a glamorous one, by *Star Tribune* Executive Editor Joel Kramer. The investigative process that revealed "a culture of arson" in St. Paul was anything but glamorous. And pinpointing the day, week or month that the story became clear to us is impossible, for it emerged one tiny piece at a time over nearly a year of full-time investigation.

Arson was far from our minds in the fall of 1988 when we stumbled upon a decade-old investigation that filled four file drawers in the St. Paul Police Department. The reports, which had remained sealed by a judge's order for years, dealt mostly with illegal bar ownerships. But buried in those hundreds of pages were several mentions of arson, and evidence of a curious loan from the city's fire chief that helped launch a local public insurance adjusting firm years before.

Several weeks of investigation would raise troubling questions about that loan. We learned that the adjuster, who by this time owned a near monopoly on the business in St. Paul, often represented arsonists, helping them negotiate insurance settlements for fires they'd set themselves or were suspected of setting.

The next 12 months led us through a maze of more than 10,000 documents from nine states and a foreign country, hundreds of sources and hundreds of fires. We interviewed arsonists and suspected arsonists, investigators, cops, jailbirds, firefighters, fire victims, insurance agents, accountants, politicians and housewives.

State and county records, fire reports and interviews revealed that the adjuster employed not only moonlighting firefighters, but also two men later convicted in major arson-for-profit conspiracies. Review of hundreds of building permits showed that the adjuster also steered fire repair work to a nearly invisible construction company owned by the fire chief's brother. A survey of hundreds of fire reports showed that the fire chief, his brother and 15 of their friends and associates had suffered 51 fires over the past 25 years.

An expert hired by the newspaper found that the fire chief had tolerated shoddy investigations of many of those fires and others handled by the adjuster. One fire killed a resident at a local hotel, and another killed a young child in an apartment building.

Understanding this cozy St. Paul fire industry meant uncovering associations that had developed over a quarter of a century. It became clear that seeing the forest for the trees would require more than routine organization. Hundreds of names were entered into a computer data base created specifically for the project. Significant events covering 25 years were entered into a second, chronological data base. A third data base recorded hundreds of property ownership histories. A fourth kept detailed records of nearly 200 fires with connections to the adjuster, the chief or his brother.

If the record-keeping aspects of the project seemed less than glamorous, the "gumshoe" parts offered little relief. It seemed a glamorous job on the sunny day when we paddled a canoe across a lake to get a peek at a remote house whose entrance road was consistently blocked by two well-trained guard dogs. But all glamour was gone three sweaty hours later when we paddled back after negotiating a half-dozen thickly wooded tributaries with nary a glimpse of the house.

At least we got tan. Our midwinter, door-to-door survey of dozens of St. Paul fire victims afforded no such luxury. We stood on doorsteps in the wind and snow, recording details of the victims' fires, their adjusters and their fire repair contractors. And while some were suspicious about a couple of bearded reporters asking probing questions, others were generous enough to invite us in and offer invaluable information.

Writing the story, a two-month process, was as tedious as reporting it. The *Star Tribune* imposes a grueling process known as "line-by-lining," in which the reporters and an editor fact-check each story one line at a time. It is that commitment to accuracy that helped us sleep at night. And it was the late-night, seven-day-a-week contributions of *Star Tribune* editors, photographers, librarians, artists and designers that brought the project together despite tight deadlines and two cranky reporters. Some who deserve special mention include Executive Editor Kramer, who broke from tradition to personally handle the editing of each of the stories; deputy Managing Editor John Ullmann, who directed the project from its inception; and Assistant City Editor Bill Loving. Trout Lowen and Steve Lowe, two interns hired specifically for the project, provided months of tireless research.

At this writing, the fire chief, who has denied any wrongdoing, remains suspended without pay, and the mayor has initiated proceedings to dismiss him. The Federal Bureau of Investigation, Internal Revenue Service and Federal Bureau of Alcohol, Tobacco and Firearms are investigating all aspects of the newspaper reports. Firefighters now are prohibited from moonlighting for public adjusters, and the state legislature has passed a new law regulating the state's public adjusting business.

> —Lou Kilzer
> Chris Ison
> *Minneapolis–St. Paul Star Tribune*

A CULTURE OF ARSON

INDUSTRY PROFITING FROM FIRE INVOLVES ST. PAUL FIREFIGHTERS AND HAS LINKS TO THEIR CHIEF

SUNDAY, OCTOBER 29, 1989

BY LOU KILZER
AND CHRIS ISON

A multimillion-dollar industry profiting from arson and suspicious fires is flourishing in St. Paul with the assistance of several key firefighters. And much of the money has flowed to two men linked to Fire Chief Steve Conroy.

A yearlong Star Tribune investigation shows that Conroy has contributed to a culture in which arson has thrived. He has tolerated shoddy fire investigations and allowed firemen to moonlight for a firm that has represented alleged arsonists in fire insurance claims.

In addition, two convicted arson conspirators appear to have had ties to both Chief Conroy and his brother.

"I've never seen such a pattern of impropriety as in the St. Paul Fire Department," says Elden Boh, a fire investigation expert hired by the Star Tribune.

Fire has so permeated St. Paul that Conroy, his brother and 15 of their friends and associates have suffered 51 fires in the past 25 years. Nearly half of those were clearly arson although it is not known who set them. In another 24 percent of the cases, investigators did not determine a cause.

Millions of dollars in insurance money from St. Paul fires has flowed to two companies:

• The first firm, Public Adjusters Inc., was financed by Conroy through a series of loans in the 1960s shortly before Conroy was promoted from captain to fire chief. In return for a commission, the firm helps fire victims collect as much as possible from their insurance companies. Headed by William J. (Billy) Whelan, the firm has used hustle and connections to attain a near-monopoly in the business in St. Paul. Whelan has employed two men who were later convicted of arson conspiracy, and within the past year alone has represented several people who were found to have set their own fires.

• The second firm, Conroy Construction Co., is run by the chief's brother, Pat. This nearly invisible company has had more than a million dollars in fire repair contracts steered its way by Whelan in the 1980s.

Chief Conroy says he has no financial interest in either company, and his brother and Whelan agree.

Of more than 100 fires from the past six years in which the Star Tribune was able to determine that Whelan or Pat Conroy became involved, about 32 percent were labeled arson; another 25 percent of the fires were suspicious or undetermined. Who set the fires was seldom determined.

One factor contributing to the success of the industry is the St. Paul Fire Department itself.

Several St. Paul firefighters, including three of Conroy's district fire chiefs, have worked for Whelan—sometimes testifying for people their own department suspected of arson.

And over and over again, the Fire Department's investigation of suspicious fires that were later handled by Whelan and Conroy Construction has been sloppy and grossly inadequate, according to Boh, the arson expert who reviewed the probes.

Fires were ruled as being caused by smokers' materials when residents weren't even asked if they smoked. And investigators overlooked obvious patterns, failing to note when a person had suffered a second, third, fourth or even fifth fire.

The Fire Department's failure to identify arson means that the property owner would probably have no problem collecting from the insurance company and paying Whelan and Conroy. Even in cases where arson is identified, a poor fire report could discourage the police from trying to find out who did it. In many cases, the commander at the fire scene, the person partly responsible for deciding whether the fire was arson, was one of the firefighters moonlighting for Whelan.

Although Boh said a few investigators repeatedly performed substandard work, management problems in the department could account for much of the problem, he said.

In more than 50 of the cases studied by the Star Tribune, the people suffering the fires were the fire chief himself, his brother or business associates and friends of the Conroys. In the past 25 years, fires have occurred at three properties owned by Chief Conroy. His brother Pat has reported at least eight fires, three at the same address. Pat's most recent fire was last month.

In the years when most of these fires were occurring, Steve and Pat Conroy allegedly have had ties to two major St. Paul arson conspirators: Vernon Hermes, currently serving prison time for a 1986 arson conspiracy conviction, and Tony Hartman, a convicted torch.

The Conroy brothers say they have no more than passing acquaintances with Hermes and Hartman.

About the time the fire chief financed the adjusting company in the 1960s, Hermes, a longtime acquaintance of the chief's, was hired.

Hartman was working in a bar owned by Steve Conroy's brother and managed by the chief's nephew at the time of his 1986 arrest for arson. Hartman's ex-wife says that for years, the fire chief regularly called her husband at home to gossip. Like the Conroys, Hartman also has reported an extraordinary number of fires at his own properties.

Most of the Star Tribune's findings are new, but 10 years ago, St. Paul police and the state's Bureau of Criminal Apprehension (BCA) told Mayor George Latimer that Chief Conroy might have had hidden investments in bars where arson and suspicious fires had been reported.

According to a police memorandum, Latimer first said that the investigation should proceed. But it soon died amid a political storm in 1979, with the most serious allegations against Chief Conroy never being made public. Latimer said he cannot recall if he ever asked his chief about the allegations.

Arson expert Boh, who has been involved in nearly 1,500 fire investigations, says: "The associations you have with the St. Paul Fire Department are not normal associations that I have ever seen."

Based on a year of investigation, here is how profits are made from suspicious and arson fires in St. Paul:

BILLY WHELAN: CENTER OF THE PROFIT-MAKING FIRE TRADE

At the center of St. Paul's fire industry is "Billy" Whelan, a pugnacious 68-year-old East Sider who portrays himself as the firefighters' friend and the insurance industry's nemesis.

Whelan, who got his start in the business with the help of a series of loans from Steve Conroy in the 1960s totaling more than $10,000, has attained a near-monopoly in St. Paul in the business called public adjusting.

Despite its name, public adjusting is a private affair, with adjusters viewing themselves as modern-day Robin Hoods, coming to the aid of fire victims before impersonal insurance companies can rip them off.

But unlike Robin Hood, public adjusters get paid for their services. For a fee of usually 10 percent of the eventual insurance settlement, the adjuster will appraise damage to a building and its contents, then represent the property owner in dealing with the insurance company.

On its surface, public adjusting was an unusual business for a firefighter to finance. Although the adjuster usually aids innocent fire victims at a time of stress and confusion, the money involved often has attracted both professional and amateur arsonists. It is this persistent taint of arson that has given the field a black eye with fire officials around the nation.

"If you're guilty (of arson), you generally don't want to face anybody. You'd just as soon somebody else do it. And that's why you'd have a public adjuster," explains Peggy O'Brien, who actually helped arrange arsons for a St. Paul public adjuster.

And there are cases where the public adjuster is on the scene even before the fire. O'Brien's boss, for instance, would recruit would-be arsonists, teach them how to make their fires look accidental, pack their homes with junk furniture and then wait for the fire engines.

The "victim" would then hire O'Brien's boss to adjust the damage. He would inflate the fire damage—the cheap Salvation Army sofa would suddenly become a priceless heirloom—and the group would have plenty of money to divide.

One curious item about O'Brien's boss, federally convicted arson racketeer Eugene P. Gamst, is that he was once president of the firm started by Billy Whelan, the company that Chief Conroy helped fund.

Gamst testified that he left Whelan's firm around 1971. Soon afterward, he came to the attention of arson investigators in Minneapolis and St. Paul. They began examining records of Gamst fires as far back as 1968. No cases were ever brought.

In federal court testimony, an Omaha police officer testified that in 1972, Gamst and an associate met him at a St. Paul restaurant and tried to entice him into an arson ring.

And further evidence of Gamst's longstanding arson associations comes from O'Brien, who turned state's evidence to help the FBI crack Gamst's interstate arson ring in 1980. She said Gamst told her that he'd been arranging fires for 20 years without ever being suspected.

Gamst isn't the only person convicted on arson-related charges to have worked for Billy Whelan. Vernon (Lefty) Hermes was identified in a St. Paul police report as being an arson suspect while working for Whelan in the early 1970s. Whelan agrees that Hermes solicited business, but says he didn't know of any arson connections.

Hermes was convicted on federal arson conspiracy charges in 1987 while working independently as a St. Paul public adjuster.

"He got greedy," Whelan says.

While Gamst and Hermes were working with Whelan, so was one and perhaps two fire captains who later would be promoted to district fire chiefs.

One of them, Warren Cook, has been with Whelan for 25 years—even before the loans from Conroy began. The other, Steve Conroy's brother-in-law Anthony Connelly, was unsure of the exact years he worked for Whelan, but thinks it was in the early 1970s.

Still another district chief, two other fire captains and a firefighter have worked for Whelan on occasion over the past three years. And their jobs with Whelan have also brought them into contact with arsonists: Whelan clients who needed help in fraudulent insurance claims.

Such contact is almost inevitable. Cook, for instance, agrees with O'Brien that arsonists prefer using public adjusters in their insurance claims. And yet, Cook could not recall a single fire of the 2,000 or so that he's handled in which he or Whelan turned down the fire adjustment because of suspected arson.

And the inevitable has, in fact, happened. In the past three years, at least 12 Whelan clients have been accused of arson or fraud by their insurance companies. Two of them pleaded guilty in criminal courts. Two others were adjudged to be arsonists by civil courts.

In those civil cases, Whelan's firefighters have taken the stand to defend their work for the alleged arsonists. Also testifying, though on the other side, were St. Paul arson investigators.

In one case, District Chief Cook took the stand to defend his determination that a television set and a photocopying machine were destroyed, although they were in a part of the house that was removed from the fire.

He admitted that he made the determination despite the outward appearance that the equipment was undamaged and without actually turning on the machines to see if they worked.

Another district fire chief, a fire captain and a firefighter—all working for Whelan—also defended their work in this "contents inventory."

The jury was not impressed. It found that the insurance claim the firefighters helped prepare was fraudulently inflated.

The jury also decided that the homeowner set the fire as part of an arson-for-profit scheme.

In another case this year, Cook had to explain why a couch that the insurance company proved had been bought for $400 was listed in his inventory as a $1,200 loss. The insurance company had the receipt for the couch because the homeowner had claimed it as a loss in an earlier unrelated vandalism case.

In this case as in the first, the jury decided that the claim that the firemen helped prepare was fraudulently inflated. The firemen had estimated that the homeowner lost $18,000 on her contents. The jury said the value was actually $5,000. But the homeowner couldn't collect even that, because the jury ruled that she arranged her own fire.

The insurance company maintained that the homeowner had a motive to raise money through fraud, having squandered (partly on cocaine) most of an earlier $200,000-plus personal injury settlement.

Helping alleged arsonists with claims is only one of the potential conflicts for the firefighters. For instance, the Star Tribune has discovered that Cook was the commanding officer in at least 11 fires where the victims later hired Pat Conroy or Billy Whelan. There may be more.

Cook says his role in those fires—as in all that happens while he is on duty—is to "work with the investigators to decide how the fire started."

And therein lies the potential conflict. If Cook labels a fire an arson, he could jeopardize insurance payments. In other words, too many arson findings could be bad for Whelan's business.

Cook finds all of the Fire Department's connections to this network normal, legitimate business. When he works for Whelan he takes off his firefighter's hat, he says, and no longer is involved with looking for evidence of arson.

And he says he resents the inquiry into Public Adjusters Inc., saying it's a matter of somebody "trying to make something out of nothing."

Perhaps Whelan himself best summarizes the prevailing attitude. "Who do you think are the worst crooks," he asked a reporter recently, "insurance companies or arsonists?"

A FIREMAN'S BEST FRIEND

Even firefighters not on Whelan's payroll have benefited from the feisty adjuster. Billy Whelan is a friend of the fireman.

"He would buy dinners for a whole fire station," recalls Ralph Samalla, who was a partner in Public Adjusters with Whelan in the 1960s.

"He would tell 'em, 'you don't have to plan on dinner for Friday night. I'm going to bring dinner over.' And he'd have a catered dinner."

It's a tradition that has lasted into the '80s. Firemen have been served prime-rib meals on Whelan's tab catered from Hafner's, a restaurant on White Bear Av.

Whelan's good relations with the firefighters appears to be good business. For example, fire scenes have been turned over to him to board up windows and doors, even in cases where arson is suspected and before the owners have been notified of the fire.

Linda Foster, a St. Paul woman who suffered a 1984 arson fire in which she was not a suspect, said a fireman pointed to Whelan while her fire was still being extinguished.

"Do you know who that man was who gave you that card?" Foster recalls being asked by a fireman. She said she didn't.

"His name is Bill Whelan and he's a public adjuster. . . . You're going to need a public adjuster. I can't tell you what to do, but I'll tell you what I told my wife. I told her (that) if we have a fire to call Bill Whelan before you call the fire department." Foster said she was very happy with Whelan's work for her.

To see how pivotal Whelan can be in a fire, consider the case of Victor Hawkins, whose house at 362 Sherburne Av. burned in an arson last year, a few days after he moved in some of his belongings. According to Hawkins, who police say was never a suspect in the fire, he experienced the following:

He was away from the house on the morning of the fire, when Whelan reached him by phone and told him about the blaze. Hawkins says he has no idea how Whelan got the number.

When Hawkins arrived at the scene, Whelan had already been inside and had arranged for someone to board up broken windows.

Hawkins says Whelan asked him who his insurance company was. When he named the company, he says, Whelan exclaimed: "I know a guy with them down in Iowa. This will be a breeze."

And, in fact, it apparently was a breeze. The insurance company settled for $83,020, including $28,700 for contents that the Fire Department had valued at $1,000.

Hawkins says that at one of several meetings he had at various restaurants with one or more firefighters, Whelan made "derogatory" remarks about Mike Morehead, an arson detective with the St. Paul Police Department.

Hawkins said that Whelan "didn't like Morehead cause Morehead was such a gung-ho guy. He wanted to find out who did all the fires."

STRUCTURAL REPAIRS: WHERE THE BIG MONEY IS

The big bucks in fire insurance settlements come in checks to repair the actual structural damage.

Peggy O'Brien, the arson recruiter who worked for Gene Gamst, says that some public adjusters have a special arrangement with certain contractors allowing them to share in the repair portion of the insurance settlement. And that's on top of the adjuster's usual 10 percent fee.

Says O'Brien: "You can really make a load with a contractor."

And, she says, it's easy to steer business to a preferred contractor. Often, she says, an adjuster simply tells a client: " 'Listen, I've got a guy who will do this, just as cheap as he can.' And of course you are going to listen to him. . . . 99 chances out of 100, you will take who your adjuster recommends."

Terry Joy, a Twin Cities attorney specializing in fire insurance work, says that if a public adjuster steers work only to certain contractors, the possibility of collusion exists.

O'Brien puts it bluntly: "It's all kickback city."

O'Brien's involvement in the adjusting business ended in 1980 when she began testifying in arson cases in Omaha. By then, she had met adjusters in several states, including many in the Twin Cities. However, she has no knowledge of how the business now works in St. Paul, nor whether specific adjusters there are involved in kickbacks.

O'Brien says that she has met Billy Whelan, but was unaware of his arrangement, if any, with contractors.

Whelan has used several contractors. But the one he's used most often in recent years, based upon a review of building permits, is Patrick A. Conroy Sr., brother of St. Paul's fire chief.

And Pat Conroy appears to get nearly all of his fire repair business from Whelan. Of 60 fire repair jobs done by Conroy in which the Star Tribune has been able to determine the public adjuster, 57 were handled by Whelan. Most of the clients interviewed by the newspaper said they hired Conroy on Whelan's advice.

Whelan says that all his dealings with Pat Conroy are above-board. Pat concurs.

Shoehorned into an unmarked second-story office in a West Side industrial building, Conroy Construction is nearly invisible.

Its name does not appear on the building's directory; it's listed in the Yellow Pages under "contractors," but not under "fire repairs." The pickup truck that Pat Conroy uses on the job carries no company logo. Conroy Construction is so insulated that even a professional process-server reported that he couldn't locate its headquarters. And many of Conroy's own customers say they have trouble reaching him, except through Whelan, with complaints about the quality of repairs.

Conroy, however, says that in every case, the homeowner endorses the insurance check covering the repairs, and that they wouldn't do so if they were dissatisfied. He also says that grumbling over contracting work is common in the industry.

Many clients say they are confused about exactly how their insurance funds were handled, and report varying degrees of control over those funds. At least nine Whelan customers report that while they got the money from insurance checks to replace their damaged contents, Whelan controlled the funds for the repair of structural damage. They say that although they endorsed the checks, they received none of the funds. That money typically went to Whelan, then to Conroy.

At least four other clients, however, said they had control over the funds to repair structural damage to their homes.

The size of the insurance payments for a typical fire is driven by a modern invention in homeowners insurance called a "replacement cost policy." It's the biggest weapon in a public adjuster's arsenal because it requires an insurance company to pay for repairs that bring a property back to its pre-fire condition.

Because of the clause, hundreds of modest or slum-like dwellings in St. Paul that have sustained limited fire damage have received large insurance settlements, sometimes exceeding the market value of the entire house.

It's simply done. For instance, no matter how many layers of linoleum might have covered a hardwood floor before a home suffered a fire, a public adjuster typically will insist on restoring the original hardwood flooring—and not just in the room that burned. If new flooring in the room that burned doesn't exactly match the rest of the hardwood in the house, the adjuster can insist on re-flooring the entire house.

The same is true of carpeting, crafted moldings and the heavy plastering found in many of the city's core housing districts.

Faced with large claims by the public adjuster, insurance companies often agree to compromise, paying less than the full replacement cost for the damage but giving the homeowner and the adjuster wide latitude in use of the funds. After satisfying lien holders, the homeowner can quite legally spend any leftover money any way he wants.

Several clients of Whelan and Conroy who were interviewed by the newspaper said they did not understand that process. At least four said they believed that the entire settlement to cover structural damage had to be spent on repairs.

What they do receive are proceeds from the check to replace their personal belongings damaged in the fire. And most say they are very pleased with how Whelan handled their contents claim.

However, some homeowners say they suspect that the real value of the repairs Conroy Construction made is less than the insurance settlement, but that they received none of it back.

Building department records appear to bear them out. In 17 cases reviewed by the Star Tribune, insurance payments for structural damage average $35,660—over four times the $8,300 average on Conroy's building permits.

Conroy explains that he may have misunderstood how the permits are supposed to be filled out. He says that he doesn't include the value of his subcontractors' work for his permits, although building department regulations say that contractors are supposed to do so. Even with the subcontractors' permits figured in, the total paid to cover structural damage repairs averages 3.9 times more than what the permits indicate.

Whelan suggested that Conroy might deliberately underestimate the value of repairs because the higher the amount of the stated repairs, the higher the fee the contractor must pay the city. "If you do a $30,000 (construction job), are you going to take out a building permit for $30,000?" he fumes.

Interestingly, on two occasions Conroy Construction fire-repair permits were dated before there was a fire at the property. Conroy says there must have been a mistake.

As for handling the settlement for structural damage, Whelan says he does everything according to the book. Where the replacement clause is invoked, the replacement is made. Where there is a negotiated settlement, the money goes to the homeowner after mortgage companies and contractors are paid.

Hawkins, the homeowner who got an $83,020 settlement for a fire, says he has real problems with how the insurance money in his claim was spent.

He says he cleared $19,500 after Whelan took his commission from the personal property settlement. The bulk of the settlement—about

$54,320 to repair the house—Hawkins never had control over, he says.

Hawkins says he was told by a Whelan employee that the value of the repairs totaled $29,000, roughly $25,000 less than the insurance check for structural damage.

FIRE CHIEF'S BROTHER HAS CONNECTIONS TO ARSONIST

In recent interviews Pat Conroy has appeared less than forthcoming, choosing to deny some things that can be demonstrably proven.

The subjects range from such matters as ownership in bars to fires on his own property. Also at issue is his alleged relationship with one of the state's more prolific arsonists.

For instance, Pat says he had almost no interest in a St. Paul bar called the Park Rec that was damaged by fire in 1969 and 1973. Yet he admitted a secret half-interest in that same bar in a 1981 sworn deposition.

He denies ever having an interest in a St. Paul bar then called Conroy's, though he was the license holder and though he was listed as an owner in a lawsuit over the bar's sale.

The same is true with a bar in Mounds View. Conroy denies ownership, though the bar was licensed in his name and run by his son.

And Conroy is equally oblique in discussing his ties to Billy Whelan. For one, he said Whelan doesn't steer fire business his way—though building permits and interviews clearly demonstrate that scores of fire repair jobs are directed to him by Whelan.

And both Pat and Steve say they have almost no connections with each other. However, records show their paths have crossed. They were listed as directors of a corporation that ran a bar operated by Pat in the 1960s. A lawsuit from the same era lists the two and Conroy Construction as co-defendants. Outside of the cover page, however, the old suit has been destroyed by a judge's order.

In the 1970s, Pat built a bar that Steve secretly owned, and built a restaurant on land that Steve sold to two associates. Pat has also done contracting work on a bar financed by Steve. Pat has also managed that bar.

In a 1980 sworn deposition, St. Paul bar owner John Keena said that when Pat Conroy planned to claim an interest in a Keena-owned bar because of an old $30,000 debt, it was Steve Conroy who told him about it. And not only once, but "several times." Steve Conroy says that never happened.

And John Pfaff, a longtime friend of Steve Conroy, says he recalls that Pat and Steve shared an interest in the mid-1970s in a planned Pfaff real estate venture called Woodbury Center.

But it's in matters concerning Tony Hartman that Pat Conroy's comments are most troubling. Conroy says he has almost no connection to Hartman, one of the state's more prolific arsonists. He says Hartman may have worked for a subcontractor on a Conroy repair job many years ago.

But that's not the story that Hartman told the Star Tribune last year when he was interviewed in a federal lockup in Missouri, where he was serving time for arson conspiracy. His story, which paints a far more intimate picture of his alleged ties with Pat Conroy, has been filled in by subsequent interviews with Hartman and others.

Hartman is an avuncular and often charming 67-year-old retired contractor with past convictions for theft, drug possession and—most recently—arson conspiracy. In three interviews, he talked freely of his many friends, a virtual cross section of St. Paul culture: from alleged gangsters to a prominent doctor, lawyer and several businessmen. Many of those relationships have been corroborated by the Star Tribune.

Of Pat Conroy, Hartman says he's been a close friend and occasional business associate for three decades. In fact, since his release from prison this year, Hartman says, he's continued seeing Pat Conroy at a bar run by Pat's son. He said he talks to Pat's son at least twice a week.

Hartman says that 20 years ago, he worked so closely with Conroy that Pat "thought I was (his partner), but I wasn't."

In later years, Hartman says, he liked to socialize at Conroy-owned bars. And it was at just such a bar that Hartman met his eventual partner in arson, Vernon Hermes. Pat Conroy introduced them, says Hartman.

Hartman's former wife, chief operating nurse at an area hospital, confirms the relationship. Tony worked for Pat Conroy for years, she says. Her ex-husband, Janet Hartman continues, was asked by Pat to watch over employees at Conroy-owned bars, making sure they weren't dipping into the till.

Hartman, she says, would tell her: "I've got to go out. I'm checking to see if these guys are stealing money from them or charging too much for the drinks." She said that in some of these cases she thought Tony was working with Pat Conroy's son.

Hartman's son, an admitted armed robber named James Churchill, said his father considered Pat Conroy a close friend. "They were card-playing buddies and pool-shooting buddies and drinking buddies," Churchill said. "I think they were pretty close."

But perhaps the strongest evidence that Hartman had a closer relationship with Pat Conroy than Conroy acknowledges comes from testimony by an agent of the Federal Bureau of Alcohol, Tobacco and Firearms. Agent Robert Williams testified that two to three days after Hartman's arson conspiracy arrest in 1986, agents found him working at Muldoon's, the Mounds View bar owned by Pat Conroy and managed by his son.

Hartman says he was doing a construction project there. Williams testified that when he saw Hartman, he was "doing a small remodeling job in the stage area of Muldoon's."

Tony Hartman doesn't limit his association with the Conroys to Pat and Pat's son. Steve Conroy, too, was a friend, although a more distant one, says Hartman.

The chief denies any friendship, saying he has perhaps said "hello" to Hartman four times in his life.

Janet Hartman says she recalls that a man named Steve Conroy would frequently call Tony during the 1970s. She says she thought the man had some relation to the St. Paul Fire Department. As far as she knows, the discussions were merely gossip.

Valerie Churchill, a longtime Hartman associate, says she also is sure that Tony was a friend of Steve Conroy's and that Tony would visit Patrick's, Steve's bar on Larpenteur Av.

Although James Churchill says he knows of no friendship between his father and St. Paul's fire chief, he recalls that one of his father's favorite watering holes was a bar called the Parkside, near Lake Phalen.

Insurance salesman Jim Malone, a former Parkside bartender, said that Hartman was so well known there that when he would walk through the door, patrons would shout "Tony!"

The Parkside was financed by Steve Conroy. It was run by a former St. Paul firefighter.

Tony Hartman may not have been the only arsonist to have had more than a passing acquaintance with St. Paul's fire chief. Another arson conspirator to cross the chief's path was Vernon Hermes, the former solicitor for Public Adjusters Inc.

William Flaherty, a public adjuster who was a former business partner of Pat Conroy, says that Hermes was part of a "clique" that included the Conroys, Whelan and Flaherty.

"Sure, we all knew one another. We were all brought up in the same era," Flaherty says. "You're talking about a Catholic-Irish town. We all played together. . . . We all took apples out of the same guy's tree together."

In fact, Flaherty says that he thinks it was Steve Conroy who put Hermes to work on Billy Whelan's staff to watch over Conroy's financial interest. "Billy Whelan and Hermes were buddy-buddies for years," says Flaherty.

Vernon Hermes was convicted of arson conspiracy in the same 1986 case that landed Tony Hartman behind bars. Federal agents believed he'd arranged arsons in at least three states.

Conroy said he did not put Hermes in business with Whelan. Asked two weeks ago if Vernon Hermes was a friend of his, St. Paul's fire chief replied: "He's not my enemy."

PROBE LINKED CHIEF CONROY TO FIRES IN THE LATE '70S

The fire chief's alleged relations with people suspected of or convicted of being on the other side of St. Paul's fire trade should not be a surprise at City Hall.

In fact, former St. Paul Police Chief Richard Rowan told Mayor George Latimer a decade ago that his fire chief allegedly held interest in bars that had been torched.

That 90-minute meeting took place Aug. 14, 1978, as a political gale was raging in St. Paul. The gale concerned a two-year state and local police investigation into perhaps the strongest political lobby in the city: St. Paul's liquor dealers. Before it was over, investigators were accused of illegal wiretapping, personal vendettas and attempted entrapment.

What the public knew at the time was that the investigation was into hidden bar ownerships. But Latimer was told that the investigation in Steve Conroy's case had gone far beyond that. What it concerned, Chief Rowan explained, was arson.

A police memo describing the Latimer meeting is succinct: ". . . the Chief told Latimer that much more serious allegations had been brought up against Conroy. For example: several bars that experienced arson fires allegedly were linked to or financed by Steve Conroy; that Conroy had loaned fire adjuster Billy Whelan $10,000 to start his adjusting business. . . .

"Latimer agreed that these allegations were of a more serious nature than a hidden ownership in a bar, and urged the chief to explore them."

That resolve soon waned and Latimer joined others in criticizing the investigators.

Reflecting on the probe a decade later, Latimer told the Star Tribune that the information Chief Rowan presented him was "so horrendous that if there was any merit to it I would have hoped that it would have been prosecuted."

But it's clear the mayor did little on his own to determine whether there was merit to the charges.

"My job was not to try to judge the truth or falsity but to make sure it was all being pursued, that there wasn't any favoritism."

"It seemed to me," Latimer said in an interview last year, "that we turned everything over to the county attorney."

Asked if the county attorney adequately pursued the matter, Latimer responded: "I don't know. How do I get to evaluate the county attorney? It was a county attorney thing, wasn't it?"

But the county attorney's office reports receiving no information about Conroy and arson. Paul Lindholm, the assistant county attorney who handled the liquor probe, said recently the issue of arson was news to him. He did recall a meeting with Latimer, Rowan and others to discuss the probe. He said Latimer was growing impatient with the probe and wanted an answer to a pivotal question: "When is this going to end?"

Lindholm said he didn't recall any discussion of arson during that meeting.

County Attorney Tom Foley says he, too, saw none of the police reports concerning arson until reporters showed him a stack of the files this month.

He said he would need time to study the files in depth, but said some of it appeared to be "gossip." And Lindholm said he was convinced that the BCA and police probe had "no focus."

Both prosecutors said the BCA wanted to call an "investigative grand jury," something Foley's office doesn't believe in.

The man who might be able to explain what was and wasn't given to the county attorney and why—Raymond DiPrima, the BCA agent who headed the probe—isn't talking. Richard Bacon, head of special investigations for the BCA, says there was enough evidence to warrant an investigative grand jury probe of several matters uncovered by detectives, although he did not single out Conroy. As it was, "a lot of things (were left) unanswered." And he tosses the blame back to Ramsey County: "What we didn't have is the cooperation of the county attorney."

It's clear that some of the information in police and BCA files is a mixed bag. Some of it is raw intelligence from unnamed and unevaluated sources. Other information, though, is from named sources or from people known to the police as highly reliable and who had detailed information to offer concerning the chief. And when viewed in context with information gathered by the Star Tribune, the strongest sections from the liquor probe paint a plausible picture of Conroy's ownership of bars that burned.

To be sure, some of the hardest evidence against Conroy concerned alleged hidden ownership in bars that hadn't burned. At the time, it was illegal to own more than one bar.

For instance, a St. Paul police report dated June 22, 1978, says that officers stopped the owner of Patrick's Lounge as he was heading into the fire department. The man, according to police reports, pulled out an envelope "full of paper money and said, 'I've got to deliver this to Steve Conroy. It's from the bar.'"

Investigators later obtained bank records showing Conroy's interest in the bar. He borrowed the money to build the bar and both people who claimed ownership told investigators that Conroy was a 50 percent owner. Hidden interests are possible only through falsified liquor licenses, which was one focus of the probe.

BCA records state that one of those owners was prepared to testify before a grand jury that he "skimmed money from the receipts" of a bar "and gave this money to Conroy."

But the allegation of most concern to investigators when they talked with the mayor was arson.

Overall, various sources had claimed that four bars in which Conroy allegedly had investments at one time had burned. Most of the probe centered on two major nightclub fires that occurred a month apart in the summer of 1975.

The first was at McDonough's Supper Club, 107 Concord St., which burned to the ground on June 22 from a fire reported at 2:59 a.m.

One BCA source, identified as a member of the city attorney's staff, tried to investigate Conroy's alleged ownership in the bar a year or two after the fire.

The investigator alleged that he was stopped short "in his efforts during the first day of the investigation by his boss, (Deputy City Attorney) Philip Byrne. He was called by Byrne and told that Steve Conroy was 'hot' about the questions being asked about him, and to 'knock it off.' "

He did so, but not before he "learned that McDonough's bar was or had some Conroy money in it," the report said.

Today, Byrne says that police source was Tom Weyandt, now an assistant city attorney.

Weyandt says his investigation started when he mentioned to Byrne that Conroy allegedly had hidden ownership in McDonough's and Patrick's on Larpenteur. He says Byrne told him to check it out.

He phoned two of his sources, but within 45 minutes, Byrne told him to stop his investigation. "I can't remember if he said Conroy or (liquor license inspector Joe) Carchedi already called him and asked why we were checking into Steve. And he said drop it. . . . And that was that." He says he never did confirm the tip.

Weyandt says he has always wondered how the word got out so fast.

Byrne says he only asked Weyandt to stop because the quick reactions indicated that the investigation was not being conducted with "discretion and judgment." He said police should handle the matter. Byrne also says he does not remember who called him to complain about the investigation, but that it was not Conroy.

Other sources also told police they knew of Conroy's interest in McDonough's.

Police records say that Conroy called the St. Paul vice squad three times in the two months before McDonough's burned, voicing concern that the arrest of a stripper there might endanger the club's liquor license.

Conroy denies making the calls.

Conroy's department never determined the exact cause of the $210,000 fire, but investigators focused on an electrical panel in the basement. The nightclub later sued an electrical company that had done work at the bar. A jury, however, determined that the electrical firm was not negligent.

The listed owner of the bar—Fran McDonough—says Conroy was not his partner in that nightclub, and Conroy denies it, as well.

(Star Tribune research of available public records shows the two did have business interests in common. Corporate records show that Conroy and McDonough were partners in a travel business before the fire. Conroy was one of two references on McDonough liquor license applications both before and after the fire.)

The second fire to get the most attention of detectives occurred 26 days after McDonough's burned. The 3:25 a.m. fire at 435 St. Peter St. gutted the Showboat nightclub, which, according to the liquor license, was owned by Blackie Landreville.

Investigators developed sources who said Conroy was a partner in the establishment, and that he took an interest in the subsequent fire investigation. Conroy denies having had an ownership interest or showing special interest in the investigation.

According to their records, the liquor probe investigators developed indirect evidence of Conroy's alleged business dealings with Blackie Landreville and his brother Jerry from IRS agent Jim Kuperski. The agent said that "the Landrevilles and Conroy are constantly going back and forth on different business deals," according to the police document.

Kuperski has been unavailable for comment.

And Billy Whelan appeared to supply information about the chief and the Showboat. Whelan, according to a BCA report, told a fireman that the cause of the $150,000 nightclub fire—which the fire department had described as suspicious and possibly arson—was in fact arson. Plus, according to the source, "Whelan alluded to the fact that Conroy was a hidden owner at the club."

Whelan was the public adjuster hired by the nightclub's owners.

(The Star Tribune has been able to confirm business and personal connections between Conroy and Jerry and Blackie Landreville. Among the findings: Two years after the Showboat fire, Conroy helped arrange the sale of a bar he controlled to Blackie Landreville, and he retained a contract for deed on the property. The Landrevilles and Conroy have also been partners with others in a 1980s mining venture.)

The bottom line seems clear: The BCA and St. Paul Police Department investigators were confident that they had enough sources of information to warrant further investigation of the fire chief and others. In Conroy's case, they had firm evidence of illegal hidden ownership in two bars that hadn't burned, and wanted to investigate the more serious allegations of ownership in bars that had.

But they were deterred by the political uproar, which portrayed the investigation into bar ownership as a "witch hunt."

Officials lamented that they were legally barred from disclosing to the public the breadth and seriousness of the investigation. Instead, they were blasted by members of the St. Paul City Council for allegedly improper investigative techniques.

Chief Rowan, who soon left office, said in a written report that the probe had been forced "on the defensive, causing it to divert its attention from the investigation and respond to charges initiated by persons it was investigating."

" . . . The response," he wrote, "to this investigation by the city council is without precedence in the memories of police officials."

FOR CONROYS AND FRIENDS, A TRAIL OF FIRES

Although the only fires the liquor probe dealt with were on properties that Steve Conroy allegedly owned, Conroy has also had fires on properties he unquestionably owned. And so have his brother and 15 friends and associates.

Steve Conroy's major fire started on the night of March 4, 1983, and by the time it was over, "there wasn't anything left to get suspicious about," said Hudson (Wis.) fire inspector Terry Bauer.

An insurance company adjuster says he recalls that the loss was between $100,000 and $150,000.

Conroy explains that he wasn't living at the house at the time of the fire, but that his fiancée had been there a few hours before the blaze to turn on a furnace. There was going to be a birthday party at the house the next day, and she wanted the place pre-warmed.

Out of curiosity, Conroy says, he asked two of his own fire investigators to research the fire. The chief investigator sent by Conroy gave the chief an oral report, saying that the fire started accidentally in the basement furnace room, Conroy said. Conroy has had two additional small fires on property he's owned.

Other fires have dogged Conroy's relatives and associates. And, as with Steve Conroy's fires, it isn't known who set them, if anyone.

Between 1965 and 1989, Pat Conroy had at least eight fires on property he owned, including three at the same address. Four of those were listed as arson and two others were listed as undetermined in origin.

In one of the fires listed as undetermined, firemen noted that there was a "strong odor of gasoline" at the scene. No one was prosecuted in any of those fires.

Pat also suffered fires in a St. Paul bar called the Park Rec, in which he held a hidden 50 percent interest.

One fire produced an $80,000 insurance check, none of which was put into repairs. Instead, as Pat Conroy testified in a 1981 deposition, each partner took about $20,000 off the top and most of the rest was used to pay bills. That bar closed within a year.

According to a sworn deposition by Pat Conroy's partner, Chief Conroy knew of his brother's interest in the bar. He apparently didn't tell his men, who listed a bank as the owner on a fire report. Pat Conroy is not mentioned.

Fire investigators also did not determine the fire's cause, although they said there were three possible explanations. All involved accidental causes. A fire report did note, however, that there were "two 5-gallon flammable liquid containers partly full and two 1-gallon flammable liquid containers near the fire scene. One was badly burned."

The person in charge of liquor licensing at the time was Joe Carchedi, an associate of Chief Conroy. He has had three fires.

Tony Hartman, the arsonist with alleged ties to Pat and Steve Conroy, has personally had at least eight fires on properties he owned or controlled. Most happened in St. Paul, although one was in White Bear Lake, another involved a fourplex in Minneapolis and one happened in Waverly, Minn. The Waverly fire was adjusted by Billy Whelan. Vernon Hermes adjusted the Minneapolis blaze.

Walter Montpetit, who says he is one of Steve Conroy's friends, has suffered four fires, one an arson, two undetermined and one accidental.

William Schally—a man who once told undercover investigators that a bar he managed had been secretly owned by Conroy and has purchased property from the chief—suffered a house fire in St. Paul.

Frank Fabio, a man who moved houses for Conroy in the 1960s and sold a bar to a corporation directed by Pat and Steve Conroy, was convicted in 1971 for an arson at his house.

McDonough, Conroy's onetime business partner, has lost more than his supper club to fire. He recalls three other fires, the latest at his Lakeland home in 1981. Whelan adjusted the loss and Pat Conroy did the remodeling.

Lyle Triviski suffered two arson fires. Pat Conroy has remodeled two bars for Triviski. George Schaumburg, former manager and business partner in a Pat Conroy bar, has suffered fires. Vernon Hermes has suffered a fire, Billy Whelan has suffered a fire, and various other friends and business associates of Conroy have suffered fires.

And the fires have not abated with time.

Just last month a home owned by Pat Conroy at 913 E. Orange Av. was gutted by fire. Conroy's son was living there at the time. Investigators said that the "fire started behind an electric stove, extended up the wall, burning across the ceiling through the kitchen into the adjacent bedroom, with some extension into the living room."

"This fire," the report continued, "appears to have started from a faulty 20-year-old stove." Insurance on the house, the report quotes Pat Conroy as saying, ran out three days before the fire.

The 19-line report does not say what insurance company it was. It also contains no indication that the stove was examined for an electric short. It doesn't say if the fuses in the house were checked. In fact, it leaves as "undetermined" the box on the fire form called "Form of Heat of Ignition."

There's no identification of the person who reported the fire, nor any mention of interviews with witnesses. The report calls for no investigative follow-up. And there's no mention in the reports that Pat Conroy, the owner, had suffered seven previous fires, including four arsons.

In St. Paul, it is an old story.

CONROYS AND ASSOCIATES SAY THEY'VE DONE NO WRONG

S U N D A Y ,   O C T O B E R   2 9 ,   1 9 8 9

Steve Conroy steadfastly maintains that he has no connections to a fire industry in St. Paul profiting from arson or suspicious fires.

His friend "Billy" Whelan says just as strongly that he never represents people he knows are arsonists.

And Pat Conroy, the chief's brother and Whelan's business associate, says fire repair work is only a small part of his business and that Star Tribune reporters are seeking controversy where none exists.

Conroy, chief since 1966, acknowledged lending Whelan an undisclosed amount of money to help the former sandwich-shop owner begin his public adjusting business.

"Before I became chief, I told (then) Mayor (Tom) Byrne and the city attorney, Joe Summers, about my involvement with Whelan," Conroy said in a letter to the Star Tribune. "Mayor Byrne remembers this conversation. They advised me that there was no conflict. On my own, after becoming chief, I chose to have no more involvement with public adjusters."

Conroy also wrote that he has "nothing to do with my brother's business," adding, "My brother is an honest hardworking man who attends Mass every morning."

As for allowing his men to work for Whelan's firm, Conroy says he has no legal power to stop them. "Regarding my employees, the city attorney tells me that I am not allowed by law to regulate what off-duty firemen do for employment."

(St. Paul city attorneys say they know of nothing that would prevent Conroy from limiting such outside activities by firefighters.)

As for a firefighter testifying for accused arsonists on the subject of their insurance claim, the chief said: "If he's testifying only to the value of the merchandise lost, I don't see that that's a conflict, no."

In general, the chief said he did not feel negatively toward the field of public adjusting. "Generally, I feel that there is a need for them or they wouldn't be there." Asked if arsonists tend to use public adjusters more frequently than others, Chief Conroy said: "I've never thought about that."

The chief also said his department—including the arson investigation unit—"is looked on as one of the better fire departments in the country."

Whelan attributes his success in the St. Paul public adjusting business to hard work, not to his connections.

Asked why many of his cases involve "incendiary" or "arson" fires, Whelan said: "I have no idea." At times Whelan said he would not take a case if he thought it involved arson-for-profit. During another interview, he said, "I have no concern" about who started a fire. Arson, he said, is the fire department's business.

Whelan also said that his company and the firefighters never engage in fraud nor artificially inflate claims, and pass through to each homeowner everything that is due.

The arsonists who have worked on his staff were not known arsonists at the time, he said.

Whelan said it doesn't make any sense for him to represent arsonists because if they're caught, he doesn't get paid. The accused arsonists he's defended have mostly been unjustly accused, he said, and one who actually pleaded guilty had fooled him.

Pat Conroy said he is in a competitive market and gets no favorable treatment from Whelan. As for those who complain about his work, Pat responds: "I try to do my best to satisfy them all. . . . Some of them, no matter what I do, I can't satisfy them."

The chief's brother said he's never been involved in arson. And he steadfastly denied anything more than a passing acquaintance with convicted arson conspirator Tony Hartman.

Warren Cook, the district fire chief who has worked for Whelan the longest, also sees no conflict in his moonlighting. He explained that when he commands a fire scene, he doesn't know if Whelan will land the job, so he's not influenced in his judgment on whether the fire was incendiary.

He also said there is no conflict in doing property inventory and preparing insurance claims for people his own department suspects of arson. He said he's working for Whelan, not the suspected arsonists.

INVESTIGATIONS OFTEN FALL SHORT

DEPARTMENT FAILS TO ASK OBVIOUS QUESTIONS IN SUSPICIOUS FIRES

MONDAY, OCTOBER 30, 1989

BY LOU KILZER
AND CHRIS ISON

Tasslean Parker's fires defy the odds.

Her home at 863 Hague Av. in St. Paul burned six times between 1974 and 1984. For an average U.S. house, the odds of that happening by chance are more than 2 million to 1.

The fires weren't all chance; one was possible arson and two were suspicious. Three others were determined to be accidental. Reports contain no evidence suggesting that Parker set the fires, and she says she did not.

But records show that St. Paul Fire Department investigators did little to determine how any of the fires started, even though several circumstances should have raised suspicions.

Some of the fires had something else in common: They were cases in which two people close to Fire Chief Steve Conroy stood to profit *if* the Fire Department didn't call it arson.

Parker's cases fit a pattern.

After examining records of more than 100 St. Paul fires, an arson expert hired by the Star Tribune concluded that there is a pattern of sloppy or incomplete investigations by the Fire Department, often on fires with suspicious circumstances. In many cases, investigators failed to take fundamental steps that are followed by many fire departments and recommended in basic investigative manuals.

The cases examined by the newspaper are not a random sample. Nearly all were chosen because they brought business to an associate of the chief or the chief's brother, Pat Conroy, or because the fires were on property owned by the Conroys or their associates.

For instance, many of the fire victims, such as Parker, hired William (Billy) Whelan to prepare their insurance claims, paying him 10 percent of their settlements. Whelan started his business in the mid-1960s with the help of more than $10,000 in loans from Steve Conroy, a fire captain at the time.

Whelan has employed at least six moonlighting St. Paul firefighters since then, a situation that fire officials from other cities say is an obvious conflict of interest. He also employed two people who later were convicted in arson cases, and he has represented people suspected of setting their own fires.

And like Parker, many of the fire victims hired Conroy Construction Co. to repair the fire damage. The company is run by Pat Conroy and gets most of its fire repair work through Whelan.

There's nothing to suggest that investigators on the fires are involved with Whelan's company or Conroy Construction, and investigators insist that the outside interests of fellow firefighters have no effect on their work.

Yet the investigators' duties clearly conflict with the interests of Pat Conroy, Whelan and the firemen Whelan employs. If the investigators find evidence of arson, the insurance company may suspect the property owner and refuse to pay. And that means no insurance money for Pat Conroy and Whelan.

But Conroy, Whelan and his employees have received insurance money, much of it from suspicious fires that sometimes receive little scrutiny from Steve Conroy's fire department.

Arson expert Elden Boh of Denver, Colo., said the pattern of poor investigations is too widespread and covers too many years to be attributed to only the individual failures of investigators. Much of the responsibility, he concludes, rests with the chief, who has tolerated substandard investigations and clear conflicts of interest for nearly two decades.

"Chief Conroy may have been satisfied with his very incompetent investigative division," said Boh, who has investigated about 1,500 fires in nine states. "I would say there's probably no motivation from within the administration—which is primarily the chief and the department head."

Chief Conroy said he believes his arson unit is one of the better ones in the country.

"I think we have a good arson investigation (unit)," Conroy said. ". . . Our investigators are very thorough, do a very good job."

Boh disagrees. Based on reports provided by the Fire Department —most from the past five years but others dating back to the early '70s—Boh cited these frequent failures by investigators:

• They didn't interview owners or occupants of buildings that burned.

• They didn't check for a history of fires attributed to one person or one address, a fundamental step that can raise important suspicions.

• They failed to ask basic questions. For instance, some fires were attributed to careless smoking, yet there is no mention in reports that investigators asked if the occupants smoked, if they'd been smoking just before the fire, where they might have been smoking or where they might have discarded cigarettes.

• They failed to seek financial information that could point to arson motives by building owners.

• They listed causes as "possible electrical" without reporting any rationale for that.

• They ignored "red flags" that suggest arson, such as the presence of accelerants or the possibility of break-ins around the time of the fires.

• They failed to test for flammable or combustible liquids, a basic step in determining if a fire has been set.

• In a few cases, even when investigators were suspicious, they sometimes understated the possibility of arson. That means police might not have considered the cases high priorities for follow-up investigations.

To be sure, the St. Paul Fire Department fully investigates some fires and often discovers arson, including many cases involving Whelan and Pat Conroy. But in many of those cases, arson was obvious, Boh said.

Too often, when finding the fire's cause required more digging, he said, the job simply didn't get done.

"In the fire service in St. Paul, the fire investigations are conducted very poorly," said Boh. "They're substandard. They're worse than shoddy in comparison with national standards. . . . There are certain investigators who do not follow through with investigations—period."

Since 1977, the job of the St. Paul Fire Department's investigators has been only to determine the cause and origin of fires. If it determines a fire is an arson, the case goes to the Police Department to determine who is responsible.

Still, experts agree that for the initial fire investigators to find arson, they often must probe into more than the fire itself. The arson investigation guide of the Federal Bureau of Alcohol, Tobacco and Firearms lists many steps to be taken at fire scenes, steps that often fail to appear in St. Paul reports.

For example, the manual lists questions that investigators should ask of owners, occupants and witnesses. Investigators should first see if they can eliminate all accidental or natural causes of the fire. They should check to see if the color of smoke or flame is unusual, if doors or windows were forced open, whether any vehicles were seen leaving the area or whether the owners had been doing anything unusual before the fire. They should search the general area for unusual circumstances.

Those and other steps can help determine what started a fire. And if arson is found, a much deeper probe is necessary to establish motive, means and opportunity. The St. Paul Police Department now handles the deeper investigations, but before 1977 that, too, was the Fire Department's job.

Boh found that both before and after 1977, the Fire Department dropped the ball too often.

Take one of Parker's fires in 1974.

Upon arrival at the scene, firefighters found a blaze in a second-floor closet. Investigator Roy Chial's report contains only three sentences:

"Tasslean (Parker) dropped her son . . . age 10, off at the house to play records that were bought for him. He was home alone for a short time before fire was discovered. Cause of fire: Possible child playing with fire."

The report makes no mention of an interview with the child. There was no mention of matches or a lighter being found, no investigation to see if another cause was possible. No neighbors were questioned about unusual activity by the homeowner just before the fire, and no financial information was sought to detect any motive for arson, according to the report.

Any of those fundamental steps might have led to a solid determination of the fire's cause.

The investigation of Parker's 1975 fire is similar—the report indicated almost no investigation, although the investigator noted the fire was "of a suspicious nature."

The sloppy investigations are not restricted to residential fires, but include major commercial fires, as well.

In 1975, for instance, fire destroyed a large downtown St. Paul nightclub called the Showboat. The club had been owned by longtime associates of Chief Conroy. During a 1970s police probe of hidden bar ownerships and alleged arson, a state agent had obtained information that the chief himself had an interest in the club, a charge that Conroy denies.

Regardless, it is clear that Conroy's department did little to investigate the early-morning fire, even though it was listed as suspicious and possibly arson, and caused an estimated $150,000 damage.

Besides the routine two-page form, the investigative report totals just six pages, two of which simply include a few jottings with cursory information. There is no narrative of what the investigator found; nothing is typewritten. Parts of the report are barely legible.

"You've got a multi, multi-thousand-dollar fire here in a commercial building," Boh said. "And this is all you've got. I can tell you right now this is not a complete investigation. There's no investigation. This is just unbelievable."

Since the Police Department took on the burden of criminal investigations in 1977, the Fire Department often has failed to determine causes of fires—some of which had suspicious circumstances—or has failed to provide evidence supporting the causes they list on reports. That means some fires that might be arson are not forwarded to police, Boh said.

Take Parker's $12,000 blaze in 1984.

Investigator James Syvertsen did not find the exact cause and failed to follow fundamental investigative procedures. For instance, he said the cause of the fire was "electric failure" and "possible lightning." But there was no evidence collected to support either reference.

"By reading this one-paragraph report, I can't see why they came to the conclusion that it was an electrical fire," Boh said. The fire burned down through the floor, rather than burning up and out, as most fires do, Boh noted. That suggests it was not an electrical fire, and that accelerants might have been present. Plus there was nothing in the report to back up the reference to lightning as a possible cause, he said.

"It would definitely need more work," Boh said.

Parker gave Syvertsen permission to return for follow-up investigation, but there are no reports indicating that a follow-up was done.

"I think we went back," Syvertsen told the Star Tribune when asked about the report. But he said he's unsure why he listed the cause as electrical or why there is no mention of further investigation. "It looks like I wrote it off as an electrical fire," Syvertsen said.

It was the second fire in which Whelan handled Parker's insurance claim; Pat Conroy repaired the damage.

In cases where arson was found and cases were forwarded to police, Boh generally saw good investigations. But he also found fires that were clearly suspicious and appear to have been forwarded to police but were never followed up.

He said that may have been due in part to poor reports by the Fire Department that understated the suspicious nature of the fires.

Police Sgt. Mike Morehead, who Boh said conducted many good investigations, said he believes police and fire investigators generally work well together. But he added that because of manpower problems, police usually will give low priority to cases that aren't specifically listed as arson by the Fire Department.

Even when the Fire Department labels a fire as arson, the quality of its investigations can affect the Police Department's ability to make a case, Morehead said.

For instance, the newspaper found four arsons at one address between 1983 and 1986. The house was owned—secretly at times but later on paper—by prolific arsonist Tony Hartman. But the investigators, before forwarding the cases to police, focused on burglars, teenagers and children as possible culprits in the first three fires. Even in the fourth fire, which happened after Hartman had been arrested in a federal arson sting, there was no mention of the owner's past involvement in arson.

Police never made a case on any of the fires.

Boh said that the Fire Department's failures were not uniform.

Syvertsen's work on Parker's fire, for instance, was not typical for him. He conducted thorough investigations and found what started the fires in almost all of his cases reviewed by the newspaper.

Others, such as Louis Chapdelaine and Roy Chial, conducted poor investigations or failed to determine fire causes much more often. Chapdelaine didn't find the cause of fire in one-fourth of his cases reviewed by the newspaper. (Chapdelaine retired last year.)

Chial, who retired in 1982, failed to determine a cause in more than one-third of his cases reviewed.

Chial declined to answer questions, although he said that failing to find the exact cause of fires was common. He added that he thinks investigators were motivated and had adequate resources.

Chapdelaine, too, declined to answer questions, except to blame manpower shortages for some problems.

"Did you ever try to do 14 investigations in one day and do a good job?" Chapdelaine asked. ". . . I think I did a good job while I was there, and my record will pretty well speak for that. . . . If there was a mistake made, I suppose it was human. I'm admitting I possibly could have made a mistake."

But Boh said that work done by Chapdelaine and Chial was simply inadequate.

"Really, in fire investigation nowadays, there's no such thing as an undetermined cause of fire. And even years ago, and I'm going to go back to the time that I started in '77, it was, you know, uncommon to have an undetermined cause."

Chief Conroy provided statistics showing that in the past five years, his department failed to determine a cause of fire in only 1 to 7 percent of the city's structure fires. Those rates are lower than the national average of about 12 percent undetermined for 1986 and 1987, as recorded by the U.S. Fire Administration.

But Conroy's figures may overstate his department's success rate in determining cause. Of the 104 cases involving Whelan or Pat Conroy that were reviewed by the Star Tribune, 17 percent were undetermined.

The discrepancy may be, in part, because the newspaper found cases where investigators listed a fire cause on the front of their reports, yet their description of the fire shows they really weren't sure of the cause. In other cases, investigators listed "possible" causes of fires but found little evidence to support the causes.

In defending his arson unit, Conroy pointed to a study released this year by a consulting firm in Vienna, Va. The study goes into little detail on arson investigations, and its overview of the arson problem in St. Paul has good and bad news.

The percentage of structural fires caused by arson in St. Paul is below the national average. But more than half of the dollar amount of fire damage in St. Paul was caused by arson in 1987, twice the national rate, according to the report. In 1987, 303 St. Paul fires—15 percent of those investigated—were suspicious or arson, and arson caused $2.4 million in damage.

And while the number of arson and suspicious fires declined by 37 percent nationally from 1977 to 1987, St. Paul saw a nearly 13 percent increase from 1983 to 1987.

The report said that the number of deaths due to fire is "extremely low" in St. Paul and "reflects very favorably on the city."

Former and current fire investigators lay some blame for investigative problems at the chief's feet. Former arson investigator Thomas Weyandt, who retired in 1984, said the investigative unit just wasn't a high priority for Conroy.

"It's hard to get convictions. Without convictions you don't get too much publicity, and it's fairly costly," Weyandt said. "There's a lot more glamorous things. . . . You can show your picture in the paper. . . . You can have another unit running around the city in parades and stuff like that."

District Chief Steve Pizinger disagrees. An investigator for six years until being transferred this year, he said that a lack of manpower hurt the investigative unit, but that the chief "was real progressive in getting us the schools and the equipment we needed."

But Syvertsen, currently the department's senior investigator, said he's asked for more resources several times, with no results. He cited problems such as poor record-keeping, a lack of manpower and work schedules that inhibit communication among investigators.

For instance, he said, information about the many previous fires at Parker's address would have been important for investigators. But he said he didn't know about them because investigators lack a good system to check fire histories.

Such a system is fundamental to good fire investigation, experts say

But St. Paul's record-keeping system is fraught with problems. Fire officials said they couldn't find many reports requested by the newspaper for several months, and they still haven't produced several reports. They also found that they'd failed to input hundreds of reports into the computer system that's used to track fires.

The chief said the police and fire departments are merging their arson investigation offices to improve communication.

Investigators also may be spread too thin. One investigator works each shift, and he responds to every fire. That means a single investigator might conduct 200 to 300 investigations a year, Syvertsen said.

National arson expert John Barracato says that's simply too big a caseload to handle properly.

"You can't have an in-depth investigation when that happens," said Barracato, the former New York City fire marshal. "It's impossible. It's impossible because of the volume, not because of the lack of expertise.

Barracato said the maximum caseload should be about 120 a year. But he added that large caseloads and lack of training are common to fire departments around the country.

The Virginia consultants recommended that the St. Paul Fire Department re-evaluate sending the only on-duty investigator on all structure fires "to determine if this is the most efficient use of the captain's time."

Chief Conroy's links—and those of other firefighters—to public adjuster "Billy" Whelan are known in the Fire Department. Syvertsen said he's heard that Conroy helped finance Whelan, and although he often runs into Whelan at fire scenes, Syvertsen said that hasn't influenced his work.

"Whelan, I know that he knows firemen and I know that he knows the chief," Syvertsen said. "I try to remain neutral. . . .

"That's the farthest thing from my mind at the time, what they (the adjusters) are going to do. Philosophically, I feel that if a person commits a crime, he should be punished for it, not rewarded for it."

But Syvertsen also said that during his six years in the arson unit, he's seen no sign of personal interest by Conroy in making the unit better or addressing problems.

"They don't know the problems we have here. And I don't think Conroy knows, either," Syvertsen said. "I've never, really, since I've been here six years, sat down and talked with Conroy. He works everything through his chiefs. I go through my deputy (the deputy chief in charge of the arson unit)."

The chief acknowledged he has a hands-off approach to running the arson unit. His reason?

"I have kept hands off from arson investigations so I'm not accused of steering them. . . . I did that purposely so no one can say that I interfered with the investigation on that."

And he said he doesn't see a conflict in firefighters working for Whelan, or any public adjuster, as long as they don't solicit business on the fire scene.

But officials from other departments say the conflict is obvious.

Of six fire departments in medium-sized cities that were contacted by the newspaper, all said that firefighters would be prohibited from working for public adjusters in the same city in which they fight fires. Most said they'd never heard of firefighters doing such work.

When Minneapolis Fire Chief Thomas Dickinson found such a case, he took quick action, issuing a warning and later disciplining the man when he continued doing adjustments.

"There's no doubt in my mind that's a conflict of interest," Dickinson said.

Dickinson said that working for an adjuster can provide an incentive for not fighting fires aggressively, because adjusters make more money on bigger fire losses.

He added that firefighters who also help prepare adjustments could end up in court testifying on behalf of suspected arsonists—which has happened in St. Paul three times just this year. "We can't tolerate that," Dickinson said.

The city of Minneapolis requires employees to get permission from their department heads before they take outside jobs to assure that they don't take work that could conflict with their public responsibilities.

Conroy said he's been told he has no authority to limit his employees' work outside the department. But St. Paul city attorneys said they're unaware of any such restrictions.

And the St. Paul Police Department has a detailed policy that prohibits several types of outside employment. A general clause states that police can't work for an "establishment which would tend to lower the dignity of the police service in any manner or where a conflict of interest is seen to exist."

The Star Tribune has found eight cases in which District Fire Chief Warren Cook, who moonlights for Whelan, helped put out fires that Whelan's company later adjusted. Cook has said he usually gets paid by the hour, not a percentage of the loss, however.

Although his first responsibility as a district chief is to put out fires, Cook also has a duty to help determine their causes and origins, if possible.

Cook said that he doesn't believe his outside work is in conflict with his firefighting responsibilities. He said that when he fights fires, he has no way of knowing whether Whelan will get the adjusting job.

However, he also noted that Whelan gets much of the adjusting work in St. Paul.

FOUR

TOM TOLES'S OUTRAGE

1990 WINNER IN THE EDITORIAL CARTOONING CATEGORY

"For a distinguished example of a cartoonist's work, the determining qualities being that a cartoon shall embody an idea made clearly apparent, shall show good drawing and striking pictorial effect, and shall be intended to be helpful to some commendable cause of public importance . . ."

The Buffalo News
Tom Toles

Through his drawings, editorial cartoonist Tom Toles hits hard at the duplicity, insincerity, hypocrisy or just fuzzy-headedness shown by public figures. Says Toles of his craft: "Drawing a political cartoon every day is the equivalent of holding a gun that never stops firing."

Tom Toles is not the run-of-the-mill editorial cartoonist. His style cannot be categorized as that of a particular school, as can that of so many editorial cartoonists in the field today. His work is unique, different.

Toles's cartoons are distinguished by a sense of humor that those who support his point of view and those who oppose his viewpoint never can deny exists. His work is marked by a strong sense of outrage on the nation's meaningful issues, such as the environment, or military spending at the expense of social programs and education.

His cartoons on local and state issues are direct, hard hitting, pull no punches. They are effective weapons in our editorial arsenal, and local and state politicians and opinion makers are always mindful of Toles's message.

His national and international cartoons, carried in more than 150 newspapers through the Universal Press Syndicate, are just as meaningful. Here is the distinguished work of a unique talent.

—Murray B. Light
The Buffalo News

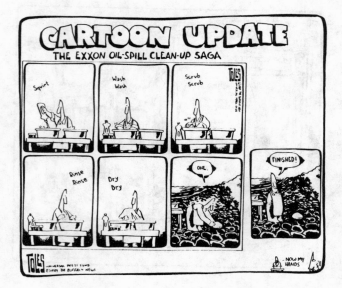

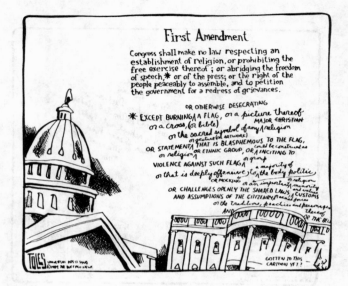

FIVE

THE *EXXON VALDEZ* OIL SLICK

1990 WINNER IN THE NATIONAL REPORTING CATEGORY

"For a distinguished example of reporting on national affairs . . ."

The Seattle Times
Ross Anderson
Bill Dietrich
Mary Ann Gwinn
Eric Nalder

Exxon quickly accepted responsibility for the worst oil spill in U.S. history, but, as *The Seattle Times* reported, a huge gap rapidly developed between Exxon's publicly stated plans and actual cleanup results.

Ship groundings 1,300 miles away aren't usually front-page news in Seattle.

Nor, at first, did the wreck of a vessel in Alaskan waters on the early morning of March 24, 1989, seem particularly riveting. But then the details trickled in: The *Exxon Valdez,* a massive oil supertanker, had split apart on a reef, spilling millions of gallons of its toxic cargo into scenic Prince William Sound.

It was clear this was a full-fledged environmental disaster. And it was clear we were in a special position—had a special responsibility, in fact—to cover it.

Seattle and Alaska have ties dating from the 1890s, when fortune hunters bound for gold fields stocked up on whatever provisions they could afford in the bustling settlement on Puget Sound before heading north.

Nearly a century later, the fortune-hunting connection persists. These days, the gold is Alaskan salmon.

More than half the boats that pull the prized sockeye and chinook from Alaska's frigid waters are based in Seattle. And one of the richest fishing grounds, for salmon and for even-more-precious roe herring, is Prince William Sound. The economic implications for our region were clear.

This was, of course, much more than a business story. There would almost certainly be devastation to birds, otters and other marine life, and scarring of some of America's most enchanting shorelines.

Other, more obscure implications—what the largest spill in U.S. history reflected about consumption of natural resources and humanity's relationship with the earth at the end of the 20th century—inspired us further to try to report it as well as or better than we'd reported anything before.

To that end, Managing Editor Alex MacLeod gave us freedom to spend whatever money and staff time seemed necessary—no small commitment in that part of Alaska, where a trip to the next town means a $200-an-hour air charter. It didn't hurt that MacLeod was himself once a Prince William Sound fishmonger, having worked in the port of Cordova in the early 1970s.

Nor did it hurt that we had at hand a group of veteran reporters with a rich and varied grounding in Alaska: Ross Anderson, *The Times'* chief political reporter, had made an avocation of studying the Alaskan fishing industry; Bill Dietrich, environmental reporter, had written extensively about both the natural and the human resources of the 49th state; Mary Ann Gwinn, Sunday magazine writer, had established contacts in both Alaska's oil industry and the environmental community in reporting on the Arctic National Wildlife Refuge.

These people started out with both an understanding of the fascination for Alaska and Alaskans, and, unashamedly, with a personal sense of loss for what had been tarnished. From their passion was born the persistence to cover this story over many months, under difficult and sometimes even life-threatening conditions. Even through that passion, however, they maintained clear and balanced vision.

Dietrich went north first, the day of the spill. Accompanying him was photographer Craig Fujii. They were among the first to portray the magnitude of the disaster, to cut through Exxon's public-relations pablum and Alaska state officials' hysteria.

They found their truth by leaving the pack of journalists in Valdez —which itself was unscarred by the spill—and finding their way to islands stained purple-black with the viscous oil.

As Dietrich describes it: "The oil hits you like a hammer. You can smell it. You can taste it. It makes your eyes burn. Until you're in the middle of it, you can really have no idea what's it's like."

Once the severity of the spill was established, we set out to examine its origins. Anderson flew to Juneau, Alaska's capital, and to Anchorage, its largest city and oil-industry hub, to look at the conditions that allowed such a disaster to happen.

While most of the national media focused on Joseph Hazelwood, the captain suspected of being intoxicated when his ship went aground, our reporting found him to be more a symptom than a cause.

Anderson and a team of investigative reporters working in Seattle found, among other things, that:
• The oil industry had lobbied successfully for years in Juneau to minimize requirements for oil-spill preparedness and was the single most powerful force in Alaskan politics;
• A decade of cutbacks in oil-spill workers, equipment and budgets had left the oil companies with only a shadow of what was once a model cleanup program on Prince William Sound;
• The federal government had ignored warnings about the need for better radar equipment on the sound;
• The Coast Guard and the oil industry had long tolerated alcohol abuse by mariners.

Anderson went on to Cordova, the center of fishing on Prince William Sound, to chronicle the desperate and ultimately successful struggle to save salmon fingerlings from the encroaching oil.

Other animals were not so lucky. As we looked around the newsroom for a third reporter to send to the spill, we sought someone who could capture that tragedy.

Enter Gwinn. She brought a magnificent talent for description to bear on a piece that brought tears to the most hardened among us—a first-person account of finding an oil-soaked loon on a remote beach.

Dietrich, Anderson, Gwinn and photographers Fujii and Harley Soltes spent week upon week on Prince William Sound, battling the elements and increasingly recalcitrant business and government officials. (Soltes had the most harrowing experience, being tossed into the icy sound when a skiff in which he was riding capsized.)

There was another important element to this story, one that would be found largely on our own sound. Four times a day, 365 days a year, tankers that take on the oil pumped from the Trans-Alaska Pipeline at Valdez cruise into Washington state's inland sea to deposit crude at waterfront refineries. If Prince William Sound could be so ravaged, what of Puget Sound, or of hundreds of other waterways around the world?

In May, investigative reporter Eric Nalder boarded an oil tanker in Valdez and rode it to a refinery in northwest Washington. For the next six months, he compiled an unprecedented body of information on tankers and tanker safety. His findings revealed an alarmingly fragile layer of protection against oil spills. They told how the Coast Guard—the government's first line of defense against ship disasters—had cut back on its vigilance while turning its attention to the drug war. They described how the Coast Guard and the justice system had merely slapped the wrists of crewmen whose drunken behavior caused accidents and hazards. And most significantly, they presented overwhelming evidence that a requirement for double hulls on oil tankers would almost certainly prevent another *Exxon Valdez* incident.

Coincidentally, the day before the Pulitzer Prizes were announced, we published news we found gratifying: Conoco Inc., a major oil shipper, had decided to replace its fleet with double-hulled tankers.

Words to warm the heart of the loon.

—David Boardman, Assistant City Editor
The Seattle Times

ANGER, FRUSTRATION IN VALDEZ

RESIDENTS, ENVIRONMENTALISTS CRITICIZE DELAYS IN CLEANUP; HUMAN ERROR BLAMED FOR SPILL

SUNDAY, MARCH 26, 1989

BY BILL DIETRICH

VALDEZ, Alaska—Angry residents and environmentalists yesterday criticized delays in the cleanup of the 11.1 million-gallon oil spill here that has been blamed on human navigational error and could get worse.

The tanker Exxon Valdez remained punctured and crippled late yesterday on a reef in Prince William Sound as 240,000 barrels of crude oil spread through the intricate environment and workers got frustrated in attempts to offload remaining oil.

The stricken tanker, as long as three football fields, is tilted at a slight angle about two miles from the nearest land.

As the sun set yesterday, airplanes spewed a dispersant agent on the oil in hopes of breaking it up, and oil skimmers were at work around the ship like waterbugs, trying to round up what they could. But the spill is so vast that the oil booms available could not begin to deal with the mess.

Residents of this community are peppering oil company officials with questions after watching what seemed to them a slow and sometimes hapless effort to corral the oil before it harms wildlife and fisheries.

Among the most frustrated observers was Alaska's Gov. Steve Cowper, who called the cleanup efforts "slow and inadequate."

The spill already ranks as the worst oil spill in U.S. history, and observers are bracing for its potentially devastating effects on the environment and a multimillion-dollar fishing industry.

"It's a major disaster I consider as dangerous as the 1964 earthquake" that wiped out Valdez, said Stan Stephens, a tour boat operator in this spectacular, mountain-ringed fjord.

The spill struck on the 25th anniversary of Alaska's Good Friday earthquake.

"I'm so sick about it I couldn't sleep last night after 20 straight hours of work. The oil companies take $13 billion out of our state and then don't have the equipment to clean up their mess.

At a news conference, oil industry and Coast Guard spokesmen acknowledged several apparent errors contributing to the disaster:
• The tanker's equipment was working perfectly when it strayed at least a mile and a half outside its approved shipping lane and crashed into a reef marked by a lighted buoy on a calm, clear night early Friday. "There is no excuse" for such an error, Stephens charged.
• The Coast Guard administered blood alcohol tests to at least two crew members after the accident, Coast Guard Cmdr. Steve McCall confirmed.

Coast Guard Lt. Ed Wieliczkiewicz said the blood was still being analyzed, but because the tests came hours after the tanker left Valdez, officials were unsure whether the tests would produce evidence they were seeking.
• Although the Coast Guard gave verbal permission for the outbound tanker to shift to an inbound shipping lane to avoid ice from nearby Columbia Glacier, it did not monitor the vessel's course with available radar as the nearly 1,000-foot vessel ran even farther east up onto the reef, rupturing eight of 13 oil compartments. When Jack Lamb, representing Cordova District Fishermen United, asked why, McCall simply said such monitoring was not required by Coast Guard regulation.
• There was insufficient oil-spill cleanup equipment in Valdez Harbor despite the heavy tanker traffic from the terminus of the Alaska pipeline, and some of what was available had been removed from a barge damaged in a storm two weeks before and had not been reloaded. That, coupled with the fact that Good Friday was an Alyeska Pipeline Co. holiday, meant it took 10 hours for the first cleanup crews to reach the tanker, said Chuck O'Donnell, Alyeska terminal manager.

"We simply don't have enough equipment to contain it," Governor Cowper said after touring the spill site. "No one does. You couldn't contain it with all the equipment in North America."
• Because of the need to fly in equipment from around the globe, it

took 34 hours to get the first oil boom around the tanker to contain leaking oil. At midday yesterday, 36 hours after the spill, 12,700 feet of additional boom had been placed at the leading edge of the spill.

"We recognize time is critical," said Frank Iarossi, president of Exxon Shipping Co., but he said equipment was still being gathered.

But Cowper and Valdez City Manager Doug Griffin used the same words to describe the oil spill response: "Slow and inadequate."

"It's like using a BB gun on an elephant," Griffin said.

The accident occurred at high tide under a full moon, so there is little chance that higher tides will help lift the crippled tanker from the reef.

Wieliczkiewicz said aerial test bombing of water with dispersants failed to produce any effect, partially because of calm seas, throwing into doubt Exxon plans for more aerial bombing of the spill.

The calm seas and light winds were keeping the slick, about 50 square miles, from immediately fouling most nearby shorelines. But the response time left many local fishermen livid.

"We should have been out there yesterday (Friday)," said Pat Day, a salmon purse seiner who offered his boat to lay oil boom but as of yesterday morning had yet to hear anything.

"They can't perform when it comes down to the nitty-gritty," said Tim Lopez, harbormaster of the city's marina. "Some feel, like the rest of the community, that they could have done a hell of a lot better job a hell of a lot sooner."

"They say this was bound to happen someday," said Jim Lethcoe, who operates sailboat cruises for tourists. "So if it's going to happen, why not be better prepared? They just didn't want to spend any money."

Iarossi said Exxon will accept full financial responsibility for the spill, including compensating fishermen for "legitimate claims" of damage caused by the oil.

Spill problems may be just beginning. Exxon brought its tanker Exxon Baton Rouge alongside to begin removing some of the 1 million remaining barrels before they spill as well, but when pumping started yesterday morning, more oil began gushing into Prince William Sound.

Iarossi said that may mean internal pumping pipes are ruptured as well, making oil transfer difficult. Portable pumps may have to be used to get the oil out of the holds into new ships.

Divers found six to eight openings large enough to swim through in the hull and numerous cracks, leading to uncertainty about whether the ship can be refloated. Experts from Europe were expected to begin examining the ship today.

Iarossi said Exxon's first priority was to offload the remaining oil before it also leaks into the water; the second is to clean up oil already spilled; and the third is to investigate the cause of the accident.

The National Transportation Safety Board was expected to begin investigating the cause today.

The spill has temporarily closed the port at Valdez to both tankers and other vessels. As a result, the flow from the Alaska pipeline has been cut from 2 million barrels a day to 800,000 barrels, with the impact of that on oil markets or Alaska state revenues still unknown.

Valdez was crammed with oil company officials, biologists, journalists and public officials.

British Columbia officials expressed concern that the oil might flow southward toward their province, and Fred Olsen, deputy director of Washington state's Department of Ecology, flew over the site and expressed similar concerns.

"We just want to keep an eye on it and if it has the potential to move south, we want to control it," Olsen said.

The oil has only spread a few miles southward, however, and is many miles from breaking into the open sea.

"I think we have a good chance of recovering large parts of the oil spilled at this time," said the Coast Guard's McCall.

Stephens reported seeing sea lions coated in oil from the spill, but the seriousness of biological damage was still unknown yesterday. It may take days, or even weeks, before it becomes apparent how much oil can be cleaned up and how much will wash ashore or kill marine life.

The massive spill posed an environmental nightmare for emergency cleanup crews, primarily because the scene is easily accessible only from the air and sea and Prince William Sound is a complex environment of pristine islands, channels, bays and icebergs.

After recent spills in Hawaii and off the coast of Washington, 1989 is becoming the "year of the oil spill," said Kelly Quirke, ocean ecology coordinator for Greenpeace in San Francisco. "Alaska is perceived as an energy colony, and we're just beginning to see the environmental costs."

The sound supports a variety of birds and marine animals that include whales, seals and porpoises.

"It's kind of like sailing through a zoo," said Lethcoe, who lives on a boat in the sound.

"There's a high concentration of sea otter, waterfowl, sea birds and pink salmon in that area," said Steve Goldstein, a spokesman for the Interior Department in Washington. "Some birds have already died, and we are doing our best to try to save the fish by containing the oil to the area where it presently is and by trying to skim it."

"The herring fishery will be almost totaled," said Lopez, the marina harbormaster. "Exxon is spending a lot of time worrying about its ship and much less about the oil spill. I know what I'd be doing if I was a fisherman—I'd get a lawyer. Somebody's going to pay."

SPILL CLEANUP CRIPPLED BY CUTS, EX-OFFICIALS SAY

TWO SAY STAFF, EQUIPMENT WERE SLASHED

TUESDAY, MARCH 28, 1989

BY ROSS ANDERSON AND BILL DIETRICH

A decade of cutbacks in oil-spill workers, equipment and budgets has left the Alyeska Pipeline Co. with only a pale shadow of what was once a model cleanup program on Alaska's Prince William Sound, former company officials say.

Cutbacks were so severe that, when the supertanker Exxon Valdez began leaking oil into the ecologically rich sound last Friday, the oil consortium was left with ill-maintained booms, no barge to take on oil and virtually no properly trained people to respond to the disaster, the ex-employees say.

James Woodle, retired Coast Guard commander and general manager of the Port of Valdez from 1982 to 1984, said Alyeska's lack of equipment and trained staff meant it could not respond promptly—despite ideal weather conditions.

"You can't clean up everything in 48 hours," Woodle said. "But you can contain it, and they could have done it with this one if they had the manpower, the initial response."

The Port of Valdez was built and is operated by Alyeska, a consortium of eight oil companies including Exxon. Alyeska is responsible for the oil-spill contingency plan and for emergency response to spills in the sound.

Woodle and Jerry Nebel, Alyeska oil-spill response coordinator in 1981–82, said they were fired by Alyeska after they complained about cuts in the company's oil-spill program.

Don Cornett, Alaska coordinator for Exxon, said yesterday he was not aware of any such cutbacks. He declined further comment.

An Alyeska spokesman said this morning the company needs more time to respond to questions and had no response to the charges by Woodle and Nebel.

Another former Alyeska oil-spill coordinator, who asked not to be identified, said that the company's cleanup program "was all up to snuff" until his retirement in 1982. "But I don't know what's up there now."

Woodle and Nebel describe a steady deterioration in Alyeska's oil-spill response capacity, reinforcing complaints by local fishermen who say the oil consortium has failed to live up to promises made before construction of the oil port. In particular, the former Alyeska officials say:

• A full-time, professionally trained cleanup crew of 20 was gradually eliminated, replaced by dock and office workers with no training or experience with oil spills.

• A chartered, 218,000-gallon capacity barge, designed to take on oil from spill sites, was replaced by a much smaller, second-hand barge that was too badly damaged to be used in the Exxon spill.

• Modern, self-inflating booms, designed to contain oil slicks immediately after a spill, were mysteriously unavailable for more than 24 hours last week—possibly, the former officials say, because the equipment wasn't working.

• The company, which had promised to keep a full-time oil-spill coordinator, has not had one at Valdez since the mid-1980s.

As a result, Alyeska's critics say, it took 12 hours for the first cleanup crews to reach the Exxon Valdez, instead of the five hours called for in the company's own contingency plan. Only five oil skimmers—designed to collect oil from the water's surface—were deployed, instead of the 13 called for. And it was nearly three days before any substantial cleanup was launched.

Dave Kennedy of Seattle, the scientific support coordinator for a large National Oceanographic and Atmospheric Administration team that is assessing the cleanup program in Prince William Sound, said the lack of a full-time oil-spill crew at Valdez is not surprising.

"It's real easy to throw stones," said Kennedy, but the practicality of keeping a large work force trained to do nothing but wait for an oil spill is questionable.

But Larry Safford, vice president of VRCA Environmental Services, a firm hired by the state of Alaska to monitor the cleanup on Prince William Sound, said Alyeska was not prepared.

"You have to approach a spill the same way you do a battle," he said. "You have to have the equipment ready and you have to have people ready and you have to have the generals knowing the sergeants. That didn't happen. If you really hit it in the first 36 to 48 hours, you might win."

Woodle and Nebel, both of whom now live in Washington state, agreed. In lengthy interviews with The Times, they said Alyeska was complying with its own contingency plan when it opened the new oil port in 1977.

"You had a dedicated, full-time response team," said Woodle, who was the Coast Guard commander at Valdez until he retired and went to work for Alyeska in 1982. "That was all they did. They worked on a contract basis, not as Alyeska employees."

Early oil-spill crews were trained at specialized schools in Texas and Britain, equipped with the latest technology, and staffed so that as many as 16 trained people were on duty on any shift, he said.

The program met the requirements of a contingency plan, which in turn was part of the decision to allow the oil consortium to build the oil terminal at Valdez—the northernmost ice-free port in Alaska.

"Initially, Alyeska was sort of under a microscope," said Nebel, a four-year Alyeska employee who also served eight years on the Valdez City Council. "They followed that contingency plan to the letter.

"Then they started to talk themselves out of it. They started paying more attention to shareholders' profits. And things started to get out of hand."

The former officials said the cutbacks started in 1979—when world oil prices were at their height. That's when Alyeska dropped the independent contract and established its own oil-spill response team.

Next, the full-time cleanup crew was cut to eight per 12-hour shift, they said.

"About 1982, they started a severe cost-reduction program," Woodle recalled. "It became competitive to see how much cost you could cut in your operation."

Since the oil-spill response costs were primarily labor, the only way to cut was to lay off workers, he said.

"The two years I was with Alyeska, the crew was cut in half, from

20 to 10," Woodle said. "And you had no dedicated oil-spill response people. They were all involved in daily operations, with nobody on standby."

The result was a shift from the equivalent of a full-time fire department to a volunteer force, where workers must drop what they're doing to respond to an oil spill.

Nebel, a Seattle pleasure-boat salesman, was fired as oil-spill coordinator in 1982 after he revealed the cost-cutting policies to his cleanup staff, Woodle said.

Meanwhile, Woodle said, maintenance on the oil port was allowed to lapse. The plant that takes on ballast water from arriving tankers deteriorated so that huge quantities of oil-laden ballast were allowed to pollute Valdez Arm, the fjord which connects Valdez with the sound.

The Anchorage Daily News, which reported the ballast water situation, also recently revealed that the heavy seas of the Gulf of Alaska have taken their toll on the Alaska tanker fleet, which has made 17,000 voyages up the coast since the oil port opened. Federal records indicate that the number of oil spills, mostly small, have increased—mostly due to stress cracks in tanker hulls, the paper reported.

Oil-spill cleanup equipment also deteriorated, the former Alyeska officials say. The primary tool of the trade is the Vikoma Seapak, a British-made device that is towed to the scene of a spill and inflated to form 1,500-foot sections of floating boom around an oil slick.

Alyeska would haul out and inflate one of its five Seapak booms to impress members of Congress, environmentalists and other visitors, Woodle and Nebel said. But booms began to suffer from lack of maintenance, they said.

"The quantity of boom available started to decrease right away," Nebel said. "It would get damaged, ravaged by the weather. And it's expensive equipment. So when one would wear out, they'd grab another one from the emergency response warehouse, and it dwindles down to nothing."

Woodle said he was fired by Alyeska for "insubordination" after he wrote letters to Alyeska and the member oil companies complaining that cutbacks severely limited the companies' capacity to respond to a spill.

In his letter, dated April 1984, Woodle warned the company that "due to reduction in manning, age of equipment, limited training opportunities and lack of experienced coordination personnel, serious doubt exists that Alyeska would be able to contain and clean up effectively a medium- or large-sized oil spill."

The last professionally trained oil-spill coordinator retired to Whidbey Island in 1982, Woodle said. The job was handed over to an untrained office manager, then eliminated altogether, its responsibilities added to the chief engineer's job description. "They turned it into a situation where the terminal engineer became everything."

OIL SPILL: ONE WEEK OF FRENZY

BEST EFFORT INADEQUATE

FRIDAY, MARCH 31, 1989

BY BILL DIETRICH

VALDEZ, Alaska—Oil-industry experts and government officials say they have done their frantic best to cope with America's biggest oil spill.

A week after the spill in Prince William Sound, it is clear their best has been woefully inadequate.

Of the 240,000 barrels—10.1 million gallons—of crude oil spilled from the tanker Exxon Valdez early last Friday, fewer than 7,000 had been mopped up a week later.

Errors, hesitation and folly have illustrated how poorly prepared the petroleum industry is to respond to a superspill in a scenic and sensitive environment.

The feebleness of the human cleanup is in odd contrast to the sudden bustle of Valdez, where cars back up in a town with no streetlights, phone lines are jammed and planes lumber in with experts and supplies from around the world.

Exxon Corp. has brought in 160 spill experts and managers, hired nearly 400 workers and flown in 37 cargo planes of equipment. The skies buzz with the company's 10 helicopters and four planes.

All this shoreside frenzy has produced little tangible effect at sea, with the spill running 50 miles across Prince William Sound to slap against a series of wilderness islands.

Exxon officials have conceded here that technology can't really cope with a spill of this magnitude. Environmentalists readily agree.

"We cannot afford to drill in sensitive areas," said Karen Jettmar, Alaska representative of The Wilderness Society. "No amount of preparation can alleviate human error."

Exxon, conceding early that an on-site fleet of seven skimmers and four miles of boom was inadequate to the task, chose to promote two relatively untried and controversial technologies: burning and chemical dispersants.

Neither has made a significant dent, despite unusually favorable weather, because of delays in their use. The oil has now emulsified enough so that neither is very effective.

But behind the physical dimensions of this calamity are a series of human errors and miscalculations with no excuse. Consider:

• Exxon has yet to explain why the skipper of its biggest and newest tanker was Capt. Joe Hazelwood, who had three drunken-driving convictions in his home state of New York. Hazelwood, who has since been fired by Exxon, had a blood-alcohol reading of .061 when measured nine hours after the ship rammed Bligh Reef, according to National Transportation Safety Board investigators. Under federal navigation laws, the limit is .04.

While a Coast Guard warrant officer says he smelled alcohol on Hazelwood's breath two hours after the accident, the Coast Guard did not test Hazelwood and two crew members for seven more hours—by which time much of the alcohol would have dissipated. Availability was not a problem: An alcohol testing kit was on board to help enforce both government and company regulations against drinking on oil tankers.

• Hazelwood turned over command of his tanker to Third Mate Greg Cousins eight miles north of Bligh Reef and retired to his cabin— even though Cousins didn't have the pilot's certificate required by the Coast Guard to master a ship through those waters. The tanker subsequently ran up onto the reef.

The contingency plan prepared by Alyeska Pipeline Service Co. for a 200,000-barrel spill states: "It is highly unlikely a spill of this magnitude would occur (because) tankers calling on Port Valdez are of American registry and all of these are piloted by licensed masters or pilots."

Alyeska is a consortium of eight oil companies. It operates the Trans-Alaska Pipeline and is responsible for emergency response to spills near Valdez.

• The Coast Guard gave permission for the outbound Exxon Valdez to shift to an inbound shipping lane to avoid ice floes, but then failed to use radar to discover the tanker was steering 20 degrees off the approved course before smacking into the reef. The Coast Guard is now saying a newer, weaker radar station installed at Potato Point in

1984 does not have the range to pick up a supertanker past Busby Island, a dozen miles away. Local fishermen have risen at press conferences to challenge this.

• When oil tankers first began leaving Valdez in 1977, local ships' pilots accompanied them not just to Rocky Point 15 miles down the inlet as is done today, but all the way to Hinchinbrook Entrance at the edge of Prince William Sound, more than 80 miles. The practice was stopped in the early 1980s. Coast Guard Cmdr. Steve McCall said he doesn't know why; the change was made before he came to his Valdez job.

• The Exxon Valdez, just 2½ years old and one of the two biggest ships in the company fleet, was built with only a single instead of a double hull, despite the fact it traveled some of the most environmentally sensitive areas in the world.

Asked why, Exxon Shipping Co. President Frank Iarossi has said only: "We need an assessment to see if a double hull would have made a difference."

• The oil-spill contingency plan lists 13 oil skimmers as the equipment to be stockpiled to cope with a big spill, but only seven were on hand, according to Charles O'Donnell, the terminal superintendent for Alyeska.

The plan also called for 22,000 feet of boom to corral spilled oil, but on the night of the accident only 7,500 feet were ready.

Another 7,000 feet had been unloaded from an emergency response barge that needed repairs but had remained unfixed for two weeks. A newer barge had been ordered from Houston, but was still in Seattle when the spill occurred.

The remaining 7,500 feet had been used as boom around oil-terminal docks and was not immediately available.

The plan called for a barge with skimmers to be on site in five hours, but Alyeska took 10. Noticeable use of booms and skimmers did not take place until Sunday, the third day of the spill.

• The contingency plan called for rapid use of chemical dispersants to break up the oil, since they are most effective before the slick begins to evaporate and congeal. But while the Coast Guard had the authority to allow dispersants, Alyeska spokesman Tom Brennan says it refused to give permission when Alyeska asked at 2:30 a.m. Friday.

Instead, the Coast Guard sought the approval of state and federal environmental authorities, even though such use had been agreed to in a dispersant plan adopted just a few months before. Officials waited for tests to be completed, delaying approval until Sunday—too late to use them before high winds drove the oil into the surrounding islands.

The contingency plan states: "It becomes very apparent how important it is to have dispersants approved so they can be used very effectively to prevent the continuing input of oil into the small bays and shorelines in Prince William Sound."

Even if approval had been obtained immediately, however, neither the dispersant nor the C-130 cargo planes needed to deliver it were ready in Valdez; they had to be flown in.

• Also delayed for approval was burning of patches of oil. The oil is scooped by towed fireproof oil booms and then set afire. The first test burn was ignited near the Aleut Indian village of Tatitlek without warning, frightening the inhabitants and choking them with smoke.

When initial results seemed encouraging, however, and permission to use burning was approved Sunday, high winds that night disrupted the operation. By the time an attempt was resumed Tuesday, the oil had coagulated enough that it would not burn.

• The contingency plan states that "private commercial vessels from the Valdez small-boat harbor would be employed to assist booming and logistical support." The lack of transport to the remote grounding site was one reason spill response took so long. The Coast Guard had closed the marina, and fishermen's offers to employ their boats were mostly ignored for the first three days after the spill.

Cordova fishermen finally organized their own flotilla to try to attack the spill.

• Of immediate importance was draining the remaining 1 million barrels of crude oil from the grounded tanker so that a ship break-up would not spill that into the water as well. But when attempts showed internal tanker piping was apparently ruptured, Exxon was forced to bring in portable submersible pumps. These too were not stockpiled in Valdez, and the need to fly them in meant the transfer of oil to a new tanker was at a trickle until Tuesday.

In sum, Exxon and the Coast Guard seemed almost paralyzed for the first four days of the spill, first by the lack of necessary equipment and second by high winds Sunday night and Monday. In that period, the opportunity to possibly corral the spilled oil in deep, open waters around the ship was lost. The simple act of putting an oil boom around the ship took three days.

In response to this record, Alaska state officials have been blistering, calling Exxon's performance inexcusable and initiating a criminal investigation into the grounding itself.

The company's record is not all bad. It immediately accepted full financial responsibility for the spill and cleanup, promised to reimburse fishermen for any lost income and mounted a frantic effort to airlift people and equipment in.

Exxon publicly pledged to return the area to as near its previous purity as possible. "We're going to be here a long time," said Iarossi.

But the industry's performance in this spill shows a huge gap between promise, when the Alaska pipeline was built, and performance, residents of the sound have repeatedly charged.

Suggested solutions include local pilots for the trip all the way through Prince William Sound, improved radar tracking of tankers, improved navigation aids, stockpiled oil-spill equipment, and immediate authority to use whatever it takes to contain or disperse the spill.

"We want to learn from what happened here," said George Nelson, president of Alyeska. "Something obviously didn't work as well as we would have hoped."

"We certainly have to do some reconsidering," said William Stevens, president of Exxon USA.

Indeed. Oil continues to spread inexorably across western Prince William Sound.

But oil executives also continue to insist they were defeated by an insoluble disaster, not their own unpreparedness. It is, they contend, the risk society takes for cheap oil.

That position was indirectly embraced today by President Bush. He reaffirmed his decision to open the fragile Arctic National Wildlife Refuge for oil exploration. Bush said, "I don't think there is any way you could plan" for a situation like the one in Prince William Sound.

"I'm not sure you can ever design a policy anywhere to guard against that," he said.

CLEANUP GEAR GOES NOWHERE

EXPERTS SAY EXXON TURNED DOWN OFFERS OF EQUIPMENT, HELP

FRIDAY, MARCH 31, 1989

BY ERIC NALDER

As weary crews fight a losing battle against an ugly oil spill spreading over Alaska's Prince William Sound, dozens of oil-skimming boats and machines remain docked and warehoused in cities up and down the West Coast.

Exxon Corp., the giant oil company that accepted responsibility for the spill near Valdez, has declined and even ignored offers for some of the equipment that could have blunted the impact of spill on the environment, according to officials with oil-spill cleanup consortiums in Seattle and Vancouver, B.C.

Exxon officials counter that the time necessary to ship the skimmers and equipment to Alaska has rendered their use impractical. They say moving the equipment to Alaska would leave other areas of the coast vulnerable to spills.

And some of the equipment that would have been useful early in the spill is no longer needed as the oil becomes thicker and harder to sweep, they say.

In any case, interviews with a dozen experts who fight West Coast oil spills raise many questions about Exxon's handling of the nation's largest oil spill, which occurred in the early morning hours last Friday.

Bill Lerch, vice president of a Seattle company that builds oil-skimming boats, compared spillfighting tactics to the techniques used by firefighters. In his view, firefighters do it better. He said a fire department sends more than enough equipment to a fire immediately, and then it sends back what isn't needed.

"You don't send someone down with a watering can to see what else is needed," said Lerch, who builds skimmers for oil companies and the Navy.

"They bring in some equipment and then keep adding and adding."

WORKING OVERTIME

Exxon and the Alyeska Pipeline Service Co. so far have put a dozen oil-skimming machines to work on Prince William Sound, according to Exxon spokeswoman Sharon Curran-Westcott.

Companies as far away as Florida have been working overtime making oil-containment booms, said George Lobenz, president of an Alaska company that has shipped 27 miles of booms to fishermen and to Exxon.

Skimming machines, booms, chemical dispersants, crews, boats and oil-burning equipment have been sent to Prince William Sound from Prudhoe Bay and Cook Inlet in Alaska and from Seattle, Portland, San Francisco and Santa Barbara and Long Beach, Calif.

But there is not enough of the material at the spill yet to blunt the spreading slick, which measures more than 850 square miles.

Thousands of gallons of Exxon-manufactured chemical dispersants have been sprayed ineffectively on the spill. Burning, too, has been tried without much success.

Curran-Westcott said Exxon is doing everything it can to prevent an ecological disaster. She said the company is especially worried about the fisheries.

But fishermen in the area are upset with the oil company for its slow response and for its refusal to bring in more equipment.

"We have roughly 10 percent of what we need today to trap the oil in its present location," said Tom Copeland, a fisherman in Cordova who has been working with his boat around the clock with hundreds of others trying to save their livelihood. "The situation is desperate."

"We're talking seven days after the spill," said Michael O'Leary of Cordova, a fishing-dependent town on Prince William Sound. "There's not much equipment on the ground. Exxon is not doing the job.

"Exxon was hoping this stuff would just float out of the sound."

The West Coast's first line of defense against major oil spills are the consortiums financed by the major oil companies. There are three in Alaska, and one each in or near Vancouver, B.C.; Seattle; Portland; San Francisco; Santa Barbara and Long Beach, Calif.; and Honolulu. They have ecological-sounding names such as Alaska Clean Seas, Clean

Sound, Clean Rivers, Clean Bay, Clean Coastal Waters and Clean Islands.

The consortiums, which have mutual-aid agreements, did participate as expected in the Alaska cleanup. Even in Honolulu, barrels of chemical dispersants were moved to the airport in case they were needed, said Jerry Willis, manager of Clean Islands Council in Hawaii.

But a quick inventory of equipment that was available indicates that there were scores of miles of booms and many skimmers available that were not used.

Here is what happened with some of the equipment that didn't get to the oil spill, or that arrived late:

• A spill-cleanup consortium near Santa Barbara offered Exxon a specially equipped vessel that can deploy any one of three skimming machines into the water to rapidly suck up oil. The ship has storage capacity for 1,200 barrels of oil and it can offload to larger barges.

NO, THANKS

The offer was declined. The ship, Mr. Clean III, would have taken nearly a week to get to Alaska, and Exxon thought that was too long, said Skip Onstad, manager of Clean Seas, the California consortium.

"I'm not in a position to second-guess the decisions they are making up there," Onstad said. "That is Monday-morning quarterbacking. That is not appropriate."

Exxon spokesman Dave Parish said his company was concerned not only with the time it would take to get such equipment to Alaska, but also with the possibility that moving the equipment would leave coasts of California, Oregon and Washington vulnerable to spills themselves. However, the Mr. Clean III is one of three such ships owned by the California consortium.

• A Seattle-based consortium offered to lend Exxon the largest self-propelled oil-skimming boat in North America, but that offer was also declined. The 73-foot vessel, docked in Bellingham, is specially designed to handle spills like the one at Valdez, with oil-sucking capacity of up to 500 gallons of oil a minute, said John Wiechert, manager of Clean Sound Cooperative.

The consortium also offered additional boats and equipment that filled a four-page list.

Wiechert said an Exxon official indicated the company would rely more on chemical dispersants and burning techniques that proved to be ineffective.

Like Onstad, Wiechert was reluctant to second-guess Exxon; their consortiums are funded by oil companies. But Roy McClymonds, general manager of a cleanup consortium in Long Beach, said there was no question Exxon should have accepted the offer of the Seattle-based consortium.

"In my experience in oil spills," he said, "there is no tomorrow. Today is when you want to react. You want to do something as quickly as possible. And I'm trying not to be critical of Exxon, who is a member of my cooperative."

• Another spill-fighting consortium near Vancouver, B.C., offered Exxon a 50-foot self-propelled skimmer complete with a crew to operate it 24 hours a day, booms and "just about anything else they felt they needed," said Martyn Green, general manager of Burrard Clean.

Green said Exxon never responded.

"I can only assume that they didn't feel it was appropriate," he said.

• The Navy has 24 oil-skimming units on three-hour standby in two locations in the continental United States and one in Hawaii, but the rules of oil-spill fighting in this country prevented any of the equipment from reaching the site immediately.

Bruce Agnew, an aide to U.S. Rep. John Miller, R-Seattle, said that by regulation the Navy equipment cannot be called to the scene unless the Coast Guard requests it, which usually requires the president to declare an emergency. The Navy equipment is usually reserved for military or federal spills, or spills that commercial companies can't handle.

Frustrated by this bottleneck, Miller, a member of the House Merchant Marine and Fisheries Committee, had been trying all week to get more Navy equipment up to Alaska, Agnew said.

Lerch, the skimming-boat manufacturer, wrote a letter to Alaska Gov. Steve Cowper on Monday complaining about the lack of Navy equipment at the Alaska spill. He said the Navy equipment, which he manufactured, is some of the best in the world because it is well-maintained and kept in a state of readiness. He said in his letter that the Bush administration should declare a national emergency to "remove that decision-making process from the bottleneck of Exxon decision-making."

SKIRTING THE RULES

William Walker, head of the operations branch at the office of the Navy's supervisor of diving and salvage, said the Coast Guard requested two Navy skimmers on Saturday night and they were deployed on Tuesday. He attributed the delay to the time it took to unpack and ship the skimmers from Stockton, Calif.

• There is a large self-propelled oil skimmer in Alaska. But the 65-foot-long catamaran Arcat was in dry dock in Prudhoe Bay surrounded by immovable ice, said Mark Jones, manager of a Prudhoe Bay cleanup consortium, Alaska Clean Seas.

The Prudhoe consortium didn't send other smaller skimmers because they were not designed for the rough waters of Prince William Sound, Jones said. He said his consortium provided Exxon with oil-burning equipment, some three miles of containment boom and chemical dispersants.

• Others in Alaska chipped in. But they, too, had to hold back some equipment in case they had their own emergencies.

In the early-morning hours after the spill, a consortium in Alaska's Cook Inlet dispatched to Valdez two small skimmers, 3,000 feet of boom, an oil burner, equipment for spreading chemical dispersants and other machines for cleaning up the oil and emptying the crippled tanker. But a 30-foot self-propelled skimmer and other equipment stayed behind in Cook Inlet.

"We have retained about half of our inventory for any problems that we might have here in Cook Inlet," explained Barry Eldridge, manager of the Cook Inlet Resource Organization.

No group is feeling the equipment shortage as severely as the fishermen at Cordova, a port some 45 miles southeast of Valdez.

According to Copeland, an activist in the tightly knit organization known as the Cordova District Fishermen United, there are 700 boats in the fishing fleet with 2,000 trained seamen ready to deploy booms.

Copeland says fishermen spent $100,000 of their own money and borrowed another $200,000 from the city of Cordova to buy booms.

The booms are guarding sensitive fish hatcheries and bays. But it isn't enough, Copeland says. He contends $1 million is needed but that the fishermen can't get any money from Exxon, the state or the federal government.

"We need that money from anybody," he said.

Exxon yesterday promised some booms, asking fishermen to cancel some orders they placed in Seattle for booms. Then the Exxon shipment didn't come in, Copeland said. Exxon renewed its promise late last night.

"We are losing our booms at our hatcheries now," Copeland said. "Ours are breaking up, we can't get more. We've had six beautiful days of weather here and Exxon has jerked us around."

UNFAIR PICTURE?

Despite the criticism, oil-spill experts say the cleanup is not being run by amateurs and that the news media might be painting an unfair picture. Several said the real problem may be simply the size of the spill, something no one could handle.

"You've got the largest oil company in the world with the resources of that corporation behind it and the best people available involved in salvaging the vessel and managing the oil spill," said Onstad of Santa Barbara.

Calling the shots at Valdez is Jim O'Brien, an ex–Coast Guard officer who operates a spill-fighting consulting firm in Louisiana.

Wiechert in Seattle praised O'Brien, although he was the man who declined to use Wiechert's skimmer.

If expertise is not the problem, then the solution to the next Valdez-like disaster may be federal legislation to strengthen the preparedness for oil spills. Agnew, Miller's aide, said there will be hearings in Congress and that one goal is to establish better-equipped spill-fighting teams in places like Valdez.

McClymonds in Long Beach said there is no doubt that Valdez was under-equipped for a major spill so far out in the sound.

"Unfortunately," he said, "it appears some really serious mistakes were made in this case. The probability of that being repeated, my guess would be, from now on would be zilch."

McClymonds, too, predicts new regulations and procedures.

A DEATHLY CALL OF THE WILD

MOURNFUL CRY OF A LOON ECHOES THROUGH A LAND DEVASTATED BY OIL SPILL

TUESDAY, APRIL 4, 1989

BY MARY ANN GWINN

VALDEZ, Alaska—I had tried to prepare myself for Green Island, but nothing can prepare you for the havoc wreaked on the creatures of Prince William Sound.

From the helicopter that took me there, the 987-foot tanker Exxon Valdez, stuck like a toy boat on Bligh Reef, was dwarfed by the immensity of the sound. It was hard to believe that we could fly 60 miles, land and walk right into the ruination of a landscape, so far from that broken boat.

The helicopter landed on the beach of Green Island. Its beaches are broad and slope gently, in contrast to the rocky, vertical shores of many of the other islands in the sound. For that reason, Green Island is favored by wildlife. Now the oil has turned the gentle beach into a death trap.

No sooner had the Alaska National Guard helicopter roared away than a black lump detached itself from three or four others bobbing in the oil-streaked water. It was an old squaw, a sea bird normally recognizable by its stark black-and-white plumage. The tuxedo plumage had turned a muddy brown and orange.

It staggered up the beach, its head compulsively jerking back and forth, as if trying to escape the thing that was strangling it. Tony Dawson, a photographer for Audubon magazine, and I watched it climb a snowbank and flap into the still center of the woods. "They move up into the grass, along the creek beds and into the woods, where they die," Dawson said. "It's like they're fleeing an invisible enemy."

Dawson used to be a veterinarian. He said documenting the oil spill makes him feel like a photographer in Vietnam: "Every day, a new body count." As in that war, helicopters drone across the sky, boats beach on shore, men land, size up the situation and depart.

Eleven days into the spill, scientists are trying to decide which beaches to clean and which to leave alone, reasoning that disruption would hurt some more than it would help. Very little actual beach cleanup is taking place. Most of the animals are going to die, a few dozen or hundred every day, by degrees.

I walked along the beach, which in some places was glutted with oil like brown pudding; in others, streaked and puddled with oil the consistency of chocolate syrup. The only sounds came from a few gulls and the old squaw's mate, which drifted down the polluted channel toward its fate. Far away, a cormorant spread its wings and stretched in a vain attempt to fluff its oil-soaked feathers. A bald eagle passed overhead.

It was then that I heard a sound so strange, for a brief moment all my 20th century rationality dropped away.

Something was crying in the vicinity of the woods, a sound not quite human. I looked into the trees.

Whooooooh. Whooooh. Whoooh. Up and down a mournful scale. Something is coming out of those woods, I thought, and is going to take vengeance for this horror on the first human being it sees.

Then I saw a movement in the grass at the end of the beach. It was a loon.

Loons have become something of a cause célèbre to bird lovers. They are beautiful birds, almost as large as geese, with long, sharp beaks, striking black-and-white striped wings and a graceful, stream-lined head. They are a threatened species in the United States because they need large bodies of water to fish in and undeveloped, marshy shorelines to nest on, and most shoreline in this country has been landscaped and pruned.

The most compelling thing about the loon is its call—something between a cry, a whistle and a sob, a sound so mournful and chilling it provoked the word "loony," a term for someone wild with sorrow, out of their head.

This was an artic loon in its winter plumage, brown instead of the striking black and white of summer. It had ruby-red eyes, which blinked in terror because it could barely move. It was lightly oiled all over—breast, feet, wings, head—destroying its power of flight. Its sinuous head darted here and there as we approached. It flapped and stumbled trying to avoid us, and then it came to rest between two large rocks.

As Dawson photographed it, it intermittently called its mournful call. Its mate swam back and forth, calling back, a few yards offshore.

I could see it tremble, a sign that the bird was freezing. Most oiled birds die because the oil destroys their insulation.

"It's like someone with a down coat falling into a lake," Dawson explained. The breeze ruffled its stiffening feathers. As Dawson moved closer with the camera, it uttered a low quivering cry.

After 10 minutes or so, I just couldn't watch anymore. It was so beautiful, and so helpless and so doomed. We had nothing like a bag, sack or cloth to hold it in. I walked around the point.

Then I heard Dawson calling. He walked into view holding the furious, flapping loon by its upper wings, set it down on the grass and said, "Come here and help me. He won't hurt you."

I was stunned by the rough handling of such a wild thing, but it developed that Dawson, the former veterinarian, knew his birds. He had grasped the loon exactly in the place where his wings would not break. He would tell me later that most bird rescuers are too tender-hearted or frightened of birds to contain them, and let a lot of salvage-able birds get away.

We had to wait for the helicopter, and Dawson had to take more pictures, so I grasped the loon behind the upper wings, pinning them together, and took up the loon watch. The bird rose, struggled and fell back to earth, then was still.

I was as afraid of the loon as it was of me in a way that touching a totally wild thing can provoke. But I began to feel its strength. It was warm, it had energy, and it could still struggle. I could hear it breathing, and could feel its pulse. It turned its red eye steadily on me. We breathed, and waited, together.

Dawson returned, took a black cord from a lens case and neatly looped it around the bird's wings. The helicopter dropped out of the sky and settled on the beach. I held the string as the loon, unblinking, faced the terrific wind kicked up by the machine. Then Dawson neatly scooped up the bird and settled into the helicopter. The loon lashed out with its needle beak until David Grimes, a fisherman working with the state on the spill, enveloped it in a wool knit bag he carried with him. The bird stilled.

Dawson and I were both streaked with oil and blood from the loon's feet, lacerated by barnacles on the beach. He gave me a small black and white feather that had fallen from the bird's wing.

We took the loon to the bird-rescue center in Valdez. I don't know if it will live. Dawson thought it had a good chance. I thought of the mate we had left behind in the water.

Afterward, we talked about whom bird rescues help more, the rescued or the rescuer. Most rescued birds don't make it. And tens of thousands more from the Valdez spill will die before they even get a chance.

I know only that the loon told me something that no one other thing about this tragedy could. If only we could learn to value such stubborn, determined life. If only we could hold safe in our hands the heart of the loon.

LESSONS LEARNED

SIX MONTHS AFTER THE NATION'S WORST OIL SPILL, ACCOUNTABILITY FOR THAT DISASTER AND FUTURE ONES REMAINS UNDEFINED AND DISPUTED

SUNDAY, SEPTEMBER 24, 1989

BY BILL DIETRICH

A summer's effort to clean up the nation's worst oil spill has yielded frustratingly meager results and means a winter of hard, hard questions.

Did the effort to mop up the 11 million gallons that leaked from the tanker Exxon Valdez six months ago today do more good than harm? Was the $1.24 billion Exxon spent wisely used? And are we better prepared for the next big spill?

A strong case can be made that the answer to all three questions is no.

What played out against the scenic splendor of Alaska was perhaps a classic example of the American way of crisis: a complacent institution, an avoidable disaster, media alarm, public outrage, special-interest demands, political posturing and reform, and the frenzied, mechanized response of an affluent, technological society.

Lots of money. Lots of noise. Lots of good intentions.

And a melodrama in which style seemed to count as much as substance, cleanup statistics warped reality, and greed and opportunism on all sides became tempting alternatives to honesty and common sense.

"It's been an extraordinary spill in an extraordinary place, and I'm not sure 1 or 2 billion dollars spent to clean it up is too much," said Sue Libenson, director of Alaska's Center for the Environment. Exxon's estimated after-tax costs of $1.24 billion amount to only three months' worth of its 1988 profits.

"But for what they accomplished, I could have done it cheaper," added Libenson. "Lots of people got paid to do a lot of B.S. this summer."

Alaska state Sen. Jay Kerttula, who represents the Prince William Sound communities hardest hit by the spill, agreed. While praising Exxon's attempt to set things right, he said: "Frankly, the cleanup is cosmetic. The ocean can take a lot of punishment, and this winter's storms will do more towards a solution than anything Exxon could do."

"The problem was, no one in this country knew how to clean up a spill of this magnitude," said Alaska Gov. Steve Cowper. "Steam-cleaning did substantial damage to some of the beaches, but frankly, public pressure was applied for Exxon to do *something*. Now it ill behooves us to say they did the wrong thing. There is a real lack of technology."

There were two tragedies on Prince William Sound.

One was the environmental and human havoc that resulted in 1,244 miles of oiled beaches, an animal death toll scientists estimate may have topped 400,000 birds and thousands of sea otters, and a disrupted salmon season.

The agony of otters having scratched their own eyes blind trying to get out stinging oil won't be forgotten soon.

The other tragedy was the ignorance, hesitation, grandstanding, role-playing and rump-protecting that made the frenzied cleanup—with truly heroic effort by thousands of well-meaning people—a disappointment.

In one sense, Exxon's effort worked: The company dumped nearly $600 million into Alaska in wages, boat rentals and liability payments to fishermen. The dollars pushed Alaska's unemployment rate to the lowest since the early 1980s, giving jobs to 15,000 people.

"What Exxon did accomplish is hiring a lot of people and keeping their public relations in pretty good shape," Kerttula said.

The cleanup did succeed in removing the worst of the slick and goo. That accomplishment was necessary, said Dave Kennedy, a Seattle-based oil-spill expert with the National Oceanic and Atmospheric Administration.

But scouring the beaches beyond that may have been a lousy investment on a dollar-per-gallon basis. The state of Alaska succeeded in skimming and washing up 13 percent of the spilled oil, or 1.37 million gallons. That means the company spent about $900 for each gallon of oil recovered.

And Exxon spent an average of $40,000 for each sea otter that was cleaned and survived to return to the wild.

Exxon's semantics of success changed as the spilled oil hardened into tar, abandoning "clean" beaches for "environmentally stable," and then abandoning that phrase for "treated." The company finally declared temporary victory and went home for the winter Sept. 15.

The state of Alaska in turn has declared Exxon's performance insufficient and vowed to continue a low-key monitoring and emergency-response effort of its own this winter, billing Exxon for the cost.

What now?

Wounded, dirtied, far from dead and far from clean, Alaska's oiled coastline is slipping into a wintertime slumber of natural healing.

Humans may sleep less easily. Despite the disaster, cleanup technology remains primitive, and tankers in both Alaska and on Puget Sound continue to ply those waters without double hulls or backup propulsion systems.

And society's tendency to penny-pinch before a crisis and splurge under the media spotlight of disaster has to raise questions.

"If we had spent that billion dollars over the past 10 years on research and developing procedures and equipment, this spill would be a lot better cleaned up," said Adm. Clyde Robbins, the Coast Guard commander in charge of the spill response.

Even environmentalist Libenson winces at the results the money bought. Exxon's own studies indicate its high-pressure hot-water washing of the beaches in many cases removed just a fraction of the oil.

"With a couple of billion dollars," Libenson said, "I might have liked to see it spent instead to buy timber rights around Prince William Sound." With the cleanup's effectiveness limited and heavy clear-cut logging scheduled around the sound, she reasoned, why not spend such dollars where it will have real environmental impact?

Sen. Kerttula said it might have made more sense to spend the same money on long-term restoration—on new fish hatcheries and wildlife enhancement.

Such debate is just beginning. Ahead are years of litigation, the trial of Exxon Valdez Capt. Joseph Hazelwood, scientific studies, legislative battles and a tough decision by the Coast Guard next spring on whether Exxon should come back and, if so, what it should do.

Exxon declined to comment on what lessons it has drawn from the spill. But others aren't averse to using hindsight to suggest some:

• *Prevention:* "The main thing that everybody's learned from this spill," said Gov. Cowper, "is that there is no available defense from an oil spill of this size."

Said Robert LaResche, Alaska's oil-spill coordinator: "The only real solution is prevention."

Since the spill, the oil industry has belatedly added a tug escort with modest skimming capabilities to outbound, loaded tankers. Sen. Brock Adams and Rep. Jim McDermott, both Washington Democrats, are pushing legislation in Congress to require double hulls on new tankers.

• *Authority:* After the spill, confusion was chronic, with a cumbersome committee structure of a dozen agencies involved in the response. Cowper said that next time the Coast Guard should be put in command immediately. "There should be no question of who's in charge."

The Coast Guard also needs its own fund to draw on, the governor said. The Coast Guard, with an annual budget of $3 billion, was like a flea trying to direct the Exxon dog, with annual revenues of $90 billion. Exxon decided what it would do, what it would spend and when it would leave. State officials advised, sniped and cajoled from the sidelines.

• *Initial Response:* Exxon, the Alyeska Pipeline Service Co. and public agencies had three days of near-perfect weather after the spill to contain the slick, and failed to do so.

Alyeska, an oil-company consortium of which Exxon is a member, operates the Trans-Alaska Pipeline from the North Slope oil fields to the Valdez terminal. Alyeska is responsible for initial response to spills.

"The real environmental damage was the failure of the pipeline company to contain the spill," said the state's LaResche. "That caused most of the expense and a great deal of the tragedy."

Cowper has prosposed building four giant oil skimmers similar to a

Soviet ship used this summer, to be based in Alaska and the West, East and Gulf coasts. He also wants tankers to carry booms, and skiffs to deploy them, to contain any slicks.

Not only was there a lack of spill equipment in Valdez, but Exxon and Alyeska initially resisted efforts of help from local fishing boats, which later proved surprisingly effective at booming and scooping oil.

The American Petroleum Institute has announced the oil industry will set up five regional spill-response centers to speed future cleanups, one of them in Seattle. A plan to immediately harness local fishing craft and use wildlife volunteers is also being urged by many fishermen.

• *The level of concern:* "One of the puzzles of this spill," said Libenson of Alaska's Center for the Environment, "is, 'Were these guys incompetent, or were they slow to respond because they were hoping the oil would go so far or disappear and they wouldn't have to deal with it?' "

Optimistic forecasts by Exxon and government scientists in the first days of the spill may have influenced decisions to put containment of the oil slick at a lower priority than salvage of the Exxon Valdez.

NOAA's Kennedy said his agency's predictions that "maybe the world hasn't come to an end" have been borne out by the facts. "We need to think more about letting nature handle itself in the future," and he contends that mechanical cleanup that sterilized beaches has actually slowed, rather than hastened, their recovery.

But others argue that scientists erred in not urging more strongly early containment of the slick. "No one ever anticipated that a spill in Valdez would end up in Katmai National Park" hundreds of miles away on the Alaska Peninsula, noted Libenson.

At the same time, the environmental impact of the spill probably never equaled the most overblown rhetoric. The spill was bad news for fishermen but hardly a complete catastrophe: 1989 was the second-best year on record for Alaska salmon catches as a whole. Even in Prince William Sound the harvest was 23.7 million salmon, down from 1987's record 33.1 million but up from last year's 14.9 million. However, low prices and the arguably unnecessary shutdown of most of the Kodiak-area fishery hurt many fishermen.

Still unknown is if the oil spill affected young salmon fry. Nor is it clear yet if the huge wildlife toll, as grim as it was, will have significant long-term impacts on species populations.

• *Needed research:* The oil industry now has three ways of dealing with escaped oil: skimming, which works best in calm weather; chemical dispersants, which work only in moderately choppy seas; and beach cleanup.

Dennis Kelso, commissioner of Alaska's Department of Environmental Conservation, noted the irony of Exxon's claiming it could not safely extend its cleanup past Sept. 15 because of bad weather, while its tankers cruise the same waters year-round. Alyeska admits that new skimming equipment it has added in Valdez will be ineffective in the stormy weather conditions that prevail for half the year.

Improved technology is desperately needed. This winter the state of Alaska will begin sifting again through an estimated 1,300 cleanup ideas submitted by outsiders in hopes, LaResche said, of "finding a few gems."

Research is also needed on the biological harm caused by oil and its natural breakdown so that policy-makers can weigh the costs and benefits of any cleanup. Chemical dispersants, high-pressure, hot-water washing and chemical solvents remain controversial, as do suggestions by some scientists that nature should be allowed to cleanse itself.

• *Legislation:* Congress has failed to pass oil-spill liability legislation for 14 years. Now both houses of Congress have bills in the works setting up $1 billion cleanup funds financed by a new tax on oil. The key sticking point is whether states should be allowed to have separate liability laws of their own.

The Alaska Legislature's long-standing sweetheart relationship with generous oil-industry lobbyists temporarily ended this spring. An oil-industry tax break was eliminated, a state cleanup fund was approved and the liability lid for oil-spill damage was raised. Still pending are 11 more spill-related bills.

"We need to make it so expensive for companies to spill oil that it is worth their while to get this problem under control," said Kay Brown, an Anchorage lawmaker.

But Kerttula, the state senator from Prince William Sound, thinks any legislative defiance of the powerful oil industry will be as short-lived in Alaska as it would be in Texas. "I see the industry coming on strong in the next election and protecting their interests," he said.

• *Fuel conservation:* While most auto manufacturers have prototypes that get more than 60 miles per gallon, federal mileage standards next year will be only 27.5 mpg. Boosting that average to 45 mpg, estimates a coalition of environmental groups, would save 46.2 million gallons of oil every day by 2000—or more than four times what spilled from the Exxon Valdez.

"How many areas do we have to sacrifice in this country before we think seriously about conservation?" asked environmentalist Libenson.

SIX

TIANANMEN SQUARE

1990 WINNER IN THE INTERNATIONAL REPORTING CATEGORY

"For a distinguished example of reporting on international affairs, including United Nations correspondence . . ."

The New York Times
*Nicholas D. Kristof and
Sheryl WuDunn*

Tiananmen Square, the nerve center of China's democracy movement, became synonymous with the popular uprising against the
Communist government. Nicholas D. Kristof and Sheryl WuDunn
vividly portray the events before, during and after the brutal military
crackdown.

The jangle of the phone interrupted our Chinese lesson, and it
would be four months before we could resume. The caller was a
Chinese journalist and a good friend—a man who would later lose his
job—telling us breathlessly that the former Communist Party leader,
Hu Yaobang, had just died.

"You might want to go to Tiananmen, or to Beijing University,"
the friend said in Chinese. "You never know what might happen."

He was right: We had no idea what would happen in the two
months after we received the phone call on April 15, 1989. Hu's
death triggered the democracy movement that shook China, and that
in part stimulated the changes in Eastern Europe later in the year.

It began as a reporter's dream. Not only were the student demonstrations vivid and exhilarating, but for about four weeks China
seemed to be the most open place in the world. We had a large number
of Chinese friends, many of them with ties to senior officials, and they
often provided us with information about Politburo meetings soon
after they dispersed. After a lunch meeting with one central government official, we were even able to give him a ride in our car to his
next destination: Zhongnanhai, the tightly guarded compound where
China's leaders live and work. Our guest showed his pass and the
guards waved us in, as if it were normal for officials to have foreign
reporters as chauffeurs.

All was not quite so glorious during the flowering of the democracy
movement, however, for a reason that readers probably did not consider: We were exhausted. Demonstrations sometimes took place at
night, and of course we had to be there too—until about dawn, when
we had to hurtle off and write our articles on deadline. Dimly, in the

hazy recesses of our minds, is a period in which we did not get to sleep for three consecutive nights; the result was an exhaustion that was physically painful and no doubt impaired our work. We felt there should have been a little warning attached to our stories: Caution: this article was written by someone who has not slept in a couple of days.

Sometimes we would fall asleep in the middle of writing the lead of a story and dream that the entire story had been written, only to wake up and discover that hours of work still lay ahead.

Reporting became much more difficult after the hard-liners rose to power and declared martial law in late May. We had close connections with those who lost the power struggle, but now we found we had no sources close to Prime Minister Li Peng. In addition, there was a mounting fear of retribution from the government, and our friends now were reluctant to talk to us on the telephone. We all knew that the phones were tapped, but until then the government had seemed benign and impotent, so it hadn't mattered much.

Throughout the democracy movement, one of our toughest tasks was to remain neutral and objective. The students appealed to all the values instilled in us since about the second grade, while the hard-liners were rather less inspiring from an American point of view— particularly after they ordered the troops to fire on crowds on June 4. It is quite difficult to feel neutral about people who are shooting at you.

When the firing began, a little after midnight, Nick rode off to Tiananmen Square on his bicycle—cars were useless because of the tank blockades that protesters had erected—while Sheryl worked the phones and covered the tank skirmishes in our area. It was a crazy bicycle ride: swerving madly around tank traps, bullets overhead, the road lit by burning tanks, and this inescapable feeling that any sensible person would be rushing just as madly in the opposite direction. After parking his bicycle in Tiananmen Square, Nick interviewed the students and workers, keeping his head down, hoping to reduce the chance it would be shot off, while they brought by the broken and bleeding bodies of their friends so that he could see and tell the world what happened.

For the next week or so, leaving our apartment was a terrifying experience. Troops were still firing fairly randomly, and on June 7 they shot hundreds of rounds into the diplomatic compound where we live—shooting out the windows in an apartment that we used as an observation post. Then the firing gradually receded over the weeks, but we faced a new risk, not to us but to our Chinese friends. In late June, we tried to bring a Chinese friend—a journalist and the daughter of a senior official—into our compound. The armed guards who stand at the gate detained her and interrogated her for four hours. Other friends of ours were arrested, and we realized that if we tried to maintain our contacts to keep up our supply of information, we would be putting our friends and sources at risk. This was a moral dilemma we had not expected. We decided to stop initiating contacts with our Chinese friends and only see them if they sent word to us that they were willing.

The other problem was reliability of information. Rumors were everywhere, but they were always presented as absolute fact. With so many rumors, and so little hard information, it was always very tempting to leave it entirely up to the reader to sort out what was what. And simply because rumors came from those close to the leadership did not make them accurate. A Chinese friend of ours asked one of Deng Xiaoping's bodyguards if it were true that the old man was gravely ill. The bodyguard confirmed that it was true. The next time they met, the topic came up again, and our friend asked the bodyguard how he could tell that Deng was ill. "Oh," the bodyguard shrugged, "I heard it on Voice of America."

Since June, life has slowly moved in the direction of normalcy, but there is still a dearth of reliable information and an abundance of rumors. Most troubling for us, the authorities dramatically stepped up surveillance of us at the beginning of 1990. Virtually every time we leave our compound, we are followed, and this has often hampered our activities. One time, Nick was to meet a friend in a hotel, but at the last minute found he had been followed. Nick saw his friend, 50 feet away, but ignored him and waited for an hour to see if the followers would leave. They didn't, so Nick returned home.

Already, some of our friends are in prison, although not so far as we know because of the connection with us. Other friends have had their careers ruined. Our thoughts dwelt on them when we won the

Pulitzer Prize, for they were crucial in helping us understand China. There is no way we can thank them enough, for they took all the risks, got none of the credit and now are suffering the consequences.

—Nicholas D. Kristof
Sheryl WuDunn
The New York Times

PRIVATELY, MORE AND MORE CHINESE SAY IT'S PAST TIME FOR DENG TO GO

MONDAY, APRIL 17, 1989

BY NICHOLAS D. KRISTOF

BEIJING—In a nation where there are no opinion polls to assess the popularity of national leaders, what people do with small bottles may be the best indication of the remarkable rise and fall in the popularity of Deng Xiaoping.

"Xiaoping" in spoken Chinese can mean "small bottle"—although the written character for "ping" in Mr. Deng's name is not the one used for "bottle"—and people seized on the symbolism a decade ago, when Mr. Deng was struggling to power and embodied the nation's hope for non-revolutionary prosperity. At that time, ordinary people registered their support for Mr. Deng by leaving small bottles in conspicuous places. These days, some people are expressing their feelings by smashing small bottles.

A decade ago, it was more talk than action, and these days, too, more people speak of breaking bottles than actually smash them. "What's the point?" explained a young man in Beijing. "If you smash it in public, you might get arrested, and if you smash it at home, you just have to sweep it up."

In any case, even Communist Party officials acknowledge that the public is growing tired of Mr. Deng. Some of the pent-up hostility has come into the open after the death Saturday of the former party leader Hu Yaobang, who was ousted two years ago after being criticized by Mr. Deng for tolerating intellectual dissidents and student unrest.

DENG'S 'STATURE ISN'T GOING UP'

In the early hours this morning at Tiananmen Square, the center of Beijing and the political focal point of China, white paper flowers fluttered in the breeze where mourners had left them to honor Mr. Hu. The only sign of litter was a freshly broken small bottle.

Public criticism of Mr. Deng remains a taboo in China, but in private it seems that few people have a kind word about him. Farmers blame him because they cannot get fertilizer. Workers blame him for the widespread corruption. Intellectuals blame him for ignoring education. And everybody blames him for rapidly rising prices.

"Everything is going up," according to a ditty now making the rounds in the capital. "Only Xiaoping's stature isn't going up"—a mocking reference to the fact that he is barely five feet tall.

The wave of discontent directed at Mr. Deng is an extraordinary comedown for a man who since 1978 has personally engineered China's "second revolution," including a policy of ecomonic liberalization that has doubled people's real incomes in just a decade. Few people in the 20th century have changed so many people's lives by so much, overwhelmingly for the better.

Interviews in the last week with Chinese and with foreign diplomats and scholars suggest three reasons for the slump in Mr. Deng's popularity:

• There is general discontent over inflation, corruption, crime and shortages, and people blame Mr. Deng since he is the most powerful person in the nation. Incomes and living standards have risen enormously in China over the last decade, but aspirations have increased even more quickly.

• Many people believe that several of Mr. Deng's children have capitalized on their father's position in their business activities. Mr. Deng no longer seems to rise above the petty corruption and influence-peddling that people see all around them.

• Some say that Mr. Deng, 84 years old, has held on to power too long. People often compare him to the aging Mao Zedong of the mid-1970's, and say that he should completely retire and leave the stage.

CALLED VICTIM OF HIS SUCCESS

Implicit in many of the criticisms is the general perception that Mr. Deng has been superseded and outdated because of the very success of the liberalization process that he initiated.

"Deng may have been right for China a decade ago, but now the people have gone beyond him," a Chinese journalist said. "It's a measure of how much China has changed in the last 10 years."

At Beijing University, where students have put up illegal posters mourning the death of Mr. Hu, there is an unmistakable edge to their grief.

"Overthrow the dictator," read one poster erected this morning. The authorities pulled it down hours later.

Another, pasted up Saturday night and meticulously copied by scores of students in small notebooks, bluntly declared, "The wrong person died."

When more than a dozen Beijing University students were loudly and simultaneously discussing their views with a foreign reporter on Saturday night, there was a sudden hush when the visitor asked what they thought of Mr. Deng. After a long pause, a woman asked, "Can't you tell?"

Wu Jiaxiang, a 34-year-old rising star in the central party organization and the author of a laudatory biography of Mr. Deng, said he is convinced not only that Mr. Deng is a great statesman but that after 50 years the Chinese people will recognize his greatness in history. But for now, he said, the problem is that the Chinese are not used to leaders who spurn divine status.

"It's an irrational attitude," Mr. Wu said in an interview. "If he's not a god, he's a devil. Chairman Mao was a god, and ordinary people wanted another god. But they find out that Deng Xiaoping is a human being. No one could assume that role of a god, and so they think of him as a devil."

While ordinary Chinese principally complain about Mr. Deng on pocketbook issues, like inflation, some intellectuals make unflattering comparisons with Mikhail S. Gorbachev, the Soviet leader. They note that Mr. Gorbachev has gone much further in opening up the political system than has Mr. Deng, and they seem slightly embarrassed that they should envy anything in the Soviet Union.

Harry Harding, a China scholar at the Brookings Institution in Washington, said that some of the most enthusiastic proponents of further liberalization also have been disappointed because they no longer regard Mr. Deng as firmly in their camp.

"What a lot of the reformers complain about is the way Deng is obstructing reform," Mr. Harding said. "Obstructing leadership reform by failing to retire, and obstructing political and economic reform by his willingness to retrench rather than push forward at this critical time."

Mr. Deng is not the only Asian leader who has been accused of staying on too long. In several of the rapidly developing countries in the region, particularly in Singapore, where Lee Kuan Yew has shaped and dominated politics for three decades, some domestic and foreign critics have argued that economic and education development have been so successful that the architect of the success should step down and give way to a younger, less authoritarian leader.

CONCERN OVER SUCCESSION

Yet in China the equation is far more complex, because people are apprehensive as well as impatient for the day when Mr. Deng will entirely give up control, especially if it happens suddenly on his death. Many Chinese worry that after Mr. Deng dies, no one may be able to control the nation and that the military might intervene.

Meanwhile, there is no indication that Mr. Deng's health is in trouble. Those who have met him say that while his hearing is failing and he is easily fatigued, he does not seem ill and his mind is still sharp. He is said to play bridge as well as ever.

Mr. Deng is said to spend his days at a heavily guarded house behind an iron gate near the Dianmen district in the center of Beijing. The two alleys on either side of the walled home are blocked to cars, although pedestrians are allowed, and a nearby garage brims with more than half a dozen limousines with the A01 license plates that are the prerogative of Chinese leaders. Mr. Deng is said to spend the mornings on affairs of state and the afternoons playing with his grandchildren, while evenings are often reserved for bridge.

BIGGEST BEIJING CROWDS SO FAR KEEP TROOPS FROM CITY CENTER; PARTY REPORTED IN BITTER FIGHT

SUNDAY, MAY 21, 1989

BY NICHOLAS D. KRISTOF

BEIJING—Huge throngs, possibly amounting to more than one million Chinese, took to the streets today to defy martial law and block troops from reaching the center of the capital, effectively delaying or preventing the planned crackdown on China's democracy movement.

Troops approaching Beijing on at least five major roads were halted or turned back by the largest crowds to have gathered so far in a month of almost continuous protests. Students and ordinary citizens erected roadblocks or lay in the path of army trucks, while others let the air out of their tires.

Reports from around the country indicated growing support for the democracy movement. The city of Xian was reportedly brought to a standstill by 300,000 protesters, and rallies were reported in Shanghai, Canton and at least half a dozen other cities, and even small villages.

MOSTLY PEACEFUL CONFRONTATIONS

A few clashes were reported, but the confrontations seemed to be mostly peaceful. More troops were reported to be making their way toward Beijing, however, and it was not clear that the people could continue to keep the soldiers out. So far, the troops have not tried very hard to enter Beijing, and a more concerted effort backed by the use of tear gas would almost certainly succeed. But after a full day of confrontation, questions were increasingly raised about the army's readiness to quell the protests.

Prime Minister Li Peng, who early this morning ordered the military crackdown on the democracy movement, did not make an appearance or comment later today. Television stations repeatedly broadcast his speech calling for the military crackdown.

As the military crackdown seemed increasingly uncertain, there were signs that the Communist Party General Secretary, Zhao Ziyang, still had a chance of recovering his authority and elbowing aside Mr. Li and the senior leader, Deng Xiaoping, to become China's next leader in an intense and increasingly bitter power struggle within the Communist Party.

Communist Party officials with access to information at the highest level say Mr. Deng has stripped Mr. Zhao of his powers while leaving him with his title. In addition, they say a meeting of the Central Military Commission on Thursday effectively stripped him of his right to order troop movements.

Mr. Zhao submitted his resignation on May 17, after being outvoted 4 to 1 on the Standing Committee of the Politburo on his proposals to grant most student demands, the official said. The resignation was withdrawn the next day before it was acted upon.

PROPOSALS GET SUPPORT

In the meantime, Mr. Zhao's bold proposals—including a plan to disclose the income and assets of officials at the level of Deputy Minister and higher—have subsequently received the support of a second member of the Politburo Standing Committee, Hu Qili. Now an intense effort is said to be under way to lobby the crucial swing vote of a committee member, Qiao Shi, whose support would mean a majority for Mr. Zhao.

Mr. Zhao's future might also come up at a meeting of the full Politburo, which has not yet been scheduled, or at a meeting of the Central Committee, which had been expected at the end of this month. How the Politburo or Central Committee might vote is likely to depend on the success of the crackdown.

"Li Peng is now in charge of the party, so he'll be scheduling the meetings," an official said. "So if he thinks he might lose, he will delay holding a meeting." The harshness of Mr. Li's speech seems to have galvanized much of Beijing's population to support the student democracy movement, and Mr. Li and Mr. Deng are now openly referred to as public enemies.

Protesters in Shanghai today carried banners reading "Li Peng does not represent us" and "Li Peng, do not use the people's army against the people," Reuters reported.

In most parts of Beijing, neither the police nor army troops could be seen today, but residents were in an exuberant frenzy to protect themselves from the threat of what is regarded as virtually an enemy invasion. All major intersections have been taken over by local residents who stand guard, waiting impatiently for the troops to arrive so they can implement careful plans to erect barricades and summon help.

"With the people behind us, we'll succeed," said Xu Shiyi, a student from Henan Province who has come to Beijing to support the movement. "No Government can survive by using the army against its own citizens."

NOT MUCH WORK IN BEIJING

While proposals in the predawn hours for a general strike seem to have been little heeded, it was clear that even if workers did not call formal strikes, they did not do much work. Beijing residents today had other things to preoccupy them, like how to keep the army out.

As rumors spread about where troops might be arriving, citizens rushed by car, bicycle and foot to do their part to turn the troops back. The crowds were larger than those last Wednesday and Thursday that the official New China News Agency had estimated at more than one million.

Truck drivers drove their vehicles in front of military convoys to block their way, and ordinary citizens lay down on the ground in front of army trucks. Many seemed to remember these tactics from the Philippine military coup that ousted President Ferdinand E. Marcos. Television footage of the "people power" revolution of the Philippines was widely shown in China at the time and now workers delight in saying that people power will defeat Prime Minister Li.

The most serious of the scattered clashes reported today occurred on a road in western Beijing, according to students, who said about 150 police officers used cattle prods to beat about 45 students blocking military trucks.

PROTESTS IN THE PROVINCES

Anti-Government demonstrations broke out in provincial Chinese cities and even rural towns today, witnesses said.

The ancient capital of Xian in northern China came to a standstill when 300,000 protesters, sympathetic citizens and onlookers packed the city's streets, a Western witness told Reuters.

On Shanghai's waterfront, 20,000 students flanked by thousands of sympathetic city workers protested for the fifth day running in support of 400 hunger strikers who have gone without food outside Government headquarters since Tuesday.

A large contingent of troops have been stationed in the European-style office buildings close to the waterfront but have not yet moved against the protesters, a reporter said.

Shanghai is also the host to a three-ship squadron of the American Seventh Fleet, which arrived for the second United States Navy visit to the port since the 1949 Communist takeover. Demonstrators have erected a 10-foot-high polystyrene replica of the Statue of Liberty in front of the Shanghai city government offices. The American sailors have been instructed to avoid the protests.

WAITING IN TIANANMEN SQUARE

In Beijing, nearly 100,000 people seemed prepared this evening to wait all night in central Tiananmen Square to protect student protesters from attack by troops. Even though there was no evidence of hostile troops within miles, many waited expectantly with clothes over their faces for the clouds of tear gas they have been told to expect.

The readiness to help has taken other forms. The Government today cut off the water supply to Tiananmen Square, but as word spread that the water fountains and taps in the area were no longer working, private business people from all over the capital contributed their motorcycles to carry buckets of water to the students.

There are still nearly 3,000 students engaged in a hunger strike on the square to back their demands for a dialogue with Government officials and for a reappraisal of the student movement.

30,000 TROOPS DEPLOYED

After the harshness of Mr. Li's speech, the lack of any strong military follow-through has raised questions about the extent to which the Prime Minister can force his will. About 30,000 troops from Inner Mongolia and Shanxi Province reportedly have been deployed, but they are vastly outnumbered by the more than one million people who took to the streets today.

Some of the troops today could be seen with tear gas canisters, and some reportedly had guns, but they seemed decidedly pacifist. Most of the soldiers seemed unwilling to openly violate their orders to advance on Beijing, but they seemed quite happy to be blocked along the way.

There also were some signs of dissatisfaction from within the party and the Government at the hard line against the students. Officials in the central party organization today circulated among themselves an appeal for a party meeting to discuss the crisis and to consider the possible retirement of Mr. Deng, according to a person who has seen the letter.

The Communist Youth League Central Committee sent a delegation to protest in Tiananmen Square, and the People's Daily newspaper today seemed to offer an implicit endorsement of Mr. Zhao over Mr. Li. The newspaper printed a photo of Mr. Zhao that was not only higher than Mr. Li's on the front page but more than twice as wide. The accompanying article included excerpts from Mr. Zhao's comments to students, and was calculated to inspire sympathy.

BITTER POWER STRUGGLE

"Of course it's an endorsement," a senior party official said. "That's as clear as it gets."

The internal power struggle between Mr. Zhao and Mr. Li has taken a much more bitter turn in the last few weeks, partly because of furious disagreements over how to deal with the demonstrating students. But party officials say that perhaps the most important element was that Mr. Zhao took the unprecedented step of challenging his longtime patron, Mr. Deng.

While Mr. Zhao is said to have felt for some time that his patron should retire fully from politics, the conflict began after Mr. Deng reacted very harshly on April 25 to student demonstrators and organized a crackdown that later was aborted. When Mr. Zhao returned from a trip abroad he made a mild speech on how to deal with students. The speech won widespread support but was resented by Mr. Deng because it pursued a much more moderate strategy.

ZHAO ATTACK ON DENG

Then, as pro-democracy demonstrations grew increasingly large, Mr. Zhao seemed to think that they represented an important constituency that he could use to gain an advantage. According to an account by an official familiar with the struggle, Mr. Zhao made his attacks, in classic Chinese style, by purporting to praise Mr. Deng. In his meeting Wednesday with Mikhail S. Gorbachev, the Soviet leader, Mr. Zhao hailed Mr. Deng as an indispensable leader who still must sign off on every important decision.

Without consulting Mr. Deng, Mr. Zhao also disclosed that the Central Committee had formally adopted a resolution saying that Mr. Deng should be consulted on important matters. While the comments were all couched in praise, the effect was to remind people that the 84-year-old Mr. Deng still makes all of China's important decisions.

The next day's demonstration was full of posters denouncing Mr. Deng, but Mr. Deng himself recognized the ploy, officials said. Mr. Li weighed in in the increasingly bitter fight by saying, in a televised meeting, that his sons were not involved in official profiteering—a clear slap at Mr. Zhao, whose two eldest sons are widely regarded as having been suspiciously successful in business.

Then last Thursday Mr. Zhao made an early morning trip to the hunger-strikers in Tiananmen Square and apologized to them for not coming earlier. "Things are very complicated," he said in what was widely taken as a reference to the difficulty of convincing Mr. Deng and Mr. Li of the need for compromise.

That was the last time Mr. Zhao has been seen in public.

FACING THE PEOPLE, THE SOLDIERS FALL BACK

SUNDAY, MAY 21, 1989

BY SHERYL WUDUNN

BEIJING—When a small convoy of military trucks used to launch tear gas and to spray water on rioters rolled through eastern Beijing early this morning, the soldiers met their first unexpected challenge. An old woman street cleaner rushed up and lay down on the road in front of the trucks.

Several hundred students immediately dashed toward the convoy, and the soldiers found themselves surrounded by Beijing residents who showered them with questions about why they wanted to repress a democratic movement, but who also gave them breakfast: bread, Coca-Cola and popsicles.

"We absolutely won't repress the people," an officer told the crowd. "We are the people's soldiers." And then the soldiers, so moved that several were crying quietly, drove back the way they had come.

THEIR ONLY WEAPON

In an awakening of sorts, the Chinese people are tapping the only weapon they can to defend themselves and their struggle for democracy against the tens of thousands of military troops ordered by the Government to move into the city: what many residents were calling "people power."

Martial law in some sectors of Beijing went into effect at 10 a.m. today. But by late tonight none of the special troops that have been brought in from outside Beijing had made much progress into the city. All over the capital, China's "desperados" and "kamikazes"—as they call themselves—were emerging from their silence and standing up for the university students who continued to fast for democracy.

"We have towels for tear gas and maybe buckets of cement to make road blocks, but besides that, we come just as we are—people," said

Kong Lingqi, a 39-year-old worker at Capital Iron and Steel Company.

Mr. Kong and the people around him in the Haidian district of Beijing were preparing for the coming of the troops, whom they said were based about seven miles away. They were hoping that every inch of the seven miles would be lined with people prepared to use their bodies to block the convoy of military trucks.

Residents tried to block soldiers not only with their bodies, but also with persuasion. They tried to engage soldiers in discussions about the democracy movement, and often they found that the troops had no idea at all of their cause. At least some of the troops said they had been told by their leaders not to read recent newspapers or watch television news.

MASSING OF PEOPLE ON ROADS

Flush with exuberance, crowds have massed along roads they think the troops may use to approach Tiananmen Square, the nation's political center. When five military helicopters encircled the area above Tiananmen Square today, thousands of fists went up in the air and angry shouts rose against the Government.

The crowd swelled at many intersections, and the hum of the crowd's voices rose into shrill shouts every so often when someone believed he had spotted the troops.

"We will lie beneath the wheels," said Wang Gang, a 30-year-old leader of a new workers organization whose members have taken an oath to risk their lives for the students. These 300 "desperados," as they call themselves, wear white bandannas to distinguish themselves from the 400 "deputies" who wear red bandannas and take fewer risks because they have families to protect.

"We are not afraid of guns or bullets," Mr. Wang said. "But we are not allowed to smash glasses, flatten the trucks' tires or beat the drivers."

Mr. Wang, a sweater factory designer who has spent most of the last few days at Tiananmen Square, spent this morning planning where the men in his organization should be placed.

Similar volunteer groups have sprung up all over the capital as angry residents form neighborhood teams that link up with others to protect the area from soldiers.

SPONTANEOUS TEAMS

Often these teams form spontaneously. In the predawn hours today in the southern suburbs of Beijing, 18 armed personnel carriers and 17 trucks holding about 850 policemen found their path impeded by a truck driver who parked his large vehicle right in front of them and then ran around the neighborhood to get the help of neighbors, witnesses said.

"I'll never come again," a lieutenant in the convoy was quoted as saying. "I'll never touch a hair of a student's head."

When troops parked three supply trucks near the Beijing Steel Institute, students drained the gas from the tanks and deflated the tires of the trucks.

This evening, people were out on the streets discussing the political state of affairs and waiting for the troops to come.

In the Xizhimen district, thousands of people crowded around the train station because they had heard that the soldiers may be forced to come in by train since they were having difficulty entering by truck or tank.

"We are waiting here," said a film worker, Wu Jianping, "because we hear there are tens of thousands of troops coming in by train."

TIDE TURNS TOWARD CHINESE HARD-LINER

LI PROCLAIMS CONTROL—ZHAO IS ISOLATED, OFFICIALS INDICATE

FRIDAY, MAY 26, 1989

BY NICHOLAS D. KRISTOF

BEIJING—Prime Minister Li Peng appeared on television today, declaring that his Government was in control, and there were more signs that at least for now he is gaining in the power struggle that is racking China.

In an indication that a military solution to the political crisis remains a possibility, Mr. Li also sent a letter to troops encircling Beijing, expressing the hope that "the troops will overcome the difficulties confronting them" and "successfully impose martial law."

Mr. Li's public appearance was the first by any of China's top leaders since the Prime Minister made a speech Saturday morning calling for a military crackdown on the nation's democracy movement. Demonstrators in Beijing and other cities have been holding large rallies calling for Mr. Li's ouster, and there were hints in official news reports earlier in the week that he might be in political trouble.

MORE ATTACKS ON LI'S RIVAL

Prime Minister Li's appearance today came amid further reports of attacks against the Communist Party leader, Zhao Ziyang, who favors conciliation with pro-democracy demonstrators.

The Foreign Ministry spokesman, Li Jinhua, said at a news conference this afternoon that Mr. Zhao was still General Secretary of the party and that there had been no changes in the nation's top leadership. But there seemed to be a growing feeling that changes were likely soon, and that Mr. Zhao might be a casualty.

At stake are not only the careers of two men, but also alternative visions of China. Mr. Li is a cautious technocrat who seems wary of moving too hastily toward economic and political liberalization. Mr. Zhao is more enthusiastic about experimenting with capitalist-style incentives and with a more open political system.

MEMORIES OF PAST INTRIGUES

While Beijing is full of rumors, all peddled as reliable, the Government has kept quiet. The extraordinary edginess of the nation, as it waits for its future to be decided, recalls the power struggles of Mao's later years, and the intrigues within the highest circles of the Government evoke comparison to imperial times, when ministers and eunuchs competed for the ear of the emperor in the Forbidden City.

There has been some modernization: party officials now have telephones. But officials say they dare not use the phones for fear they are tapped.

A working group of the Communist Party Central Committee met today to try to resolve the political crisis, a senior party official said, but it was not known what the outcome of the meeting was. The group included the governors and party secretaries of China's provinces and large cities, and it was expected to be asked to go along with criticisms of Mr. Zhao, the official said.

The official said that at another meeting a party group in the National People's Congress Standing Committee had decided that it was "premature" to call a meeting of the full Standing Committee. While such a decision is not legally binding, it was seen as an attempt to block a committee meeting that some members are trying to convene to revoke martial law.

The head of the National People's Congress, Wan Li, arrived in Shanghai this morning after cutting short a trip to the United States. Mr. Wan has been regarded by many students as a heroic figure destined to return and convene a meeting of the congress to end martial law and oust Mr. Li.

But instead he remained in Shanghai, ostensibly for medical treatment, while the rest of his delegation continued to Beijing. It was not clear why Mr. Wan, who almost certainly is not ill, stopped in Shanghai or when he would proceed to the capital.

In his television appearance tonight, Li Peng (pronounced lee pung) seemed relaxed and confident as he met three newly arrived ambassadors to Beijing. The opening segment of the evening news progam showed Mr. Li saying the troops called to Beijing had not yet reached the downtown area because they had been blocked by people who do not understand their purpose.

"Anyone with common sense can see that this is not because the troops are unable to enter the downtown area," Mr. Li said, "but because the Government is the people's government and the People's Liberation Army is the people's army."

'STABLE AND CAPABLE'

"The Chinese Government is stable and capable of fulfilling its responsibilities and of properly dealing with the current problems," he said.

Mr. Li said most of the demonstrators were young people who had good motives but did not understand "the truth of the matter." Mr. Li did not explain, but this could be read as an indication that he was encouraging the view that the "truth" was that Zhao Ziyang—pronounced jow (rhymes with now) zee-YUNG—was using the disturbances to try to seize power.

An ambassador who was present said in a telephone interview that Mr. Li did not mention Mr. Zhao by name or directly mention the power struggle. But in a clear jab at Mr. Zhao, the Prime Minister said, "The chief architect of China's reform and opening to the outside world is Comrade Deng Xiaoping and no one else."

In what appeared to be a stern warning to the United States and other countries, Mr. Li cautioned that foreign nations did not understand what was happening and should not rush to judgment.

"Foreign countries, especially those that maintain good relations with China, must not interfere in current events," Mr. Li said.

REPORTS OF MORE TROOPS

In a letter sent today to the troops, Mr. Li thanked them for restoring order in the capital. In fact, President Yang Shangkun ordered the troops into the capital on Saturday morning, apparently to suppress the pro-democracy demonstrations, but they were immediately blocked by ordinary citizens and so they still remain in the outskirts of Beijing.

There have been reports of more troops flooding into the area, as many as 300,000 of them, and it is not clear if the Government plans to send them into Beijing to suppress demonstrators. While unarmed citizens stopped the troops the last time, it seems clear that peaceful resistance would be less successful if the troops used tear gas or weapons to force their way into the city.

Major newspapers and television programs today carried a letter from the army headquarters asserting that the democracy movement had been manipulated by a small number of people and calling for a "grave national struggle" against them. The letter clearly endorsed a military crackdown.

There have been some unconfirmed reports of tension between different military units, some supporting Mr. Li and others supporting Mr. Zhao. In addition, the Beijing Garrison Command, which is believed to be sympathetic to Mr. Zhao, appears to be withholding food and other assistance to troops from other areas.

The Defense Minister, Qin Jiwei (pronounced chin jee-WAY), who has close ties to the Beijing forces, is also reported by diplomats to have been frozen out of military decision-making, perhaps because he was regarded as too close to Mr. Zhao and too reluctant to bring troops into the capital.

100,000 JOIN DEMONSTRATIONS

About 100,000 workers and students held new demonstrations in Beijing again today to demand Mr. Li's resignation, and the atmosphere in central Tiananmen Square seemed to be electric this evening. While the number of protesters was lower today than in some past days, this seemed to reflect weariness and lack of a particular event to respond to, rather than intimidation.

Many of the students occupying Tiananmen Square are from outside Beijing, and the Government issued an urgent circular tonight to stop more from coming. It ordered local officials to dissuade students from making the trip and especially to keep students from climbing on trains without tickets, as they have been doing in the last few weeks.

In a new challenge to the Government, an independent labor union announced its formation in the capital today. The group, calling itself the Workers Autonomous Association, set up a loudspeaker system in one corner of Tiananmen Square that it said was its headquarters, and its broadcasts promptly drew a large audience.

"Our old unions were welfare organizations," said Li Jinjin, a lawyer who is counsel to the new union. "But now we will create a union that is not a welfare organization but one concerned with workers' rights."

Mr. Li insisted that the new union was entirely legal, but it seemed likely that the authorities would take a dim view of its creation.

While the fate of Mr. Zhao remained unclear, a senior party official said today that Mr. Deng, China's senior leader, and other officials had turned against the party leader and that Mr. Zhao would probably soon be suspended or expelled from his post.

"There is no hope," the party official said. "It's all over."

The official described the Communist Party offices in the Zhongnanhai compound in the center of the city in virtually a state of civil war, with officials loyal to Mr. Zhao now being frozen out of all the news and decisions.

"Some of the Central Committee offices are treated like garbage now," he said.

This official and others said Mr. Deng had turned on Mr. Zhao, his longtime protégé, for two reasons.

First, they said, Mr. Deng has a deep apprehension of disorder, which he believes threatens to send China into chaos and frustrate its hopes of becoming an advanced nation in the next century.

Second, they said, Mr. Deng perceived correctly that Mr. Zhao was making his own bid for power. According to this account, Mr. Zhao upset Mr. Deng first on May 4 by making a conciliatory speech about student demonstrators without clearing the speech with Mr. Deng.

That speech conflicted with Mr. Deng's own hard-line position, but the last straw apparently came when Mr. Zhao disclosed in his meeting with Mikhail S. Gorbachev, the Soviet leader, that the Central Committee had formally voted to consult Mr. Deng on major issues.

For Mr. Zhao, the comment was his final power play—an attempt to go directly to the people by showing that the obstacle to negotiations was Mr. Deng, the man who always held the final say—and Mr. Deng promptly relieved him of his powers, though not of his title.

A small working committee on propaganda set up by Mr. Li, consisting of five close aides—Yuan Mu, He Dongchang, Zeng Jianhui, Wang Renzhi and Li Zhijian—has already accused Mr. Zhao of corruption and of being behind the student protests, in a meeting with editors in chief of major newspapers. The committee has also written an editorial, apparently critical of Mr. Zhao, that it has sent to People's Daily for publication sometime in the next few days.

In an effort to show widespread support for Mr. Li and his declaration of a crackdown, today's news programs reported that 27 of China's 30 provinces and seven of its eight military districts have sent letters or cables of support, along with other military organizations like the navy and air force.

Most of these letters have not been signed, however, and senior military officials from one unit whose letter has been published have denied writing the letter, Western diplomats in Beijing said. The military officials were quoted as saying the letter was simply fabricated to show military support.

TROOPS ATTACK AND CRUSH BEIJING PROTEST; THOUSANDS FIGHT BACK, SCORES ARE KILLED

SUNDAY, JUNE 4, 1989

BY NICHOLAS D. KRISTOF

BEIJING—Tens of thousands of Chinese troops retook the center of the capital early this morning from pro-democracy protesters, killing scores of students and workers and wounding hundreds more as they fired submachine guns at crowds of people who tried to resist.

Troops marched along the main roads surrounding central Tiananmen Square, sometimes firing in the air and sometimes firing directly at crowds of men and women who refused to move out of the way.

Early this morning, the troops finally cleared the square after first clearing the area around it. Several thousand students who had remained on the square throughout the shooting left peacefully, still waving the banners of their universities. Several armored personnel carriers ran over their tents and destroyed the encampment.

POLICE CASUALTIES REPORTED

The official news programs this morning reported that the People's Liberation Army had crushed a "counter-revolutionary rebellion" in the capital. They said that more than 1,000 police and troops had been injured and some killed, and that some civilians had been killed in clashes, but it did not give details.

The morning radio news program also reported that it would be "very difficult" to hold a meeting of the National People's Congress standing committee as scheduled. The committee, which had been scheduled to meet June 20, has the power to revoke martial law and oversee the Government, and many members of the panel are known to be deeply upset by the crackdown.

FEARS OF ARRESTS

The announcement suggested that Prime Minister Li Peng, who is backed by hard-liners in the Communist Party, was still on top in his power struggle for control of the Chinese leadership. The violent suppression of the student movement also suggested that for now, the hard-liners are firmly in control, and that those who favor conciliation, like party leader Zhao Ziyang, at least temporarily have little influence on policy.

It was too early to tell if the crackdown would be followed by arrests of student leaders, intellectuals who have been critical of the Party, or members of Mr. Zhao's faction. Blacklists have been widely rumored, and many people have been worried about the possibility of arrest.

Three hospitals reported receiving at least 68 corpses of civilians, and said many others had not yet been picked up from the scene. Four other hospitals also said they had received bodies of civilians, but declined to say how many.

[President Bush called for an end to the violence. "I deeply deplore the decision to use force against peaceful demonstrators," he said.]

Most of the dead had been shot, but some had been run over by armored personnel carriers that forced their way through barricades erected by local residents.

Changan Avenue, or the Avenue of Eternal Peace, Beijing's main east-west thoroughfare, echoed with screams this morning as young people carried the bodies of their friends away from the front lines. The dead or seriously wounded were heaped on the backs of bicycles or tricycle rickshaws and supported by friends who rushed through the crowds, sometimes sobbing as they ran.

The avenue was lit by the glow of several trucks and two armored personnel carriers that students and workers set afire, and bullets swooshed overhead or glanced off buildings. The air crackled almost constantly with gunfire and tear gas grenades.

'GENERAL STRIKE!'

"General strike!" people roared, in bitterness and outrage, as they ran from Tiananmen Square, which pro-democracy demonstrators had occupied for three weeks. "General Strike!"

While hundreds of thousands of people had turned out to the streets

Saturday and early today to show support for the democracy movement, it was not clear if the call for a general strike would be successful. The Government had been fearful that a crackdown on the movement would lead to strikes, but its willingness to shoot students suggested that it was also capable of putting considerable pressure on workers to stay on the job.

Students and workers tried to resist the crackdown, and destroyed at least 16 trucks and two armored personnel carriers. Scores of students and workers ran alongside the personnel carriers, hurling concrete blocks and wooden staves into the treads until they ground to a halt. They then threw firebombs at one until it caught fire, and set the other alight after first covering it with blankets soaked in gasoline.

The drivers escaped, but were beaten by students. A young American man, who could not be immediately identified, was also beaten by the crowd after he tried to intervene and protect one of the drivers.

MANY TROOPS REPORTED HURT

Clutching iron pipes and stones, groups of students periodically advanced toward the soldiers. Some threw bricks and firebombs at the lines of soldiers, apparently wounding many of them.

Many of those killed were throwing bricks at the soldiers, but others were simply watching passively or standing at barricades when soldiers fired directly at them.

Two groups of young people commandeered city buses to attack the troops. About 10 people were in each bus, and they held firebombs or sticks in their hands as they drove toward lines of armored personnel carriers and troops. Teen-age boys, with scarves wrapped around their mouths to protect themselves from tear gas, were behind the steering wheels and gunned the engines as they weaved around the debris to approach the troops.

The first bus was soon stopped by machine-gun fire, and only one person—a young man who jumped out of a back window and ran away—was seen getting out. Gunfire also stopped the second bus, and it quickly caught fire, perhaps by the firebomb of someone inside. No one appeared to escape.

CASUALTY FIGURES IN DOUBT

It was also impossible to determine how many civilians had been killed or injured. Beijing Fuxing Hospital, 3.3 miles to the west of

Tiananmen Square, reported more than 38 deaths and more than 100 wounded, and said that many more bodies had yet to be taken to its morgue. A doctor at the Beijing Union Medical College Hospital, two miles northeast of the square, reported 17 deaths. Beijing Tongren Hospital, one mile southeast of the square, reported 13 deaths and more than 100 critically wounded.

"As doctors, we often see deaths," said a doctor at the Tongren Hospital. "But we've never seen such a tragedy like this. Every room in the hospital is covered with blood. We are terribly short of blood, but citizens are lining up outside to give blood."

Five other hospitals also reported receiving bodies, but refused to say how many.

In addition, this reporter saw five people killed by gunfire and many more wounded on the east side of the square. Witnesses described at least six more people who had been run over by armored personnel carriers, and about 25 more who had been shot to death in the area. It was not known how many bodies remained on the square or how many people had been killed in other parts of the capital.

It was unclear whether the violence would mark the extinction of the seven-week-old democracy movement, or would prompt a new phase in the uprising, like a general strike. The violence in the capital ended a period of remarkable restraint by both sides, and seemed certain to arouse new bitterness and antagonism among both ordinary people and Communist Party officials for the Government of Prime Minister Li Peng.

'MAYBE WE'LL FAIL TODAY'

"Our Government is already done with," said a young worker who held a rock in his hand, as he gazed at the army forces across Tiananmen Square. "Nothing can show more clearly that it does not represent the people."

Another young man, an art student, was nearly incoherent with grief and anger as he watched the body of a student being carted away, his head blown away by bullets.

"Maybe we'll fail today," he said. "Maybe we'll fail tomorrow. But someday we'll succeed. It's a historical inevitability."

On Saturday the police had used tear gas and beat dozens of demonstrators near the Communist Party headquarters in Zhongnanhai, while soldiers and workers hurled bricks at each other behind the Great Hall of the People. Dozens of people were wounded, but exact numbers could not be confirmed.

It appeared to be the first use of tear gas ever in the Chinese capital, and the violence seemed to radicalize the crowds that filled Tiananmen Square and Changan Avenue in the center of the city. The clashes also appeared to contribute to the public bitterness against the Government of Prime Minister Li.

The violence on both sides seemed to mark a milestone in the democracy movement, and the streets in the center of the city were a kaleidoscope of scenes rarely if ever seen in the Chinese capital: furious crowds smashed and overturned army vehicles in front of Zhongnanhai, and then stoned the Great Hall of the People; grim-faced young soldiers clutching submachine guns tried to push their way through thick crowds of demonstrators near the Beijing train station; and the police charged a crowd near Zhongnanhai and used truncheons to beat men and women disabled by tear gas.

"In 1949, we welcomed the army into Beijing," said an old man on the Jianguomenwai bridge, referring to the crowds who hailed the arrival of Communist troops at the end of the Communist revolution. Then he waved toward a line of 50 army trucks that were blocked in a sea of more than 10,000 angry men and women, and added, "Now we're fighting to keep them out."

Most Chinese seemed convinced that the tanks and troops had been ordered into the city to crush the pro-democracy demonstrations once and for all. The immediate result of the first clashes was to revitalize the pro-democracy movement, which had been losing momentum over the last 10 days, and to erase the sense that life in the capital was returning to normal. But the use of tanks and guns came later, and it was not clear if they would succeed in extinguishing the movement or would lead to such measures as a general strike.

The tension was exacerbated by an extraordinary announcement on television Saturday night, ordering citizens to "stay at home to protect your lives." In particular, the announcement ordered people to stay off the streets and away from Tiananmen Square.

WARNINGS OF COMING CRACKDOWN

"The situation in Beijing at present is very serious," the Government warned in another urgent notice read on television. "A handful of ruffians are wantonly making rumors to instigate the masses to openly insult, denounce, beat and kidnap soldiers in the People's Liberation Army, to seize arms, surround and block Zhongnanhai, attack the Great Hall of the People, and attempt to gather together various forces. More serious riots can occur at any time."

There were some reports that the Communist Party's ruling Politburo had met Friday and given the Beijing municipality the authority to clear the square and end the protests. The People's Daily and the television news on Saturday took a hard line against the unrest, and the evening news warned that "armed police and troops have the right to use all means to dispose of troublemakers who act willfully to defy the law."

The clashes and enormous outpouring of support for the students were an unexpected turnaround for the democracy movement. Just a few days ago, the number of students occupying Tiananmen Square had dropped to a few thousand, and students seemed to be having difficulty mobilizing large numbers of citizens to take to the streets. The Government's strategy, of waiting for the students to become bored and go home, seemed to be leading to the possibility of a resolution to the difficulty.

CYCLISTS KILLED

Then a police van crashed into four bicyclists late Friday night, generating new outrage against the Government. One cyclist was killed instantly, and two died in the hospital Saturday, while the fourth seemed less seriously hurt.

Rumors were less meticulous about detail, and word spread early Saturday morning through the capital that four people had been killed by the police. Tens of thousands of people took to the streets to protest, and immediately found themselves confronting more than 2,000 unarmed troops who were marching toward Tiananmen Square.

The troops retreated, but that confrontation seemed to set the tone for the massive demonstrations later Saturday and early today.

IN THE STREETS, ANGUISH, FURY AND TEARS

SUNDAY, JUNE 4, 1989

BY SHERYL WUDUNN

BEIJING—As the crackle of automatic weapons filled the air today on the Avenue of Eternal Peace, tens of thousands of Beijing residents, even elderly men and women, rushed out to see what they could do to turn back the troops.

"The citizens have gone crazy," said a driver watching as a tank plowed its way down the main thoroughfare. "They throw themselves in front of the tank, and only when they see it won't stop, they scatter."

The driver himself was shaken by what he had seen: A tank had rammed into an army truck used as a barricade. As the truck turned over, it crushed a man to death. Elsewhere, he had seen three bloodied bodies lying in the street. Several soldiers still standing in their trucks were crying.

Students and workers threw beer bottles, gasoline bombs, lead pipes, whatever they could find, at the tanks and armored personnel trucks, which nevertheless continued rumbling down the avenue. One truck drove back and forth along the east side of Changan Avenue, as the Avenue of Eternal Peace is known in Chinese, and did not stop when people stood in its path.

Amazement had already turned to fear and defiance earlier in the evening as citizens saw the military convoys entering the city. Some troops from other provinces practically paraded their AK-47 rifles as they stood in their trucks, stranded by the human blockades that had formed around the trucks.

By dark, tensions had soared throughout the city. Hundreds of thousands of people were impelled outdoors by their disbelief and anger, yet brought back to their homes by fear of the violence. The sound of tanks whizzing by and reports of open firing fanned their fears.

"You beasts! You beasts!" shouted the people at the troops.

'WE HAVE TO OBEY ORDERS'

Around a convoy of about 45 military trucks in the eastern part of the city, people pushed and shoved their way to the troops, shouting and urging them to consider their role as fellow citizens. But the sympathy that had characterized the troops last week was gone; the soldiers seemed to have a certain resolve.

"Will you shoot at us if they order you to?" was a question asked by many of the people surrounding the truck. The soldiers gave weak assurances to the people that they would not fire, but they also admitted that they had to follow orders.

"We have to obey orders because we are soldiers," said one uniformed trooper who was driving a truck. "Otherwise we will be punished. In any case there's no way they will order us to shoot the people."

His platoon commander was firm. "We don't fear being beaten by you people," he said as he climbed out of the truck. "We just fear that our guns will be taken and then we will have chaos." Everywhere in the vicinity of the convoy was the sound of hissing, as people let out the air from the tires of as many trucks as they could.

"Why do you have guns?" shouted one man.

"A man is not a soldier without his gun, is he?" came the reply of a soldier carrying an AK-47 automatic rifle.

CITIZENS PLEAD WITH SOLDIERS

An old man took up the cause. "I tell you, there will be no good end for you if you follow your order loyally," he screamed as though his life depended upon it. "You have parents, you have brothers and sisters. You should not beat your fellow citizens under any circumstances."

The nearly crazed citizens were climbing onto the trucks, trying to intimidate the soldier. But everywhere in the vicinity, anger was mixed with horror as the people saw how the soldiers handled their rifles and watched as several tanks pulled up.

"Is this the way Li Peng shows how martial law protects the people?" said an old man sitting on a rail.

Another young man said, "When they shoot with real bullets, it will be doomsday." Only hours later did the troops open fire.

In the afternoon, the scene near the walled-in Communist Party compound, where about 30 tear-gas bombs were released, had been the first site of violence. But now that seemed tame. A 20-minute conflict between 300 to 400 riot policemen and hundreds of citizens seemed to have galvanized the citizens. They began to believe that the Government was willing to use force—rubber bullets, broken bricks, truncheons—against the people.

CHAOTIC SWIRL OF PEOPLE

"I couldn't keep my eyes open because of the dense tear gas," said Lu Baochun, a 26-year-old assistant engineer. "It was the troops that first used bricks and tiles to attack, and the citizens fought back."

Mr. Lu had rushed back out to the scene, a chaotic swirl of thousands of people darting back and forth inspecting broken bricks and glass and examining the white powder-like splotches on the street apparently from the tear gas.

"When I went into the house of a nearby citizen to wash my eyes with fresh water, I saw several children lying on their stomachs on a bed," said Mr. Lu, whose own face and neck were reddened from the gas. "They had wet towels covering their mouths, and an old woman was beside them weeping."

He was standing at the Communist Party headquarters shouting with rage now at the two-dozen military troops with long truncheons and green helmets, sweating in their heavy green uniforms under the pelting sun.

Some citizens gathered in small huddles around people they thought had been witnesses to the attack. Others crowded together discussing the event, many apprehensive about how far the Government would go.

"They are simply ruffians and bandits," said a young well-dressed woman who had gotten caught in the cross-fire of bricks and stones as she was on her way to the office. "They bit people just like mad dogs."

A Chinese journalist was trying to comfort her. "We are shocked," he said. "We thought that this kind of thing only happened during the reign of the corrupt Government of the Kuomintang. Yet this happened in our People's Republic. The troops and the police, they are supposed to be our brothers."

BEIJING DEATH TOLL AT LEAST 300; ARMY TIGHTENS CONTROL OF CITY BUT ANGRY RESISTANCE GOES ON

MONDAY, JUNE 5, 1989

BY NICHOLAS D. KRISTOF

BEIJING—Army units tightened their hold on the center of the Chinese capital on Sunday, moving in large convoys on some of the main thoroughfares and firing indiscriminately at crowds as outraged citizens continued to attack and burn army vehicles.

It was clear that at least 300 people had been killed since the troops first opened fire shortly after midnight on Sunday morning but the toll may be much higher. Word-of-mouth estimates continued to soar, some reaching far into the thousands. Outbreaks of firing continued today, as more convoys of troops moved through the city.

The bloodshed stunned Beijing and seemed to traumatize its citizens. Normal life halted as armored personnel carriers and troop trucks rumbled along debris-filled roads, with soldiers firing their automatic weapons in every direction. Smoke filled the sky as workers and students vented frustration and outrage by burning army vehicles wherever they found them separated from major convoys, in side streets or at intersections.

SQUARE IS SEALED OFF

The area around central Tiananmen Square was completely sealed by troops who periodically responded with bursts of automatic-weapons fire whenever crowds drew close to the square.

By ordering soldiers to fire on the unarmed crowds, the Chinese leadership has created an incident that almost surely will haunt the Government for years to come. It is believed here that after the bloodshed of this weekend, it will be incomparably more difficult to rule China.

Many fewer people than normal were in the streets Sunday and today, and some of them ended up in the hospitals or in the morgues. The number of casualties may never be known, because the Government has asked hospitals not to report any numbers on deaths or injuries. However, based on accounts pieced together from doctors at several hospitals, it seems that at least 200 died in the hospitals and that many other corpses were probably left in the hands of the military.

SAVING THE LIVING

"We had to concentrate on those who were still living," one doctor said today. "We had to leave behind most of those who already were dead."

When troops finally seized Tiananmen Square early Sunday morning, they allowed the student occupiers who held on to the center of the square for three weeks to leave and then sent tanks to run over the tents and makeshift encampment that demonstrators had set up. Unconfirmed reports rapidly spread that some students had remained in the tents and were crushed to death.

The troops sealed off Tiananmen Square and started a huge bonfire. Many Beijing residents drew the conclusion, again impossible to verify, that the soldiers cremated corpses to destroy the evidence.

A HIGHER ESTIMATE

The student organization that coordinated the long protests continued to function and announced today that 2,600 students were believed to have been killed. Several doctors said that, based on their discussions with ambulance drivers and colleagues who had been on Tiananmen Square, they estimated that at least 2,000 had died. But some of these estimates, based principally on antipathy for the Government, appeared to be high.

Soldiers also beat and bayonetted students and workers after daybreak on Sunday, witnesses said, usually after some provocation but sometimes entirely at random.

"I saw a young woman tell the soldiers that they are the people's army, and that they mustn't hurt the people," a young doctor said after returning from one clash Sunday. "Then the soldiers shot her, and ran up and bayonetted her. I ran away, so I couldn't tell if she lived or died."

News of the killings quickly spread to other parts of China, principally by radio reports from the Voice of America and the British Broadcasting Corporation.

Chinese-language broadcasts have been jammed recently, but not on all frequencies.

In Shanghai, some supporters of the democracy movement reacted to the killings in Beijing by going on strike, a diplomat there said in a telephone interview. However, few factories are open on Sundays, so the real test of a strike will come today, and many people doubt that a strike will be successful because of a lack of organization among workers.

STRIKE POSSIBILITY

In addition, Shanghai residents expressed protest by erecting barricades throughout the city to block traffic.

In northeastern China, small demonstrations to protest the killings in Beijing were held in Shenyang, Dalian and Changchun. However, in those areas there has not been much talk of a general strike, a diplomat said.

Huge convoys of scores of army vehicles, led by tanks, continued to roll through the main roads of Beijing this morning and early afternoon, skirting trucks that had been set on fire by civilians with molotov cocktails. Troops in the vehicles fired their submachine guns constantly, mostly in the air. However, some casualties were reported.

Troops still fired periodically when clusters of people gathered near the Beijing Hotel, and several people were reported killed and injured. Among them was a middle-aged Western man who was hit in the leg and stomach, according to a witness. He could not be immediately identified and his condition was not known.

In a sign that the troops' mission is not over, the television news today broadcast a letter from the army headquarters to the soldiers, congratulating them on their "everlasting historic exploits in defending our republic" and warning that "the struggle is a long and complicated one."

"Arriving at the scheduled positions and restoring order at the square is only the first elementary victory we have achieved," the letter added, without elaborating. "More difficult and challenging tasks remain before us."

China's television news on Sunday night showed the army knocking down a replica of the Statue of Liberty that students had put in place on the square. The broadcast hailed troops for "victoriously crushing this counterrevolutionary rebellion."

The broadcast did not mention civilian casualties, but said that three soldiers had been killed and two were missing.

In fact, one of the three, a man who was described as "beaten dead by ruffians on Jianguomen Bridge," had actually been run over by an armored personnel carrier.

The official news also indicated that people had destroyed 31 military trucks, 23 police cars, two armored personnel carriers and 31 buses. But those numbers seemed much too low, for everywhere in Beijing people reacted to the killings by torching vehicles and creating blockades. The troops only controlled a few major thoroughfares, and elsewhere citizens continued to control the streets.

One soldier who had shot a young child was overpowered by a large crowd in the Chongwenmen district early Sunday, and then hanged and burned as he dangled from a bridge. Troops later arrived at the scene and cut down his smoking corpse.

The Government issued an announcement calling for the return of weapons it said had been taken from the army, as well as demanding that "kidnapped" troops be returned. The announcement could be interpreted as preparing the way for an attack on several universities, on the ground of recovering stolen weapons.

Student leaders apparently have some submachine guns that were taken from soldiers or from supply trucks, but at least so far they have seemed more interested in displaying the weapons than in using them. Students at People's University also seized an armored personnel carrier this afternoon and drove it around their neighborhood, but there was no indication that they planned to use it against troops.

There was no announcement from the senior leader, Deng Xiaoping, Prime Minister Li Peng or other officials who presumably ordered the military attack on student demonstrators. Mr. Li is believed to be winning so far in a major power struggle with the Communist

Party General Secretary, Zhao Ziyang, who favors a more moderate line toward protesters.

Some accounts had Mr. Deng in poor health, and even in a hospital, but diplomats noted that such rumors invariably surface whenever the 84-year-old leader has been absent from view for a period of time. Mr. Deng has not appeared in public since he met the Soviet President, Mikhail S. Gorbachev, on May 16.

The demonstrations began after the death April 15 of a former Communist Party leader, Hu Yaobang, who was widely admired for his moderate policies. Until the weekend, both the Government and the demonstrators had been very restrained, but the army's use of violence seemed to radicalize many protesters.

Students at Beijing University were busy today making firebombs that they planned to hurl against troops whom they expected to assault the campus. Rumors of such an assault circulated throughout the day but by the early hours of Monday morning, none had taken place.

A STUNNED RESPONSE

Beijing residents seemed stunned by the violent attacks on the protesters for democracy, but unsure how to respond. While many students and young workers are militant and insist that they will win in the long run, older people already seem to have accepted defeat.

"The democracy movement is already finished," a Chinese journalist said despondently.

After the first attacks Sunday, calls for a general strike were heard from the outraged protesters. However, a physician said that there was little chance for a stoppage to succeed because the army would immediately force people to do their jobs on threat of death.

"We have no guns so we can't fight," the doctor said. "But after a few months, the movement will bubble up again."

A long drive through much of the capital on Sunday—on almost deserted streets filled with the twisted remains of barricades run over by tanks and armored personnel carriers—suggested how far the city must go to restore normal conditions. Smoke rises at major intersections from the carcasses of military trucks that have been turned over and set alight, and automatic-weapons fire is now part of Beijing's background noise.

The northern section of the second ring road was a tangle of debris from road blocks that tanks had pushed aside, as well as long buses that are arranged to block traffic. At every intersection, curls of smoke rose from burning trucks, and in some places when the air is still, the air is so acrid that it is quite uncomfortable.

It remains very difficult to find out what is happening in other parts of the capital. Telephone services are overloaded and unreliable, and so are the rumor networks. Indiscriminate firing by troops discourages people from staying on the main roads, and barricades make it difficult to take narrower routes.

No foreigners are known to have been killed in the recent shooting, but at least two suffered minor bullet wounds and several other foreigners have been beaten, usually for taking photographs. Two CBS News employees, Richard Roth, a correspondent, and Derek Williams, a cameraman, were released Sunday night after spending the entire day in detention.

SEVEN

DESTRUCTION ALONG THE FAULT LINE

1990 WINNER IN THE SPOT NEWS PHOTOGRAPHY CATEGORY

"For a distinguished example of spot news photography in black and white or color . . ."

The (Oakland) Tribune
Staff

Photographers for *The* (Oakland) *Tribune* fanned out over the path of destruction caused when the earth came unglued in the Bay Area. The rich photographic harvest is presented in the following gallery.

This is a story of peak performance. It is also about courage.

The devastating earthquake at 5:04 p.m. on October 17, 1989, found *Tribune* photographers scattered all over town. Some were at Candlestick Park in San Francisco. One was at Jack London Square in Oakland. One was on a freeway heading home. One was on his way back from giving a photography class. A couple were in *The Tribune* tower as it swayed like a cornstalk in the wind.

Our photo team rallied quickly. Phones to the paper were temporarily cut off. By instinct, the photographers zeroed in on the key trigger points, angled past police barriers, climbed atop buckling freeways, and, with little regard for their own safety, recorded the poignant and heroic dimensions of the disasters.

Roy H. Williams has a 40-year career and 35 awards notched in his shoulder strap. He was on a freeway heading home to Hayward when he felt the earth's terrible rattle. The police radio barked the news that the Cypress Freeway, a mile-long double-decker road in downtown Oakland, had collapsed.

He arrived to find a huge stretch of pancaked concrete as far as the eye could see. Within was a chain of inhabited rush-hour automobiles, crushed to the height of their license plates. Before Williams's unbelieving eyes, a man was being helped from the lower deck to safety. Williams began snapping. Then, a woman (the man's wife, it turned out) was ushered to the ground, both of them rescued by a courageous bystander.

Trembling, the couple embraced and stared back at the death tunnel they had miraculously escaped. Williams's lens fluttered.

Paul Miller has shot pictures around the world in his career. Rushing to the Cypress, he didn't know what to expect. Seeing the desolation, he began shooting at a machine-gun clip. There, at the foot of the crumpled concrete, a paramedic placed a hand tenderly on the forehead of a victim on a stretcher. Miller's photo captured a mix of chaos and compassion that marked the long night.

That night is seared in his memory as the saddest situation he ever covered. "It was hard to take pictures," he said later. "I was crying and trembling."

Reginald Pearman had the evening lab shift, which meant he would be developing pictures for the third game of the World Series. He was grabbing a bite at Oakland's Jack London Waterfront when the shaking began. Unsure of the scope of the temblor, Pearman began shooting whatever he saw.

Ultimately, his police radio alerted him to the scene at the Cypress, where, blocked by police lines, he used his long lens to get his shots. It was a fearsome experience. "I was afraid I'd have to climb to the top, and I'm afraid of heights," Pearman recalled. "I was going to do it if I had to, but I thought about my family, my kids. What if something happened to their dad?"

That sensitivity worked for Pearman days later when he captured the poignant anxiety of a woman resident, Lucy Reed, about to be evacuated, gazing through her window at the Cypress, which was in danger of collapsing.

Michael Macor arrived at the Cypress at 5:35 p.m., within a half hour of the quake. He could see people on the top level of the structure. He knew he'd have to get up there quickly, before police sealed it off. He found a concrete pillar, once a freeway support, now toppled into crude steps by which he mounted to the top. It was only later that he thought that the whole freeway could have caved in at any time. He spotted volunteers and paramedics hoisting a stretcher over the side. He raised his camera arm length over his head and started shooting. "I was mostly reacting," he said. "There was no way to set the stuff up. I was recording history as best I could."

That particular piece of history made the front pages of newspapers around the world the next morning.

Angela Pancrazio was at San Francisco's Candlestick Park preparing to cover the A's-Giants third Series game. The stadium rumbled as if "something was coming up from the ground to swallow us up," Pancrazio said.

She raced to her car and tried in vain to reach the paper by radio. Finally, a shaken editor answered and told her to go to the Marina District, a high-class residential area built on landfill along the Bay.

"It was an inferno," she remembers. "Buildings that were five or six stories were now one story. Very, very eerie."

Pancrazio spotted a team of firefighters pulling a woman from one of the buildings. She followed them toward the ambulance. "For an instant there was a break in the crowd surrounding her. I saw one of them look down and smile, and she smiled back. I was able to make a photograph of that brief moment."

Pancrazio captured a series of other brief moments, each packed with emotion.

Other photographers' experiences echoed these: Tom Duncan, on his way from teaching a photography class, borrowed a student's amateur camera and started snapping away; Matt Lee conned his way to a rooftop for a better vantage point; Pat Greenhouse captured the pathos of a homeless mother holding her infant son beneath a Red Cross sign; Gary Reyes snapped a fan at the ballpark holding up a homemade sign that read, "Wait until the Giants bat."

In the chaos of that first night and throughout the week, *The Tribune* was a clearinghouse for the national and world press. Graphics and photography director Tom Faupl coordinated the interaction between the photo lab and the rest of the news operation. Chief photographer Ron Riesterer and lab technician Steve Hotvedt filed photo requests that surged in from all over the world, developed and edited mountains of film, dispatched photographers and helped wire services get their pictures out.

"We have smaller quarters and fewer processing resources than most papers," says Riesterer. "But on that first night, 15 of the photos that went out on the AP wire were ours."

And, on that first night, *The Tribune* managed to get its computers and telephones back in working order, bring its work crews in, and get the paper with its prize-winning photos to all subscribers on time.

> —Leroy Aarons, Senior Vice President for News,
> and Tom Faupl, Photography Director
> *The* (Oakland) *Tribune*

By Roy H. Williams

Maedell Stafford is rescued from the lower deck of the Cypress Structure at West Grand Avenue. "John and Maedell Stafford were on the lower deck of the Cypress Freeway when the quake hit. Their car was crushed, but they had only minor injuries. I was in my car when the quake struck, and after hearing news reports, I headed for the collapsed freeway. When I arrived, John Stafford was being rescued and Maedell was clinging to the outer railing of the lower deck. When John was safely on the ground, she [Maedell] was helped to safety. After thanking their rescuers, the couple shared a hug."

By Paul Miller

Driver injured in the I—880 collapse is comforted while waiting for an ambulance to arrive. "Seeing the devastation of the Cypress Structure, I was glad to see the quick response of the paramedics, firefighters and police. I helped move power and water lines and tried to stay out of the way of emergency crews as they were doing the most important work of saving lives."

By Reginald Pearman

Lucy Reed looks out the window of her Cypress Gardens apartment before being evacuated. "It was Sunday, October 22, at the Cypress Structure, and I heard that the police were evacuating the Cypress residents as a safety precaution. I walked a 10- to 12-block circle to where the evacuation was taking place and met Lucy Reed."

By Michael Macor

A man is rescued from the upper deck of the I–880 Cypress Structure, where hundreds initially were believed to be trapped.

By Angela Pancrazio

Rescue workers pull a woman from the rubble of a damaged home in the San Francisco Marina District. "Just as I
was about to photograph the World Series, the quake
struck. After realizing its seriousness, I left Candlestick and
radioed *The Tribune*. I was sent to the inferno in the Marina
District. A crowd of firefighters was rescuing a woman from
a flattened building. I ran with them toward the ambulance.
There was a break in the crowd as one of the rescuers and
the woman exchanged smiles."

By Michael Macor

Emergency personnel and a passerby aid a victim injured when a 1½-mile stretch of the Nimitz Freeway collapsed. "After reaching the collapsed freeway, I made my way north, walked up an on-ramp and crossed to the other side. Walking between the two decks and across four lanes, I looked down the length of the freeway and saw medical personnel working on a victim. I moved in closer and lower to the ground to show the medical team as well as the destruction."

By Angela Pancrazio

A clock in the Alameda County Courthouse in Oakland stopped at the time of the earthquake. "The day after the earthquake, I was sent to the Alameda County Courthouse. The courtroom was a mess. Law books made the judges' quarters impassable. The California flag was across the court reporter's chair. Out of the corner of my eye I saw shards of glass and a clock on the floor. I read the time—it was a little past 5:04, the exact moment of the quake—and made the photograph."

By Angela Pancrazio

Dorothy Lee of Piedmont prays for earthquake victims at an Oakland memorial. "A week after the quake, community leaders, residents and rescue workers gathered at Taylor Methodist Church in West Oakland to mourn the dead. Dorothy Lee, a Piedmont resident, came to pray for those she didn't know who had been killed in the Cypress Structure. During the service she stretched her arms upward in prayer."

A badly damaged building in San Francisco's Marina District is propped up with lumber. "The October 17 quake found me in San Francisco without cameras and with very little gas in my car. Borrowing photo equipment from one of my San Francisco State students, I headed toward the black smoke rising from the Marina District. I first encountered this apartment building that had been thrown into the street, what was left of it being propped up by scraps of wood."

By Tom Duncan

By Tom Duncan

Firefighters are framed against a silhouette of flame as a five-alarm fire races through a block in the Marina District. "Beyond the destroyed apartments a massive fire that had consumed a quarter of the block was raging and was still burning strongly as night fell. Manning fire lines close to the blaze, volunteers outnumbered firefighters 10 to 1."

By Matthew Lee

Coroner's office workers remove a body from the top of the collapsed Cypress Structure. "When I arrived at the Cypress Structure, the entire block was lined with TV trucks. Police lines kept residents and onlookers separate from the media. I set up about a block away. The angle was low and pretty far away, so I scanned the skyline and spotted people on a roof. I explained to the owner of the building that I was from a local paper and he seemed to like me and allowed me on his roof. All I had to do was wait and shoot."

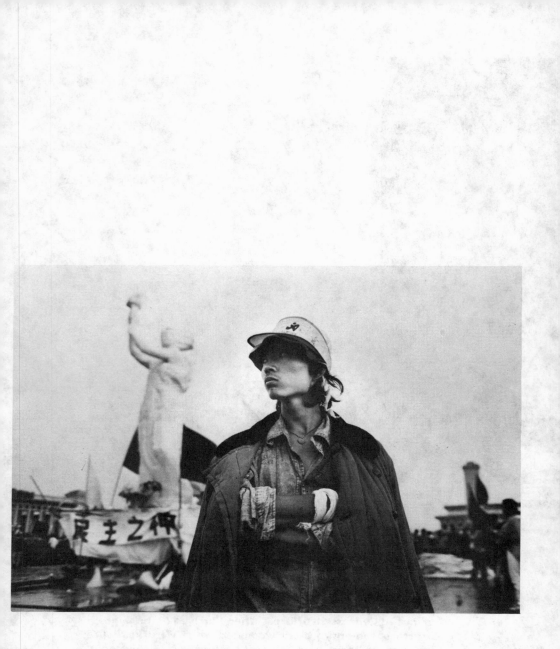

A student stands in Tiananmen Square near the students' version of the Statue of Liberty.

A student pleads with Chinese soldiers to listen to what the students were saying in their pro-democracy speeches. This picture was taken prior to the violence.

A student lies dead in Tiananmen Square on the night of the massacre.

On the night of the massacre, students carry the dead and wounded from the square.

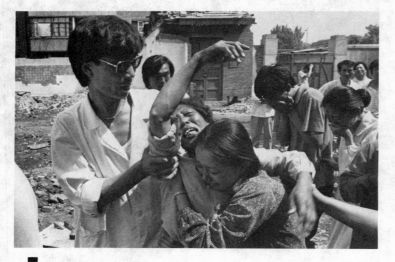

The mother of a slain student grieves at the knowledge that her child had been one of the victims of the Tiananmen Square violence.

On the day after the massacre, people roam through the street where burned-out military equipment can be seen.

Order is restored. This picture was taken a few days after the violence in the square and after the cleanup.

An East Berlin youth uses a sledgehammer on the Berlin Wall. This picture was taken within a few days of the wall opening.

In Prague, a young Czechoslovak rings a bell and shouts his support for pro-democracy sentiments during one of many rallies last fall.

Romanian women mourn the deaths of revolutionaries who were killed during the uprising that swept Nicolae Ceausescu from power. This picture was taken at Belu Cemetery in Bucharest, where 400 new graves were dug for those killed in the uprising.

Romanians ripped the Communist symbols from the middle of their national flags. Soldiers occupying Republic Square in Bucharest joined thousands in relishing their liberty, snatching up editions of a newly free press.

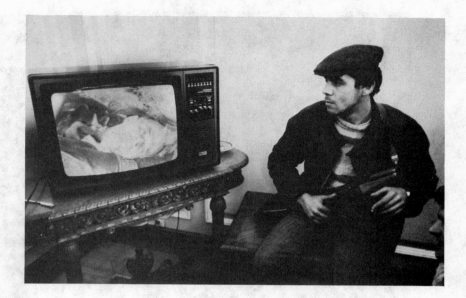

A Romanian militiaman sits in the office of former president Ceausescu at the Communist Party headquarters. The soldier is watching a film of Ceausescu's execution on the television.

As reports spread on Christmas Day that leader Nicolae Ceausescu had been executed, people in the streets celebrated. For a few, the news was overwhelmingly emotional.

EIGHT

FACES OF DEMOCRATIC CHANGE

1990 WINNER IN THE FEATURE PHOTOGRAPHY CATEGORY

"For a distinguished example of feature photography in black and white or color . . ."

Detroit Free Press
David C. Turnley

David C. Turnley of the *Detroit Free Press* followed the "winds of change" from China to East Germany, Czechoslovakia and Romania, and recorded each country's varied response to popular demands for democracy.

David C. Turnley's work in 1989 was a compelling chronicle of both the joy of freedom and the pain of the struggle to achieve it.

His camera captured the celebration in Berlin as citizens smashed the hated wall, and the waves of jubilation in Prague, where Czechs cheered the return of Alexander Dubcek.

But his most compelling work—accomplished under the most difficult and dangerous conditions—was in Beijing and Bucharest.

In Beijing, Turnley stood side-by-side with students on the June night that demonstrations for democracy became a tragedy of repression.

With his camera, he documented the deaths of scores of students in Tiananmen Square and stayed with them even as soldiers shot into the crowd with machine guns. When soldiers attacked him and stomped his cameras beneath their feet, he continued to file using borrowed equipment.

Turnley stayed in Beijing long after many Western photographers had left, working surreptitiously so as to avoid troops that had been ordered to shoot journalists on sight.

Turnley was one of the first photographers to get into Romania amid the chaotic overthrow of the Ceausescu regime. He recorded the violence as people fought in the streets of the capital and the grief of Romanians burying friends and relatives who had been killed in the government's brutal effort to crush the rebellion.

Turnley's ability to get great pictures under extraordinarily difficult circumstances is unique. We believe these photographs would be special even if they hadn't been taken under extreme conditions.

—Heath J. Meriwether, Executive Editor
Detroit Free Press

NINE

AMERICA'S ENDANGERED FARMLAND

1990 WINNER IN THE EDITORIAL WRITING CATEGORY

"For distinguished editorial writing, the test of excellence being clearness of style, moral purpose, sound reasoning, and power to influence public opinion in what the writer conceives to be the right direction . . ."

The Pottstown (Pa.) Mercury
Thomas J. Hylton

To Thomas J. Hylton, editorial writer for *The Pottstown Mercury,* the proposition was simple: Don't destroy the local environment to gain prosperity and in the process lose both. Readers apparently agreed and voted for a bond issue to protect farmlands from development.

If I have one natural talent useful in my profession, it is my ability to see the obvious—like the little boy in "The Emperor's New Clothes."

In 1986, when I was named *The Mercury*'s first full-time editorial writer, it was obvious to me—if to no one else—that the destruction of southeastern Pennsylvania's farmland was the biggest issue and would remain so for years to come.

The region is a paradox. With nearly half of Pennsylvania's residents, it is the most densely populated area of the state. But it also produces two-fifths of its agricultural output. And despite its manufacturing image, Pennsylvania's leading industry is agriculture.

Since the early 1980s, a tremendous economic boom in southeastern Pennsylvania has threatened its farms. Antiquated zoning laws, together with a public mind-set that suburban development is not only inevitable, but actually necessary for prosperity, have accelerated the process. Chester, Bucks and Montgomery counties, which surround Philadelphia and suburban Delaware County, lost a fifth of their farmland in just the five-year period from 1982 to 1987.

Nobody wanted to do anything about it. Nobody seemed to think there was anything to do about it.

I felt otherwise. To me, suburban sprawl is a modern evil—bland, inefficient, and environmentally destructive. In 1986, I visited England, and I was impressed by how carefully the English protect their countryside and encourage people to live in towns.

As a student of history, I know that towns are as old as civilized man, because they represent an eminently sensible way of life. I have lived in Pottstown for 19 years and find it far superior to the suburbs, where people are completely dependent on their cars.

Editorial writers can be more visionary than politicians. I therefore continually advocate that promoting city and town life is the only way we can accommodate a growing population without further degrading the planet. At the same time, there are very few problems Philadelphia has that wouldn't be solved by an influx of 500,000 middle-class residents.

That's a long-range goal, of course, and in the meantime I concentrate on more practical ways to protect open space.

Early in 1987, I discussed farmland preservation with Rep. Sam Morris, a Chester County farmer and chairman of the Agricultural Committee of the Pennsylvania House of Representatives. Sam is a pioneer in land preservation techniques and gave me several good ideas.

I talked with the directors of farmland preservation programs in Maryland and Massachusetts. I talked to the former county executive of Suffolk County, New York, which floated a $26 million bond in the 1970s to buy development rights from farmers.

The culmination of this research was a seven-day series of editorials in April 1987 on proven methods to preserve farmland and open space. Since then, I have written scores of editorials on the need to protect rural life and encourage development in and near existing towns.

Because new developments are the major item on most townships' agenda each month, I find no shortage of opportunities to repeat *The Mercury*'s land-use gospel.

Later in 1987, Rep. Morris persuaded Gov. Casey to sponsor a referendum on the November ballot asking state voters to approve a $100 million bond to buy development rights from farmers. The referendum passed handily.

Divided among 15 or 20 participating counties, however, $100 million didn't go very far. In November 1988, I recommended that Chester County float its own $50 million bond to protect farmland. It was enough to make a difference, but not so much as to be dismissed out of hand.

Two weeks later, the head of the Chester County Agricultural Development Council recommended a $100 million bond issue to save 50,000 acres of farmland by the year 2000. Suddenly, $50 million didn't seem so outrageous.

The Chester County commissioners appointed a task force on preserving open space. In June 1989 that body recommended a $50 million bond issue. The commissioners decided to place a non-binding referendum on the November 1989 ballot.

As far as I was concerned, this was the most important vote on the most important issue of my generation. If the referendum passed, it didn't necessarily mean farmland would be saved, but if it failed, it meant the eventual demise of agriculture in southeastern Pennsylvania.

I decided to write a week-long series of editorials summarizing everything I had written in the previous two years, packaged with accompanying cartoons. The series would be published two weeks before the election, enough time for a pro-farmland group, Chester County Citizens to Save Open Space, to photocopy the editorials and ensure their distribution to key leaders throughout the county. I believed the sheer volume of material, as well as the words, would help demonstrate the referendum's importance.

I asked my brother, Bill, a book editor for Rodale Press, to edit the series for me. He polished the text, tightened it, and suggested I conclude each editorial with a direct plea to the voter to save open space. "Don't ever let the reader forget why you're writing these editorials," he said.

On Election Day, we ran a brief Page One editorial urging voters to visit the polls and save the farms.

The referendum passed by an overwhelming 81 percent of the vote. The commissioners have vowed to follow the will of the people. They plan to issue the first bond in September.

The fight to protect farmland has only begun, however. I am continuing to write about two editorials a week on the need for regional efforts to protect open space and revitalize Philadelphia and nearby towns. The prestige of the award, I'm sure, has given new credence to our position.

A small-town paper gives writers far more freedom to pursue their own causes than a big-city paper where space is at a premium and decisions are made by committee. Because a small paper has limited resources, however, almost everything worthwhile has to be done on the journalist's own time. The paper gives you the forum, but it rarely can give you the time needed for major projects.

It took me years to become an editorial writer. I now write about 500 editorials a year, dummy every editorial page, and check off each one in the composing room. This has enabled me to earn the respect and confidence of the two publishers I've served, Sandy Schwartz and Joe Zlomek, and to keep the editorial page clearly and consistently focused on our objectives.

Since its inception in 1931, *The Mercury* has made local news its overwhelming priority. The editorial page is devoted almost exclusively to local and regional issues. People get wrapped up in national and international events they can't influence, and ignore the local issues that have far more impact on their lives. At *The Mercury,* we concentrate on things we can change.

—Thomas J. Hylton
The Pottstown (Pa.) *Mercury*

BOND ISSUE IS ESSENTIAL TO PROTECT CHESTER COUNTY'S FUTURE

MONDAY, OCTOBER 23, 1989

BY THOMAS J. HYLTON

The Chester County commissioners have placed a non-binding referendum on the November 7 ballot asking if $50 million in bonds should be issued during the next four years to preserve farmland and open space.

The Mercury wholeheartedly endorses the bond issue. We urge every resident to vote *yes* on the question, which the commissioners are using to gauge public support for conserving open space.

Each day this week, we will discuss a different aspect of the bond proposal. We hope to show why it is vitally important, not only to the future of Chester County, but to all of southeastern Pennsylvania.

The referendum is crucial for two reasons:

First, the bond money is desperately needed to preserve open land against the unprecedented tide of development that has been engulfing Chester County in the last three years.

Second, the referendum itself is a watershed event.

If the people vote overwhelmingly in favor of the bond issue, it will clearly signal a change in public attitude about the management of our most precious natural resource—our land.

It will give our elected officials confidence to explore changes in the tragically misguided land-use policies that have ravaged southeastern Pennsylvania for three decades.

If we act in time, perhaps the magnificent countryside—some of the richest farmland in the world—can be saved for future generations. Perhaps we will temper development, accommodating growth without needlessly diminishing open space.

But if the referendum fails—or passes only by a narrow margin— then Chester County will be doomed to the same congestion that strangles much of metropolitan America.

Although we are squarely in the center of the densely populated corridor between Washington and New York, the suburbanization of Chester County is not inevitable.

There are ways for the millions to live in harmony with farms and woodlands. The English, the Belgians, the Dutch, and the Germans have been doing it for years. We can adapt their methods to our needs; we need only the will to do so.

Time is of the essence. Political reality says it will take years to change Pennsylvania's antiquated land-development laws to allow Chester County to control its own destiny.

We don't have those years to wait. We must begin immediately to protect our most endangered land before it's too late.

The bond issue is the crucial first step.

RAMPANT DEVELOPMENT MAY DOOM CHESTER COUNTY'S FARM INDUSTRY

MONDAY, OCTOBER 23, 1989

BY THOMAS J. HYLTON

This is the last fall harvest for Horace Mowrer.

"It's no longer farming country," said Mowrer, an East Vincent Township supervisor. Development has taken over.

The first Mowrers came to Chester County from Germany in the 1740s. For six generations, the family tilled Chester County soil. Mowrer has worked his own 104-acre farm and planted several hundred acres rented from neighbors.

Mowrer's son, Michael, will continue the tradition. But not in Chester County. The Mowrers have bought two farms, of 348 acres and 202 acres, in central Pennsylvania.

"The main reason I'd say I'm looking forward to getting out of here is the traffic situation," Mowrer said. "With all the building going on, traffic's going to get heavier." The Mowrers considered another spot in Chester County, but "we couldn't afford anything in this area here."

The Mowrers are not alone. Between 1982 and 1987, Chester County lost 252 farms and 30,037 acres of farmland, not to mention thousands of acres of woodlands and other open space. All went to development.

Aside from a few rural counties with small populations, Chester County is the fastest-growing county in Pennsylvania. Lancaster and Bucks counties are close behind.

The urban megalopolis is surging down the Route 202 "high-tech" corridor from King of Prussia into the very heart of the county. Strip malls and luxury-class Levittowns are elbowing into the Brandywine Valley from Delaware. Development spatters from the new Route 422 expressway onto the northern townships.

Last year, 32,400 acres—an area one third the size of Philadelphia —was approved for commercial and residential development.

The Chester County Planning Commission expects the county's population to grow from 340,000 in 1987 to about 400,000 in the year 2000—an increase of 60,000 people in just 13 years. But the planning commission has underestimated growth in the past.

According to existing zoning laws, there is room for more than one million people in Chester County.

This proliferating growth is coming at the expense of Chester County's number one industry—agriculture. Last year, Chester County's 1,800 farms employed about 14,000 people, more than any other industry. With $290 million in cash receipts last year, Chester County ranks second in agricultural output among Pennsylvania's 67 counties, and 11th among the 1,566 counties east of the Mississippi River.

Not only does Chester County have soil that is as fertile as any in the world, a stable climate, and a solid agricultural support industry, it is conveniently adjacent to the fourth largest metropolitan marketplace in the United States.

Does it make sense to destroy the farms to accommodate suburban sprawl?

"Every year we lose 2 to 5 percent of our dairy farms," said Richard Breckbill, president of the Chester/Delaware County Farmers Association. Unless something is done, he said, "there're not going to be any left in 10 or 15 years."

Something *you* can do to ensure there will be farms in Chester County a decade from now is vote *yes* on the $50 million bond issue for farmland and open space preservation.

SPRAWLING GROWTH WILL ERODE CHESTER COUNTY'S QUALITY OF LIFE

TUESDAY, OCTOBER 24, 1989

BY THOMAS J. HYLTON

From the days of William Penn to those of Dwight D. Eisenhower, Chester County remained much the same. The rolling landscape dotted by stone farmhouses, the small villages, and the forested hills looked just as they did 300 years before.

In the late 1950s, America's love affair with the automobile introduced the first conspicuous development. The next two decades brought moderate but significant growth.

Now development is absolutely exploding.

Construction projects yielding 35,000 housing units have been proposed in just the last three years. At this rate, megalopolis will sprawl unchecked from border to border by the year 2000.

When Hough/Loew Associates built the first industrial park in Exton nine years ago, ". . . people were saying, 'Where's Exton?' " said developer Jack Loew. Today there are nine industrial parks in Exton, 40 in Chester County.

Three corridors of development are thrusting across Chester County from east to west: In the north is the Schuylkill River corridor from King of Prussia to Pottstown. In the center is the Route 202 corridor from King of Prussia to Coatesville via Exton. In the south is the Route 1 corridor from the Delaware state line to Lancaster County.

Exton promises to supplant King of Prussia as the center of commercial development in suburban Philadelphia. If all the office, retail, and light industrial buildings proposed are actually constructed, Exton will have as much commercial space as the rest of the county combined.

Immediately to the east of Exton, developer Willard Rouse III has proposed a 1,500-acre mixed-use community called Churchill. It will contain 2,000 residential units and 7 million square feet of office space —as much as currently exists in the entire King of Prussia area.

Churchill will introduce 5,000 more residents, 30,000 more workers, and 100,000 more daily car trips to a region that is already one of the most congested in southeastern Pennsylvania.

For more than a decade, Chester County officials have lobbied the state and federal governments to build the Exton bypass, a 5.6-mile limited access highway to connect Route 202 east of Exton with four-lane Route 30 west of Exton.

Major developers, including Rouse, are seeking a new interchange from the Pennsylvania Turnpike to Route 29 and the widening of Route 202.

But such new arteries inevitably generate more traffic.

"Most communities are trying to overcome the traffic crisis in ways that actually perpetuate it," said Douglas Porter of the Urban Land Institute in a recent transportation journal article. "Most projects being planned in fast-growing areas build in automobile dependency, which leads to congested highway arteries, which results in cries to reduce densities of development, which in turn creates greater dependency on automobiles."

Welcome to Chester County, where two-thirds of the households own at least two cars, and less than 4 percent of the people use public transportation.

Unless land-use policies are changed, the future of Chester County is as grim as the smog that covers Los Angeles, the city that pioneered sprawling development.

"In the Los Angeles area, we cannot, in our wildest dreams, solve the traffic problem," a California transportation planner recently told the *New York Times*. "No matter how many freeways we build, it's only going to get worse."

Things have deteriorated to the point where a *Los Angeles Times* poll this summer showed that half the residents have considered moving out within the past year.

Chester County's proliferating development presages major changes in its residents' way of life:

• Because the area will be far more crowded, people will spend more of their lives sitting in traffic on the way to work, school, or shopping.

• Air quality will diminish. Last year, Chester County failed to meet federal ozone standards for 17 days. It was the highest number on record and only four days fewer than Philadelphia.

To curb air pollution in southern California, draconian measures such as limiting the number of cars per household and banning gasoline-powered lawn mowers are being implemented. Similar restrictions may eventually be needed in Chester County.

• The county is headed for severe water problems, warns Bill Sellers of the Brandywine Conservancy. More than 60 percent of the county's population depends on groundwater, and soon more water will be taken from the ground than nature can replenish.

That's happening in New Jersey. In a 1986 study, the New Jersey Department of Environmental Protection concluded that because of overdevelopment, wells in southern New Jersey were being over-pumped. The Department ordered a 35-percent reduction in pumping and recommended that a reservoir, fed by the Delaware River, be built to increase the area's water supply.

In southeastern Pennsylvania, though supplies have not grown, water consumption has spurted from 5 billion to 7 billion gallons of water a day during the last decade.

This rise in consumption is caused more by changing lifestyles than population growth. Suburbanites use far more water than city dwellers because of their large lawns, pools, shrubs, and gardens. Meanwhile, Chester County has had five drought watches in the last eight years.

• Septic systems—used by 60 percent of the county's residents—are failing in many areas. For example, the Chester County Health Department has pressured all three Coventry townships to provide public sewers because hundreds of on-site systems are failing. But township officials are resisting, both because of the high costs and because of the accelerated growth they know sewers will bring.

Ironically, the major benefit growth is supposed to bring to Chester County—economic prosperity—may be a chimera. Long Island, one of the most overdeveloped regions of the Northeast, is experiencing a severe downturn in its economy after a decade of explosive growth.

The Island's two suburban counties have lost 5,000 jobs in the first six months of this year, consumer spending has dropped, the inventory of unsold homes has swollen and new residential construction has plummeted.

High housing prices, labor shortages, and congested highways—all the problems facing Chester County—have been blamed for the bust.

"We should replace our frantic effort to expand with a careful effort to improve," said John O'Brien, chairman of Grumman Corp., the Island's largest private employer. "We don't have to make (the economy) bigger anymore. We just have to make it better."

Quality of life has become a major consideration of any business looking to expand. It would be tragic if Chester County destroyed its environment to gain prosperity and ended up losing both.

One way to control growth in Chester County is to tie up development rights on key lands. That's what the proposed $50 million bond issue to preserve farmland and open space would enable the county to do. It's essential the bond issue be approved. Vote *yes* on Election Day.

SUBURBIA PAYS A HEAVY PRICE FOR NEGLECTING PHILADELPHIA

WEDNESDAY, OCTOBER 25, 1989

BY THOMAS J. HYLTON

Three Sundays ago, the Rev. Leon Sullivan, a prominent Philadelphia civil rights leader, told a congregation of fashionable Chestnut Hill churchgoers that suburbs must do more to help the inner city.

"If we do not . . . deal soon with the problems of the homeless, the drug-addicted, the unemployed, the poorly educated—and the helplessness and hopelessness that festers every day—within three years at least 30 American cities will explode," he said.

While the particulars of Sullivan's warning may be disputed, the grim reality of Philadelphia's poverty and hopelessness cannot be. And while Sullivan's sermon implied the suburbs don't care very much about Philadelphia's problems, the truth is worse than that.

We in suburbia tend to regard the people of Philadelphia as foreign foes rather than fellow citizens. Suburban legislators speak in terms of battling Philadelphia interests, getting what's rightfully ours, making sure Philadelphia doesn't get a dime more than it deserves.

Last year, state Rep. Sam Morris, D-Chester County, was vehemently attacked by his Republican opponent for being *too concerned* about Philadelphia.

But why shouldn't Morris be concerned about Philadelphia? The true citizen of a democracy is, as Isocrates said, one "who considers poverty among his fellow citizens as his own disgrace and measures his well-being not by trying to outdo each other, but by the absence of want among the whole people."

Moreover, by thumbing our noses at Philadelphia, we're undermining our own way of life.

The drugs and crime that breed in the city have spread to every suburban county. And while block after block of Philadelphia housing lies abandoned and crumbling, we're paving over the woods and farms to build sprawling new communities that are destined to collapse by their own inefficiency.

Consider the evolution of southeastern Pennsylvania.

In the days of Ben Franklin, Philadelphia was the pride of America and the second-largest English-speaking city in the world. The people of Philadelphia were as prosperous as any on earth.

During the next two centuries, Philadelphia's population multiplied 20 times over. A wonderful and efficient system for housing and employing 2 million people was developed. All the elements of daily life—houses, parks, schools, hospitals, places of work—were concentrated in a user-friendly community. A huge system of public transportation whisked people all over the city. People could walk to many of the places they wanted to go.

Those who worked in Philadelphia but lived in the nearby suburbs were also served by the system. They lived in little communities clustered around stations on the rail line that connected them to the city.

After World War II, the proliferation of cars and new fashions for living changed all that. As the middle class left for the suburbs, the standard of living declined for those left behind, which encouraged yet more people to leave. About 400,000 have abandoned the city since 1950, leaving a magnificent-but-declining infrastructure in the hands of people who seem unable to maintain it.

The sprawling suburbs that supplanted Philadelphia as the home of the middle class are not nearly as well planned as the original community. Sweeping new developments not only take away irreplaceable farmland, they require hugely expensive and wasteful expenditures of public resources.

Each new mile of electric and telephone line, water and sewer pipe, and highway serves fewer people than ever before. Police and ambulance services must cover vast areas. People find themselves unable to buy even a loaf of bread without driving a two-ton car to do it.

Meanwhile, the region's public transportation system, considered one of the best in the world, is falling apart. Louis Gambaccini, general manager of SEPTA, said the system needs $3.5 billion in maintenance over the next 10 years just to keep functioning.

SEPTA's system needs to change, as well. Since the suburbs have replaced the city as the region's major employer, most workers now commute from suburb to suburb rather than from suburb to city. And Philadelphia has thousands of residents who desperately need suburban jobs but have no way to get to them.

At bottom, the Philadelphia problem and the suburban problem is a land-use problem. We cannot continue to ignore the city, and we cannot continue to fuel new economic growth by stretching suburban sprawl over an ever-widening area.

It will take years to reverse the trends of two generations, but there is one step Chester County residents can take immediately to protect rural areas. The Chester County commissioners have placed a non-binding referendum on the Nov. 7 ballot asking if $50 million in bonds should be issued to preserve farmland and open space.

The funds will be used to purchase parks and to buy development rights from farmers, ensuring their land can only be used for agriculture.

Vote *yes* on the bond issue.

SOUTHEAST PENNSYLVANIA MUST MAKE BETTER USE OF ITS LAND

THURSDAY, OCTOBER 26, 1989

BY THOMAS J. HYLTON

Gov. Casey has declared October as recycling month to promote public awareness of the state's new recycling law. "We're doing more to control the amount of trash we generate than any other state in the nation," he said.

The new law is ambitious in scope. It requires people to recycle at least 25 percent of their trash within the next decade. Currently, only 1 percent is recycled.

While Pennsylvania is setting new standards in reusing manufactured goods, it remains shamefully extravagant with its most precious resource of all—its land.

When George Washington was president, there were 430,000 people living in Pennsylvania. Today, there are nearly 12 million of us, and each one puts far more strain on the environment than our ancestors.

We drive cars that spew pollutants into the air. We use heavily manufactured products and vast quantities of electricity. We create mounds of garbage. And everyone wants to live on a two-acre lot.

Unfortunately, while there are 25 times more Pennsylvanians than there were 200 years ago, there's not one square inch more of Pennsylvania.

We must begin to use Pennsylvania's land far more wisely than we do now.

Just as we needed a revolutionary recycling law to manage our trash, we need far-reaching changes in our development laws to conserve land.

To its great misfortune, Pennsylvania has an antiquated system of local government. Each of the state's 2,572 municipalities is supposed to regulate growth within its borders. However unwise it may seem, each is supposed to allow for every type of development—from malls to housing projects to heavy industry.

Land use is best regulated on a regional basis. It is impossible in a lone township like West Vincent, for example, to maintain farmland when highways and offices and housing are proliferating around it.

The issues are too overwhelming for small townships. Watching a group of part-time supervisors deal with a major developer is like watching the Polish cavalry fend off German tanks.

Counties, or a regional authority, must have the power to direct growth into some areas and forbid it in others. Prime agricultural areas must be held safe from development.

In Europe, this kind of thinking is second nature. If it wasn't, its open space would have vanished long ago.

At the end of World War II, the English strictly zoned every piece of land in the nation. A greenbelt was created around each city, which the government has maintained in a successful effort to keep the countryside intact. Thanks to that approach, a country smaller than Pennsylvania but with four times its population is world famous for its rural charm.

France and the Netherlands have instituted comprehensive national farmland preservation programs. Even though its population density is nearly four times that of Chester County, Holland's No. 1 industry is still agriculture.

Recently, several states have taken the first steps toward managing growth on a regional scale.

In 1986, the New Jersey Legislature created a State Planning Commission with a mandate to find a balanced way to guide development. The most densely populated state in the nation, New Jersey lost half its farmland between 1950 and 1985.

Early next year, the New Jersey Legislature is expected to adopt its first statewide land-use plan. It aims to curtail growth in more than half the state while encouraging the redevelopment of the cities and older suburbs.

In southeastern Pennsylvania, new development must be concentrated into compact areas. One- and two-acre residential zoning should be discouraged.

Philadelphia and outlying towns, linked together by rail, must be revived. Cities and towns were created because they make sense. For example, people can walk places. They can use public transportation to get to their jobs and back.

So far, Pennsylvania hasn't considered any sort of regional mechanism to manage growth. Except for the southeast, the state is eager for growth and sees little need for stricter land regulation.

Since 1978, the Pennsylvania Municipalities Planning Code has allowed neighboring municipalities to voluntarily create a regional zoning law, but only one such law—in lower Bucks County—has been drawn up. Because each municipality jealously guards its prerogatives, most state and local government officials have resigned themselves to accepting the status quo.

We believe major changes in land-use laws are imperative—especially in southeastern Pennsylvania.

We believe the public is far more receptive to change than the elected officials themselves. People will support strong measures to curb suburban sprawl, save farms and open space, protect the environment, and ensure a better life for our children. But the public needs a way to voice its will.

The Chester County $50 million bond referendum to save open space provides that instrument. If it passes by a wide margin, elected officials may be emboldened to consider strong steps to preserve Chester County from the onslaught of development. Lancaster, Berks, York and other agrarian counties may follow Chester County's lead.

In his annual message to Congress in 1862, Lincoln proposed a bold plan to end the war and free the slaves. The slave-holding states would order immediate emancipation, and the federal government would compensate each slave-owner for the loss of his property.

At the time, the plan was considered dangerously radical, but Lincoln defended it with these words:

"The dogmas of the quiet past are inadequate for the stormy present. The occasion is piled high with difficulty, and we must rise with the occasion. As our case is new, we must think anew, and act anew. We must disenthrall ourselves, and then we shall save our country."

Chester County has lost more land to development in the last three and a half years than it has in the previous 300. The present laws governing growth are inadequate for the stormy present. Stronger laws can and must be adopted.

But enlightened public attitudes will take years to translate into workable laws. Chester County doesn't have years to wait. In the short run, funds from the proposed bond issue are vital to preserve land until adequate land-use measures are adopted.

"A nation may be said to consist of its territory, its people, and its laws," Lincoln said. "The territory is the only part which is of certain durability. 'One generation passeth away, and another generation cometh, but the earth abideth forever.' "

If rural Chester County is to be preserved for future generations, the bond issue must be approved. We urge you to vote *yes* on Election Day.

BOND ISSUE WILL PRESERVE FARMLAND AND OPEN SPACE

FRIDAY, OCTOBER 27, 1989

BY THOMAS J. HYLTON

Last April, as concerns mounted over the loss of farms and woodlands, the Chester County commissioners appointed a task force to formulate a strategic plan for preserving environmental resources and open space.

Headed by then-Commissioner Irene Brooks, the task force comprised 12 county residents, including two developers, two farmers, a senior Commonwealth Court judge, a veterinarian, a county planner, and an oil company executive.

After two months' study, they recommended that the county issue $50 million in bonds over a four-year period to buy parks and protect farms.

Specifically, the money would be used as follows:

• $10 million to purchase development rights from farmers. If, for example, land is worth $5,000 for agriculture and $20,000 an acre for development, the county would pay the owner $15,000 an acre— in cash—for a deed restriction committing the land to agricultural uses *only*.

This not only protects farmland, it provides farmers with capital.

• $2 million to match state funds to acquire development rights from farmers. In 1987, Pennsylvania voters approved a $100 million bond issue to protect farms statewide. Chester County should receive at least $8 million through this program during the next 10 years, but it must match every four state dollars with one of its own.

• $18 million to buy and develop two county parks. Though no specific sites were recommended, the parks would be in the southern and eastern ends of the county and encompass 400 to 600 acres each.

• $2 million for the creation of greenways along streams and a series of trails connecting parks and other public facilities. The trails would use utility corridors and abandoned rail lines, supplemented by easements negotiated with private property owners.

- $11 million for municipal park and open space acquisition programs. These funds would be channeled to the county's 74 cities, townships and boroughs through a revolving loan fund and matching grants.
- $5 million for private conservation groups. Again, the funds would be disbursed through a revolving loan fund and outright grants, and would be used for purchases of farmland, stream corridors, and unique natural areas.
- $2.5 million for grants to historical organizations to protect historically significant sites.

By leveraging grants to municipalities and conservancies, the $50 million in county funds can be stretched to save $75 million worth of land, the task force suggests.

The bond proposal is not unprecedented. In the 1970s, Suffolk County in eastern Long Island spent $21 million to protect farmland from development. "In retrospect, it is about the only thing that made all the agony (of office) worthwhile," said former Suffolk County Executive John Klein, who pioneered the program.

Last year, voters in Broward County (Fort Lauderdale), Florida, approved a $75 million bond issue to preserve open space.

The Chester County commissioners have scheduled a public referendum for Nov. 7 on the proposed bond issue. "It's a true test of what the people want," said Dominic Marrone, commissioners' chairman. "If we want this program in place, each and every one of us must pay for it."

The task force proposes three bond issues, one in 1990 ($20 million), the second in 1991 ($15 million), the last in 1993 ($15 million). The bonds would be repaid with county property tax revenues.

For a residential property valued at $126,000 (the countywide average), the bond issues will add $12.80 to the tax bill the first year, rising to $32.43 in the fourth year, and then decreasing slightly until it is paid off in 16 years. The average residential county property tax is currently $227.

How much would it cost to wait? Last year, Lower Makefield Township in Bucks County became the first in Pennsylvania to propose a major bond issue to preserve dwindling open space.

Development is so widespread and Lower Makefield land values are so high that $45 million would preserve just 1,000 acres of farmland

and 500 acres of environmentally sensitive land along the Delaware River. The bond issue would have nearly doubled the average township tax bill from $390 the first year to $700 in the sixth year. Though the proposal was defeated, *45 percent* of the voters were prepared to shoulder the cost to preserve the open spaces.

Last November, Dr. Colin Johnstone, chairman of the Chester County Agricultural Development Council, said the county should set a goal of saving at least 50,000 acres of farmland by the year 2000.

"This is some of the richest farmland in the world," he said. "As a matter of public policy we cannot afford to squander our farmland on two-acre developments."

He said $100 million could save 20,000 acres of farmland, and expressed hope that another 30,000 acres could be saved through private efforts.

The $50 million bond proposal falls short of Dr. Johnstone's goal, and the bulk of the funds will go toward parks, rather than preserving productive farmland. But the bond issue proposal is addressing a range of concerns. It's designed to balance the need to preserve farmland with the need to provide parks people can actively enjoy.

Yet with its $50 million price tag, the proposal is the most ambitious county open space acquisition program in Pennsylvania.

The task force has done an admirable job. Its plan merits enthusiastic public support. Not only is the money necessary to protect open space, the referendum itself is essential to mandate land conservation. Vote *yes* on Nov. 7.

BENEFITS OF OPEN SPACE BOND ISSUE FAR OUTWEIGH ITS COST

SATURDAY, OCTOBER 28, 1989

BY THOMAS J. HYLTON

Chester County residents are being asked to vote *yes* on the upcoming open space referendum by a coalition of farmers, businessmen, and environmental groups.

Called Chester County Citizens to Save Open Space, the group is promoting the bond issue through mailings, phone banks, and endorsements.

Not everyone is enamoured of the proposal.

One newspaper recently editorialized that "the county has no business competing with developers to buy land."

Others have complained that taxpayers can't afford the price tag, that creating parks means removing valuable land from the tax rolls, that the bond issue may become a boondoggle, that it will primarily benefit the rich.

These objections deserve answers.

Governmental intrusion: The business of government, said Lincoln, is to do those things for the people which they cannot do for themselves.

Chester County is being developed so rapidly that only swift, forceful intervention can protect agriculture and preserve a balance of land uses.

While farmers would like to continue their operations, they face taxes that rise as property values soar, increased traffic, and an agricultural support system that is waning as the number of farms dwindles. At the same time, they are being offered fortunes for their land.

Most Chester County residents may want to preserve the county's rural flavor, but as individuals they cannot. Only through their county government can they unite to purchase development rights from farmers, thus preserving open space and keeping agriculture viable in Chester County.

The program is voluntary; no land will be condemned.

The cost: The bond issue will raise property taxes 3 mills ($32 for the average residential property) until it is paid off in 20 years. In return, it will preserve thousands of acres of open space and protect the county's agricultural base.

County real estate taxes are currently 23 mills. By contrast, the Owen J. Roberts School District levies a 166-mill real estate tax (in addition to an income tax), and its property tax will rise 9 mills in each of the next two years just to pay for the teachers' current contract. Little public objection has been voiced.

At 3 mills, the bond issue provides a major public benefit for a small price. It would be foolish to reject a program costing the average property owner but 60 cents a week when far more dramatic tax increases go unquestioned. The positive impact of this bond issue will far outweigh its cost.

The loss of taxable land: Preserving farmland and open space will help hold the line on taxes, not raise them. Whenever land is developed, it creates a demand for government services that costs money. Agriculture places a smaller demand on government than any other land use. North Coventry Township, which has the largest shopping mall in northern Chester County, charges a mercantile tax in addition to a 10-mill real estate tax. Neighboring South Coventry Township, which is mostly farmland, levies only a 2-mill property tax.

To finance a $10 million bond issue to expand one elementary school—an expansion made necessary because of increased development—the Owen J. Roberts School District recently raised taxes 10 mills.

And don't forget that the farmland protected from development, though reduced in taxable value, does remain on the tax rolls. The farm will continue to contribute to the county's economy and to its tax base.

Fear of a boondoggle: A legitimate concern wherever government is corrupt or incompetent, ask yourself if this is truly a legitimate concern in Chester County.

It is the responsibility of the minority party, the press, and conscientious citizens to be vigilant as the program is carried out. Considering the keen interest of many environmental and public service groups in open space, it seems unlikely fraud or waste would go undetected or unremedied for long.

Benefits for the rich: Cynics seem to believe the county will buy land or easements only from *wealthy* property owners. This is a classic red herring. The farmer who is land rich is usually also cash poor. Selling development rights is unlikely to make him rich, but it will commit him and his land to farming. Those farmers willing—and many are in fact anxious—to commit their land to agriculture deserve the program's top priority.

As far as parks are concerned, the primary consideration should be the suitability of the land, not the financial condition of the seller.

Two hundred years from now, it will make little difference *whose* land was purchased in Chester County. Future generations will only remember, with gratitude, that county government saved the forests and farms while they could be saved.

But Chester County will only do this if you, the voters, get out on Nov. 7 and vote *yes* on the bond issue referendum. It is in *your* best interest to do so.

THE LAND IS OURS TO PROTECT FOR OUR CHILDREN AND GRANDCHILDREN

SUNDAY, OCTOBER 29, 1989

BY THOMAS J. HYLTON

As this century dawned, Rotterdam was Europe's greatest harbor and one of its most ancient cities. It was a fairytale setting of clocktowers and gables, tile roofs and narrow cobblestone streets.

Then, on May 14, 1940, the German bombers came. In less than three hours, 600 years of history were wiped from the face of the earth.

The paving over of rural Chester County lacks the drama, the malevolence—and the shocking suddenness—of the blitzkrieg on Rotterdam.

The result will be the same.

The Dutch rebuilt Rotterdam, and it is a great and vibrant city. But its history is confined to the library, and we are all the lesser for it.

Chester County will always have Valley Forge, Longwood Gardens, the Wyeth museum, and other monuments to its magnificent past.

But when its gently rolling hills are covered with housing projects, and its quiet country roads are widened, straightened, and lined with convenience stores, then the heart and soul of Chester County will be gone forever.

The transformation of historic countryside into modern suburbia will come not at the hand of a madman, but through our own folly. Unfortunately, many people do not realize the scope of recent commercial and housing construction. They don't appreciate how close Chester County is to permanently losing its rural character.

A sense of identity, a pride in our home and surroundings, is what we need. Chester County is beautiful beyond compare. The rolling farmland, the wooded hillsides, the streams and wildlife are precious endowments we all enjoy. They have been handed down to us from generation to generation, and they are ours to protect for our children and grandchildren. We have a responsibility to be good stewards of our land.

It makes no difference how much farmland is left in the Midwest; or how many forests there are in the Appalachians. Chester County is our home.

The proposed $50 million bond issue on the Nov. 7 ballot will provide funds for open space and farmland preservation. The bond issue is indispensable to protect our heritage. The cost is small; measured in terms of generations, it is trivial.

Last fall, Mercury columnist Cindy Mitch described feelings that many of us share:

A few days ago I trekked up a hill in Chester County. You get to this hill by making your way through a tangle of branches and fallen tree limbs. Your feet slide off small rocks hidden by a thick carpet of moss and dead leaves. If you look up at just the right time, and are very, very quiet, you come eyeball to eyeball with a doe and her fawn. There is no sound except for the birds and the movements of small animals and the rhythm of your heart beating in unison with the life of the forest.

I sit up here on this hill and I think about the vegetable stand next to the Country Tavern. I think of how my grandmother used to chop firewood on cold winter days just a few yards down the hill from where I'm sitting. I think of my grandfather and how he once broke wild horses on this land.

I remember nights in this forest when the only illumination was the light streaming down from the moon and stars. I remember how we could stand out here alone and not be afraid in the darkness, because there was nothing out here that would hurt us. When I was a kid I knew the land would be good to me simply because I was good to the land. Back then, we had an unspoken pact with Mother Nature. In the ensuing years, we broke it.

There are people coming around here now destroying this land. They pay lip service to it. They claim they have a feel for the land and its history. They're lying.

When you have a feel for this land you don't destroy it to build houses and resorts and office complexes. When you have a feel for the land you nurture it. You respect it. You treat it the way you would like it to treat you.

And then you pick up a multi-colored leaf and some cool, damp moss and a dried twig or two. And you hold these things as close to your heart as you possibly can before they slip away from you.

The Chester County we love is slipping away from us. Once it's gone, it's gone. The $50 million bond issue is essential to protect what we have left. We urge all Chester County voters to go to the polls Nov. 7 and vote *yes* to save open space.

TEN

THE SOCIAL PROMISE OF ARCHITECTURE

1990 WINNER IN THE CRITICISM CATEGORY

"For distinguished criticism . . ."

San Francisco Chronicle
Allan Temko

Architecture critic Allan Temko of the *San Francisco Chronicle* urges a new vision for architects and citizens, reserving sharp words for the onslaught of thoughtless technological civilization as well as for "thorny" preservationists.

The articles by Allan Temko, the *Chronicle*'s architecture critic, are beautifully written even when openly combative.

Perhaps the most far-reaching of all of Temko's contributions to sound regional planning and civic vision are the two magnificent articles on San Francisco's Presidio. The two articles elevated public discussion of the future of the military base to a new level of understanding, and led to new planning policy by the National Park Service, which previously had been drifting toward piecemeal dismemberment of the Presidio.

Dealing with another problem of supreme importance to Californians—the necessity to prepare for the next major earthquake—Temko pointed out that "the Great Building Inspector in the Sky" had given us a superb lesson in environmental education.

His article made the lesson clear to ordinary readers without putting the slightest obstacle between their understanding and complex technical matters. Only a critic with a rare command of engineering practice and theory could have written that article on short notice—and with such grace and lucidity—just a few days after the quake.

As a historian who for many years taught at Berkeley and later at Stanford, Temko is also a learned and lively reviewer of books, museum exhibitions, TV programs, and other public events that fall beyond the usual range of architectural criticism.

His criticism—no matter what the topic—is always as insightful as it is gracefully written.

—The Editors
San Francisco Chronicle

THE SOCIAL ART OF ARCHITECTURE FOR POOR AND SICK

MONDAY, FEBRUARY 6, 1989

BY ALLAN TEMKO

Public-interest architecture for the poor and helpless is so rare nowadays that when a pro bono outfit such as Asian Neighborhood Design emerges, creating humane environments on low budgets, it deserves thanks from everyone who cares about the unfortunate.

Asian Neighborhood Design, known as A/N/D to do-gooders in San Francisco, does wonderful things not just for Asians, but for all kinds of people who need help.

Architecture is only one facet of A/N/D's four-part operation, which includes housing management, community counseling and job training for unskilled youths in a furniture shop where recently arrived Asian craftsmen teach.

All that is impressively managed by a staff headed by Maurice Lim Miller, who is of Mexican, Chinese and German descent, but it is the architecture and planning division of Asian Neighborhood Design that is most remarkable.

Financed principally by San Francisco's creative use of federal community block grants, which were cut severely during the Reagan years, the design group offers its services to other nonprofit organizations at fees they can afford, and sometimes for no money at all.

The four young architects on the staff are of Chinese and Japanese ancestry, although A/N/D welcomes collaborators of other ethnic background. Tom Jones, who was its director of design until he became Mayor Art Agnos' adviser on low-cost housing a few months ago, is conspicuously Anglo-Saxon, and studied at Cornell when its architecture school was one of the most elitist in the Ivy League.

ARCHITECTURE STUDENTS

A/N/D was started in the early 1970s as an outgrowth of the civil rights movement by Asian American architecture students at the

University of California at Berkeley, and the designers were volunteers. For the past 10 years, they have received modest salaries, but because young architects are notoriously underpaid, they make about as much as they would if they were beginning with big commercial firms.

They are expert in low-cost housing and particularly adept in transforming flea-bitten hotels into decent dwellings in the Tenderloin and other neighborhoods, as well as in Chinatown.

The group's best work to date has been the inspired renovation of the old Swiss-American Hotel, above the empty restaurant that used to be New Joe's, at 534 Broadway.

Lately it has branched out into two specialized buildings, each a mix of new and recycled construction: the Coming Home Hospice for dying AIDS patients at 115 Diamond Street in the Castro and the equally remarkable Women's Alcoholism Center at 2261 Bryant Street in the Inner Mission, which includes accommodations for children who usually would be separated from their mothers as they undergo a cure.

It is possible to pass these three unassertive buildings without realizing that they are serious works of architecture, and that is one of their virtues. Vulnerable people need calm and solace and whatever joy inexpensive surroundings can give them under very tight budgets.

The exterior of the Swiss-American Hotel, where Lenny Bruce fell out of a window in 1965, is virtually unchanged except for fresh paint. To discourage graffiti, the soft colors have been applied in imaginative patterns on the side wall along the steep rise of Romolo Alley. So far, the building has not been seriously defaced.

BRIGHT AND CHEERFUL

Inside, all is bright. The somber workingmen's hotel and sometime brothel, later a hippie flophouse, is cleaner, more cheerful and surely safer than at any time since it opened around 1910.

The 65 rental rooms have been completely redone and seem perfectly tailored to single elderly people or couples. Some accommodate families with small children and look cramped to visitors, but they are incomparably superior to the hives of single-room-occupancy units that infest the tenements of Chinatown. There also are four two-room units for sick residents who may require an overnight nurse or attendant.

But the vital point is that the rooms that once held such loneliness and despair have been transformed into a community. This is especially apparent in the handsomely equipped communal kitchens and dining areas, very neatly kept, and the new communal bathrooms—thoughtfully designed for the differing needs of women and men—that have replaced the dank old toilets.

Corridors have been rearranged and broadened in some stretches to provide sitting areas. Playful little pediments and moldings are really directional markers that help elderly people not to lose their way.

Skylights bring light to the center of the building. The old staircases have been saved, together with most of the old interior walls, and sensitively repainted in soft blues or rose, again in order that the elderly may know where they are. The wiring is all new, as is the plumbing. Smoke detectors and sprinklers have been installed. Most important, as in all of the group's projects, the building is carefully but unobtrusively managed.

REVITALIZED HOTEL

The revitalized hotel is only a few miles across the city from the hospice for AIDS patients, but the distance in human experience is immeasurable. This is America's first hospice for the dying on the British model, and hundreds more are needed across the country.

Nothing in their lives can prepare patients for the sorrow and suffering within this former convent, part of the Most Holy Redeemer Church complex along Diamond Street.

Yet if there is no hope in the hospice, there is almost limitless love expressed for the 15 patients, both by the attending staff and in the care the architects have lavished on the project.

The mutual regard between patients and staff is tactfully enhanced by the design. Little was done to the building, but the interior was reorganized and refurbished almost inch by inch to provide maximum comfort. The nuns' parlor is a discreet reception room. An outdoor deck now adjoins their dining room. The bedrooms, formerly shared by nuns, are now nearly filled with hospital beds, but there is no extensive medical treatment here, only an attempt to reduce the pain, and the spaces are dimly lit to protect the patients' eyes.

In these quiet spaces, the design group received much help from community volunteers, including some of the best artists and interior designers in town, who not only contributed some excellent paintings and furniture, but stained glass to complement existing glass in the lofty upstairs chapel, which is now a lounge room for this special community and its visitors.

Next door, in what had been a sacristy, a soundproofed room with heavily padded walls allows for the release of grief.

By contrast, the Women's Alcoholism Center is almost a place of joy. In this sunny Mission neighborhood of stalwart old Victorians, A/N/D found a three-story, bow-windowed house with an empty lot next door, which perfectly suited the expanded program of the Women's Alcoholic Center, created 10 years ago by a group of recovered alcoholics and community leaders as a facility for working-class women.

The problems of such women, defenseless and frequently battered, are radically different from those of their more affluent sisters. Without household help, and usually with no household at all, they cannot properly care for their children and invariably lose them, often forever, while they try to kick their habit.

TRADITIONAL DESIGN

The design problem was to transform the old house into a residence for the women and their children and to build a therapy and counseling facility and child-care center on the adjacent empty lot. The architectural problem was gracefully solved with a three-story wooden building that is not literally Victorian in detail, but so traditional in spirit and scale that it resembles old San Francisco row houses.

From the street, the adjacent buildings seem to be separate dwellings, each with a tall staircase. A gate between them leads to the child-care facility and outdoor play area in the rear, serving not only the children living here, but other children whose mothers, having partially recovered, are now outpatients of the center.

They are in much better shape than the women who are in the desperate early stages of a cure. The refurbished interiors of their residence, like the new offices next door, are unexceptional architecturally but are socially and psychologically of considerable interest.

CHILDREN AT HAND

Small groups of children, not necessarily brothers and sisters, share bedrooms separate from their mothers, who sleep two to a room. The women often cannot perform the simplest tasks for themselves or their offspring, but there are kitchens and dining areas where they can help prepare meals and, if they are able, eat with the children, who are looked after by the staff.

All this is far from luxurious, but somehow not Spartan. The architecture, unobtrusive to the casual visitor, is part of the healing process. As the women learn to nurture the children and to respect themselves, the significance of architecture as a social art becomes powerfully clear.

For helping to teach us that half-forgotten lesson in an age of private extravagance and public squalor, when the homeless sleep in doorways and these women might otherwise be on the streets, bravo to Asian Neighborhood Design.

HARMONY IN DESIGN

NATIVE AMERICAN ARCHITECTURE

BY PETER NABOKOV AND ROBERT EASTON
(OXFORD UNIVERSITY PRESS)

SUNDAY, FEBRUARY 26, 1989

Reviewed by Allan Temko

"In the beginning God gave to every people a cup, a cup of clay, and from this cup they drank their life," a Digger chief told the anthropologist Ruth Benedict more than half a century ago. "Now," he said, "our cup is broken."

Nothing can undo the shattering of a culture, but if a book can recapture the essence of a lost way of life—its everyday human meanings and supernatural myths expressed in buildings and spaces that have been largely destroyed or abandoned—it is this long-needed study of "Native American Architecture" by Peter Nabokov and Robert Easton.

Between them they have put together the shards and fragments of the great cup of life in a brilliant and beautiful book.

Not for 100 years has there been an attempt to describe the full range of Native American buildings, but it has been worth the wait for this magnificent survey that covers the breadth of the continent from the Arctic to northern Mexico.

Every type of Native American architecture is presented with flawless scholarship, including portable or impermanent structures such as Sioux tepees and Eskimo tents as well as tremendous Iroquois longhouses that lasted for years until they were so dirty and flea-infested that they were torn down and rebuilt on different sites.

But nothing could deprive tribal life of an innate nobility, based on harmony with the natural world, in which even modest buildings could carry intimations of the cosmos. Like all architecture, which is not merely construction but the art of building, this was environmental design of a high order, with innumerable regional variants possible within a universal respect for the Earth.

Nabokov and Easton, without fixing their focus on any single historic or prehistoric era—which would be impossible in a study of so many peoples—show the continuity that in most cases lasted for centuries. They bring the story down to the fragmented present, as TV antennas poke above the roofs of open-frame Seminole chickees in Florida that are still thatched with palmetto fronds, but which ride out hurricanes that topple modern buildings.

This gives the book a majestic scale, with profound lessons for our inchoate technological civilization. Sweeping through nine vast regions between the Atlantic and the Pacific, each larger than many countries in the rest of the world, Nabokov and Easton show the flexibility and grace of lightweight architecture that permitted seasonal movement of many different peoples, without scarring the earth.

The land, of course, played a profound structural role in this indigenous architecture, not only in pit houses and earthen lodges, but in monumental mounds and circles such as the perfect circular form at Newark in Ohio, 1,200 feet in diameter, which dates from 200 A.D., and still can be clearly seen from the air.

It was at least as great a technical achievement as the planned "street" and "plaza" pueblos of the Southwest, where adobe dwellings —stepped-back in pyramids at Taos, but flat in other settlements— frame public spaces where kiva and church each have honored emplacements, in some of the most striking examples of mixed cultures that followed the advent of the Europeans.

Yet everywhere across the continent, structural technologies were admirably fitted to local problems. A photograph of the hands of a Tipai man of Southern California in 1925, lashing together the branches of a grass house frame, shows a technique as appropriate to regional needs as the great plank houses of the Pacific Northwest.

To the immensity of their task in bringing such varied architecture to vibrant life—buildings are virtually constructed on their pages— the authors in a rare scholarly partnership have combined architectural history and anthropology, in its fullest meaning as the study of man.

Nabokov, a relation of the great novelist and a very good writer, is an anthropologist at the University of California in Berkeley. Easton, a professional architect who is an authority on vernacular buildings, has taught design at UCLA.

The authors do not say precisely how they shared the work, but the reader senses that this is an "interdisciplinary" collaboration in which each crossed easily into the other's terrain without insisting on academic niceties. They needed the widest view possible because, besides trying to re-create the past, they had to deal with the tragedy of Native Americans, who had drawn their strength and health from the natural world. After the land was taken and spoiled by strangers, the once-populous peoples were decimated and degraded.

There is no more heartbreaking illustration in the book than a photograph of 1,700 tepees within an imprisoning fence at Fort Snelling, Minn., in 1862, after troops crushed an uprising of the Santee Sioux against white settlers.

For of all the cruelties inflicted by white men on Native Americans, the most terrible—short of genocide itself—was the destruction of organic environments that were inseparable from wonderfully ingenious architecture. All was united by reverence for the natural world and its creatures. Thus the mighty woodworkers of the Northwest, creators of magnificent totem poles, also fronted plank houses with the carved and painted beaks of monstrous ravens, which opened to "swallow" visitors as they entered.

Always the authors show individual buildings in larger social groupings and towns, laid out in cosmic patterns, or according to tribal organization that determined community forms, for instance dividing settlements on two sides of streams, or centering ceremonial buildings on an axis between the sky world and the underworld. This is similar to ancient shrines elsewhere in the world that the historian of religion, Mircea Eliade, has shown were believed to have their original models in heaven.

Yet if a dwelling could be a divine revelation, it was also a rationally ordered center of family life. In many tribes, male and female children slept to either side of their father and mother, the youngest closest to the parents, the eldest farthest away, until they married and moved to dwellings of their own. Life continued in immemorial forms until the onslaught of mechanical civilization. Every aspect of construction bore the touch, the loving skill, of human beings. Women raised tepee poles. Saplings were bent to form structural frames for wigwams. Bark, grass and animal skins served for enclosure. Only in harsh and remote locations did such traditions survive, such as Arctic igloos and the pueblos and hogans of the arid Southwest. Otherwise, nearly everything perished.

The loss seemed irretrievable until this book. Much had been written about Native American folkways, but relatively little about buildings, except for specialized studies that stopped far short of the informed comparisons and penetrating insights of Nabokov and Easton. Before their grand synthesis, the history of more than 1,000 years of Native American design and construction was a vast, drifting miscellany of anthropological and archaeological research, often resting on conjecture.

A paucity of physical remains complicated the problem. Except for rebuilt wigwams, earth lodges, often over-repaired cliff dwellings and tourist-ridden pueblos—unable to escape the lifelessness of museum exhibits—few buildings survived to show Native American architecture in unadulterated condition. Everything was affected by the white man's technology and social outlook, even in the longhouses still being built and maintained on Iroquois reservations in upstate New York and southern Ontario.

Gone are the thousands upon thousands of tepees on the Great Plains, arranged in cosmic circles and adorned with astounding "spirit animals": Horse, Snake, Deer, Eagle and mythic Thunderbird. But their veracity persists in what may be the most moving passages of a book that has pieced together nearly every shred of evidence, including a stunning collection of early photographs and drawings.

These are complemented by fine color plates and diagrams made expressly for the book. Behind all this is a decade of research that included on-site visits to every part of the country and conversations with Native Americans who, against great odds, are loyal to their culture. Their words are as clear and bracing as the winds that once swept over the unspoiled land, from which they drew their health and strength.

CAREFUL PLANNING A MUST FOR S.F.'S PRESIDIO TREASURE

MONDAY, MAY 15, 1989

BY ALLAN TEMKO

Now that the Army must surrender the Presidio to the National Park Service, it is high time to make sure that this unique opportunity is not frittered away.

The stakes are enormous. The magnificent old base deserves an equally magnificent new use, not merely as a great historic park but as a cultural institution—perhaps a new kind of "World University" —that could be the key to San Francisco's whole future as a center of Pacific civilization.

If Nirvana, the final beatitude, had floated down on San Francisco from on high, it might bear some resemblance to the 1,440-acre forested preserve, which has the most spectacular natural open space in any large city in the world.

That the Presidio is also an architectural treasure, with the finest ensemble of U.S. Army buildings this side of West Point, only enhances its cultural value. Dating back to the 1850s, but largely from the late 19th and early 20th centuries, 400 buildings (out of a total of 900 on the base) contribute either historically or aesthetically, usually both, to the Presidio's status as a national landmark.

Under no circumstances should this heritage be trashed. Even if its uses were as fine as Fort Mason's, which we don't need two of, the Presidio must be much more than a recreation facility.

But therein lies the danger that this literally priceless resource will be chopped up and degraded by a strange mélange of opportunistic politicians, mid-brow bureaucrats, populist nuts, arts and crafts innocents and Fisherman's Wharf concessionaires. A stampede of would-be squatters is already under way.

Paradoxically, there is also a certain danger from environmentalist purists who think that the western edge of San Francisco, once barren dunes that have been almost entirely planted by man, are the wild Mendocino coast.

None of these piecemeal approaches will work. The Presidio must be seen whole, as an incomparable urban resource. All of its secondary uses must accord, or at least not conflict, with its highest possible use as a cultural and educational resource.

There is no question that it can be transformed into a university— not a conventional University of California campus, but as I shall show in detail tomorrow, an unprecedented, profoundly democratic international institution that all nations could share.

The stage is ready for this great intellectual drama.

Two campuslike spaces especially recall university environments: the immense parade ground of the Main Post, degraded to a blacktop parking lot but easy to restore as a splendid greensward, and the long grass centerpiece of Fort Winfield Scott, used by the soldiers for sports and seldom visited by tourists, although it is almost directly on axis with the Golden Gate Bridge and commands one of the most thrilling views of the great reddish web of steel.

Each of these "campuses," put to peaceful purpose, could in time become as famous as the central lawn of Jefferson's University of Virginia. Their strong surrounding architecture could easily accommodate many uses: the Main Post as the university proper, Fort Scott perhaps as a low-cost conference center—much needed in San Francisco—on the order of Asilomar, but in a setting of rare grandeur.

VARIETY OF RESOURCES

Even then, plenty of buildings and spaces would be left for a wonderful variety of other uses, from nature study to child care. The officers' and noncommissioned officers' clubs, with few alterations, can be opened to the public. So can the golf course and clubhouse, whose civilian membership is now snootily limited. The beautiful stables, disused for decades, could again be filled with horses, and bridle paths opened. The chapels already are virtually public places of worship.

The Park Service, of course, will require many facilities for its expanded operations. Down near Crissy Field, the nearly completed commissary, part of a $30 million Army construction program that never should have been undertaken in the 1980s, can become a visitors' reception center.

The military police station, guardhouses and fire station would be turned over to the Golden Gate National Recreation Area, just as warehouses, repair shops, garages and other utilitarian structures will be occupied by park crews. And a good chunk of the Presidio's ample housing should go to national park rangers, who make as little as $16,000 per year and are priced out of the local residential market.

Opportunities for museums abound. I'm not thinking of mass-cult shrines, such as a College Football Hall of Fame, which state Senator Quentin Kopp wants to move from the Ohio boondocks and dump on the Presidio, but of cultural institutions of very high order, which would be worthy neighbors of a university.

A "Smithsonian of the West," for instance, superseding the fascinating little Army museum installed in a 19th-century infirmary building, could be distributed in period structures as authentic as the airplane hangars near Crissy Field that date from pioneer days of Army aviation.

The Palace of Fine Arts, with its incomparable Exploratorium, presently cut off from the Presidio by major traffic arteries, should be brought into the whole cultural complex and perhaps allowed to expand within the Presidio's walls.

Added to this is a huge stock of housing—ranging from monumental barracks to family dwellings for officers and enlisted personnel, including fine houses for the brass—that are arranged in formal groups or meander along tree-shaded roads.

At the moment, it all seems up for grabs while our liberal congresswomen, Mesdames Boxer and Pelosi, foes of the battleship Missouri, fight to prolong the Army's departure, in a bitter irony, for the sake of a Pentagon payroll.

But sooner or later, the soldiers must go, and then the Presidio by law, thanks to the vision of our late Representative Phillip Burton, will become part of the "crown jewel" of the Golden Gate National Recreation Area.

VIEWS OF THE BAY

Topped by wind-swept ridges of pine, cypress and eucalyptus, opening to tremendous views of the sea, the bridge and the bay (that could still be improved by selective clearing and replanting), the

Presidio has turned out none the less handsomely for never having had a master plan.

Only after World War II, when some truly terrible buildings went up, replacing nice old ones, was the site desecrated by monstrosities such as Letterman Medical Center, a third "campus" that is seismically unsafe for hospital use and mars the whole view westward to the Presidio.

Letterman may be a candidate for demolition when the Golden Gate National Recreation Area takes over, but almost everything else seems worth saving, except the hideous Wherry housing, overlooking the ocean beaches, which was built in the 1960s and should be returned to nature forthwith.

How such decisions will be made is still a very open question. The planning process is just starting, and public hearings on the future of the Presidio will not begin until late June or July.

Some proposals, such as the rock-and-pop amphitheater that Bill Graham thinks would be dandy beside the Golden Gate, are bound to be outrageously inappropriate. Others may make sense, such as a museum commemorating the role of minorities in the armed forces as well as the history of American Indians, whose extermination was conducted partly by Presidio-based troops.

After sorting out popular notions of what the Presidio should be and conducting specialized studies of the site (for example, of 100-year-old trees that are cracking and dying and perhaps should be replaced in slightly different patterns), it will take a couple of years to complete a general plan and still longer for it to be approved.

Because the Presidio is in fact urban, locked into the very fabric of the city, it is seen by many worthies as a heaven-sent chance to relieve the housing crisis in general, and in particular to shelter the homeless, AIDS patients and crack addicts. Fast-buck artists would like to install motels and hotels (there goes Letterman Hospital and rehabbed barracks), fast-food joints and souvenir shops.

NOT FOR SALE

Fortunately, the Presidio cannot be sold off by panicked federal officials—right up to the environmentally incompetent Interior Secretary Manuel Lujan—who are scared stiff of assuming heavy new responsibilities when, after years of Reaganish parsimony, there is hardly enough money to run the Golden Gate National Recreation Area as it is. Parts of the Presidio may be legally leased, however, presumably on the Yosemite model, and Park Service officers, prodded by the press, have spoken of potential "revenue centers" that sound ominously like tourist traps.

May heaven forfend such an omen. For one thing, if a World University is created, there's no reason for hand-wringing over money, even if the Presidio, according to slightly overwrought present estimates, will actually cost $17 million annually to operate and maintain as a park once the Army departs.

That will probably occur in a phased withdrawal, lasting well into the 1990s, which gives time to the nation—for this is too important for local sages alone to decide—to consider the Presidio with the intelligence and respect it deserves.

AN IDEAL SETTING FOR A GLOBAL CENTER OF LEARNING

TUESDAY, MAY 16, 1989

BY ALLAN TEMKO

If the Presidio is transformed into an unprecedented "World University," it should be a supreme work of social art.

As the finest urban site in the world, grander and wilder than Golden Gate Park, twice the size of the central campus of the University of California at Berkeley, about as large as the main academic and research complexes at Stanford, it would be a unique emplacement for a new kind of university—one so audacious in concept and mood that the very term "university" may be misleading.

To create such an institution means nothing less than inventing the future.

At a time when sentimental, tourist-ridden San Francisco is being overpowered by Southern California—politically, economically and in some ways culturally, except for our top universities, civilized amenities and beautiful natural surroundings—the new Presidio in a single stroke could give us a head start into the 21st century.

Hardly anyone is thinking of the Presidio in such exalted terms. A notable exception is William Penn Mott Jr., former National Park Service director, who has just returned to the Bay Area to act as chief planning adviser at the Presidio. He wishes to make the Presidio the world's foremost center of ecological policy and research, dealing with global problems such as the "greenhouse effect" and acid rain.

The worldwide scale of his proposal is right, but surely its intellectual scope can be broadened and deepened to admit a limitless array of interests, from science and art to politics and law, that could bring nations together.

So far, the most promising proposal along these lines is for a "Pacific Rim University," advocated by Lewis H. Butler, a public-spirited lawyer and health-care expert who is also president of California Tomorrow, an organization occupied with social and physical planning of the state.

"Pacific studies," subsidized by Asian businesses, are a hot item in U.S. academic circles these days, but they were hardly thought of eight years ago (except in a few places like the rather sleepy East-West Center at the University of Hawaii) when Butler saw the possibility of a demilitarized Presidio as a home of innovative social policy for the diverse peoples of the Pacific Rim.

Inspired by his experience as a Peace Corps director, Butler was particularly eager to help Third World countries in Asia and Latin America. He did not foresee a conventional university, but a clearing-house of practical information provided by developed nations such as the United States and Japan, which would also exchange ideas of mutual interest to themselves.

But as military budgets rose by 15 percent each year during the 1980s, and the Army seemed ensconced in the Presidio forever, But-ler's program remained vague, with no specific reference to buildings and grounds, still less a detailed curriculum or financial strategy.

'SWORDS INTO PLOWSHARES'

Now it is alive again, but its real merit, to my thinking, is to open the still nobler prospect of a "World University," conceived as an unprecedented emblem of international understanding and peace.

That would be an all-time "swords into plowshares" scenario. What is more, it can come true. The venerable military post, enriched by more than 200 years of history under four different flags, could be transformed into a cultural complement of the United Nations at relatively little cost to American taxpayers.

If it were financed by many different nations—although the United States rightly should pay the largest share—the concept not only would be financially feasible but perfectly compatible with the Presi-dio's role as a unique historic park.

Precisely how such a program would be accommodated in the charming old Army buildings—and probably some handsome and tactful new buildings, too—is less important at this stage than the vision of an "open" university for which no overall model exists.

Taking advantage of the Presidio's tremendous stock of housing, it would be literally a democratic home for learning and creative imagination, which could be taught and practiced at many different levels. The very highest standards—say, those of Nobel Prizes—could co-exist with popular education of extraordinary vitality and richness. Subjects could be as vast and complex as the cleansing of the sea and the farming of its waters, or intercontinental monetary exchange, and as unassuming as folk arts, regional costume and indigenous cuisine.

The point is that nobody who wished to learn more about the world would be shut out, even for a day or two.

AMERICAN INSPIRATION

The prevailing spirit of the place could not help being profoundly American, in its boundless aspirations, historic architecture and the splendor of the natural surroundings, as well as the large numbers of American teachers, students and invited guests. Ordinary visitors, on holiday in California or bused over from San Leandro, could simply wander in for edification and delight.

Over time, an international ambience would set in. Every nation and region, from Chile to Alaska and New Zealand to Siberia, around the world to Sweden and Spain, Britain and Brazil, could maintain a distinct presence, each paying what it could toward the upkeep of buildings and grounds, with the more affluent—especially the United States and Japan—making up the difference for Pakistan or Bangladesh.

Admirably suited to this diverse array of cultures would be the Presidio's variety of housing. Majestic old barracks, for instance the great row of brick and wooden structures on the west side of the Main Parade Ground, would be made-to-order national pavilions, recalling the separate residential halls of the Cité Universitaire at Paris rather than the International Houses at Berkeley and Columbia. Closer still, perhaps, are the French, German, Italian and other "theme houses" at Stanford.

The best comparison would be to the foreign "houses" or colleges that were established in medieval universities in Europe. There was an English "nation" at Paris, and French representation at Oxford.

These national or ethnic establishments—Soviet Armenians, conceivably, could have their own—could also produce revenues. Each could have its own dining facility, possibly a deftly recycled mess hall, which logically might also be a delicious public restaurant (without altering the exteriors of historic buildings).

There could be shops, even multinational bazaars, in the former post exchange, for the sale of art and crafts, from peasant fabrics to haute couture, pottery to blown glass. Every nation might have its own art exhibitions and presentations of music, drama, dance and cinema, or demonstrations of science and technology.

Any kind of cultural overture, allowing a nation to reveal its best self to the world, would be welcome. Larger and wealthier countries could sponsor their own displays; others could share central facilities, such as the existing Presidio movie house, no great piece of architecture but inoffensive enough.

AN ARCHITECTURAL GEM

These suggestions are offered only to stimulate other proposals. A formidable counterargument could be made that the university should not be centered on the Main Parade Ground, as handsome as it will be when the ugly blacktop surface of the vast parking lot is returned to original greensward. Some suggest that Fort Winfield Scott—a less well-known architectural gem—is a made-to-order campus commanding an unmatched view of the Golden Gate Bridge.

Built between 1910 and 1912 as a coastal artillery headquarters, quite separate from the Main Post, the splendidly unified Mission Revival architecture of Fort Scott—considered as a group—deserves comparison with anything else of the period except for a few masterpieces like the Quad at Stanford.

Mostly barracks, the cream-colored buildings, capped by curving Spanish Revival parapets and red-tiled roofs, compose a half-circle—closer to a "J" than a "U"—around the southern end of a long grassy oval, used by the soldiers for sports. This inevitably recalls the central lawn of Jefferson's University of Virginia, which opened to a great perspective of the Blue Ridge before its end was filled in.

Here the view has lost none of its glory. Straight ahead, almost on axis, rise the burnt-orange towers of the bridge, their cables tautly strung, with the Marin headlands lifting beyond and Tamalpais in the distance. With fog swirling through the Gate, there is an incomparable sense of grandeur and peace.

Because of its isolation, I had thought of Fort Scott as a contemplative place, a retreat, beautifully suited to be a conference center on the order of Asilomar. On the slopes behind the main complex are some of the best officers' houses in the Presidio, stately Colonial Revival residences in brick, with white classical trim.

CENTER OF ACTION

The Main Post, on the other hand, is a center of action. The surrounding buildings—by no means of equal value, especially on the east and the north—can be carefully studied, with an eye to razing some of the more unsightly examples and improving views toward the bay and the dome of the Palace of Fine Arts.

Looking down toward the surf-pounded shoreline of Crissy Field, already ceded to the Golden Gate National Recreation Park, it is obvious that this maltreated expanse should be completely developed as a public recreation ground and not as a prissy little Japanese garden, totally out of scale with the breathtaking scene of water and distant hills, which the park agency for a time intended to perpetuate.

When all that is done, and the playing fields, picnic areas, tennis courts and especially the restricted Presidio golf course are made accessible to the public at large, the old Main Post can come into its own as an exciting cultural center. Classes could be held in dozens of buildings, including officers' housing that could provide comfortable lounges and seminar rooms. Sixth Army headquarters is already an administration building where deans could replace colonels tomorrow. Red-brick Pershing Hall, with its white pillared veranda and classical pediment, looks borrowed from a college campus.

The interiors of many of these buildings, much altered over the years, are not sacrosanct. Yet Park Service preservationists are notoriously thorny types. They are most intractable—in their silly bickering over redoing parts of Fort Mason, for instance—when they should be helping more gifted and creative designers from the private sector.

Certainly, the recycling of Presidio buildings should not be left to the Smokey-the-Bear bureaucracy alone.

And that brings up the planning process itself, well-intended by the park staff, headed by Douglas Nadeau, but no guarantee that we shall get a great concept for the Presidio from the local powers that be. When park superintendent Brian O'Neill submits the planning policy to the park's advisory commission later this month, it will predictably call for a "blue-ribbon committee," presumably composed of prominent Northern Californians who, I'd guess, will be fervent Sierra Clubbers.

BROADER PERSPECTIVES

There is no reason that these worthies alone should decide the fate of the Presidio, or that the decision should depend on the whims of the Bay Area alone. Even though the committee will consider ways to attract or create a "lead institution" such as a university or a "Smithsonian of the West," we need the finest minds in the nation—in the world—to conceive what such an institution could truly be.

Surely, it should not be merely another branch of the University of California (which, by the way, has already ruined sites of surpassing beauty at Santa Cruz and La Jolla, to say nothing of the environmental butchery of Parnassus Heights in San Francisco).

Still less, with no disrespect to a school I like, should San Francisco State University take over the Presidio as an expansion campus, as its president cheekily suggested.

Ultimately, many universities may have a role at the Presidio, but it is too precious for academic politicians to slice up and reduce to an ordinary place.

Not only superb architects and planners, but poets, writers, composers, artists, scientists and philosophers—professional designations matter less than unswerving devotion to excellence—must strive to make the new Presidio one of the creative triumphs of our age. The stakes are forever.

QUAKE SHOWS US HOW TO REBUILD

THURSDAY, OCTOBER 26, 1989

BY ALLAN TEMKO

If Caltrans hadn't been ponderously inefficient and understaffed, bereft of research funds and otherwise reduced almost to a maintenance agency by the parsimony of Jerry Brown and the belatedly furious George Deukmejian, a mile of Interstate 880 might not have been swatted down by an earthquake it should have ridden out easily.

Whatever else the quake was, it was superb environmental education. The Great Building Inspector in the sky simply shook the bay region, singling out structures that needed repairs or removal, and flattening a few on the spot.

But not a single well-built modern building was lost. There was no wholesale destruction of densely settled areas, no uncontrollable fire.

The lights went off long enough to scare people, but there was no panic.

Now that the rather fevered media coverage is calming down, the disaster can be seen in perspective as chiefly a failure of massive transportation structures and older, inadequate buildings on improper sites.

Some two-thirds of the 63 deaths occurred in the crumpling of I-880 in Oakland—an awesome display of the power of nature that is far more horrible in reality than it appears on television. By far the worst inconvenience was the failure of a single section of the Bay Bridge, which like the fallen and battered freeways had been expected to withstand shocks of much greater force.

The worst-hit dwellings, especially close to the rural epicenter, were either shacks or decent structures that out of carelessness or false economy were never bolted to their foundations. If such strengthening were made mandatory, under a statewide code that would include financial help for the needy, the whole problem of residential safety would be solved in a single thrifty stroke.

There are many other inexpensive measures, such as the installation of smoke detectors and easily shut off gas and electric lines, that the quake showed are urgently needed.

342

All this can be done. Still, the surprise of October 17 was a damned close thing, a terrifying rehearsal of the 8.0 Big One—a jolt that will be much stronger when it inexorably strikes.

REBUILDING THE REGION

The earthquake's painfully instructive warning offers a ready-made agenda, a profoundly new approach to reshaping the regional environment that should make this a safer and more beautiful place, starting with the demolition of the monstrous Embarcadero Freeway to transform the waterfront into the sunny and open place it once was.

What is needed now is a reconciliation with nature and respect for its laws. They have been violated in innumerable ways, but rarely more recklessly than in random filling of the bay, mercifully stopped by the Bay Conservation and Development Commission since the 1960s, but paid for this time around by enormous damage and deaths that mainly occurred on unreliable soil.

So now we should have a greening of our part of the world, where the improved environment would pay for itself in a generation.

Despite the wild cost estimates—billions picked out of the air— the clearing of the wreckage and a rational program of retrofitting structures that are worth saving should not be as expensive as generally thought. New structures will be required anyway as the region grows.

RATIONAL STRUCTURES

Within the great regional frame, individual buildings of every conceivable type are the places in which we live and work—and die, if they crumble when a big one strikes.

Here again the 7.1 quake has furnished us with a full-scale demonstration of how structures behave under enormous seismic stress—not as models on the great shaking table of the University of California's lab at Richmond, but as real buildings standing on sites that vary from solid rock to dredged-up mud.

The result is a lesson in structural dynamics that from the tops of the tallest office towers such as 345 California Street to the vast underground hall of Moscone Center strikingly vindicates principles of structural design developed in the past 20 or 30 years.

For although the quake flattened the Nimitz and unhooked a Bay

Bridge section, the downtown highrises simply swayed and held, quite unharmed, as if in deep harmony with natural law.

Put simply, the highrises fared well because they could move. The freeways failed because they were too stiff.

The tall frames were designed to resist heavy winds as well as quakes, and although the individual stories are rigid and soundly connected from floor to floor, the buildings are quite flexible as a whole.

The lithe frames, at once resilient and rigid, give under stress without yielding completely, vibrating in relatively long movements, much more slowly than the violent, rapid motion of the earth.

This is not at all a recommendation for tall buildings, but simply an illustration of a dynamic response to seismic forces.

The principle of movement applies to structures of an infinite variety of sizes and shapes, regardless of their architectural pretensions, which can be vulgarly at odds with good engineering.

They can be slabs such as the Bank of America world headquarters or slender towers such as McKesson, standard rectangular frames such as the Hartford, complete or partial vertical "tubes" such as Crocker Center, diagonally braced within their cores or with X's expressed on the outside (a bit fictitiously), as in the Alcoa Building. Even a form as crazy as the Transamerica Pyramid, which flicks like a whip in the wind, perversely makes a kind of structural sense, and did very well in the quake.

In a vivid phrase of our foremost structural engineer, Professor Emeritus T. Y. Lin of the University of California at Berkeley, the towers are designed "to roll with the seismic punches."

Engineers call this ability to move "ductility."

The counterpart of ductility is rigidity, the ability to resist.

Rigidity is as old as the history of construction and can be understood by pushing against a wall (you can feel ductility by bending a branch). Innumerable structures are designed almost entirely on the principle of rigid resistance, most notably nuclear power plants. Of course, no building can be a completely immovable object when it encounters the irresistible force of a major earthquake, but in theory a sufficiently rigid structure should move all in a piece with the earth.

The ill-fated Oakland freeway, a rigid structure, was not built nearly that well. Designed according to conventional wisdom 40 years ago, before the great advances in structural theory of the past quarter-century, the crude double-decker was locked in an outmoded concept and built on soggy soil close to the bay.

UNEXPECTED FALL

Whatever its faults of design and construction, 880 was not expected to fall in such a shake, and neither should a section of the great Bay Bridge. These structures were not expected to move so violently in a relatively moderate quake, and several engineers—including UC Berkeley Professor Ray Clough, a specialist in the new field of "soil-structural interactions"—have been led to wonder what effect the bottom of the bay, and even more the porous sand, gravel and watery earth beneath Cypress Street, may have had on the paths and acceleration of the earthquake waves.

Did the superstructure of the freeway, vibrating from the shock, go into "phase" with the earthquake's vibration period? If they went into resonance, like a tuning fork that starts to sound when another starts nearby, the destructive force of the earthquake could have been greatly amplified.

This happened in the recent Mexico City earthquake, where many structures (mostly on the unstable edge of an old lake bed) went into the same vibration period as the tremor.

If a similar resonance developed at Oakland, very large lateral forces would have been generated in the stiff decks, knocking the weak columns off their pins.

Whatever happened will not be clear until detailed records of earth movements and damage are collated by seismologists, geologists and engineers, who, with analytical methods largely unavailable a generation ago, must decipher a bewildering array of phenomena.

Some of these are not hard to figure out, but there is no clear pattern of structural behavior.

That wood-framed apartments collapsed on haphazardly filled land in the Marina is not startling to anyone who had considered their flimsy construction and unstable site. On the other hand, even worse buildings on better land in Chinatown and the Tenderloin were expected to go down, but didn't (although some have suffered internal injuries that make them candidates for demolition).

Then again, the precarious bayfront developments of Foster City and Watergate in Emeryville didn't vanish as expected in liquefied mud like Jell-O, but don't count on these places staying firm the next time.

If nature gives us a breather before the Big One, scientists' studies of this patchwork destruction will lead to profound changes in structural design and building techniques.

In the meantime, several unproved but promising technologies can be used immediately.

SHOCK ABSORBERS

The most interesting is "base isolation" of low or midsize buildings by placing shock absorbers between their foundations and the structural frame. The isolators take the brunt of the seismic shock. The only system installed so far in California (although there are several dozen in Japan) is in a new courthouse in San Bernardino County, designed by San Francisco engineer Alexander Tarics. It has performed well during several small quakes.

Another enterprising engineer, with his own version of seismic resisters, is Marc Caspe. He had the happy idea of urging the Pentagon —the only branch of the government with pots of money for technical experiments—to retrofit risky military hospitals, such as the vulnerable Oak Knoll in Oakland.

But ingenious mechanical devices cannot accomplish the enormous task ahead. Each earthquake, each site, each building is a separate problem, and only great principles of engineering can be applied to them all.

Lin, showing the way as he has in many fearless designs, such as the 300-foot arches of Moscone Center, which took the 7.1 quake with seemingly effortless grace, has in a more prosaic job—the 30-story Pacific Park Plaza apartments beside Interstate 80 in Emeryville— shown precisely the universal approach needed.

Architecturally this is an absolute dog of a building, but structurally it is a wonder, the highest ductile-frame concrete building in the West. Rising on deep pilings from the bay-shore mud, the supple tower flexes before the winds blowing in through the Gate, but when the quake hit, it responded to the impact—as Frank Lloyd Wright said a building should—like "a willow" in a breeze.

A mile away, unable to move, Interstate 880 and about 40 people died at the same moment.

ITALIAN LOOK FOR DELANCEY STREET COMPLEX

MASTERPIECE OF SOCIAL DESIGN

THURSDAY, DECEMBER 28, 1989

BY ALLAN TEMKO

Delancey Street has built up so much good will by turning former addicts and convicts into self-respecting citizens that no one except a heartless Modern architect could object to the Italian stage-set design of its nearly completed headquarters on the Embarcadero.

Architecturally, all that this Venetian or Roman street scene needs is a sound track of "O Sole Mio."

But this is camouflage. Delancey Street's architecture, beneath its traditional exterior, is a masterpiece of contemporary social design.

For Delancey Street's new home is far and away the greatest halfway house in the country, and probably the world. In plan, organization and mood, the design is tailored to suit perfectly a program that is unsurpassed in making winners out of losers.

Jauntily facing the outer world on the prime triangular site bounded by the Embarcadero, First Street and Brannan Street, the complex of three long buildings also looks inward—again, in a very Italian way —to a protected interior court.

Here, among an array of support facilities, workshops, meeting rooms and recreational spaces, with flats and dormitories upstairs, vulnerable people can work out problems within an extended "family" where almost everyone, from murderers to ex-prostitutes, has done time.

'OLD-FASHIONED' VALUES

It is a place where Mies van der Rohe and Le Corbusier, or even Frank Lloyd Wright, are not exactly household names. What counts in this unique community are "old-fashioned" values, in architecture and everything else, that all of its members can share.

What's more, they themselves have built their healing environment, performing about 95 percent of the work with little professional help from outside.

In a stunning example of "affirmative action," for many of them had few previous skills except bad ones, they have beautifully finished the stucco facades, replete with loggias and balconies, flower boxes and ornamental ironwork they have made with their own hands.

They have installed the fine copper flashings, gutters and drain pipes. The red-tiled stairs and terraces, like the overhanging tile roofs, are almost all theirs. They have cut and shaped the cedar corbels beneath the eaves.

Inside, the craftsmanship is equally impressive. Union plumbers and electricians provided instruction, but the bathrooms and kitchens, like flooring and fireplaces, were all put in by people who formerly built nothing at all. Stained-glass windows came from Delancey Street's glass shop.

Thanks to its own labor, plus some materials donated or marked down by the construction industry, Delancey Street got about $28 million worth of architecture for half that much in actual cash.

It also obtained a good deal on the land. The valuable site just south of the Bay Bridge, owned by the port but leased to the Redevelopment Agency, was slated for low-income housing in the midst of upscale residential developments. When ordinary below-market-rate housing proved unattractive to investors, Delancey Street stepped in, cajoled neighboring developers to accept its presence and negotiated an excellent 66-year lease for one of the best spots on the waterfront, opposite Pier 36.

Even so, the project could not have gone ahead if Bank of America, and especially its chairman, A. W. Clausen, had not opened a $10 million line of credit. Delancey Street is repaying the loan regularly through income from its various businesses and from sales of other properties from a ragtag collection of buildings that it now can vacate.

Although Delancey Street's current "family" of 500 men and

women won't start moving in from other places in the city until February or March, and the buildings won't be altogether finished before summer, it is already possible to see why this picturesque but very controlled environment should become a model for comparable institutions everywhere.

NONINSTITUTIONAL ARCHITECTURE

If such architecture is to succeed, it must be as noninstitutional as possible—the rationale of Delancey Street since it was opened in improvised premises by the late John Maher in 1971.

Since then it has expanded prodigiously and embarked on a number of profitable ventures. Without taking a cent in public money, although the private sector helps a lot, it has evolved into a partly self-sustaining community, with shops of its own that will occupy the arched Roman storefronts at street level.

The residents will live above the stores, recalling European immigrants who settled in the tenements of Delancey Street on the Lower East Side of Manhattan.

According to Mimi Silbert, the extraordinary UC Berkeley Ph.D. who founded Delancey Street with Maher and now heads the whole operation, the idea is that the residents, after a hard journey, are also newcomers to American life, with a full future before them.

And if she has not actually designed the buildings, it is her thinking that has enabled the architects Backen, Arrigoni & Ross, with Howard Backen as partner in charge, to create the remarkable communal image that suddenly rises up on the Embarcadero.

Seen from the north, the great rounded corner of the main building, where Brannan Street intersects the Embarcadero, is a welcoming presence—and will seem much more welcoming when the construction fence is removed and the ground-floor restaurant opens.

Directly above the public restaurant is Delancey Street's own lofty dining hall, reached not from the street but from the interior court. On the level above, the facade opens in a deep-set loggia, with theatrical balustrades sweeping around the curve of the building. It serves a spacious social room for the residents, with one of the finest views in the city of the Bay Bridge, but at the same time the loggia establishes a vigorous three-dimensionality that travels down the strongly modeled facades, extending 260 feet along Brannan and 390 feet along the Embarcadero.

Both of these long perspectives could seem arid, as the flat bare-bones Modern of the Bayside Village apartments in fact appears on the other side of Brannan Street. But the facades are saved from monotony by robust projections and indentations, slightly varied from one another, that give the effect of row housing.

These are not row houses at all. Behind the facades are ingenious living arrangements that vary from rudimentary shared flats for fresh arrivals to gracious apartments, overlooking the bay, for the most senior residents. It is a little like the old Ivy League system of assigning the worst rooms to freshmen and the best to seniors, as a reward for lasting the course.

The logic of the Delancey Street program is strikingly revealed when one enters the courtyard through the rather grand entrance on the Embarcadero or the corner gardens at the far end of the site. The center of the court is occupied by three key buildings: a central meeting hall for rap sessions and socials, a fitness center and swimming pool, and a cinema, equipped with the latest technology by Lucasfilms.

The perimeter of the court is lined by rows of "practice shops," which provide goods for Delancey Street residents and serve as training facilities. The rears of the practice stores meet the rears of the exterior stores, which serve the public.

CLEVER ARCHITECTURE

This is clever architecture. The question is whether it is to be considered fine architectural art.

Backen, Arrigoni & Ross are among the leading residential designers in the country. They are not only excellent Modernists, but also avowedly "eclectic" and "contextual" architects, and even "historicists" on occasion, not only for Delancey Street but at Jordan Winery, say, where they have unashamedly imitated a French château, in reinforced concrete.

Even though they have done tens of thousands of units of commercial housing, none of it, I'd say, comes close to Delancey Street's feeling of community in which people help each other to live with great kindness and candor.

Could the same be achieved, or surpassed, in richly organized Modern architecture—instead of ersatz Italian traditionalism? Neither Backen nor Delancey Street, confronted by overwhelming social realities, was willing to take the chance.

ELEVEN

MURRAY'S LAWS OF SPORTS (AND LIFE)

1990 WINNER IN THE COMMENTARY CATEGORY

"For distinguished commentary . . ."

Los Angeles Times
Jim Murray

Discarding conventional wisdom, Jim Murray, sports columnist for the *Los Angeles Times,* sprinkles a heavy dose of common sense into his columns, which are as much about humanity as they are about sports.

I don't think anybody sets out to win a Pulitzer Prize. If they do, they won't.

I don't think anyone ever shut the cover on his computer or typewriter and said, "There's a Pulitzer!" If he did, it ain't.

What any journalist, sportswriter or cityside, foreign, or weather correspondent tries to do is get through his ride every day. I remember once asking a friend of mine, a war hero who flew missions off a carrier in the South Pacific and had I don't know how many victories to his credit, how it felt to be a hero. "You don't want to be a hero—all you want is to get back from your ride," he told me.

I remember when I took over the job of sports columning. My old pal, Tex Maule, veteran of columning on several papers, offered a word of advice. "Every one doesn't have to be a Pulitzer," he counseled.

Well, maybe not. But every one has to be the best you can do at that time. You never want to let a column go until you have polished it to the best of your ability in the time allotted.

The first thing a newspaper story has to be is on time. Thereafter, columning gets to be a trick like twirling a rope. You have to get yourself in a rhythm. Sometimes you go into what golfers call "the Zone." This is ether country where the words seem to flow out of an unseen source. Unfortunately, these episodes do not come every edition. Sometimes they do not come at all or not for months at a time.

Writing is hard work. Even sportswriting. No one but a writer understands that.

Writing used to be simpler for a sportswriter when all he had to do was tell the public who won. And why. But the public already knows that now. You don't get to tell them who won the Super Bowl. Or even how. They just saw it on television—in slow motion and in minute detail.

You have to go down to the locker room and tell them the story behind the instant replay. Maybe you find the loser. The one who isn't going to Disneyland. Maybe you find the unsung hero. Maybe you find Joe Montana, too. But you better find something besides how many yards he gained, how many passes he completed.

I have always tried to entertain the reader first. Not to inform him. He can find the score and the details elsewhere. I think people read the sports page to be amused. Or bemused. I don't find this disenfranchises you from informing them. On the contrary, they will take information, and much more palatably, in the guise of fun and laughter.

Our object is the same as that of other journalists. It's to make the public read the paper.

The paper picks the Pulitzer candidates. It's no use to ask the author about his articles. He likes all his columns. He could no more reject one than he could keep one of his kids out of an air raid shelter.

The editors picked a few on deadline. The Kentucky Derby story, for example. Here was a race won by a 3-year-old brown colt who was by Halo and out of something, but to me it was a win for the plain folks. He was a kind of Hans Christian Andersen's ugly duckling. His own connections kept trying to auction him off. He was knock-kneed, wobbly, and I suggested his owners were afraid he was going to turn out to be a camel. This was hyperbole, or exaggeration for effect, but it gets the reader interested and that, after all, is what you have to do whether you're Ernest Hemingway or Matthew, Mark, Luke or John. That's what writing is all about.

I rely more heavily on observation than on adroit questioning. I can write better about Joe Montana if I study him from a distance when he doesn't know he's being studied than I can if I sit and grill him for an hour with these terribly penetrating questions they ask in the interview room, like "What does it *feel* like to win a Super Bowl, Joe?" I will never do a telephone interview with a subject I haven't met, because if I can't *see* a subject I feel like the proverbial blind man describing an elephant.

Finally, you have to take some wild risks occasionally. I plunged, foolhardily, into the touchy subject of why black athletes, in most cases, are superior to their white brothers. I'm no anthropologist, but I have covered sports and locker rooms long enough to know a simple truth: Show me a great athlete and I will show you a poor person—a person who comes from a long line of people who slept on dirt floors, chopped cotton or cane, baled hay or cleared stumps. You don't get heavyweight champs out of silk sheets. The closer you are to the soil, the better you are able to perform feats of strength or speed.

I didn't expect this simplistic view to go unchallenged, but you have to stick your neck out in this business. Besides, I knew I was right. You see, that goes with the territory, too. You have to be an opinionated jerk. If you're going to play it nice and safe, the reader will get bored. What's worse, you'll get bored.

—Jim Murray
Los Angeles Times

THEY WRAPPED THIS UP AND PUT A BO ON TOP

TUESDAY, JANUARY 3, 1989

BY JIM MURRAY

You want to check out your window today and see if the birds are chasing the cats? Maybe the rivers are running uphill? The sun still rising in the east, is it? Maybe Cuba will turn Republican.

Anything can happen now. The South can rise again.

Are you sitting down? You might want to take a nice stiff drink.

You may not want to tell it to just anybody—not everybody will believe you.

Bo Schembechler won a Rose Bowl Monday. Honest! Trust me. Would I lie about a thing like that?

There's hope for Harold Stassen yet, the Minnesota Vikings. Shoot, Custer might have got it right if he stuck to it long enough.

Pasadena had been to Coach Bo Schembechler what the iceberg was to the Titanic, the flood to Noah. He should have taken out an insurance policy against ever even hearing about the place. The first time he came there, he not only lost a football game, he almost lost his life. He had a heart attack, almost on the sidelines. He watched the game from an oxygen tent.

His health improved but his record didn't. One of the best football coaches who ever blew a whistle or screamed at a cornerback, Bo won 223 lifetime games, he was the scourge of the Big Ten. Nobody knew the X's and O's or the secrets of motivation better than Bo.

But, when he'd get to Pasadena, he kept ending up second. No one minded in the Midwest when he couldn't beat USC and UCLA. Happens to a lot of people. But when he couldn't beat Stanford, people began to think he was in the wrong business. Even Arizona State beat him. That was going too far.

They grumbled about him. He was too conservative. Maybe the game had passed him by. He belonged to the Flintstone era of football. And so on.

It was all hogwash. As the USC Trojans and the wise guys of Vegas found out in Rose Bowl LXXV Monday. When Bo has better players and his heart doesn't start missing, Bo Schembechler can play football with anybody. Anywhere.

The story of the 75th Rose Bowl game Monday is that Bo Schembechler knew he was going to win it. He took the measure of the USC team he was facing and he knew it wasn't one of those cat-quick, bury-you-at-the-line-of-scrimmage SCs you usually run into at Pasadena.

Bo is ordinarily one of the crankiest individuals you will ever see when he's behind in a ballgame. But, when he came into the locker room behind, 14–3, at the Rose Bowl Monday, he didn't throw any chairs, question the ancestry—and the courage—of his secondary. What Bo did was tell his players they should have been 17 points ahead, that they didn't have ahold of the Lombardi Packers here, or even the John Robinson Trojans. What they had here was a team that not only could be beat but could beat itself.

The Trojans could have broken the Schembechler losing streak all by themselves. In a sense they did. You have seldom seen—outside of a Kennedy family picnic on the White House lawn—so many slap tackles by one team in one game. The Trojans appeared to think the game was tag.

Michigan didn't put you in mind of the Olympic relay team. They were not blindingly fast. They were just a typically good, strong-arm, ball-control Big Ten team. They didn't dazzle you, they just put a chokehold on you.

Games, like wars, have turning points. The 1989 Rose Bowl game's came in the third quarter. With some 12:54 left to play in the period and the score SC 14, Michigan 3, the Michigan team had the ball on its own 42-yard line, first and 10.

Schembechler's team tried a reverse. A schoolyard play. The ball ended up in the hands of a back named John Kolesar, a hard-working flanker who never put anybody in mind of Lynn Swann. Kolesar was trapped by 3 Trojan tacklers some 20 to 25 yards behind the line of scrimmage.

It wasn't as if King Kong had the football. In the old sandlot, we used to have a technique called "pants-slapping" in which you just made a halfhearted swipe at some boulder-thighed guy going by. You hoped to fool your teammates into thinking this was a sincere, reckless effort.

The Trojans had this technique down pat Monday. John Kolesar, who should have been screwed into the ground on his own 15 or 20 got away from the thigh slaps for a gain all the way to the Trojan 42.

Shortly thereafter, Michigan drove in for their first touchdown. The elation was palpable. So was the realization that they might have the better football team this day.

SC made more mistakes than a politician who takes his secretary on a cruise, but the Trojans' biggest mistake was failure to finalize a tackle. Their flag-football endeavors turned the Michigan backfield into the new Four Horsemen. In a sense, Michigan and Bo didn't win the game so much as they inherited it. You might say, they Hoarded it. Thigh slaps didn't stop Leroy Hoard, a rugged specimen who rolled up 142 of his team's 208 rushing yards, much either. Hoard should be immobilized by a rope tie like a running steer.

SC's coach, Larry Smith's brow was as black as a Canadian Rockies cold front when he came into the interview room after the game. "We didn't block, we didn't tackle. We didn't wrap up. We let the ball-carriers out of jail all day. We were sloppy. We'd get to people and relax. You got to tackle 'em."

Bo Schembechler is now 2–7 in the Rose Bowl. Every Rose Bowl game he lost, he lost by a touchdown or less save for one 24–14 defeat by UCLA.

But, when you don't gang-tackle and play muscle football against a Schembechler team, you not only bury a jinx, you make him notice for the first time that Pasadena is not a place where people turn into wolves at midnight or sleep in coffins, but it is a place where they have snow-capped mountains, they parade flowers down the main street and the temperature is nice and the people dress for dinner and have good manners.

Bo might even grow to like it better than South Bend or Columbus. Now that he has turned it into a winner's circle. If he's going to start to win here every 9 years, he may start to like Disneyland and oranges. He'll want to come out every year if he gets teams that give you "Oh, excuse me!" tackles.

And pretty soon, the Pacific 10 will be flinching at Pasadena instead.

COUNT ON JOE TO MAKE MOST OF HIS HAND

MONDAY, JANUARY 23, 1989

BY JIM MURRAY

MIAMI—Well, as Yogi Berra said, It ain't over till it's over.

The Cincinnati Bengals had the XXIIIrd Super Bowl well in hand and almost in the bank Sunday. They had the lead, 16–13. They had the San Francisco 49ers on their own 8-yard line. There were 3 minutes and 20 seconds to play.

The only trouble was, Joe Montana had the football. And, he had Jerry Rice.

I don't know about you, but whenever I see Joe Montana standing in a huddle licking his fingers, if I were an opposing coach, I'd want to cover my eyes.

When Montana licks his hand like that, it's like John Wayne beginning to drawl, Cagney balling his fists and bouncing up and down on his heels. It's Wyatt Earp walking down Main Street at high noon with his hands just above the holsters.

You can't give Joe Montana the football and 3 minutes on the clock, even if there are 92 yards to go. It's like giving Nick the Greek the deal, Van Gogh a brush, or Gene Kelly something by Gershwin and rain. Caruso an aria with a high C in it.

What you're going to get is not so much a football game as a work of art.

You had a feeling of inevitability as Joe began to play his hand. "That is as good as you can play," the losing coach, Sam Wyche, was to say at the end of the recital.

Joe licked his fingers and went to work. He didn't get desperate, greedy. He just got deadly. Bogart in a room alone with a murderer.

The stats at the end of the game told the story in dull prose: "Montana passes to Craig for 8. Montana passes to Frank for 7 and first down. Montana passes to Rice for 7. Montana passes to Rice for 17 and first down. Montana passes to Rice for 27 and first down."

All of a sudden, the 49ers weren't on their 8, they were on Cincinnati's 18 and there were only 39 seconds left to play.

The world was thinking field goal and a tie game and overtime.

Joe Montana licked his fingers and thought, Bet it all. The Super Bowl was right there to be grabbed.

Joe Montana threw a pass to Roger Craig over the middle. Eight yards. Only 10 more to go. Montana threw a pass to end John Taylor. Touchdown.

You can't say Cincinnati lost the game. They really had very little to say about it. They were just flummoxed by a guy who has been doing this between finger licks for most of his life. Joe Montana was born to throw a football. As probably was an Otto Graham, John Unitas, Sammy Baugh. Just as Hogan was born to hit a golf ball, they were born to pass a football.

Montana, afterward, was probably less impressed with what he had done than anyone in the ballpark. Was this his greatest game, someone wanted to know? Joe looked at him as if he lost his mind. "No, not nearly," he said. "I did a whole bunch of dumb things I shouldn't have done. I threw some bad passes. I missed some open people."

Even the final drive did not make Joe choke up with sentimentality. He allowed carefully as how the drive the 49ers put together to defeat the Dallas Cowboys and put themselves in their first Super Bowl 7 years ago might have had a higher quotient of virtuosity.

Try telling that to the Cincinnati Bengals. "As good as you can play," repeated Sam Wyche.

Montana admitted he was not the cool frontier marshal he appeared to be. "When I overthrew Jerry Rice, I was hyperventilating so much that I was getting dizzy. I was trying to call time out and couldn't even get attention."

A man who plays his hand close to the vest to the last, Montana refused to divulge what the play that won the Super Bowl was.

"I hope nobody else does either," he grinned. "We may want to keep it in."

If there was a false note to the game-ending recital, it was that the winning touchdown was not scored by Jerry Rice.

There may be better football players than Jerry Rice but none more graceful. There may have been better games played than the one he played on Super Sunday 1989—but don't bet on it. There may be more graceful athletes than Jerry Rice on his way out for a long pass —but I've never seen one.

He practically took charge of Super Bowl XXIII, pulling down 215 yards worth of passes, some of them on balls that were so far over his head or out of his reach as to seem to be reachable only by phone.

Jerry Rice catches a football the way Baryshnikov dances Swan Lake. It's an art form, too, not an athletic contest. The football world hasn't seen anything exactly like this since Lynn Swann retired. Neither one of them ever seemed to just catch a football out in the open. They seemed to do it in the process of leaping a tall building or diving out of a low plane.

I thought the 49ers had blown the game in the second quarter. With the ball on Cincinnati's 2, fourth down and a yard to go, the 49ers elected to go for a field goal.

Now, the 49ers have this reputation of this wide-open, leather-slinging, go-for-the-jackpot football team. With the ball on the other guys' 2 and a yard to go for first down and 2 to go for touchdown, what you do when you go for 3 points instead of 7 is say, "I'll play these, I'll stand on 17." You fold the hand, so to speak. Join the ribbon clerks.

When you have a guy on the ropes, you don't clinch. I mean, do the Yankees bunt with 2 on or go for the big inning?

The Niners missed that field goal. It served them right.

But they got in character for the last drive. With their cool hand Joe at the controls, they swept right through field goal territory this time and bet the hand and won their third Super Bowl this decade. They are, certifiably, a dynasty.

Any team that has the other team right where it wants when it has the length of the field to drive and only 3 minutes to do it should last as long as the Hapsburgs. As long as Joe Montana stands there licking his fingers, they are the royal family of football today.

HE WAS AMERICA'S COACH, A COWBOY IN A WHITE HAT

FRIDAY, MARCH 3, 1989

BY JIM MURRAY

I always figured one of the reasons the Dallas Cowboys were "America's Team" was Tom Landry.

I mean, Tom was everything you expected a real cowboy to be. He had this prairie squint to his eyes like a guy looking for the dust clouds of an oncoming posse or the smoke signals of a redskin raid. He was laconic, fair, obliging, polite. Tom Landry never thought he was better than anyone else. He respected you. You had to respect him.

I always thought that no other coach could have brought Roger Staubach back into the game of football and brought him along till he became one of the three or four best quarterbacks ever to play the game.

I remember when Staubach showed up at Cowboy camp in Thousand Oaks, a crew-cut lieutenant j.g. who had just spent four years in the Navy, playing mostly what amounted to touch football. And he was trying to beat out some of the registered stars of the game in the quarterbacks, Don Meredith, Craig Morton and Jerry Rhome.

I don't think any other coach would have given Roger the fair shake he got from Landry. But Landry gave everybody a fair shake. That's what Tom Landry was all about.

I remember all those years when Landry's teams seemed to come up a yard short, a placekick shy. I particularly remember that standard TV shot. It showed Landry closing his eyes and looking heavenward in the standard aggrieved grimace of pain as he accepted yet another dose of undeserved misfortune.

It was the Landry Look. The my-God-there-goes-another-one look. But it was gone in an instant. Later, in the locker room, there would be Landry patiently and politely explaining what had happened without tantrums or outbursts or locked doors. Landrys took their medicine.

Tom Landry is a Christian. It's a term that has come under a certain public obloquy because of the actions of a lot of people who seem to mix up religion with hypocrisy. But Tom Landry was not one of those inquisitorial types.

I never saw him inflict his views on anyone else or even condemn anyone else for behavior that was antithetical to his. If he sometimes seemed like a parson running a wild animal act, he did it with dignity.

When one of his players, frustrated because Landry wouldn't brawl in public print with him, called him "a plastic man," Landry just grinned. And kept going to church.

On the field, he was so unflappable, you would have thought he didn't care. The expression never changed. You couldn't tell by looking at Tom Landry whether he was behind or ahead, whether he was holding three aces or a busted straight.

He always wore the matching clothes of the middle-class office worker who got two pair of pants with the jacket. I remember a Texas journalist once spotting him in the distance and saying, "It's either Tom Landry or an FBI agent."

He wore felt hats long after they were fashionable and sometimes they had little brooms or feathers in them. Comedian Don Rickles once cracked, "There's 80,000 people in the stands and they're going crazy, the game is in an uproar and there's Landry trying to square his hat!"

But that was Landry, too. He didn't show up in sneakers or running shoes—or jeans and a T-shirt with a picture of Schubert on it. Where Tom came from, the gentry dressed with care and the collar was starched or buttoned down and the necktie matched the socks.

He was meticulous. He always looked as if he had just taken a shower. Landry's eyes were never bloodshot and neither was his mind.

His teams had a dash and style to them that the public liked. They didn't out-muscle you, they outwitted you. They were fun to watch. They brought in things such as the "Hail Mary" pass and the "flex" defense—bend but don't break.

It was not that Tom couldn't recognize a great football player from a car window. He could. But he wanted to get a Cowboy-type player, not just another troglodyte with a 20-inch neck.

Landry's teams were in five Super Bowls. They won two, and lost the others by a total of 11 points.

Class is an overworked word. Landry had more than class. He had integrity. He cared about his players. It just wasn't his nature to gurgle over them. Vince Lombardi used to show his players he cared by yelling at them. Landry wasn't a yeller. The part of the Rio Grande Valley he came from, only the dogs made noise.

But despite the stoic exterior, I always felt there was a warmth about Tom Landry. His attitude always reminded me of that French general who once said: "There is no use getting angry and raging at facts. It is a matter of indifference to them."

The Cowboys were Landry's team, his creation. No one else ever had them. He must have felt about them the way Rodin felt about his sculptures. They kicked this man out into the street in Dallas the other day. Some man who made his money in commerce has bought himself Tom Landry's statue, the way some butter-and-egg man might buy a Monet.

I guess it was not like Tom to insist on ownership in the franchise. Where Tom comes from, there was a difference, I guess, between owning the ranch and working the cows. Tom was, actually, a humble man. He never wanted to be anything but what he was, coach.

I really wouldn't want to be the new coach. Jimmy Johnson, by all accounts, isn't a humble man. He can't be. He just stood there while they fired America's Coach and gave him his team. It's as if the rustlers just shot John Wayne.

I guess we'll all just have to get another team.

ONE MAN'S SUN-BAKED THEORY ON ATHLETIC SUPREMACY

SUNDAY, APRIL 30, 1989

BY JIM MURRAY

A few days ago, NBC, which should have known better, presented a one-hour seminar-type TV program that undertook to show that blacks are better athletes than whites. Next week, presumably, they're going to have one to show the earth is round. Water is wet.

But it's when they got into the reasons for blacks being superior that they got into water they couldn't tread. They brought in grave scientists to give learned discourses. And when they traced it to physiological racial differences, they raised the hackles on large segments of the populace.

Any sportswriter could have told them that would happen.

You see, none of us likes to be told we're different. Even if the differences are advantageous. With the exception of a few Anglo-Saxon eccentrics who despise the rest of mankind, we're a conformist lot.

If we're good at something, we don't like to be told it's because we have this twitch muscle not given to the rest of human beings. It's like being able to see better because you've got three eyes.

Great athletes, like great musicians, of course, have some gift the rest of mankind doesn't. Sam Snead, the great golfer, is double-jointed. Ted Williams, in his prime, had the eyesight of a hungry hawk. But these were hardly group legacies.

Do black athletes have some edge that accounts for their preponderance of representation in all sports they undertake? Well, of course they do. There's an old saying that when a thing happens once, it can be an accident. Twice, it can be a coincidence. But if it keeps happening, it's a trend.

The poor doctors on the network, a physiologist and an anthropologist who stuck their test tubes into this liquid dynamite of an issue, appeared on television to be politically and sociologically naive.

They seemed startled that their innocent research could arouse such vehement passions as when the Berkeley sociologist, Harry Edwards, with whom few dare to cross adjectives and prepositions, thundered that their study was racist. You learn never to cross points of view with Harry. He's bigger than you are. Also louder.

The scientists are not only naive, they were a little unscientific. To understand why American blacks were succeeding in such boggling numbers, they studied *West Africans*. Figure that one out.

It didn't take Harry Edwards long to point out—correctly—that American blacks are a long way genetically from any African blacks. The American black, like the American anything, is a mixture of races, cultures and pigments. Sherman's army has descendants in every ghetto in America, you can bet me. Edwards himself reminded the panel that he had great, great grandparents who were Irish. So did I but I never had a good jump shot.

Harry likes to think racism and segregation drove the young blacks into the one avenue open to them in a closed society—sports. They got good at them because they were desperate.

I can buy that. Up to a point. Deprivation is a powerful motivating force. So is hatred. There's very little doubt raging hatred made Ty Cobb excel after the day he came home and found that his mother had shot and killed his father by "accident." Cobb set out to make the world pay.

But I would like to offer my own theory of athletic supremacy.

Unweighted by any scientific gobbledygook, not bogged down by any documented research, not even cluttered by facts, Murray's Law of Athletic Supremacy is beautiful in its simplicity, based on a long-time non-balancing of the issues, a resolute refusal to entertain any other points of view. Charles Darwin, I'm not. I base my findings on that most incontrovertible of stances—total ignorance. Compared to me, Darwin was equivocal.

First of all, I don't think it is twitch muscles or long tendons or larger lungs or even that old standby, rhythm, that contrives to make African-Americans superior athletes.

In the second place, I have never been able to understand the convoluted scientific efforts to explain away the darker pigment on some human beings. To me, it is a simple matter of geography. The closer you get to the Equator, the darker the skin.

I mean, aren't southern Italians darker than Swedes? Skin coloring is a function of climate. I will cling to this notion until a blond, blue-eyed baby is born to natives in Zimbabwe or a black-skinned child emerges in Scandinavia.

I am absolutely positive that if you had put a colony of Irishmen in the Sudan in, say, 5000 BC, their descendants would be black today. If you had put a Sudanese population in Dublin in 5000 BC, their descendants would have red hair.

Now, we come to athletic prowess. Murray's Law is simple: Athletic prowess is bestowed on that part of the population that is closer to the soil, deals with a harshness of existence, asks no quarter of life and gets none.

Nothing in my business, journalism, makes me laugh louder than to pick up a paper and find some story, marveling wide-eyed, at how some deprived youngster from a tar paper shack in Arkansas, one of 26 children, rose to become heavyweight champion of the world, all-world center in the NBA, home run champion or Super Bowl quarter-back. Well, of course he did. That's dog-bites-man stuff.

A much bigger, more astonishing story would be if a youngster came out of a silk-sheets, chauffeur-to-school, governess-at-home atmosphere in the mansions of Long Island to become heavyweight champion of the world, or even left fielder for the Yankees.

You always get great athletes from the bottom of the economic order. That goes back to the days of ancient Rome, when the gladiators were all slaves (later Christians, and we all know the early Christians were the poor).

In this country, the lineups of professional teams were always filled with the names of farm boys or the sons of the waves of immigrants who came over here from the farmlands of Ireland or Germany or Italy or Poland. How do you think Shoeless Joe got his nickname? Why do you think he couldn't read or write?

The African-Americans are simply taking up where the Irish-Americans, German-Americans, Jewish-Americans, Italian-Americans and the home-grown farm boys left off. Like their predecessors, they come from a long line of people who worked long, hot hours in the sun, growing grapes, chopping cotton, cutting cane. This makes the belly hard, the muscles sinewy, the will stubborn but accustomed to hardship. This is the edge the black athlete has. The same edge the boys from the cornfield, the boys who came from a long line of Bavarian stump-clearers, had in another era.

And what happened to them may happen to the American black. Already, as blacks migrate from the levees and cotton fields of the Old South and get more than one generation away from it to the metropolises of the North and East and live their lives by radiators and soft beds and eat junk food instead of soul food, they are losing their places, increasingly, to the hardy breeds from Central America and the Caribbean. That's the way it goes.

Don't ask me to explain any of this. Trust me. I'm fresh out of test tubes. Don't burden me with facts. Or twitch muscles. As Harry Edwards and I could tell you, Irishmen don't have twitch muscles.

CHALK UP A VICTORY FOR OUTCASTS

SUNDAY, MAY 7, 1989

BY JIM MURRAY

LOUISVILLE—A horse they thought so little of they did every-thing but leave him on a park bench with a note on him won the Kentucky Derby Saturday and may be the greatest thing to come down a homestretch in this decade and maybe in several.

If he was a cat they might have drowned him at birth. He was knock-kneed, he wobbled when he walked like a teen-ager in high-heels. He was so ugly he was almost 2 years old before they were sure he wasn't going to be a camel.

Twice, they tried to auction him off. But the horse-buying public was too smart for that.

Nobody wanted Sunday Silence till Charlie Whittingham took a look at him.

Charlie Whittingham has been around race horses since the days of Dan Patch. He knows they don't have to look like something out of a Roy Rogers movie. You judge a horse with a clock, not a mirror. Man o' War might have had a lousy profile.

Charlie liked Sunday Silence so much, he bought half of him. The horse the tuxedoed auctioneers could not get a nibble on looked to Charlie like a bigger bargain than a hot diamond.

The horse who won $574,200 Saturday and $980,000 in his life wouldn't bring $17,000 at a dispersal sale two years ago. When Arthur Hancock III declined that sale price, his partners backed out. "You take him, then," was their attitude.

Whittingham, on the other hand, reacted as if a rich uncle had just left him an oil field. He couldn't believe a horse this good would be available at any price. The horse was not only good, he was as well-behaved as a Boy Scout and as trainable as a circus seal. Talent often comes coupled with moodiness, truculence, temperament. Talent often hates to be told what to do and how to do it. Good Soldier Schweiks, they're not. Sunday Silence was like a kid who eats his vegetables and cleans the blackboards. If he could talk, he would say "Yes, sir!"

That's all Charlie Whittingham needs—a fast horse who will do what he tells him.

So, the horse nobody wanted is the toast of Kentucky today. He won the coldest—and the slowest in 30 years—Kentucky Derby on a gelid May Saturday when sleet swept down the backstretch and a cold wind whipped in the horses' faces on the turn for home.

Was the winner much the best? Well, look at it this way: How many Kentucky Derbies do you see with the winner running sideways in the stretch?

The race was run in the slow-freight time of 2:05. Horses move faster than that pulling surreys. That was the slowest Derby since 1958. There's no telling what Sunday Silence might have run if he hadn't come down the stretch like a guy carrying a football—or being thrown out of a waterfront bar. Saddle broncs in a rodeo do less jumping around. Patrick Valenzuela must have thought he was trying to stay on a Brahma bull.

The least surprised guy in Kentucky was Charlie Whittingham. Whittingham has been telling everybody who would listen for months that his horse was something special. It was such a startling change of posture for Charlie that the public chunked in $592,058 on his horse to win.

It has always been considered an act of faith back here in the bluegrass country that horses who come over the mountain from the Pacific are, by definition, "nice little California sprinters." They're not supposed to like it when anything draws alongside them.

The horse who was supposed to expose them at Churchill this year was a speed demon infelicitously named Easy Goer. Tracksiders couldn't make up their minds whether he was another Man o' War— or merely another Secretariat. Wonder Horse III. He didn't even need to be whipped. He had won the Wood Memorial under a hand ride like a horse on a bridle path being ridden by a debutante. He had come within a click of a world mile record with nothing chasing him. No one had ever shopped him around or put an ad in the paper or offered to throw in the saddle if someone would bid on him.

Charlie Whittingham was unimpressed. "Maybe he's a wonder horse," observed Charlie. "He better be."

He wasn't. It was a case of easy come, Easy Goer. He did finish second. It was the second time he had lost at Churchill in six months. Maybe he didn't care for the track. It was hard to. It was greasier than a truck stop hamburger. The field often looked like Charlie Chaplin trying to cross a waxed dance floor.

It was vindication of two sorts for his principal owner, Arthur Hancock III. He not only refused to sell Sunday Silence short—twice —but he had the laugh on those who said he was not serious enough to run the family heirloom, Claiborne Farms. When Arthur Three got out of college, he passed up mucking the family stalls in favor of playing a guitar in honky-tonks and writing songs about guys whose wives left them for truck drivers and took the kids with them. He even named Sunday Silence from a Kris Kristofferson lament titled, "Sunday Morning, Coming Down."

The family wasn't sure they wanted a guy who would rather be Willie Nelson than a stud farmer, rather have a hit record than a Derby horse. Arthur took his guitar and left home.

Claiborne Farms had 34 horses in 28 Derbies, winning two of them. Arthur Three has been in four Derbies and won two.

The horse nobody wanted and the owner the family didn't want either hauled down the biggest prize in racing Saturday. If he—they —win the Triple Crown, they may set a new trend in the sport of kings. Get owners out of rock concerts and horses out of the Yellow Pages.

NOT ONLY DOES HE UNDERSTAND, HE SHOWS HE CARES

TUESDAY, JULY 18, 1989

BY JIM MURRAY

Too often, the major league ballplayer is portrayed as a churlish, graceless individual who comes into public view brushing the little kid autograph seeker aside, refusing to pose for pictures, announcing irritatedly that all he owes his public is a .293 average or an appearance at a baseball card show for which he gets $10,000.

There are, to be sure, a few who fit this unflattering image. They take the $2 million and run. The fans' love is unrequited. The record books sometimes identify these worthies as most valuable players. The public concept of what these letters stand for is quite different.

So, it gives me great pleasure today to check in with a different kind of story, the account of a major league player who belongs to the world at large, is a citizen in good standing with the rest of the community, a man who cares.

So far as I know, Jim Abbott is the only man in a big league uniform ever to win the Sullivan Award as the nation's outstanding amateur athlete. He's the only one in a big league uniform who only has one hand. Jim Abbott is the only reason I know of to be glad there's a designated hitter rule in the American League.

We all know what kind of pitcher Jim Abbott is—eight wins, six losses, 62 strikeouts in 101⅔ innings, an ERA of 3.45. But I have a clipping from an Indianapolis newspaper that shows what kind of a person he is.

The circumstances require a bit of explanation. On the morning of April 17, little 5-year-old Erin Bower went with her mother to the local K mart store in the Castleton Farms section of Indianapolis. There was this tube of toothpaste on the counter. Erin picked it up. It exploded. Some cretin with a grudge against the store—or the world—had placed a bomb in it.

It didn't kill Erin. It just blew off her left hand. You don't even want to think about it.

In all the outpouring of sympathy for little Erin, one letter came marked with the logo of the California Angels. It read:
"Dear Erin:

"Perhaps somewhere later in your lifetime you will properly understand this letter and the feelings that go behind it. Regardless, I wanted to send something along now after being made aware of your terrible accident.

"As your parents have probably told you, I was born without a right hand. That automatically made me different from the other kids I was around. But you know what? It made me different only in their eyes. You see, I figured that's what the good Lord wanted me to work with. So it was my responsibility to become as good as I could at whatever I chose to do, regardless of my handicap.

"I just won my first major league game. When the final out was made, a lot of things went through my mind. I thought of my parents and all the help they provided; my brother and his support; and all of my friends along the way. The only thing, Erin, that I didn't pay attention to was my handicap. You see, it had nothing to do with anything.

"You're a young lady now with a tremendous life ahead of you. Whether you want to be an athlete, a doctor, lawyer or anything else, it will be up to you, and only you, how far you go. Certainly there will be some tough times ahead, but with dedication and love of life, you'll be successful in any field you choose. I'll look forward to reading about you in the future.

"Again, my best, Jim Abbott, California Angels."

Now that, you have to say, is the way to get an autograph. And the news from Indianapolis, as reported in the Star, is good: Erin, who turned 6 today, has been fitted with an electrically powered hand at the Medical Prosthetics Center in Houston. It'll do everything a real hand will do—except throw the curve. If Erin wants to do that, she'll have to learn to do it with her other hand. As Jim Abbott has shown, that's no problem.

AT GAME 3, NATURE TOOK AWESOME SWING

WEDNESDAY, OCTOBER 18, 1989

BY JIM MURRAY

SAN FRANCISCO—God put the World Series in perspective here in San Francisco Tuesday night.

He shook the ballpark, like a dog would a rag, just minutes before the start of Game 3.

A baseball game is about as trivial a pursuit as you can imagine when nature is in a rage. The earth growled, heaved and, suddenly, a World Series that had been as deadly dull as a chess game in a firehouse became more wildly exciting than you would want.

It was the worst earthquake I had ever been in. And I've been in them since January 1944. It was as if the earth first shrugged, then went into a violent spasm of hatred. I remember leaning over to my colleague, Ross Newhan, and murmuring hopefully, "They never last more than a minute."

If you have ever been in one, you know a minute can seem an eternity. An earthquake disorients you. It is a world gone crazy. I kept watching the center field stands in horror, expecting to see them come tumbling down in a mountain of rubble any minute. The monstrous malevolence of an earthquake is impossible to overstate.

When it finally stopped, there was relief, then uneasiness, and then mild panic in the ballpark. But it soon gave way to a kind of festive atmosphere.

"When the aftershocks come," I reminded myself, "they are rarely the intensity of the initial shock."

Then rumors began to surface:

"The Bay Bridge collapsed!" was the first.

"San Francisco is burning!" was the next.

A few, fueled by beer, were undaunted. "Play ball!" they screamed.

But there was no ball to be played this night. The teams were out on the field. The police cars emerged out of nowhere. The PA system, before it burned out, reminded people to go onto the field or head for the exits. It suddenly, soberingly, occurred to people that a disaster had struck. Fatalities had been totted up to maybe 200.

San Francisco is a black hole in the firmament of American cities tonight.

They do not know when and if the World Series will resume. The important thing is to get San Francisco to resume. It is a city living with an unpredictable sociopath. It may go years, even decades, living as normal as a postal clerk. Then it goes into maniacal rages.

The ballparks, the bridges, even the highways and electrical circuits are at its mercy. A World Series is the least of its victims.

TWELVE

THE TRIUMPH OF ADAM AND MEGAN WALTER

1990 WINNER IN THE FEATURE WRITING CATEGORY

"For a distinguished example of feature writing giving prime consideration to high literary quality and originality . . ."

Colorado Springs Gazette Telegraph
Dave Curtin

Having survived a blast that caused disfiguring burns over most of their bodies, Megan and Adam Walter embarked on the most painful part of their recovery: being reunited with a society that overvalues physical beauty. Their painful journey is sensitively told by Dave Curtin.

On June 21, 1988, Adam and Megan Walter and their father, Bill, were critically burned in a propane-gas explosion in the home they were renting in rural Ellicott, Colorado, 16 miles east of Colorado Springs.

I was on the cop beat that night, and when the call came in, I drove to the Penrose Hospital Burn Unit, where I saw Adam, then 6, and Megan, 4, arrive at the emergency room by Army helicopter. Their father arrived a few minutes later by ambulance. In the hospital waiting room, I saw 80 people of all ages gathered in prayer and realized this was much more than a fire story. This would be a story of how a family's tragedy brought together a community.

Our news stories in the days after the fire focused on the children's struggle to survive, their dramatic transfer to the Shriners Burn Institute nearly 1,000 miles away in Galveston, Texas, in a medically equipped Lear jet traveling at 700 miles per hour, and the investigation into the cause of the explosion.

About this time, the children's aunt, Candy Entingh, said something to me that set the wheels in motion for a more in-depth account of the Walter family and how it would face this disaster.

"Do you know how they're going to feel when they get home?" Entingh asked me. "Like misfits. They're going to feel ugly, different, like they don't fit in. We want people to see them and say, 'Hi Adam! Hi Megan!' "

Soon after the Walters returned home from the burn center, Deputy City Editor Carl Skiff, photographer Tom Kimmell and I met with the family and told them we thought we could help re-integrate them into the community. Telling their story, we told them, might even help others cope with similar disasters or misfortunes.

Bill and Cindy Walter had been told at the burn center that other children may look at a masked Adam and Megan wrapped in pressure-garment suits and ask them why they look like "monsters" or "mummies." The Walters wanted to do what they could to help their children overcome being ostracized.

They agreed to let Kimmell and me be their shadows for six months.

"We had so many things to deal with physically and emotionally, we were skeptical about having a reporter and a photographer always on our doorstep during our time of crisis," Bill Walter recently told us. "But after we met the three of you, we had a favorable feeling about your honesty and sincerity."

Kimmell and I watched as two children—a kindergartener and a first-grader—took us on an incredible journey of fear and courage, despair and hope, insecurity and inner strength. Less than a week after meeting the family, we traveled with them to the burn center in Galveston for an examination. Three days together of airplane flights, hotel arrangements, meals and medical clinics enabled us to get to know one another in a hurry.

Doctors and therapists at the burn center supported our theme. They told us that when it is time to leave the supportive environment of the burn institute, many of the children treated there are afraid to return to the outside world.

"Their behavior ranges from withdrawn to panicky," said Andrea Royka, head of the center's child-life department, which promotes self-expression by the children. "They start to feel that it's much better to stay at the hospital. It's almost a panic that they're leaving this place that they first despised."

Once Adam and Megan found out we liked to play hide-and-seek and slurp chocolate pudding, they quickly befriended Kimmell and me. Kimmell worked to make the children comfortable around his array of cameras. Soon they were asking if they could help carry the cameras through airport corridors. The cameras, hanging almost to the floor from their frail, bony shoulders, swung awkwardly with the limping gaits of Adam and Megan.

Adam seemed to take to his celebrity status. On one trip to the Texas burn institute, everywhere the boy went—the motel lobby, a cafeteria line, the hospital—Adam would reach as high as he could, tap a stranger on the hip, point to us and announce, "He's a cameraman. He's a writer."

He affectionately referred to us as "the camera dude" and "the writin' dude."

One day, Adam was asked by his father to say the breakfast prayer. Everyone held hands around the table and Adam said, "Dear God, thank you for this food. And for Tom to take the pictures. And for Dave to write the words."

Interaction with Megan also came easily. Wherever we traveled— by plane, car or bus—Megan would ask, "Tom, can I sit next to you?"

Megan said she wanted to marry "Dr. Bill"—Shriners Burn Institute surgeon Bill Baumgartl. But later she decided she wanted Tom and me as boyfriends. "I have three boyfriends!" she proclaimed excitedly one day.

As our relationship with the family grew over the months, the Walters entrusted us with cassette tapes the children had made for their father when they were fighting for their lives. The family also granted us permission to read their diary documenting their thoughts in the days and weeks after the accident.

By knowing what they were faced with—physically and emotionally—we could better report what they had to overcome. When it came time to write the story, Skiff warned me to resist the temptation to overwrite. "Let the story tell itself," he said.

This is the story we told. While our story ended after 200 inches, theirs goes on for a lifetime.

—Dave Curtin
Colorado Springs Gazette Telegraph

ADAM & MEGAN

A STORY OF ONE FAMILY'S COURAGE

SUNDAY, JANUARY 8, 1989

BY DAVE CURTIN

Six-year-old Adam Walter and his 4-year-old sister, Megan, were burned severely along with their father on June 21 when a propane-gas explosion ripped through their Ellicott home east of Colorado Springs. Their lives were drastically changed.

Now, the Bill and Cindy Walter family is looking to the new year with great hopes and optimism. This is the story of their courageous triumph over disfiguring burns, and of the strength they have received from the warm responses of friends and strangers.

□ □ □

Megan Walter carefully arranges brightly colored ornaments three and four deep on the Christmas tree branches within her reach. Consequently, all the branches at the 3-foot height bend toward the floor from the weight.

"Megan, we need to spread out the ornaments a little more," her mother, Cindy, says gently, rearranging the bulbs.

Members of the Walter family had hoped to be back in their ranch home for Christmas, but construction is not completed. They are trimming their tree in an Ellicott rental home on a crisp, clear night, as they listen to a church-service program over the radio.

In the room illuminated only by the blinking of the multicolored lights on the tree, Cindy turns on a cassette tape. It is one the children had made to their father, Bill, five months earlier when they were in hospitals 1,100 miles apart.

In the background on the tape is the humming and beeping of hospital monitors. The children's voices quiver, their breathing is labored. Their words are more like gasps.

In the explosion, all suffered third-degree burns: Megan over 75 percent of her body, Adam over 58 percent and Bill over 38 percent of his body.

Third-degree burns—the most severe—destroy all skin layers. Bill, Adam and Megan were in critical condition for several weeks.

The blast killed the family's black Labrador retriever, Max.

"Dad, I think you're the specialest dad in the world," Adam begins on the tape. "And you're the only one I have. I'm glad we're still one family. I'm glad I don't have a stepdad or a stepmom. I'm so glad you guys don't fight and that we can be together. And that we can see each other, and that we can pray for each other, and that we can try to get better."

Then Megan's voice comes onto the tape. She is whispering, "Mom, can Dad talk back to me?"

"No," Cindy is heard to explain in the background. "Dad will have to talk back to you later on another tape."

Then, Megan begins: "Dad, you know what? Max is dead, Dad. And do you know why he's dead? Because he was standing right behind Adam and the wind blew him. The wind blew him so hard that it blew him right out the door and he broke his back. And now he's dead, Daddy. I'm really sad about that. I bet Adam's sad, too. When Mom talked about it to me, I got really scared. I thought Max got his fur burned. Mom told me his fur didn't get burned, he just got killed. Don't be sad, Dad, because when we get home, we're gonna get another puppy. Do you know what Dad? When you come see me, I'm going to start walking and you're going to see me walk."

Bill, sitting by the twinkling Christmas tree, quietly weeps as he listens to the tapes.

"What's wrong with Dad?" Adam asks.

"This tape is very special to Dad," Cindy says. "He has special feelings when he listens to it."

JUNE

It is another summer evening on the plains 16 miles east of Colorado Springs. Ominous, black clouds roll in as a weary Bill Walter comes in from the fields of the 1,120-acre cattle ranch he manages. Bill, 36, the son of an Illinois dairy farmer, is a big man with a hearty laugh.

His 34-year-old wife, Cindy, arrives home with groceries in one arm and 7-week-old Abby in the other. Adam, 6, and Megan, 4, scramble into the house ahead of her. Cindy and the children have been in Colorado Springs shopping and getting Megan a new hairdo.

Cindy and Bill, married for 14 years, met at Grand Rapids (Mich.) School of Bible and Music. They sing in their church choir, and she is a director of the youth ministry.

The family likes living on the Ellicott ranch, their home of three years since moving from Savanna, Ill. In the mornings, sunlight decorates the sprawling fields. In the evenings, thunderclouds rattle the windows like a temperamental neighbor.

But most importantly, the children are happy here. Adam loves horses, riding his bicycle and helping his dad feed the cattle. When he grows up, he wants to be a policeman, "so I can go fast and not get a ticket."

Megan can't wait for Abby—"my baby"—to grow up so she'll have a girl to play with. Megan loves to play hide-and-seek and, like her mother, she is meticulous. She follows her mother around the grocery store straightening the cans on the shelves. And Megan loves to hug, especially Abby and the family dog, Max.

□ □ □

Now, Adam and Megan are sitting on the floor of the mud room at the top of the basement stairs to change their shoes before going out to play. Max is wagging his tail, waiting for them. Adam is hoping his mother will make his favorite dinner, macaroni and cheese. Megan wonders what will be for dessert. Even after breakfast, she had asked, "What's for dessert?"

Cindy removes Abby from the blanketed infant seat in front of the kitchen window and places her in her crib in the children's bedroom. As Cindy prepares dinner at 5 p.m., she realizes there is no hot water. Bill, still wiping the sweat from his sundrenched brow, heads down to the basement to light the pilot light on the hot-water heater. He doesn't know that propane has leaked into the basement. He lights a match.

Suddenly a fiery explosion rocks the house.

"There was a boom and I saw a fireball," Cindy says later. "I didn't know what happened. I thought the house was hit by lightning."

"Call the hospital!" Bill shouts breathlessly. Trying to run, he staggers up the basement stairs. Only the collar of his shirt is left dangling from his neck.

The children are swept up in the sudden tunnel of fire. Most of their clothes are plastered to the walls of the mud room. The rest are melted onto their bloody bodies.

Six windows and a door are blown out into the yard. The blanket that had covered Abby moments earlier shoots through a shattered window and lands about 100 feet from the house.

Megan, her eyes stinging, wonders why Mommy is talking on the phone *now*. She thinks her mother is calling a friend.

The children and their father blindly stumble to the shower. They stand under a stream of cold well water to douse their burns.

"Daddy, my knees are weak. I'm falling," Megan cries.

"Hold on to me, Meggy," Bill says. "Hold on to me for support."

"I'm cold!" cries Adam. He has little skin to keep him warm.

Paramedics wrap the screaming children in wet sheets and carry them to the ambulance. Megan is crying out that her eyes hurt. Her corneas are burned and doctors at first fear she will be blind. But that fear will disappear after further examination.

In the ambulance, paramedics work desperately to keep the three conscious.

When Cindy sees her children at the Penrose Hospital emergency room in Colorado Springs, they are burned beyond recognition. She can't tell Adam from Megan.

"They didn't look anything like them," Cindy later recalls. "But their eyes, their eyes were the same and I knew it was Adam and Megan inside."

Megan is calm. "Look, Mommy, my foot's burned," she says, not knowing that her entire body is burned.

Adam is calm until he sees how badly burned Megan is. Then he becomes hysterical. He is struggling against the doctors, battling the oxygen, fighting the intravenous tubes. "His eyes, they were crazy," Cindy remembers.

"Adam, it's Mommy," Cindy calls to her son. But she can't make contact with him.

Not far from his children, Bill is hallucinating from the morphine anesthetic and shivering so violently that he is bouncing on the gurney.

Cindy walks alongside Megan into the operating room. Just one tuft of hair is left from the girl's new hairdo. When Cindy tenderly strokes it, it falls out.

"They're very critical," Dr. John Marta, an anesthesiologist, tells Cindy. "They might not make it. They're your kids out here. But they're mine in there," Marta says, pointing to the operating room. "I'll do everything I can. But I can't make any guarantees."

Cindy to this point has had unfaltering strength in living out this horror story. But now, she feels her strength pouring out as if through a sieve.

She buries her head in her hands.

"I prayed," she says later. "I prayed that my children would die.

"I didn't want them to have to go through it. I knew they had accepted the Lord as their savior. I knew they were going to heaven, that they would be with him. I didn't want them to go through all the pain and disfigurement. I didn't pray for Bill to die. He wasn't going to leave me all alone."

□ □ □

"I have to change my thinking," Cindy thinks the next morning when her children are still alive. "The Lord has not taken them to be with him. We can work through this."

Later, Bill is put in a wheelchair and pushed in to see his children. Megan doesn't recognize her father.

"Megan, it's Daddy," Cindy says.

The girl seems unconvinced. Then Bill speaks.

"Megan, honey, I love you," Bill says.

Megan's eyes keep circling her father's face, trying to piece it back together as she remembered it. Finally, she speaks.

"Daddy, you stepped on me!" she moans, remembering the frantic moments on the basement stairs after the explosion.

Since Megan did not immediately recognize her father, Cindy decides to prepare Adam for Bill's visit.

"Adam, your Daddy's coming to see you," she tells him. "He'll look different. Just look at his eyes."

Six days after the explosion, Megan and Adam are transferred to the Shriners Burn Institute in Galveston, Texas, which is 1,100 miles away. But doctors warn they may not survive the flight.

Bill sees his children moments before they are boarded onto the specially equipped medical jet. "I knew it might be the last time," he says.

□ □ □

"Am I going to die?" Adam asks daily from his Galveston hospital bed. "I'm not going to see Dad again, am I? Either I'm going to die or Dad is."

Nanny—the children's grandmother, Audra Shoemaker—and Cindy cannot truthfully tell Adam that he is not going to die. Instead, they work to calm his fear by changing the subject—"The Lone Ranger" is on television. This seems to brighten the boy.

"How come he's called the *Lone* Ranger when he always has a friend with him?" Adam wants to know.

Adam and Megan will spend seven weeks in the burn institute. Both are suffering from pulmonary edema, an excessive buildup of fluid in the lungs. Megan has a partially collapsed lung, and Adam had a cardiac arrest earlier.

Doctors work around the clock to prevent a collapse of circulation, a shutdown of the stomach and bowel system, upper lung and wound infections, kidney failure, pneumonia and prolonged shock.

The children are covered with cadaver skin as a temporary covering, and they undergo several blood transfusions and skin-graft operations. Back in Colorado Springs on one July day, 104 people from the Walter family's church, Mesa Hills Bible Church, respond to a call for blood.

The children are suffering from relentless nausea, burning fever and excessive chills. An automatic cooling blanket and fans control Megan's 104 fever.

The children relive the explosion in nightmares that might recur for months or even years.

Adam says the hospital isn't the solution—it's the problem. "Get me out of this hospital," he demands of Nanny.

During the final weeks of their first stay at the Galveston hospital, Adam and Megan are taught to sit up, to feed themselves and eventually to walk.

One day, Megan sees her reflection for the first time in a bedside cart and exclaims, "I think my hair's growing faster than Adam's."

On a bright day, Megan announces her wedding plans. She will marry "Dr. Bill"—surgeon Bill Baumgartl. Cindy and Nanny tell her she can't marry Dr. Bill, but she can have him for a boyfriend for now. Megan considers this for a moment and then declares, "I'll be a kid nurse!" Surely, that would be next best to marrying Dr. Bill.

Each child is given 3,200 calories of milk a day as part of a special diet rich in calcium, protein and potassium. Megan and Adam are fed a pint of milk an hour, 24 hours a day, for six weeks through a gastric-nasal tube.

Burn victims use calories at two times the normal metabolic rate. Not only is their rate of protein breakdown increased, but they lose protein through their wounds, says Shriners dietitian Megan Duke.

Doctors have learned how to replenish the tremendous amount of fluids lost through burn wounds. Before that, some severely burned people starved to death because they couldn't be fed fast enough, Duke says.

□ □ □

Adam is horrified when he sees the silicone-rubber face mask he and his sister will wear. "Take it away," he demands. "It scares me."

The masks, made from plaster molds of the children's faces, put pressure on the skin to control scarring.

The children will wear the $800 masks 23 hours a day for 1½ to three years, until the scars are mature and can no longer be changed.

"It's hot, it's itchy, it burns, it makes people afraid. There's a lot of reasons not to wear it," says Roland Morales, the medical sculptor who made the masks.

"It comes down to the parents. Kids start telling their parents, 'I hate you,' and the parents let it go and say, 'A plastic surgeon will correct it later.' A lot of people think a plastic surgeon can correct anything. That's not true."

The children also will wear pressure garments called Jobskins. Invented 20 years ago by an engineer, Conrad Jobst, the $1,000 elastic suits are custom-made to tightly fit their bodies like second skins to control scarring.

When skin is severely burned down to the third underlayer, it loses the benefit of the tight skin pressure that once was on top. The underlayer literally grows wild as it heals and forms a scar. If no pressure is applied when a scar is forming, skin will grow into irregular knots and swirls.

Without the mask and Jobskins, ugly, disfiguring and constrictive scars will develop.

The Jobskin must be worn for 12 to 18 months. Before pressure garments were used, burn victims were forever unable to function and grotesquely scarred.

Megan and Adam will wear a mouth spreader, a taut rubber-band contraption that keeps the mouth opening from growing shut. "You won't be able to eat a Big Mac unless you wear it," Morales tells the children.

They also will wear pads underneath their arms to prevent their armpits from growing shut.

Meanwhile in Colorado Springs, Bill is able to feed himself applesauce for the first time since the explosion five weeks ago. He now can shake hands, brush his teeth and blow his nose.

On Aug. 11, Adam, Megan, Cindy and Nanny return from Galveston.

But before they had left the burn institute, Cindy and Nanny were reminded that the children are returning to a world that may not be ready for them—a world that values physical beauty. They were told that severely burned children are stared at and often avoided. Other children may ask them why they look like a Martian, or a mummy or a monster.

Cindy and Nanny learned that some children live through their burns only to die a slow, social death.

"Do you know how they're going to feel when they get home?" asks the children's aunt, Candy Entingh. "Like misfits. They're going to feel ugly, different, like they don't fit in. We want people to see them and say, 'Hi Adam! Hi Megan!' "

AUGUST

"Hey!" Danny Spanagel shouts to Adam. "You lost two teeth, too!"

They are at children's church at Mesa Hills Bible Church on West Uintah Street. Adam and Megan are being reunited with their friends for the first time since the explosion, eight weeks earlier.

Danny doesn't seem to notice Adam's face, blotched red with open wounds. Or his shaved head. Or his awkward two-legged hop forced by constrictive scarring of the joints.

Danny sees only that Adam has lost his two front teeth.

Adam smiles and pats his best friend on the shoulder as only 6-year-old pals can do.

There are three dozen children ages 4 to 8 sitting in tiny chairs in the crowded room.

When Megan walks in, she sees little girls with long, flowing hair. Their skins are silky, their complexions radiant. They are in their Sunday dresses.

Megan's head is shaved. Her scalp has been used for donor skin for most of her five skin grafts. Her hands are gnarled and knobby, her fingers webbed together. Her face is scarred. Her body is bandaged from neck to toe.

The children stare. A tear rides unevenly down Megan's pock-marked cheek.

"Hi Megan," comes the squeaky call of a young, hesitant voice from across the room. This starts a flurry of greetings, and Megan quietly acknowledges them.

On the bulletin board is a poster of the Walter family with the words, "Can You Help?" In the portrait, the family is smiling, un-burned, unscarred.

The children in the class look at the poster, then at Adam and Megan.

"Kids are curious by nature," teacher Sybil Butler says after class. "They've heard Adam and Megan have been burned. Now here they are in front of them and they're trying to figure it out. I told them that Adam and Megan will look different. But they're still Adam and Megan."

After church, family members go to their temporary home—the house of "Auntie" Candy and Uncle David Entingh.

There, Adam and Megan are shuffling around in rigid, robotlike motions with their cousins. Adam can't push his Hot Wheels cars along the floor as he used to. So he cradles them in his bent arms, drops them on the floor and pushes them with his feet.

"Eight weeks ago, we didn't know if they were going to live," Bill says. "Now they're running around. It's a miracle."

Then Bill turns solemn. "You don't wake up everyday and say I might die today. People are too preoccupied with what they're doing —where they're going—to think like that. What happened to us took

30 seconds and changed our lives forever. Things will never be the same for us," he says.

"We don't want to just be alive," Cindy says. "We want to be normal."

SEPTEMBER

"How come your face is the same?" Adam asks his father during a two-hour therapy session at Penrose Hospital. "How come you don't have to wear the Jobst thing?"

"Because I'm not burned as bad as you are," Bill tells him.

Later, as Bill waits for his therapists, he tries to explain Adam's questions.

"What he's getting at," says Bill, "is 'How come you weren't burned as bad? Weren't you in the same explosion? You lit the match.' "

Adam denies he is burned, his father explains, and becomes angry when he is reminded. Sometimes Adam goes into uncharacteristic rages when he is forced to wear the mask or when he must go through another painful daily bath, Bill says.

"Sometimes . . . he'll yell and scream. I'll pick him up and Adam won't be inside."

One day, when Bill paddles him, Adam screams, "I hate being burned!"

"Then this look comes over his face like 'Oh-oh, I admitted it,' " Bill says.

Another day, Bill asks his son, "How come you never say 'Thank you' anymore?"

"Why should I say 'thank you' for something I don't want?" Adam fires back.

"It's like he's saying, 'I didn't ask for this,' " Bill says. "He doesn't want this anymore. He just wants to be a kid."

While Adam is at times overcome with denial and anger, Megan struggles with feelings of shame, Bill and Cindy say.

Earlier in the week, when the children were going to a monthly checkup in Galveston, Megan was following her Auntie Candy through the Colorado Springs airport. But Auntie wasn't aware that Megan, in her mechanical straight-legged gallop, was trying desperately to keep up with her. Finally, Megan stumbled, falling breathlessly to the cold tile floor. She was unable to pick herself up.

On the plane, a disheartened Megan muttered for an hour, "I want to be burned. I'm glad I was burned. Take my ears off."

In an effort to relieve such feelings, the family is seeing a psychologist. "The kids have feelings that they don't know why they have," Bill says. "Sometimes I think if the Lord took them, they wouldn't have to go through this. They're tired. Tired of the pain."

"They don't know this is going to last a long time," Cindy says. "They think it's just for now."

□ □ □

Across the Penrose Hospital therapy gym, therapist Cathy McDermott asks Megan to make a fist. The girl strains with all the fury a 4-year-old can muster and succeeds in cupping her hand. "That's very good!" Cathy says.

Recognizing her own progress, Megan wiggles the knuckles on her right hand as if to wave and exclaims, "Look!"

The children's burns cause severe pain when they try to move their arms, legs and fingers. Thick scarring of the joints keeps them from moving normally. Therapists will work to mold the scar tissue while it is still active. When the scars mature, they will turn white and cannot be changed.

Cathy asks Megan what she is going to do on her birthday. Megan shrugs and says, "I'll eat cake."

Megan also hopes she will get earrings for her birthday. "Before I was burned, I used to have lipstick," she says in her best ladylike manner.

Later, another therapist, Janese London, places Megan on a large mat and removes her bandages. She encourages Megan to lie on the mat and point her toes "like a ballerina."

"I don't want to be a ballerina," Megan says.

"Why?" Janese asks.

"Because," Megan giggles, "they wear purple shoes and a pink dress!"

Megan tells Janese that she bathed herself today. "But I couldn't put the shampoo on," she laments. Which reminds her, "I have more hair than my baby does," she says of her sister Abby. "I'm gonna have long hair. Before I was burned, I had it all the way past my back."

As the therapy session comes to an end, Adam and Megan eagerly ask if they get to dance. Their father asks also, because he knows how much dancing means to them: During these minutes, Adam and Megan can forget they are scarred and burned. They can forget the painful struggles of eating, brushing their teeth, bathing. They can escape.

Adam and Megan put on oversized sunglasses that dwarf their shaved heads, and therapist Patty Stafford leads them in energetic, gyrating moves to the thumping sound of "Walk Like an Egyptian."

The children's excited laughs fill the gym. Without realizing it, their sudden exuberance equates to therapeutic exercises that it is hoped will one day allow them to do the things others take for granted —walking normally, dressing without pain, grasping a fork and a spoon.

As the session ends, Patti waves goodbye and the music fades.

Adam and Megan silently continue their high-stepping, arm-flinging liveliness. Into the elevator, they're still dancing. Down three floors, they're still shaking their heads rhythmically to the imagined beat. Then they bop out of the elevator and into the parking lot of the hospital—the same hospital where 10 weeks ago, 80 friends had gathered to hold hands and pray for the two critically burned children. Praying that Adam and Megan would again smile and laugh. And dance.

□ □ □

Adam arrives at his seventh birthday party wearing the hated mask. Ten other first-graders are with him at The Boardwalk, an amusement center.

Adam at first had demanded, "No girls." But his mother had explained that girls *will* be there and that he *will* be nice to them.

The party is the first time he has seen all but one of his school friends since the explosion.

Sharing the party is Adam's friend Roy Webb, also turning 7. Cindy didn't want Adam to think he was being showered with gifts because he had been burned. The joint party should help dispel such a notion.

"I don't want him to be ugly and I don't want him to be spoiled. I just want him to be normal," Cindy says.

"Mom, take my mask off so I can go play," Adam says. His mother relents. After all, it is his birthday.

"Adam wants to get this over with by forgetting about the mask," Bill says. "With Adam, it's 'bring on the scars. I'm going to play. This isn't going to last.'"

"The first expression you get of someone is by the expression on their face," Bill says. "But if you can't see the face, Adam thinks the mask scares people."

The maskless Adam has made his way to a bumper car. His gloved hands clutch the levers. At first, the other children are afraid to bump into his car, afraid that perhaps his frail body will break. But Adam quickly sets them straight. He bumps their cars with reckless abandon and sports a large smile that everyone can see.

In contrast to her brother, "Megan wants to get it over with by wearing her mask," Bill says. "She is very conscious of being pretty. She wants everyone to know that she's a girl. She saw what the Jobst gloves did for my hands."

Megan has been hiding behind her mask, Bill says. The masks must be removed to eat, and when it's time for meals, she says she's not hungry.

Megan arrives at the party fashionably late, with her mask on. She's wearing a party dress over her Jobskin and a ribbon—not in her hair, but atop her Jobst hood. Her fingernails are painted red, and her earrings sparkle.

Auntie had fashioned the ribbon, following an incident two nights earlier. A pizza delivery man, upon leaving the Entingh home, waved goodbye to Megan and said, "See ya later, fella!"

"I hate it when someone calls me fella," Megan says, rolling her eyes.

Her eyes tell it all. You can tell whether she is smiling or frowning underneath her mask by the glint or sorrow in those sky-blue eyes. At the moment, she is frowning.

Some of the children at the party shy away from the masked girl. But not Justin Herl, one of Adam's classmates. Without a word, Justin grabs Megan's gloved hand and, gently but deliberately, marches her to a video game. He has become her protector.

"Kids are so compassionate," says Jan Henderson, Adam's kindergarten teacher who is at the party. "How come we can't carry that compassion with us all our lives?"

□ □ □

In Galveston the night before she and Adam go through their monthly clinic at the Shriners Burn Institute, Megan stares at her dinner. She quietly describes the other children she has seen at the institute.

"I see little children with no feet and no hands." She pauses. "Children with their ears and noses burned off."

The family is eating at Western Sizzlin'. Megan sticks a piece of steak with her fork and struggles to lift it to her mouth. Others in the restaurant watch curiously. Although it is a battle for Megan to feed herself, Bill and Cindy believe their children must learn to do everyday tasks for themselves.

During dessert, a chocolate chip takes a long plunge from atop Megan's sundae to the table. It takes her 30 seconds to pick it up in gloved fingers and hoist it to her mouth. "I got it!" she boasts.

At the daylong clinic, Megan and Adam go through a painful, comprehensive examination. They will undergo the checkups indefinitely. The Shriners will pay for their care at the burn institute until they are 18 years old.

The possibility for reconstructive surgery won't be known for at least two years, when the scars mature, says Dr. Bill Baumgartl. But the surgeons are optimistic.

"They were burned very severely, and they were here initially for only two months," Baumgartl says. "People with half the burns have stayed six months. Their progress has been remarkable."

□ □ □

Therapist Stephanie Bakker, who three months ago had taught the children to walk again, today will lead them in exercises to increase their range of motion, strength and endurance.

"The family as a unit must be very involved with the burned victims," Stephanie says. "Cindy was a rock through the whole thing. She's a great source of strength. She was determined they were going to make it. . . . She's been a real inspiration for the other parents, and she's been admired by all the staff. Because we're so impressed

397

with Cindy and Bill, that tells you about the rareness of their strength," Stephanie says.

"These kids are really a pleasure to work with—their smile, their big hug. That's the reward for working here—seeing them go from critically ill to being independent children again."

When the children go to therapy, they think it's a place to play. But therapists with psychology backgrounds are trained to learn what the kids are thinking by how they play. "If a 4-year-old is playing with dolls, and the doll who's supposed to be mommy is nagging the doll representing the child saying, 'That's what happens when you don't mind Mommy,' we know that's something we have to work on," says Sara Bolieu, a hospital spokeswoman.

"Children think that everything bad that happens to them is a punishment," says Andrea Royka, head of the child-life development department. "We had one boy who dressed up for Halloween as Freddy Krueger, the burned character in 'Nightmare on Elm Street.' Then he was burned two months later. He thought God was punishing him for dressing up as Freddy Krueger.

"The kids will ask, 'When I'm 21, will my scars go away?' Then it's time for reality therapy."

Across the room, music therapist Rocio Vega hands Adam bongo drums and instructs, "Beat it like you're really mad."

The exercise serves as a release for anger and tension, she explains.

"Music therapy is actually psychology," she says. "The kids will handle stress through music, and often are encouraged to write their own songs. Maybe they're real angry and have no other way to express it. It's OK to be mad or sad, and Adam and Megan know that."

Therapists have made a "re-entry" video that will reintroduce Adam and Megan to their classmates at home.

"You can prepare a child only so much for going back to school," Andrea says. "But when you don't prepare everyone else . . . everything we've done with Adam and Megan is shot. It's scary to the other children because their friends look different."

In Adam's re-entry video, the therapist tells Adam's first-grade classmates that he is "scared about going back to school. He wants people to know he is the same inside although he looks different on the outside. Adam is still the same Adam, and Megan is still the same Megan."

At the end of the film, Adam, dressed in hospital pajamas, tells his classmates, "I hope I can see you soon. Maybe the first day, I won't come."

□ □ □

Adam and Megan usually do not display an abundance of affection for each other. But on this day, after having gone through so much together, they are being separated for the first time. Adam is going home. Megan is staying in Galveston 10 more days. She will have skin grafts tomorrow on her chest, elbows, knee and thigh. She is devastated by the unexpected turn of events and she is crying uncontrollably. Adam is trying not to cry.

Adam limps toward the van parked near the hospital entrance. Megan waddles after him the best she can. Because of contractures in the elbow joints, she can't straighten her arms and he can't bend his.

Megan stops at the curb. Adam, bawling, turns to his sister. As he works desperately to curl his frail arms around her, Megan tries just as hard to unfold her bent arms to receive him. Finally, they hug.

As the van rolls away, Adam tells his father through gasping sobs, "I didn't think it would be so hard."

OCTOBER

Five days before Halloween, the family goes to see "Bambi" at the Super Saver Eight theater at Citadel Crossing.

The cashier looks down at the two masked children. "Oh, great masks," he says. "I've never seen one of those before. Those are funny. Hey, those are great."

As the family walks in, Cindy corrects him. "Those aren't Halloween masks. My children have been burned."

A pallor stretches across the cashier's face, and he is speechless. After the movie, he approaches Bill. "I'm sorry. I didn't know. I really didn't know."

After the movie, the family goes shopping for tricycles. Therapists at Penrose Hospital have recommended the tricycles for the children to exercise their knee joints and improve their ability to grip by grasping the handlebars.

For Adam, the decision to accept a tricycle is tough. He was adept at riding his bicycle "very fast." He already had picked out a new bicycle for Christmas. It was the bike of his dreams.

"It's *very* fast," he had said. "And it has *very* good brakes. . . . It's an adult bike."

Bill explains to Adam that he's not yet strong enough to balance a bicycle and that he wouldn't be able to grip the handlebars.

After much consternation, Adam decides he'll accept a trike. But not until Bill tells him he can pick out any horn he wants.

While they are shopping, a small boy spots the children. "Look Mom, they're wearing masks," he says.

"They have to wear the masks," his mother explains, "because they have 'owies.' " The boy appears to accept the explanation.

Moments later, a little girl sees Megan and says, "Look Mommy, she has a pig nose."

Megan's feelings are hurt, and she runs to Cindy. "Mommy, I don't have a pig nose."

"No," Cindy assures. "You don't have a pig nose. She just doesn't know about your mask."

□ □ □

On a moonless night, the family returns to the Ellicott ranch for the first time since the explosion four months earlier. Megan naps during the 16-mile ride. When she awakens, she's home—at last.

But she's troubled because it doesn't look like home.

The mud room—at the top of the stairs where Megan and Adam were nearly killed by the fireball—is dark, vacant and hollow. It echoes. The doors and windows, blown out by the blast, are boarded.

The washer, dryer and freezer have been moved into the kitchen.

Megan walks into the kitchen. Cindy opens a cupboard, and scorched, wilted rose petals come fluttering out. She had kept a basket of the petals on top of the refrigerator. "What a mess!" Megan says. She limps quickly across the kitchen and into the children's old bedroom. She is comforted when she sees her bedroom is undisturbed.

Adam, meanwhile, has romped straight to the big wooden toy box made by his father and is digging feverishly for his cars and trucks. Megan soon arrives at her toy box. Side by side, they are absorbed in their long-lost toys.

This is Bill's second visit to the house. He had been here a couple of weeks ago. He had spotted melted pieces of clothing and skin, plastered to walls from the force of the explosion, and removed what he could.

Now he hesitates before going into the basement. "How will this make me feel?" he asks himself. "Can I handle this?" But he continues down, each of the 11 steps taking him closer to the source of the tragedy that so drastically had changed their lives. A cardboard box next to where Adam had been seated on the stairs is unscathed. The blast also hadn't disturbed a plastic bag, tennis rackets and baseball mitts in the basement.

"Sometimes I think the kids would have been better off if they were standing right behind me," Bill says. "But I can't change it."

For Cindy, this is the fourth trip to the home since the explosion. She had gone to the house the day after to get some clothes, and at other times to clean up the rooms. "It doesn't bother me anymore," she says. "I didn't like to go at first because of the smell. It was the smell of burned flesh. It was a people smell. It was the same smell as in the burn unit."

The family walks out the door of the mud room and stands at the evergreen bush where Max had gone to seek his final refuge. Max, with broken back and scorched lungs, had crawled under the evergreen to die.

NOVEMBER

Adam and Megan are wearing new winter coats and mittens on a cold, windy day in Ellicott. Their old coats were destroyed in the explosion. They each carry a sack lunch, and Adam carries a book bag for both on his back. Today is their first day of school.

Cindy and Bill escort them to their classrooms at Ellicott Elementary.

Adam and Megan are not wearing their masks so their new classmates can see that they have features and hair.

Without hesitation, Cindy introduces Megan to the hushed kindergarten class. Then she holds up Megan's mask and carefully explains that her daughter must wear it. "If she doesn't, the bumps on her face will get real big and ugly," Cindy says.

The 20 kids watch Cindy put the mask on Megan. "Megan knows

that when she wears her mask, you can't see her smile," Cindy says. "If you don't know how she's feeling, ask her. Ask her if she's feeling sad or happy."

Teacher Jan Henderson asks the boys and girls whether they are glad to see Megan. They respond with a resounding "yes!"

"Megan, are you happy to be here?" Mrs. Henderson asks. Megan nods, but unconvincingly.

The teacher tries again. "Megan, are you happy or sad?"

"Happy," Megan says, softly.

Her classmates, still silent, continue to look at the masked girl for several minutes.

Down the hall, Cindy repeats the introduction in Adam's class, where he is a celebrity, at least for today, among the 18 first-graders who are competing for his attention.

"Adam's face is red because his blood is working hard to heal it," Cindy tells them. "Underneath his suit, his skin is OK. It's just real red. After a year, Adam can take the suit off. You can touch Adam's skin if you want. Adam will let you.

"If he needs help, he will ask, 'Will you please help me?' but don't rush up to do things for him because we make him do a lot of things for himself," Cindy says.

After Cindy and Bill leave, the first-graders are asked by teacher Lynda Grove what they learned.

"He can do most things we can do," says one student.

"You can touch his skin and it won't hurt," another says.

"He can do things by himself," another says.

When first-grade teacher Jolynn Olden brings her students into the room to meet Adam, she asks the children if they have questions for him.

"Can you go across the monkey bars?" asks one.

"Not yet," Adam replies.

"Can you go down the slide?" asks another.

Adam nods.

"Can you run?" another wants to know.

"Yes," Adam says.

Now the true measure of worth for a first-grader becomes evident. "Fast" to a 7-year-old is everything important.

"Can you run as fast as in kindergarten?" a youngster carefully queries. "Faster," Adam says unflinchingly.

"Can you ride a bike?"

"No," Adam answers reluctantly. "We're still working on balance."

Miss Olden turns Adam's answer into a lesson. "Class, what's balance?" she asks. The answer is universal. "It's staying up on two wheels," the pupils chime.

"Were you scared to come to school today?" a classmate asks.

"A little at first," Adams says. "But I got over it."

The questions continue to pour in. "Do you have fingernails? (Yes). What do you do at home? (Homework). Does your neck get tired of holding your mask up? (No).

"Can we touch you?" one boy asks. Adam nods.

The children scramble to their feet and rush to circle Adam. All at once, they begin touching him. They are convinced that he's just like them.

□ □ □

A cutback in their daily therapy allows the children to attend school three days a week. Cindy and Bill want to get their children back into the mainstream as quickly as possible.

Though Adam and Megan are starting school 2½ months late, they have been working math problems and reading books at home in rare moments when not consumed by therapy and treatment.

Adam needs no practice at art. In art class today, the students are drawing what they will eat for Thanksgiving. Adam uses crayons to draw a dinosaur and what he describes as "worm pie."

Meanwhile, Megan is learning to write V's in her class. But gripping the pencil hurts her right hand. "Megan will learn by watching," says Luann Dobler, a student teacher.

In the cafeteria at lunch time, all the kids are eager to sit next to Adam. Roy Webb and Jason Harding are the winners. They and Adam recall the old days. "Do you remember when the girls attacked?" Adam asks. The two nod furtively and smile. Undoubtedly, it was a memorable event.

Two tables away, Megan wrestles with her sandwich Baggie over possession of a peanut butter and jelly sandwich. A third-grade boy who enters the lunchroom fails to notice Megan's effort to look pretty;

she's wearing her ribbons, earrings and her best dress. Having not heard Cindy's earlier lesson, he asks no one in particular, "What's wrong with Megan? She doesn't look too good. Her face is all red."

The harsh words fail to distract the little girl. Minutes later in math class, Megan is called to the blackboard to draw two of anything. On this blustery, gray day of this devastating year, Megan shuffles up to the board and draws two smiling suns.

EPILOGUE

"You always hear the cliché, 'life isn't fair,' " says Bill Walter. "I guess I've learned that. Even though it isn't fair, it doesn't mean your world has to go to pieces. This has helped me gain a better appreciation of life, what's serious and what's not.

"For my children, for myself, for my family, it doesn't seem fair. But being a Christian, I feel there's a reason for things to happen. The lives you touch and those that touch you—I wonder what the purpose is behind it all?

"More than anything, it was such a shock to me. I never really felt it was my fault. Just a freak accident. When you read of people who are hurt or see it on TV, you feel bad about it, but only for a little while. Then you go on. You never think of something like this happening to you.

"I was the one who lit the match. It seemed so unfair to the children. I've woken up many times at night with a real great sorrow. If I could, I'd like to back up to June 21 and go on from there. But in reality, you can't change that. The Lord has given us the strength to pick up the pieces and go on. Bitterness isn't going to help anyone —my being bitter or Cindy and I being bitter toward each other. Why destroy the kids with bitterness?

"It's good to be alive. More and more, the kids see that. They realize life will come back to a point of being normal. At first, they doubted if anything was ever going to be good again. Now they see that it will be.

"One thing that's really neat is to know that our community—El Paso County, Colorado Springs, Calhan, Ellicott—was pulling for us. That's hard to express. I thank everyone so much. 'Thank you' seems awful small for what we feel at a time like this."

THIRTEEN

THE MAN FROM WALL STREET

1990 WINNER IN THE EXPLANATORY JOURNALISM CATEGORY

"For a distinguished example of explanatory journalism that illuminates significant and complex issues . . ."

The Washington Post
Steve Coll and David A. Vise

During his six-year tenure as "Wall Street's top cop," John Shad tried to redefine the workings of the Securities and Exchange Commission and helped remake the rules governing the business of investing. Steve Coll and David A. Vise of *The Washington Post* assess his impact.

By the mid-1980s, when we teamed up on our first story about the king of the stock speculators, Ivan F. Boesky, Wall Street was already defining the decade. From the distance of Washington, the place sometimes looked like Circus Circus in Las Vegas—bells and lights going off, acrobats swinging on trapezes, and the unmistakable sound of money pouring through the slots.

We knew and could relate to some of the players in the takeover wars. After all, though we were only in our 20s, so were many of the rising stars on the Street. We thought we had an intuitive feel for the story. Vise had been there during the beginning of the 1980s boom, first as a business school student and then as an investment banker in the merger department of Goldman, Sachs & Company.

We both had friends who had migrated to Manhattan to become investment bankers and lawyers. Many of them were drawn to the securities business the way prospectors were drawn to California in 1849. With so many people making so much money so fast, there was bound to be trouble. We kept talking about the inevitable arrests and the inevitable crash. And then, as reporters, we were lucky enough to have a front-row seat when it all happened.

We both knew Ivan Boesky. Vise had interviewed him several times. One time Boesky came to *The Washington Post* newsroom for lunch, looked over the sprawling, buzzing, brightly lit chaos of the place and told Vise, "I love it here. It reminds me of a trading floor."

Vise asked Boesky about the suspicions that he cheated in his stock trading, but Boesky explained that some people were jealous and others were bored, and those who were tired with their own lives found it exciting to speculate that he was somehow a crook.

In the fall of 1985, when Coll was a newly arrived feature writer in

The Post's Style section, he wandered across the cavernous newsroom to search for Vise in the Business section. Coll was spending time with Boesky to write a profile of him, and he'd heard that Vise knew Boesky.

We talked, traded information, enjoyed working together, and within weeks produced a story raising questions about whether Boesky traded stocks illegally based on inside information. One year later, in November 1986, the Securities and Exchange Commission made the stunning announcement that it had reached a record $100 million settlement with Wall Street's most aggressive speculator and that he had agreed to finger those who had helped him violate the law.

It seemed natural for us to collaborate again. A few months after Boesky's fall, Coll moved to New York to become *The Post*'s Wall Street correspondent and to team up with Vise to cover the raging bull market and the unfolding insider trading scandal. We wrote a lot of breaking news stories about the investigations and the markets and longer analyses and profiles to bring the story to life. We also tried to dig out scoops.

After the stock market crashed in October 1987, we began to look for a way to pull all the strands of the story together to enhance our own—and our readers'—understanding of what had taken place.

As reporters, we were frustrated by the Securities and Exchange Commission. It seemed the agency had been running the key Wall Street fraud investigations, and regulating the exploding financial markets, largely in secret. We both wanted to get inside the place and open it up a little, but we knew it would take time and that the barriers to entry were formidable.

In February 1988, we wrote a memo to Peter Behr, *The Post*'s assistant managing editor for business coverage, proposing a major investigative project on the SEC in the 1980s. Because of the agency's penchant for secrecy, we proposed that the project be guided both by *Post* business editors Behr and Tom Dimond and by *The Post*'s lock-smiths, editors Bob Woodward and Steve Luxenberg. With remarkable alacrity, given the risk to the newspaper's daily coverage of what was a hot, unfolding story, Behr approved the project and off we went.

A few weeks later, Vise was at La Guardia Airport in New York City, putting his briefcase through the security check when he looked up and saw John Shad only a few feet away. The former SEC chairman, Shad had become United States ambassador to the Netherlands, and he was living in The Hague. Vise was stunned to see him. Their eyes met and Shad extended his hand.

"I just finished meeting with a partner of yours at Morgan Stanley," Shad said.

Vise realized that Shad must have mistaken him for an investment banker at Morgan Stanley and joined him on the escalator toward the Eastern Airlines shuttle. Shad, it turned out, was flying to Boston for a meeting at the Harvard Business School. Vise had been on his way to Washington, but he quickly told Shad he was a reporter, swapped his boarding pass and flew instead to Boston with Shad. Vise explained that he was working on a major project to understand the SEC's role in the 1980s. It was a good beginning.

One year later, after thousands of hours of interviews, review of thousands of pages of documents, and much solid advice from our editors, we put the series together, but only after a memorable all-night editing session with Luxenberg in *The Post*'s newsroom. When the series appeared in the newspaper, the era at the SEC and on Wall Street that had inspired our collaboration was nearly over. There was a new President, George Bush, who talked about moderating the excesses that had gone before him. Within a short time, the mightiest and most notorious investment firm of the 1980s, Drexel Burnham Lambert, went bankrupt. Remarkably, former SEC Chairman John Shad was at the helm of the firm when it went down.

When it was all over, what lingered was the image of Boesky's fall.

During the 1980s, the fit-looking arbitrageur, clad in his uniform three-piece suit with gold pocket watch, had been at the pinnacle of Wall Street, even as he secretly paid briefcases full of cash for inside information. By the time 1990 arrived, a decaying Boesky with long hair and scraggly beard had been pictured on the front page of the New York *Post,* and former inmate Boesky was explaining how he had learned to cope.

"Now Mr. Boesky," he was asked under oath, "under your cooperation agreement with the United States government, you agreed not to break any laws of the United States or of any state. Is that correct?"

"That is correct."

"While you were at Lompoc prison, did you break any laws of the United States?"

"I think I did."

"And tell us what you did."

"Well, there were a couple of chaps who did laundry there. And I gave them a few quarters and they did my laundry."

"And that was a violation of the law of the United States. Isn't that right?"

"I think it was."

—Steve Coll and David A. Vise
The Washington Post

REMAKING THE NATION'S MARKETS

IN SIX YEARS AT SEC, SHAD SPURRED RADICAL CHANGE

SUNDAY, FEBRUARY 5, 1989

BY DAVID A. VISE
AND STEVE COLL

On March 19, 1980, John Shad, a chainsmoking bulldog of a man with an imposing manner, ushered future president Ronald Reagan through the New York Stock Exchange—across the boisterous trading floor, up to the exchange club and finally to a richly appointed conference room full of select leaders from business and Wall Street.

Shad waited outside. After 31 years on Wall Street, rising to become a multimillionaire and vice chairman of E.F. Hutton Inc., he was restless. He was no politician, but he wanted to make his mark in government.

The door swung open. Laurence A. Tisch, who would later become chief executive of CBS Inc., came out first and flashed a "thumbs up" sign—the group approved of Shad's candidate.

Eight months later, Reagan won the White House and rewarded the 58-year-old Shad by making him chairman of the Securities and Exchange Commission, Wall Street's top cop. Shad resigned from Hutton and headed for the capital, the first Wall Street executive to chair the SEC in 50 years.

When he departed six years later, the SEC, Wall Street, the stock market and the economy had undergone radical changes—spurred in many ways by Shad's policies, and shaped by his forceful, passionate personality.

Shad's policies contributed to fundamental changes in the nation's stock markets that cannot feasibly be reversed. He quickly cut a political deal that gave birth to new, highly speculative financial products. While Shad brought a record number of insider trading cases, he chose not to use the SEC's considerable powers to aggressively regulate the debt-financed hostile takeovers that rocked the economy. He redirected the SEC's vaunted enforcement division, seeking to prevent large companies from being prosecuted for wrongdoing by individual employees. He threw out SEC regulations that he considered duplicative and expensive for companies, freeing billions of dollars for other uses.

Without the SEC peering as closely over their shoulders, some of the biggest investment firms witnessed a breakdown in discipline among their stockbrokers, especially in the area of fraudulent sales practices. Many institutional investors evaded federal rules designed to control speculation in the new financial products, a contributing factor in the 1987 stock market crash. While Shad's actions alone did not cause the crash, they helped unleash economic forces that went beyond what he anticipated or any government agency was able to control.

This is the first of four articles examining how John Shad remolded Wall Street and the SEC between 1981 and 1987, a period that witnessed a record rise and fall in stock prices and the biggest Wall Street corruption scandal in history, involving Ivan F. Boesky and Drexel Burnham Lambert Inc. The series is based on more than 200 interviews with present and former SEC officials, Wall Street executives and others, as well as an examination of commission documents, court files and congressional testimony.

Shad's legacy at the SEC and in the financial world amounted to much more than deregulatory tinkering: he pushed to redefine the purpose and character of the commission and its work.

In the 1970s, the SEC had become a free-wheeling, self-described enforcer of morality in the nation's corporate boardrooms, pursuing a broad mission "in the public interest." Shad believed the agency's main purpose should be narrower: to protect and enrich stockholders by making sure the financial markets were fair and orderly.

From the beginning, he met with stiff resistance from the SEC bureaucracy. He waged a kind of guerrilla warfare at times and lost many battles along the way, particularly on Capitol Hill.

Yet he was hardly one-dimensional in his thinking. Nor were his ideas strictly a proxy for Wall Street. He believed fervently in aspects of deregulation and the Reagan administration's attempt to promote freer markets, but he pushed legislation through that created stiffer penalties for insider trading.

He had made it from Mormon Utah, where he was born, to a plush apartment on Park Avenue in Manhattan, but his years on Wall Street did not smooth away all the rough edges. He had none of the elan of an investment banker, usually mumbling and chain-smoking his way through testimony before Congress, his bulldog face reflecting a deadly earnestness, not pleasure. SEC staff members talked openly about how difficult it was to understand him when he spoke.

Behind his austere demeanor was a flair for living that surprised many of his colleagues. He drove fast, whether cars or boats. He took physical risks, going skydiving and shooting white-water rapids. He loved to bet, sometimes going out with fellow commissioner Bevis Longsteth to wager on a game of Pac-Man at the Little Tavern restaurant on Wisconsin Avenue in Georgetown. And when Michael Jackson came to town for a concert, Shad went alone to the show at RFK stadium to see what the excitement was about.

He came to Washington in 1981, eager to sample the social privileges that come with being a top-ranking official in the capital. Within a few weeks, however, his wife Pat suffered a paralyzing stroke. Shad abandoned plans to buy a house in Northwest Washington, took his wife back to New York and endured a dual existence for the next six years, living in District hotel rooms during the week and commuting to Manhattan on weekends.

In the capital, he often worked past midnight, then rode alone in a cab to his hotel to eat Campbell's soup heated on a stove in his room. Come the weekend, he flew to New York and dined with his family, sometimes getting together as well with Wall Street's wealthiest bankers and lawyers.

To some of the SEC staff in Washington who opposed vigorously the changes under way at the commission, Shad's weekly commute became a disquieting metaphor: After years of proud warfare between Wall Street and the SEC, Shad had ushered in a new era of shuttle diplomacy aimed at bringing them closer together.

AN ALLIANCE IS BORN

During his many years on Wall Street, John Shad often told friends that he planned to finish his career in public service, a goal he credited to his Mormon grandmother, who had said a person should spend one third of his life learning, one third earning, and one third serving.

By the late 1970s, Shad had accomplished the earning part: he had
built a fortune of more than $10 million. But his career at Hutton
had peaked and Shad wasn't sure what he would do next.

All that started to change when Shad took a summer vacation with
some Hutton colleagues at the Bohemian Grove north of San Francisco, an exclusive, all-male summer camp for business and political
leaders. One day, Shad had a chance meeting with the former governor
of California, Ronald Reagan, who was wearing cowboy boots and sat
perched on a railing, absorbed in a performance by the ventrilo-
quist Edgar Bergen.

When the show ended, the two men took a walk and ended up at a
part of the camp known as The Hillbillies, where Shad had lunch. His
waiter was George Bush, who was taking his turn that day serving
tables at the Grove.

Shad's brief talk with Reagan that day flowered into a political
alliance. During Reagan's campaign for the presidency in 1980, his
campaign manager approached Shad and asked him to handle the
candidate's fundraising in New York.

Few on Wall Street or in the boardrooms of the Fortune 500—few
of Shad's peers—supported Reagan that early. Most favored Bush or
former Texas governor John Connally. But Shad had been impressed
by Reagan's positions on key issues. He made it known within the
campaign that he wanted a job in Washington if Reagan were elected.

Shad was pegged for the SEC chairmanship because of his strong
background in finance and because he "was probably the first business-
man on Wall Street that came out early for Ronald Reagan," said
former White House personnel chief E. Pendleton James. He breezed
through his confirmation hearings.

On Wall Street, Shad had tried and failed to gain the top job at
Hutton. It had been a painful defeat. Now, finally, he was in charge
of an institution.

A CONTEST OF WILLS

John Shad was in many ways naive about how Washington worked.
He didn't realize how much resistance he would encounter from the
SEC's vast bureaucracy and its supporters in Congress. Shad was un-
daunted. He was used to battling until he got his way. One top aide

nicknamed him "the Russian" because he was always negotiating for other people's turf.

The SEC that Shad took over in 1981 had been dominated for a decade by the ideas and personality of Stanley Sporkin, the commission's longest-serving enforcement chief. Sporkin had pushed the SEC to regulate corporate behavior through aggressive and creative law enforcement. Some on Wall Street and elsewhere believed Sporkin, who left the agency just before Shad arrived, had overreached.

Shad's early decisions signaled a new era. The chairman's office turned down a 1982 recommendation by the SEC's market regulation division to investigate alleged tax fraud at the Philadelphia Stock Exchange and the Chicago Board Options Exchange. Shad made it known that the commission would not pursue cases unless they related directly to the securities laws.

While approving some corporate misconduct cases left over from Sporkin's time, Shad pushed the enforcement division to change its priorities—he wanted the commission to go after individual crooks, especially those who engaged in illegal insider stock trading.

At times Shad seemed to regard some of the SEC staff as his adversaries, and relied on friends who were Wall Street lawyers or corporate directors for advice. Early on, Shad invited Johnson & Johnson Chairman James Burke, a classmate of Shad's at the Harvard Business School, and other corporate leaders to talk with SEC staff about what they thought the agency should be doing. Wealthy Omaha investor Warren Buffett came to discuss accounting issues with a selected group of the SEC staff.

Throughout his tenure, he talked regularly with Wall Street takeover experts such as attorney Martin Lipton about SEC policy issues. Rather than selecting Sporkin's successor from inside the SEC, as was traditional, Shad hired John Fedders, a corporate lawyer from the outside, to be his enforcement chief.

To those inside the commission, in the Reagan administration and on Wall Street who supported Shad's drive to remold the SEC, the staff's resistance was seen as an act of bureaucratic self-preservation. "John Shad had the unusual habit of asking why," Fedders said. "The staff disliked him for that at first. They were used to an unfettered environment in which they got everything they wanted."

The SEC staff learned early on that John Shad hated wasting time in transit—he called it purgatory. He held meetings in his car on the way to National Airport. He harassed taxi drivers about their speed and route selection. Returning from La Guardia Airport in New York one time during his days at Hutton, Shad instructed the taxi driver on the quickest way to reach 60th Street and Third Avenue, predicting the cost of the ride. The driver told Shad he was wrong. Shad offered to bet—double or nothing the final amount on the meter.

"It was a real contest of wills and the cabbie agreed to do it," recalled Clarke Ambrose, a Hutton executive who was along for the ride. When they arrived, following Shad's directions, the meter showed Shad had won. Shad paid the fare anyway but "the cabbie was so upset he couldn't speak," Ambrose recalled.

Shad charged around Washington the same way. He raced up to Capitol Hill and announced bold plans: He intended to cut the SEC's staff, change its internal budgeting procedures, and put in a new computer system to speed corporate filings.

Shad believed that regulation should be evaluated closely in terms of its costs and benefits—and he believed the regulations requiring companies to make repetitive disclosures were more costly than beneficial. Shad pushed his changes through despite the opposition of several major Wall Street firms, which feared they would lose lucrative business if the process were changed.

At the same time, he rejected a Reagan transition report that recommended dismantling the SEC's enforcement division in Washington and sending the staff to the regional offices. And he dismissed the theories of some conservative economists who said, among other things, that insider trading should be made legal because it would help the stock market.

But the Democrats in Congress wanted no part of Shad's programs, and they tore into him. Rep. John Dingell (D-Mich.), the powerful chairman of the House Energy and Commerce Committee, initiated investigations of Shad's personal finances. He found nothing wrong. On the budget issue, there was no conciliation—Dingell and other Democrats fought to defend the legacy of Stanley Sporkin, which they feared was being erased.

□ □ □

One day early in Shad's tenure, he was summoned to a basement conference room in the House's Rayburn Office Building for a private conference with Dingell and Rep. Tim Wirth (D-Colo.), then chairman of a key finance subcommittee and now a senator. Wirth was refusing to cut the SEC's budget.

"Shad was trying to figure out if I was serious [about not cutting the budget]," Wirth recalled. "I figured I'd bring in the big gun. . . . Dingell said this is what it is going to be and Shad got the signal loud and clear. Shad was almost shaking."

Shad moved firmly to control both the commission's internal processes and the policy positions it took in public. At times he discouraged other commissioners from testifying before Congress.

It appeared to some SEC staff and commissioners that Shad deliberately passed out copies of his own testimony, containing important policy pronouncements, at a point when it was too late for them to comment on its contents. Commissioner Aulana Peters finally insisted in 1985 that unless the full commission approved congressional testimony before it was given, it had to be labeled as personal opinion.

The effects of Shad's program were not immediately apparent outside the commission. It wasn't until 1984 and 1985 that radical changes began to occur in the stock market and the economy, influenced in part by Shad's policies, as the economy recovered from recession and roared ahead, speculative stock trading bubbled, and debt-driven hostile corporate takeovers boomed.

In the early years, Shad had few allies on the commission—the four other commissioners had been appointed by previous administrations and they did not share Shad's fervor for change. Eventually, in the mid-1980s, their terms began to expire and free-market allies of Shad were appointed, giving him an effective working majority on controversial economic issues such as takeovers.

'THE ODDEST THING'

Inside the SEC's headquarters, shrouded by the secrecy that surrounds nearly all the commission's deliberations, an incident occurred in early 1983 that demonstrated just how much had changed under Shad.

The SEC staff was locked in a dispute with the insurance giant

Aetna Life & Casualty Co. The staff thought Aetna's bookkeeping had been improper and wanted to wipe $200 million in profits off Aetna's publicly filed accounting statements, contending that this would give investors a truer picture of Aetna's financial health. Aetna officials said its books were accurate. A stalemate developed, and in January 1983 the issue was scheduled for consideration at a closed SEC meeting.

Outsiders are routinely barred from closed SEC meetings. Not only does the commission refuse to discuss or acknowledge closed cases, it does not permit defendants in enforcement cases to appear before the commission. A defendant's argument, if one is made, is submitted in writing.

Not this time. After consulting with the SEC's general counsel, Shad had agreed to allow John Filer, Aetna's chief executive, and Joe Flom, one of Wall Street's leading takeover lawyers and a personal friend of Shad's, to attend the meeting in the commission's sixth floor hearing room and present a defense. There was virtually no precedent for Shad's decision, the general counsel said, but it wasn't a violation of any rules.

There was an awkward moment as the meeting began. Nobody knew where Flom and Filer should sit. There were no assigned seats for outsiders. Flom plopped down in a high-backed swivel commissioner's chair. Two were empty; the commissioners had withdrawn from the case because they had done work for Aetna before joining the SEC.

From his perch, Flom argued that the SEC shouldn't force Aetna to make the $200 million bookkeeping change in dispute.

"It was improper," said former SEC commissioner John Evans, a Republican, of Flom's appearance. "I didn't see any reason just because it was Joe Flom to let them in—perhaps even more so because it was him." Added David Schwiesow, an SEC staff attorney who attended the meeting: "It was the oddest thing I ever saw."

Shad said the only reason Aetna was permitted to appear with counsel before the commission was because of the magnitude of the issues to it and the insurance industry.

Flom and Filer left the meeting room when the commission called for a vote. Aetna lost, 3–0. Shad voted last and joined the majority. He had made statements during the debate that some staff saw as expressing support for Aetna's position.

The image of Joe Flom in a high-backed commissioner's chair lingered long after the vote.

"Everybody was very embarrassed about it," Schwiesow said. Given the strong emotions that were stirred, it was a testament to the SEC's strong culture of secrecy that word of the incident was never leaked to Shad's Democratic opponents in Congress. Since the staff had prevailed, some in the agency said they felt no harm was done.

But others said they wondered where else John Shad's priorities—and the complicated web of ideas and friendships he had brought with him from Wall Street to Washington—would lead next.

CHAIRMAN TRIED TO COOL STAFF REGULATORY ZEAL

SHAD FOUGHT SEC CASES HE THOUGHT UNFAIR

MONDAY, FEBRUARY 6, 1989

BY STEVE COLL AND DAVID A. VISE

The Securities and Exchange Commission meeting room for cases closed to the public was packed when SEC Chairman John Shad arrived. Word of his impending confrontation with Bobby Lawyer, chief of the SEC's San Francisco office, had spread through headquarters, and the staff had come to the sixth floor to see who would prevail.

It was a winter's day early in 1985, and finally, after a two-year investigation and weeks of heated internal discussions, Lawyer was about to make his case that the SEC should lodge securities-fraud charges against Merrill Lynch & Co. Inc., the largest brokerage firm in the country.

If anyone from the public had known to ask, the SEC wouldn't have acknowledged that a discussion about Merrill Lynch was taking place. But inside the agency, the case had grown into an important symbol. The debate that day reflected nearly four years of tension between the SEC bureaucracy and Shad, who came to Washington from Wall Street believing that the SEC sometimes treated big brokerage houses unfairly. He adopted a new standard that made it tougher to bring charges against companies for wrongdoing by employees.

Shad's actions reflected his desire to steer the SEC away from what he viewed as excessive interference in the daily business of Wall Street, part of his broad interest in freeing brokerage firms and the stock exchanges from what he felt was overregulation that restrained the nation's economy.

Lawyer and other SEC staff attorneys felt that the Merrill Lynch case was a matter of law, not ideology. They argued that the firm had failed to act on accusations that a stockbroker had defrauded customers out of hundreds of thousands of dollars, and that the company should be punished. Shad objected; a firm as large as Merrill Lynch shouldn't be charged with fraud for a single employee's alleged wrongdoing, he said.

When Shad tried to block the charges against Merrill Lynch, Lawyer and the San Francisco staff insisted that they be allowed to come to Washington to present their case. They couldn't believe it was even necessary to debate the issue. Before Shad was appointed by President Reagan to head the SEC in 1981, the five-member commission had routinely approved charges such as the ones proposed against Merrill Lynch.

Shad, a self-made multimillionaire who had spent much of his career at the E.F. Hutton Inc. brokerage firm, changed all that, imposing a new policy on when such cases should be brought. Now, the staff proposed charges only in what they considered to be the most flagrant instances.

As the debate began, tensions ran high. Some of the staff members were afraid that John Fedders, the agency's enforcement chief and a Shad loyalist, would swing the vote against Lawyer. But the staff also knew that Shad sometimes found it difficult to muster the support of a majority of the other commissioners.

Although Lawyer had never appeared before the commission at a closed meeting, the overflow audience suited him fine. Ever since college, when he lived in Harlem and earned his tuition delivering carts of clothing to Manhattan's finest department stores, Lawyer told others that he wanted to be the kind of trial attorney he saw on television and at the movies—one who could dominate a crowded courtroom and triumph with dramatic cross-examination.

WHO'S RESPONSIBLE?

It was a letter to Bobby Lawyer's office in San Francisco that began the whole affair. It arrived on May 17, 1982, from Jan Haraszthy, a retired wine merchant and a Merrill Lynch customer. Haraszthy complained that a Merrill Lynch stockbroker in San Francisco named Victor Matl had made a $15,000 transaction in Haraszthy's account against his expressed wishes and while he was out of town. Haraszthy also said that Matl's superiors had been unresponsive to his complaints.

This was the core of the SEC's regulatory and enforcement work: protection of individual investors against alleged fraud, inspection and supervision of brokerage firms, and enforcement of detailed rules governing how a brokerage should treat its customers. It was less glamorous than the headline-grabbing insider trading cases then being developed at headquarters in Washington, but such work occupied much of the time of SEC attorneys in the regional offices.

Shad thought the SEC had an important role to play in protecting investors from fraud, and had vowed to crack down on insider trading, but he pulled the commission back from close scrutiny of Wall Street brokerages' operations, particularly sales practices. As a longtime executive at E.F. Hutton, Shad believed that investment firms—and the stock exchanges to which they belonged—were well equipped to police themselves. He felt that transferring some responsibility to the stock exchanges would free up SEC resources, making the agency more efficient. The SEC would do its part by monitoring how well the stock exchanges handled their new duties.

A number of the SEC staff thought Shad's approach only exacerbated the conflict within Wall Street firms between their drive for profits and their obligations to the law. Shifting enforcement responsibility to Wall Street and resisting proposals to file charges against big brokerage firms for wrongdoing by employees resulted in a breakdown of discipline at the largest investment firms, these SEC staff lawyers felt.

The debate had far-reaching implications: It raised a basic question about who was responsible for detecting and preventing fraud on Wall Street. The issue took on added significance toward the end of Shad's tenure at the SEC, when the biggest Wall Street corruption scandal in history erupted, focusing in large part on charges of fraud by employees in a branch office of Drexel Burnham Lambert Inc.

Some staff attorneys and commissioners thought the Merrill Lynch case demonstrated that the stock exchanges and brokerages could not be relied upon to carry the burden of enforcement. Lawyer, while agreeing to answer questions about his background, declined any comment about the investigation of Matl or the debate over whether to file charges against Merrill Lynch.

For Shad, Lawyer's enforcement approach was an example of how the commission's staff sometimes tried to punish big Wall Street firms unfairly. "When one out of 10,000 account executives violates the law the question is whether it is sufficient to justify sanctioning a major securities firm," Shad said in an interview. "During this period there were a thousand other situations that were properly handled by the firm. If the firm has to be perfect the cost is enormous and it has to be passed on to the investing public. I have a basic visceral reaction to sanctioning the firm for one bad account executive."

Shad said, however, that any stockbroker who abused his customers "should be prosecuted to the full extent of the law."

Lawyer dispatched SEC investigator John Bruns to the Merrill Lynch branch in the San Francisco financial district on June 15, 1983. When Bruns arrived, he found a file of 35 complaints about Matl, raising questions in Bruns' mind about Matl's conduct as a stockbroker, about the extent of Merrill Lynch's investigation into the complaints and about the company's decision to retain him.

Max L. Christensen, an Episcopal priest, complained that Matl had defrauded him of $35,000 by making unauthorized trades and by pushing him into risky investments. Robert Reeves, a junior high school principal, said that he had told Matl his goal was to earn enough money through cautious investments to help his children buy homes, but that Matl pushed him into speculative stocks, causing him to lose about $10,000 in three months.

SEC records do not reflect Matl's response to these specific complaints, but Matl said on several occasions that he was authorized to make the trades that customers were complaining about. Without admitting or denying wrongdoing, Matl settled an SEC lawsuit in 1985 and was permanently barred from the regulated brokerage industry. His lawyer declined to comment.

As Lawyer's staff took testimony from Matl's customers, they thought they discovered part of the answer to the question of why Merrill Lynch had not launched a vigorous investigation when the complaints first came in: Matl was one of the top five salesmen in the booming San Francisco office. Between 1977 and 1983, he generated about $1.8 million in sales commissions, of which his share was about $600,000.

When the SEC's investigation began, several of Matl's customers had retained lawyers to press legal claims. Merrill Lynch had settled with six customers, paying about $75,000.

In response to questions submitted by The Washington Post, Merrill Lynch said in a statement that Matl's productivity as a salesman did not influence how the company handled the complaints against Matl. "It is our policy that any employee's production is not a factor when reviewing potential or alleged improprieties on the part of the employee," the statement said.

After the SEC's surprise inspection, top officials from Merrill Lynch's New York headquarters flew to San Francisco and interviewed Matl and his supervisors at length. Matl promised to change his practices and Merrill officials, who concluded that he was a talented salesman, required him to go to New York at his own expense for a weeklong refresher course on the law governing stockbroker behavior.

Ten months later, new complaints against Matl arose, and he was fired.

"Stock brokerage firms have an inherent conflict of interest," said Cary Lapidus, then an SEC attorney assigned to the Matl case and now in private practice in San Francisco. Lapidus declined to comment about the Matl case, but noted that brokerage firms "are profit-making entities operating under a self-regulatory system. When a highly productive broker commits violations, sometimes a firm believes it is more profitable to settle or litigate customers' claims rather than to fire the broker."

In its statement, Merrill Lynch said it was "committed to the highest standards of professional and personal ethical conduct" and that its systems of employee supervision are "second to none." The statement said, "While the Matl situation was a unique one, we believe our firm acted reasonably and responsibly in dealing with it based on what was known at the time."

OFF THE CALENDAR

For more than a year, the investigation of Merrill Lynch by the SEC's San Francisco office proceeded amid tight secrecy. For nine months after the SEC's inspection, Matl continued to do business with his old clients and solicited new accounts. Neither the SEC nor Merrill Lynch warned Matl's customers of the complaints or the investigation.

The commission keeps nearly all its investigative work private. Officials at the agency say that secrecy facilitates vigorous internal debate and protects the privacy of innocent parties. Because the SEC settles most of its cases, releasing only a carefully worded document that often is the subject of extensive negotiations with defendants, it is often impossible for the public to assess whether its settlements are fair. For its part, Merrill Lynch had no desire to make public the SEC's investigation—exposure might invite civil lawsuits or provoke competitors to use the allegations to win business. "The problem is that when a firm is charged with fraud, account executives of other firms solicit their clients," Shad said.

By conducting investigations in private, SEC staff and commissioners avoid scrutiny of their decision-making processes. Such scrutiny from Congress or the public would be potentially uncomfortable—it might bring pressures on the commission to speed up, slow down or drop cases. In a few instances during the 1980s when word of a controversial SEC decision was leaked, some commissioners were publicly criticized by members of Congress who disagreed with how they evaluated evidence accumulated by the staff.

Merrill Lynch mustered its resources to stave off fraud charges. Shortly after Labor Day, 1984, as the case neared its final vote at a closed SEC meeting, the brokerage firm sent former commissioner and enforcement chief Irving Pollack and former staff attorney Robert Romano to meet with SEC enforcement chief Fedders and other staff in Washington. In a conference room at SEC headquarters at 450 5th St. NW, Pollack and Romano argued vigorously that neither Merrill Lynch nor its managers should be charged. On Oct. 19 they submitted a confidential 40-page memo with about 25 exhibits to bolster their position.

Every SEC division that reviewed the case agreed that fraud charges should be filed against Merrill Lynch, including the agency's counseling group, a unit of SEC lawyers that reviews all regulatory and enforcement recommendations headed for a commission vote. Shad was adamant that the brokerage should not be charged. He temporarily pulled the case off the commission's confidential calendar, saying that Lawyer needed to provide more information about why Merrill Lynch should be charged.

Meanwhile, Shad ordered the counseling group, through a subordinate, to draft a memo opposing charges against Merrill Lynch, according to two staff attorneys familiar with the case. "I do not recall asking somebody to oppose charges against Merrill Lynch," Shad said.

The counseling group was established by Shad's predecessor as SEC chairman, Harold Williams, largely to curtail the power and policies of Stanley Sporkin, the best-known and longest-serving SEC enforcement chief. Dismissed by some as a zealot, lauded by others as the consummate public servant, Sporkin had a far-reaching impact on business and law during the 1970s.

He established his reputation by pursuing corporations and their top executives for paying overseas bribes, maintaining political slush funds and engaging in other major frauds. "We did it in enforcement with limited dollars, high impact. . . . You can do a lot by bringing the critical kinds of cases," Sporkin said in an interview.

By the late 1970s, a growing number of people, especially in the corporate world, felt that Sporkin had gone too far. When he was appointed to the SEC chairmanship, Shad was urged to dump Sporkin. But Sporkin didn't need to be pushed; he already was frustrated by the growing resistance to his policies. In the spring of 1981 he became general counsel of the Central Intelligence Agency. He now is a federal judge.

When Shad took over as SEC chairman, he moved decisively to change Sporkin's approach. He asked the counseling group to develop a new policy describing when it was appropriate to charge corporations for wrongdoing by employees. Generally, the staff had to find evidence that the company had acted in bad faith or that the accused employees were top-level officials.

In 1983, in a "cooked books" case involving the Baltimore-based spice company McCormick & Co., Shad argued against naming the corporation publicly as a defendant. In 1984, he opposed charges against the Wall Street firm Thomson McKinnon Securities Inc. In 1985, at the same time the Merrill Lynch case was generating controversy inside the SEC, Shad fought with the staff about a similar case against Smith Barney Inc.

In each of those cases, charges were filed against the firms and they agreed to settle the matters without admitting or denying the SEC's allegations. In some instances, there was heated debate between Shad and the staff—charges against Smith Barney, for example, were approved after hot debate and a 3–2 commission vote.

But while the staff sometimes won individual votes, many SEC attorneys felt that Shad was gaining ground fast. The enforcement staff grew reluctant to initiate investigations of sales practices at big Wall Street firms because it knew such cases faced stiff resistance from the chairman's office, according to interviews with more than a dozen staff attorneys. Some investigations either never got off the ground or were dropped along the way. So strongly did the chairman feel about the issue that there were even battles about whether to put the names of big Wall Street firms on SEC subpoenas during investigations, before any decision was made about fraud charges. Shad thought the practice was unfair to the firms.

Shad's views about enforcement against large Wall Street firms were sincerely held, but they angered some staff lawyers who felt he was choosing to ignore the federal statute that empowered the SEC to bring such charges as preventive and disciplining measures—even when there was no evidence of companywide fraud. "Shad didn't fully grasp the purpose of the failure to supervise provisions of the securities laws," said Jared Kopel, the enforcement attorney in charge of the Smith Barney case, now in private practice in Palo Alto, Calif. Kopel declined to comment about the Smith Barney matter.

In Shad's view, the SEC brought more "failure to supervise" cases from 1981 to 1987 than in other six-year periods and implemented a better system for responding to investor complaints.

Bobby Lawyer became a champion of the staff's cause late in 1984. While some in Washington cautioned against pushing Shad too hard over the Merrill Lynch case, Lawyer refused to compromise—he insisted on coming in from San Francisco to argue at the commission table. Lawyer and his staff received some help behind the scenes from commissioner Aulana Peters, a Democrat who opposed Shad on some enforcement issues but maintained a friendly personal relationship with him. When the Merrill Lynch case was removed from the commission's calendar, Peters and her staff made repeated inquiries. Shad later rescheduled the matter for a vote.

AT THE TABLE

Shad and Lawyer sat across from each other at the commission's oval-shaped meeting table. The debate lasted about 45 minutes. At the start, there were presentations from Lawyer and David Schwiesow, a counseling group attorney who had been designated to present the chairman's views. Schwiesow was a somewhat reluctant advocate, since he and the rest of the counseling group opposed Shad's position that Merrill Lynch shouldn't be charged.

Shad said he didn't understand how a firm the size of Merrill Lynch —one with tens of thousands of employees and offices all around the world—could be held publicly responsible for the actions of one stockbroker in San Francisco. How could that be fair? There had not been a systemic breakdown at Merrill Lynch, Shad said.

Lawyer countered that Merrill Lynch had only one system for compliance with the securities laws—a system that depended on close involvement between the branch offices and the firm's headquarters. In this case, Lawyer said, the system hadn't worked. The failure *was* systemic, he argued.

About 15 or 20 minutes into the meeting, enough commissioners had spoken up in Lawyer's favor or asked sympathetic questions to make it plain that Lawyer had the three votes necessary for a majority. Fedders, too, spoke up for the staff's position. At one point, an attorney present recalled, Shad acknowledged that he was beginning to "feel a little bit lonely on this." The vast majority of SEC votes are unanimous, but this time Shad stuck to his dissenting position. The final tally was 4–1 to charge Merrill Lynch.

Informed of the SEC's vote, Merrill Lynch agreed to settle the case in 1985 without admitting or denying the commission's allegations, a standard formula that helps the defendant avoid additional liability in civil courts. Merrill Lynch accepted a censure and the head of its San Francisco office was suspended for two months. Former stockbroker Matl, who had entered law school in San Francisco, applied for a summer job at the SEC. He was turned down.

Bobby Lawyer's victory was celebrated by staff members in San Francisco and Washington, but they knew they were far from winning the war. "It was always very easy to bang the little [brokerage] houses, but if it was a big firm there was a reluctance to do anything under

Shad," said Ira Lee Sorkin, who between 1984 and 1986 was head of the SEC's New York regional office with jurisdiction over Wall Street. "If it was a little firm, you could name the firm, but if it was a big firm you knew you would have a problem."

Staff researcher Melissa Mathis contributed to this report.

GIVING BIRTH TO AGE OF SPECULATION

TUESDAY, FEBRUARY 7, 1989

BY STEVE COLL
AND DAVID A. VISE

Soon after John Shad became chairman of the Securities and Exchange Commission in 1981, he clambered into a bus one afternoon with a half dozen of his senior staff and headed for the race track in Charlestown, W. Va.

At the track, Shad made a proposition: For their convenience, the SEC officials could make bets with Shad rather than wagering at the betting windows. Shad played "the house," paying off on winners and raking it in on losers.

But it wasn't the money that seemed to excite him—it was the risk. He rarely went to the race track or to a casino, but he loved to wager. "Shad would bet on anything," said Clarke Ambrose, who worked with him at the E.F. Hutton brokerage firm. "He would bet on two cockroaches crossing the floor."

Shad's affection for betting paralleled his views about the stock market: some increased speculation was good and necessary. Partly as a result of his policies as SEC chairman between 1981 and 1987, speculation boomed on Wall Street. New and exotic products mushroomed in the markets and corporate takeovers attracted a new breed of professional speculator who traded rapidly to capture quick profits. Technology played a role, too, as computers speeded up the action.

Speculation and computerized trading have been blamed for contributing to the October 1987 stock market crash, but an important cause of change has gone unnoticed: Regulators did not enforce federal rules designed to control speculation by large institutional investors. In this loose environment, usually conservative institutions such as pension funds and university endowments became bold speculators, according to interviews with dozens of stock market professionals, regulators and exchange officials.

"There have to be more stringent controls" on speculators, Fred Grauer of Wells Fargo Bank, a leader in the use of computerized stock trading, told federal regulators at a hearing in late 1987.

Shad believed that some speculation enhanced the stock market's efficiency. One of his favorite words was "liquidity," which he used to conjure up the image of money flowing through the stock market and the economy like water through a fertile delta. Shad thought of faltering economies as dry gulches where the flow of money had been cut off; the solution was to open a spigot and let cash pour again, until it lapped into every parched corner and brought barren land to life.

Speculators helped promote liquidity by spilling cash into the market, Shad thought, and liquidity helped the economy by making it easier for companies to find money to pay for growth.

There were times when Shad's views about liquidity sounded almost religious. "The millennium to which mankind can aspire is that great day when capital will be permitted to flow, with safeguards against fraud and with the ease of water, into every nook and cranny of economic opportunity, first within nations, second throughout the free world, and ultimately throughout the earth," Shad declared.

CUTTING A DEAL

On a summer day in July 1981, in a rear booth of the Monocle Restaurant on Capitol Hill, John Shad lunched with Philip Johnson, chairman of the Commodity Futures Trading Commission, or CFTC, and talked about making a deal. Shad loved to make deals—he had spent a lifetime at it on Wall Street. When the meal was finished, groundwork had been laid for an agreement that would end years of regulatory bickering, reshuffle the roles of their respective agencies and change the character of the U.S. stock markets.

Shad and Johnson had much in common. They were newcomers to Washington—Shad from Wall Street, Johnson from law practice in Chicago, where he advised that city's freewheeling commodity exchanges. Both were steadfast believers in the "new beginning" promised by their president, Ronald Reagan.

Early in 1981, when Shad was picked to head the SEC, Johnson was nominated to be chairman of the CFTC, which regulates the commodity markets.

The SEC and CFTC had been at each other's throats for several years over which agency should have authority to regulate newly invented products called financial futures.

Neither agency could agree on what these futures were. SEC staff lawyers said they were like stocks and bonds, and thus should be regulated by the SEC, while CFTC attorneys said they were like commodities such as silver and gold, and thus should be overseen by the CFTC. The dispute had finally spilled into the courts.

Shad and Johnson, both free-market enthusiasts, decided that day at the Monocle to solve the problem. It took months of interagency negotiations and a big fight in Congress, but finally the deal was signed.

The agreement had many pieces, but the most important part gave the CFTC undisputed authority to regulate stock index futures. By the end of John Shad's tenure at the SEC five years later, stock index futures had become a major force in the U.S. financial markets. For many big institutional traders, stock index futures were more important than the underlying stocks themselves.

But in 1982, when Congress debated the deal cut by Shad and Johnson, about the only people who suspected that stock index futures might alter the market fundamentally were a handful of sophisticated Wall Street investors and economists. "The regulators have always been a good six or seven years behind the university [economists] in understanding these complex financial devices," said Gregg Jarrell, a former chief economist at the SEC.

A few people sounded early warnings. "In my judgment, a very high percentage—probably at least 95 percent and more likely much higher—of the activity generated by these [stock index futures] will be strictly gambling in nature," investor Warren Buffett cautioned the House Energy and Commerce Committee in a letter submitted during the 1982 congressional debate. "In the long run, gambling-dominated activities . . . are not going to be good for the capital markets."

But few paid much heed. The deal seemed to solve a nagging regulatory dispute and, perhaps most important, hardly anyone in Congress knew how stock index futures worked.

TRANSFERRING THE RISK

To understand stock index futures and how they changed the stock market, it helps to think about the weather.

A century ago, violent storms, howling tornadoes and devastating droughts gave rise to the ideas that still underlie the nation's futures markets and may help explain what went awry in the stock market during the mid-1980s.

The seasons and the weather formed a repeating, treacherous economic cycle for farmers, who have always depended on rain at the right time and in the right amount. In the spring, a farmer went deeply into debt to buy seed, fertilizer and other supplies for planting. If the weather cooperated, he profited. At harvest time late in the summer, he hauled his crop to market, sold it at the prevailing price, paid off his debts, and stashed away the profits. Next spring, he began again.

But if the weather failed, he was ruined. If it rained too much and there was a bumper crop, plummeting prices caused by the oversupply prevented him from earning enough to pay off his debt. If it rained too little and his crop failed, he might not have enough to sell to pay back his spring borrowings. Every year, then, the farmer involuntarily gambled on the weather.

In Chicago and Kansas City and other midwestern cities, a free-market answer to the farmer's predicament sprang up. Fly-by-night speculators and profiteers came west and offered to make deals with farmers. In the spring, at planting time, a farmer might contract with a speculator to "presell" the crop he would harvest later.

The farmer would get the speculator's cash, receiving the prevailing market price for wheat or whatever crop was to be planted, and agree to deliver the goods at harvest time. The speculator was betting that crop prices would rise so that he could make a killing.

The deal between the farmer and the speculator involved what economists call "risk transfer." The risk of bad weather was shifted from someone who couldn't afford to bear it, the farmer and his family, to someone who was perfectly willing to gamble—the speculator.

As time went on, the speculators started to swap crop contracts. The modern futures markets in Chicago actually began in loose, raucous crowds of speculators who gathered in the mud near the railroad depots where the crops came in. Liquidity of the sort imagined by John Shad began to develop; money changed hands "with the ease of water" among the speculators, and it became increasingly simple for farmers to minimize the risks of weather by preselling their crops in the futures markets.

It wasn't a perfect system. The speculators began to cheat. There were rigged trades, price squeezes and myriad other manipulations—some of the same kinds of alleged fraud now under investigation at Chicago's two largest futures exchanges.

Until the early 1970s, the Chicago futures exchanges were regulated by a small, ineffective office in the Agriculture Department. In 1974, a series of scandals led Congress to create the CFTC.

The CFTC's earliest challenge was posed by Leo Melamed, a science fiction writer and speculative trader who had lost his shirt in Chicago's futures pits on more than one occasion.

Stimulated by economic thinkers at the University of Chicago, Melamed realized that the risk transfer that arose so naturally a century earlier between farmers and speculators could be applied to other areas of the economy. What was the difference between a farmer worried about changes in the weather and a giant, multinational bank concerned about fluctuations in the value of the dollar in Japan, where the bank might have huge loans outstanding? The price of the dollar relative to other currencies was just as unpredictable as the weather.

Melamed, sensing that he had stumbled onto a potential bonanza, began to forge answers to these questions with officials of the Chicago Mercantile Exchange, which had long been dwarfed by the larger Chicago Board of Trade. He and his competitors came up with futures for currencies, Treasury bonds, Treasury bills, corporate bonds, mortgage-backed securities and, finally, stocks—a pension fund, for example, could hedge against a drop in the overall stock market by "preselling" some of its stocks.

The Chicago exchanges discovered that it was theoretically possible to transfer almost any economic risk on earth.

'BLESS YOU, MY SON'

As the variety and volume of financial futures grew, some regulators became unnerved by what they saw as "an unthinking crusade for every last drop of hedging, liquidity and efficiency, even when those goals become self-defeating," as former CFTC chairman Jim Stone, an outspoken opponent of financial futures, put it. "The definition of hedging is so broad that it encompasses any transfer of risk."

From that definition arose the idea of stock index futures.

Stock index futures are contracts containing promises about the future. Every contract has a date on it: an exact day, month and year sometime in the future guaranteeing the delivery of the financial value of stocks for a price negotiated in the present. The "index" part of the contract refers to the basket of stocks to be delivered. The most popular basket is the Standard & Poor's 500, made up of the stocks of 500 big U.S. corporations.

Shad wasn't even sure that stock index futures would ever become popular. Large institutions that owned a lot of stocks—university endowments, pension funds and mutual funds—tended to view the Chicago futures exchanges as seedy hotbeds of speculation. Why would a big trader abandon the venerable New York Stock Exchange for a market that started along Chicago's railroad tracks?

The answer, it turned out, was that they could buy more with less.

It takes less cash to buy a stock future than it does to buy the corresponding 500 stocks. The Federal Reserve, which regulates the use of borrowed money in the stock market, requires an individual investor buying a stock to put up at least 50 percent of the purchase price in cash. Banks and big Wall Street firms, by taking advantage of certain loopholes, can reduce their required down payment for buying stocks to about 20 percent. But the CFTC, which regulates futures, requires even less than that.

The down payment required of a speculator who wants to buy a stock futures contract today is about 15 percent. In contrast, the down payment required of an officially certified hedger is just above 1 percent. Official hedgers get more bang for their buck than anyone in the stock market, just as a home buyer with $20,000 on hand can buy a bigger house if the required down payment is 1 percent rather than 20 percent.

Stock futures regulation is based on the assumption that hedgers, who try to protect themselves against potential losses, are preferable to speculators, who tend to be treated as a necessary evil. Speculators are policed every step of the way lest they abuse the markets, but hedgers enjoy several privileges. The most important is that they can control more stock market value for less cash than other investors.

In the 1980s, nearly every Wall Street firm and sophisticated institutional investor in the stock market wanted to be an official hedger. It was easy to become one. An investor must fill out two applications: one at the Chicago Mercantile Exchange, where the S&P 500 contract is traded, and another at the investor's brokerage firm. The Merc form does not require the investor to provide much information; the brokerage firms' forms vary.

"Those things are almost a joke in some respects," said Howard Schneider, a leading futures lawyer in New York. "You file them and the exchanges say, 'Bless you, my son, you are a hedger.' "

The futures exchanges and the CFTC assert that hedging rules are enforced in vigorous audits, but a broad range of market professionals said in interviews that such audits rarely focus on whether an investor was hedging or speculating. A 1987 report by the research firm Equidex Inc. found that 90 percent of the institutional investors it surveyed who officially declared themselves to be hedgers were speculators.

After it obtained control over stock futures regulation, the CFTC assigned enforcement of the hedging rules to the Chicago exchanges. But the exchanges stood to lose business if they cracked down on speculators posing as hedgers.

"If you're Salomon Brothers and you're generating all the business at the exchange, [Chicago Merc executive] Leo [Melamed] and his boys are not going to come in for an audit," said Jack Barbanel, head of futures trading at the Wall Street firm Gruntal & Co. "You can't blame the users and the [Chicago Merc] because there's an inherent conflict of interest."

Moreover, as stock futures boomed during the 1980s, few people were sure anymore what was hedging and what was speculating. The complex, multifaceted stock and futures trading strategies practiced by many sophisticated investors, sometimes drawn up by computer programmers, made it hard to tell.

"I can argue that a hedge is speculation and that speculation is a hedge," said John D. Brookmeyer, vice president of Prudential Life, which owns a multibillion-dollar stock portfolio and trades actively in the stock futures markets. "The distinction is easy to blur."

Speculation grew like a soap bubble as institutions poured more of their cash into the stock and futures markets. Money managers and big investment firms became increasingly competitive, trading in and out of the futures markets, speculating in short-term strategies designed to outperform their rivals. Computers helped to link prices in Chicago and New York, causing stock prices to gyrate more rapidly than they ever had before.

By 1985, some on Wall Street, in Congress and at the SEC fretted that small investors were being squeezed out and that the markets were headed for collapse. Shad, from his vantage point at the SEC, was concerned about these developments. He discussed with Federal Reserve Board Chairman Paul A. Volcker ways to dampen the volatility in the market, including the possibility of higher down payments in the futures market. But no action was taken.

Neither Shad nor any of his staff publicly expressed concern that the speculation augured disaster. Shad did not want any dramatic changes that would eliminate the benefits of liquidity, including the ability of large, institutional investors to sell big blocks of stock easily.

As the exchanges took steps to combat the growing volatility, the speculation continued. By 1986, the annual volume of S&P 500 stock futures contracts traded had increased fivefold from 1982. On an average day in 1986, the underlying value of the S&P 500 stock futures contracts changing hands at the Chicago Mercantile Exchange was well over $1 billion, surpassing the value of daily stock trading at the New York Stock Exchange. "It really is a substitute for the [stock] market," said Barbanel. "The futures have been a spectacularly cost-effective proxy for the [stock] market."

Stock futures changed the way the New York Stock Exchange functioned. In the days before stock futures, a floor trader at the NYSE stood next to his post and talked about prices with other traders who gathered around him with their orders. A big order that "moved the market," or changed prices unexpectedly, was rare.

In the mid-1980s, as computer-driven trading grew, orders arrived at the floor trader's post in giant electronic bundles, whipsawing prices up and down. Money washed through the markets in great swells.

The stock market was certainly more liquid, as John Shad wanted it to be, but the waves kept getting larger and larger.

DISPATCHING TELEGRAMS

There were some people who saw it coming. John Phelan, the New York Stock Exchange's chairman, warned publicly in the spring of 1987 that the markets had been exposed to a potential "financial meltdown" because of speculation and the growth of computerized stock futures trading. Some dismissed Phelan's warning as sour grapes —the New York exchanges were losing business to the booming Chicago futures markets.

In one of Shad's last appearances before Congress in May 1987, Sen. Donald W. Riegle Jr. (D-Mich.) asked the SEC chairman whether stock prices could possibly fall as much as 500 points in a single day. "I would say I think it's highly remote, very remote," Shad said.

Five months later, the Dow Jones industrial average lost 508 points on Oct. 19, the largest one-day drop ever. The crash occurred after the Dow average posted gains of more than 400 points between the May hearing and the market's peak in August. Later, Shad would agree with those who said stock index futures should be put under the more rigorous supervision of the SEC, but he was convinced it was politically impossible to undo the deal he had cut at the Monocle Restaurant.

The crash disturbed the tranquility of the U.S. Embassy residence in The Hague, where Shad, who became U.S. ambassador to the Netherlands in June 1987, now lived. Shad dispatched telegrams to White House chief of staff Howard H. Baker Jr. and SEC Chairman David S. Ruder and wrote articles urging higher cash down payments to decrease speculation in stock futures. Shad wanted to raise the down payment so that it was 25 percent, similar to the level required in the stock market—a change that the Chicago exchanges warned would put stock futures out of commission.

"Action is needed now," Shad wrote.

Staff researcher Melissa Mathis contributed to this report.

AFTER 8 YEARS, A CHANCE TO RETURN TO THE FRAY

WEDNESDAY, FEBRUARY 8, 1989

BY DAVID A. VISE
AND STEVE COLL

On the weekend of Jan. 7, Drexel Burnham Lambert Inc. Chief Executive Fred Joseph boarded an airplane in New York bound for The Hague, capital of the Netherlands. Only a handful of Joseph's colleagues at Drexel knew of his trip, which came just weeks after the firm had agreed to plead guilty to criminal fraud charges and pay a record $650 million in penalties.

Joseph was flying to see John Shad, the U.S. ambassador to the Netherlands. Shad had hired Joseph out of Harvard Business School 26 years earlier, and for more than a decade on Wall Street had been Joseph's boss, mentor and friend.

But their relationship had changed dramatically during the 1980s, when Shad became chairman of the Securities and Exchange Commission, Wall Street's top cop. Joseph was running Drexel, the target of the biggest and most widely publicized securities fraud investigation in the SEC's history.

Now that Drexel was near an agreement with the government, Joseph wanted Shad to become Drexel's chairman and help save the firm.

It was surprising to some people that Shad, who had left the SEC in 1987, was interested in the job. But Shad liked challenges, and besides, he thought it would be good for the country if Drexel survived.

Though the commission had wide powers, Shad had done little as SEC chairman to restrain Drexel's junk-bond financed corporate raiders as they rattled the executive suites and shop floors of the country's largest companies with hostile bids during the mid-1980s.

Shad's views about takeovers and Drexel's role in financing many of them were complicated. But overall, he believed that takeovers were good for the economy because they rewarded shareholders and forced corporate managers to be more productive. The SEC finally acted to rein in Drexel after the agency staff found evidence of fraud late in 1986.

At the center of Drexel's rise was Michael Milken, its innovative and influential junk bond chief. Shad deeply admired Milken. During his own long career on Wall Street, Shad had engaged in some early junk bond financings and friendly mergers and acquisitions, though his use of these techniques was relatively conservative.

Milken should be punished if he were guilty of any wrongdoing, Shad thought. Drexel agreed to admit that Milken had rigged corporate takeovers and manipulated stock prices. But that didn't change Shad's feeling that Milken was a genius. If Milken, who has vigorously denied any wrongdoing, cut any corners, it was incidental to Drexel's success, Shad believed.

There was one other factor in the SEC's decision not to regulate takeovers aggressively that has gone unreported: At a key moment when some in the Reagan administration feared Shad was about to push for takeover restrictions, officials and economists privately told him that he was deviating from the free-market philosophy of the administration. Although the SEC is an independent agency, and not part of the administration's economic policymaking apparatus, several conservative economists in the administration lobbied Shad steadily to make sure he did not intervene.

THE LEVERAGING OF AMERICA

In June 1984, with Wall Street engulfed in a frenzy of junk-bond financed hostile takeovers led by Drexel, John Shad delivered a remarkable speech to the New York Financial Writers Association. For the first time since becoming SEC chairman, Shad spoke out about the dangers of corporate takeovers.

Shad warned that heavy borrowing to finance corporate takeovers had long-term economic and social consequences. Companies burdened by takeover debt would not be able to invest in plant, equipment, research and development of new products. Contrary to popular wisdom, he went on, many of the U.S. companies that were targets of takeovers had strong managements, not weak ones. When the next economic recession struck, many heavily leveraged companies would be pushed into bankruptcy, Shad predicted.

"In today's corporate world, Darwin's survival of the fittest has become, 'Acquire or be acquired,' " he said. "The more leveraged takeovers and buyouts today, the more bankruptcies tomorrow."

"The Leveraging of America" was the title of his talk, and it was a speech of which Shad was proud. After he delivered it, he asked one of his legal assistants to distribute copies to the chief executives of the Fortune 500—the largest corporations in the United States.

The speech, which made news worldwide, marked a potentially important turning point in the SEC's approach to the regulation of corporate takeovers.

Until 1984, the SEC had studied takeovers without advocating that anything be done about them. For two years the SEC had been under pressure from Congress, corporations and labor unions to take a stand on controversial takeover tactics, including the heavy use of high-risk, high-yield junk bond financing.

And perhaps most important, some of Shad's old friends from his three decades on Wall Street, including takeover attorney Martin Lipton and former SEC commissioner A. A. Sommer Jr., privately urged him to crack down on junk bonds and hostile takeovers. Shad defused the pressure temporarily by appointing a committee of experts, consisting mostly of Wall Street takeover professionals, to give the SEC advice about what to do.

The committee suggested tinkering with the takeover process, but recommended no fundamental change in regulations. But Shad grew more concerned as the use of debt to finance takeovers spiraled—in his days on Wall Street, he had been more cautious about the use of such leverage.

Now, in deciding to speak out, Shad had a wide impact; as SEC chairman, he was Wall Street's chief regulator, and he seemed to be taking a definite stand on a major economic policy issue. He heard warm praise from Wall Street friends who were growing worried about the aggressive, debt-driven takeover practices of Drexel's stable of corporate raiders.

Inside the SEC, Shad's speech alarmed Gregg Jarrell, the commission's recently hired chief economist. A self-described former hippie,

Jarrell had come to the SEC to promote the free market doctrine championed by the school where he was trained, the University of Chicago. Young, possessed of a sense of humor, and unconcerned about how long his career in Washington would last, Jarrell wanted to shake things up at the SEC.

On takeovers, his views were radical. "The best of all worlds is the termination of federal regulation," he wrote in a dissent to the report of Shad's committee of takeover experts. His views attracted the attention of raider T. Boone Pickens Jr., who like Jarrell was an avid racquetball player. When in Washington, Pickens would come by SEC headquarters in his stretch limousine and pick up Jarrell for a game.

When Shad provided him an advance copy of his "Leveraging of America" speech, Jarrell reacted strongly. "B.S.!" he wrote in the margin, making so many marks on the page that he turned his copy red. "You've got no evidence."

Others felt as Jarrell did. SEC Commissioner Charles Cox, a free market economist who had earlier held Jarrell's job and who had received his commission seat with Shad's help, said he was "surprised" by Shad's speech. Douglas Ginsburg, then head of the regulatory section of the Office of Management and Budget, also expressed concerns, as did other economists and officials at OMB, the Council of Economic Advisers, the Justice Department and the Treasury Department.

The conservative economists' critique was something Shad had said he wanted. One of Shad's goals when he became chairman was to transform the SEC's approach to problem solving by de-emphasizing legal reasoning and promoting an economic-based approach. He wanted all regulatory proposals analyzed by a method known as cost-benefit analysis, in which the goals of regulation are measured against predicted cost. He wanted to get rid of "burdensome" regulations.

Above all, Shad wanted to address complaints from Wall Street—which reflected his own views—that some SEC lawyers who had limited knowledge about how markets worked were making decisions about new rules with no appreciation for the economic consequences.

Jarrell and the others saw Shad's speech as a betrayal. "The administration's view was that Shad was off the reservation," Jarrell recalled.

"Number one, they wanted some communication with him, and number two, they wanted to get in there and influence" Shad's approach to takeovers.

Since coming to Washington, Shad had developed little intimacy with the White House. Once, when Shad wanted to discuss financial regulation with Vice President Bush, he had to dial 411 to find the White House phone number. When he reached Bush's office, he had trouble persuading the aide who answered that he was the chairman of the SEC.

Jarrell's concern was that Shad didn't understand what the administration wanted the SEC to do on takeovers. "I tried to move him [Shad] wherever the administration wanted to go," Jarrell recalled.

To do so, he set up lunches, meetings and other lines of communication between Shad and certain administration officials, including Ginsburg, whom Shad had met before he knew Jarrell. At the same time, Jarrell worked with other economists inside and outside the SEC to develop studies that would support the administration's position that takeovers—even the Drexel-sponsored hostile takeovers mounted by corporate raiders who had little cash to finance their bids—were good for shareholders, the economy and the country.

Jarrell said one of his tactics was to leak his pro-takeover studies to the press before Shad or the other SEC commissioners had a chance to review them. "Getting the reports out to the press in advance of their publication worked like a charm," Jarrell said. "We pushed Shad right to the limit."

When Shad confronted him, Jarrell recalled, "I had to deny, deny, deny that I had leaked my studies. . . . Our studies changed the nature of the debate." Jarrell was criticized for the leaks by Shad and others, but he didn't seem to care.

In other quarters of the administration, a similarly aggressive push was on. One official at OMB kept a big chart on his wall showing all the bills in Congress that would restrict corporate takeovers; the official's job was to stop the bills before they got too far. On May 20, 1985, OMB's Ginsburg appeared at an SEC meeting and said the administration was dubious that takeovers had reached the point where "public confidence is implicated or the financial markets threatened." Ginsburg urged that the SEC do nothing.

Those who had liked Shad's "Leveraging of America" speech hoped that it was merely the first salvo in a war that would end with new restrictions on takeovers. But Shad led no such effort.

Late in 1985, Jarrell and Ginsburg helped engineer the appointment of Joseph Grundfest, a free market economist, as an SEC commissioner. A lawyer and Democrat, Grundfest had written a chapter in the 1985 Economic Report of the President lauding the benefits of takeovers. His appointment tipped the balance of the five-member commission in favor of the free market approach.

SEC VOTES TO BACK DOWN

In January 1986, a month after Grundfest's appointment, the SEC voted to back down from nearly all the legislative proposals on takeovers it had earlier submitted to Congress. Shad, Cox and Grundfest agreed that market forces and other legislative changes had substantially cured the perceived abuses.

Shad's opponents said the commission before Shad—the SEC of Stanley Sporkin, who was the commission's enforcement chief before being pressured out of the agency in 1981—almost certainly would have attacked junk bond-financed takeovers as manipulative ploys. They felt Shad should have used the SEC rules to protect investors by forcing the raiders to disclose evidence of secure financing before launching their hostile bids.

"Lawyers in billion-dollar deals will make a close call about [takeover] disclosure and say, 'So what' about the SEC," said Ted Levine, formerly associate director of the SEC's enforcement division. "I know because I hear those kinds of conversations in transactions all the time. There's a loss of discipline."

By 1986, the shouts Shad heard about Drexel and the hostile corporate takeovers it financed had become louder.

Enormous, venerable companies such as Gulf Corp., Walt Disney Co. and others had been threatened by upstart raiders with bold plans but little money. There were allegations that Drexel had formed secret alliances with raiders and professional stock speculators called arbitrageurs to rig the process so that no target could defend itself. The SEC's enforcement division had looked into it, but it was unable to develop the kind of evidence that would stick in court.

Shad thought it would be dangerous for the SEC to attempt to slow takeovers—such regulation might have unanticipated and disastrous effects on the economy. Moreover, the 1968 federal statute governing corporate takeovers, called the Williams Act, was intended by Congress to be neutral; the SEC wasn't supposed to take sides in takeover fights, as Shad read the law.

Shad considered Fred Joseph, the man at Drexel's helm, to be a person of high integrity. They had worked together on Wall Street for almost a decade, and they were similar in many ways. Both were outsiders to the Street's blue-blooded establishment—Shad the son of a launderer, Joseph the son of a cab driver—and they shared an intense ambition to prove themselves.

Shad hired Joseph in 1963 to work with him in the corporate finance department of E.F. Hutton. During the job interview, Shad asked Joseph what his father did, what kind of name Joseph was, and what his favorite sport was. Joseph fired back: Cab driver, Jewish, boxing. It was exactly what Shad wanted to hear: He knew that Joseph was as hungry as he was, and he was impressed by Joseph's academic record, too.

Not only did Shad admire Joseph personally, he shared his views about Wall Street and investment banking. They made their mark at Hutton because they were willing to take risks, to step outside the boundaries of traditional investment banking. They concentrated on advising midsized, growing companies whose credit was not as sound and whose banking needs were not as predictable as the big blue chip corporations.

Shad broke ranks with Wall Street by raising money for Caesar's, the casino company, a deal that others credited with making casino financings acceptable on Wall Street. Later, after Joseph became Drexel's chief, that firm became the investment banker not only to Caesar's but also to nearly every major casino operator in Las Vegas and Atlantic City.

"You sure don't look like an investment banker" was the line Joseph always used to tease Shad, who was overweight and far from dashing. The line captured the identity that Shad and Joseph shared: They were upstarts, fighters, climbers.

Shad hated more than anything to waste time in cars, and he pushed cab drivers relentlessly to pick up the pace. In one trip with Joseph to the airport, Shad demanded that the cab driver move first into the right lane, then the left lane, then told him to take an exit and get back on the highway at the next entrance. The driver hit the brake, got out of the cab, and opened Shad's door. He told Shad: "If you can drive better than me, sir, you drive." So Shad took the wheel and chauffered Joseph and the cabbie to the airport.

In 1970, Joseph backed Shad in a fight for Hutton's top job. Shad lost. Afterwards, Joseph left the firm, landing eventually at Drexel, while Shad settled in as Hutton's vice chairman. Though they saw each other less frequently, Shad and Joseph continued to pursue the philosophy they had shared at Hutton. While Shad initiated a handful of junk-bond financings and many friendly mergers, Joseph and Drexel went on to pioneer a $100 billion revolution in junk bonds and fostered numerous hostile takeovers.

So when Shad was deluged at the SEC with criticism that Drexel and its junk bond genius, Michael Milken, weren't abiding by Wall Street's traditional rules, he was not easily persuaded. Intellectually and viscerally, he admired the work of Milken, partly because Milken had extended into a multibillion-dollar business some of the same approaches to investment banking Joseph and Shad had taken while at Hutton. Drexel, in many ways, was the kind of investment bank that Shad might have built himself.

ADVICE FROM BOESKY

On Feb. 19, 1986, Ivan F. Boesky was among the guests John Shad invited to SEC headquarters to discuss the problem of takeover rumors in the stock market.

Shad enjoyed his power to convene panels of experts to discuss the issues of the day. He was drawn to the ebb and flow of what he called "roundtable" dialogue, and he depended on his panels to suggest solutions to problems the commission faced. The panels were a facet of Shad's attempt to ease the traditionally adversarial relationship between the SEC and Wall Street.

Shad knew Boesky by reputation as one of Wall Street's boldest professional stock speculators. The son of a Detroit restaurateur, Boesky had accumulated a fortune of more than $100 million in just a few years on Wall Street by trading the stocks of companies involved in corporate takeovers.

Suspecting that Boesky's incredible success was based on illegal, inside information, the SEC had launched numerous investigations. The Boesky probes, along with numerous other prosecutions, reflected Shad's vow to come down on insider trading "with hobnail boots." But the commission had never been able to prove a violation.

At the February 1986 roundtable, Shad asked Boesky and other Wall Street professionals what the SEC should do about the plethora of rumors and at what stage companies should disclose merger negotiations. The earlier such disclosure, the less time there is for insiders to trade while the public is unaware of negotiations.

"I think that the goal should be the most disclosure as soon as possible for the marketplace to have a more orderly system," Boesky said.

What Shad didn't know that day was that Boesky secretly was involved in several illegal trading arrangements, including some with key Drexel executives. On May 12, 1986, one of those Drexel executives, Dennis Levine, was charged with insider trading in a scheme that had netted him about $12 million in illegal profits.

Within weeks, Levine agreed to plead guilty and began to tell federal prosecutors and SEC lawyers in New York everything he knew. Among others, Levine fingered Boesky.

Shad feared that Boesky would take his millions and flee the country. But instead, Boesky decided to cooperate, trading his knowledge for leniency. He confessed a multitude of fraud schemes to the government, including an illegal stock trading arrangement that he said he had entered into with Drexel's Milken. The arrangement, Boesky said, rigged corporate takeovers, manipulated stock prices, and evaded a host of other securities and tax laws.

As the details of Boesky's confessions about Drexel became known, several congressmen asserted that Drexel's role in the takeover boom of the 1980s had been fundamentally corrupt.

John Shad didn't believe that—Fred Joseph, he thought, did not run a corrupt firm. It appeared that Drexel might have a problem with a single branch office, its Beverly Hills, Calif.-based junk bond operations headed by Milken. Was it possible, as SEC attorneys had alleged, that Milken's group had become a runaway operation, that Milken had become bigger than Joseph or even the firm?

In June 1987, with the Drexel investigation in full swing, Shad left the SEC to become ambassador to the Netherlands, amid praise from some members of Congress who earlier had been his opponents.

Six years at the commission had made him the longest-serving chairman in SEC history. He oversaw the biggest investigations of Wall Street since the agency's creation. One investigation focused on a massive check-kiting scheme at his old firm, E.F. Hutton, a probe in which Shad declined to be involved because of his past connection with the firm.

Shaken by these scandals, Shad decided in 1987 to donate most of his fortune, about $20 million, to establish an ethics program at the Harvard Business School.

Shad had come to the SEC hoping to ease the 50-year adversarial relationship between Wall Street and the commission. Despite resistance from the commission's bureaucracy, he succeeded in reducing restraints on stock trading, including the highly speculative stock index futures.

He had shifted the SEC enforcement division's top priority from attacks on corporations to the pursuit of cheating by individuals on Wall Street. Shad transferred more responsibility for policing stockbroker sales practices to Wall Street, believing it would be more effective.

On Shad's watch, the stock market rose to the highest level in U.S. history. Soon after his departure, the market crashed, but stock prices remained higher than they had been when he came to the SEC. Corporations raised billions of dollars in new capital, aided by his elimination of "burdensome" regulations.

By the end of Shad's tenure, however, the Street's traders and bankers lived in greater fear of the government's scrutiny than they had before he came to Washington.

On his last weekend at the SEC, Shad received an honorary degree from the University of Rochester, where economist Gregg Jarrell had gone to teach.

Shad told Rochester's graduating business students, "Wall Street has long been a favorite target, and yet Wall Street's ethics compare favorably with other professions and occupations. . . . By the highest conjecture securities fraud is a tiny fraction of one percent of the enormous volume of securities transactions. . . . The few robber barons who existed were born over a century ago, and were buried in the debris of the 1929 crash. Today, the bulk of American industry and finance are managed by a generation of giants."

WEIGHING AN OFFER

Last month's meeting between Shad and Joseph at the embassy compound in The Hague was simple and direct—a negotiation between old and trusted friends.

They scratched on a single piece of paper the outline of a proposed deal that would make Shad Drexel's chairman.

Shad, who had lived by the credo that he would spend one third of his life learning, one third earning and one third serving, was concerned that any move to Drexel would be perceived as an ethical compromise.

He wanted a new job in the Bush administration, but had learned that no acceptable post would be forthcoming. Before accepting the Drexel chairmanship, Shad wanted to know more about the circumstances surrounding Drexel's guilty plea.

He told Joseph he would have to consult with his former colleagues at the SEC and with Justice Department prosecutors. Former Manhattan U.S. attorney Rudolph W. Giuliani, who spearheaded the criminal probe of Drexel, expressed enthusiasm for the idea. After Giuliani's endorsement, Shad indicated he would not announce his final decision until after he resigns as ambassador late this month.

In 1981, Shad had come to Washington from Wall Street. When he needed expert advice, he turned to Wall Street. When he considered the larger issues of economic policy, he relied on his experiences as an investment banker. Wall Street was what he knew, it was in his bones.

When Joseph offered him the Drexel job, Shad was inclined to accept. Eight years had passed since he left Wall Street. It was probably time to go home.

Staff researcher Melissa Mathis contributed to this report.

FOURTEEN

L-TRYPTOPHAN—A MEDICAL PUZZLE

1990 WINNER IN THE SPECIALIZED REPORTING CATEGORY

"For a distinguished example of reporting on such specialized subjects as sports, business, science, education, or religion . . ."

The Albuquerque Journal
Tamar Stieber

The dietary supplement, L-Tryptophan, has been used for years to treat sleep disorders, muscle tension and stress. But *The Albuquerque Journal*'s reporting on a chance connection between L-Tryptophan and illnesses in three New Mexico women led to a nationwide recall of the over-the-counter product.

At the police reserve academy in Napa, California, my teachers drummed into me and my classmates that there's no such thing as a "routine" traffic stop; a silver bullet with our name on it could be waiting for us every time we pulled over a car.

I've learned that reporting is no different. But the silver bullet in what began as a routine flu story turned out to be a Pulitzer Prize in specialized reporting.

More importantly, the series of articles linking a rare blood disorder with a supposedly benign dietary supplement may even have saved a few lives.

The story had an innocuous enough beginning. My editors at *Journal North*—a zoned edition put out by *The Albuquerque Journal*'s Santa Fe bureau, where I work—had been swapping flu stories with some stringers during a meeting about the upcoming Christmas insert.

One of the stringers mentioned that he knew of several people who were suffering particularly unusual symptoms in what was already an unusual strain of flu. He also thought at least two of them may have been taking L-Tryptophan, a synthetic form of one of 22 essential amino acids that form the building blocks of protein.

Tim Coder, managing editor of *Journal North,* dropped by my desk after the meeting, gave me a quick rundown of what the stringer had told him and said, "Check it out."

My first call was to a Santa Fe woman in her mid-30s whose name and number I got from the stringer. She reluctantly described her symptoms, which included excruciating muscle pain (myalgia) and fatigue, and acknowledged she had been taking L-Tryptophan—but only after swearing me to secrecy about her identity. She said she was scared of losing her job as a restaurant hostess.

As the interview continued, the woman became more hostile and finally hung up on me when I asked her what brand L-Tryptophan she had been using.

At that point I had a hunch that maybe I was on to something more than just a flu story.

I called the woman's physician, Dr. Kit Keith, who told me that, in addition to myalgia, her patient had a rare condition called eosinophilia—extremely high levels of white eosinophil blood cells. Keith was not, however, ready to make any connection between the woman's condition and the fact that she had been taking L-Tryptophan for insomnia. She suggested I call two other northern New Mexico physicians, each treating a woman with similar symptoms.

Dr. Phillip Hertzman, a family practitioner in Los Alamos, said, yes, his patient had been taking L-Tryptophan, but he was skeptical that the amino acid might be to blame for his patient's illness.

"Hundreds take tryptophan. I take tryptophan," said Hertzman, who has since co-authored a paper in the *New England Journal of Medicine* and given talks on the link between L-Tryptophan and the disease, which was given a name a week later by the Centers for Disease Control in Atlanta.

Only Dr. William Blevins, whose patient was in the hospital and near death, seemed open, if uncertain, about the possibility that L-Tryptophan might be a clue in the mysterious illness that, within two months, had stricken three women living within a 30-mile radius.

It wasn't until I spoke with Dr. Gerald Gleich at the Mayo Clinic, a recognized expert in eosinophilia, that a medical professional would assert what at this point seemed fairly obvious to my layperson's mind.

"The fact that one has heard of other cases makes one dubious that there is anything other than a relationship," Gleich said of the women's symptoms and L-Tryptophan.

I had my story.

But not before Dr. Ron Voorhees, an epidemiologist with the New Mexico Health and Environment Department, called *The Journal* "unethical" to print what he described as an alarmist article. And not before Dr. Mai Ting, the medical director of the clinic where Dr. Keith worked, threatened to sue us "if you use my name, Dr. Keith's name or the name of the Women's Health Services."

Concerned on both counts—we neither wanted to be alarmist nor a defendant in a libel suit—we held the story for five days. After a thorough going-over by *The Journal*'s assistant editor Kent Walz, who also happens to be an attorney, the story went to print Tuesday, November 7, 1989, with no deletions.

The day the story broke, the New Mexico Health and Environment Department received nine more reports from doctors treating patients with similar symptoms, all but three of whom had taken L-Tryptophan. Within six days, New Mexico had 30 possible cases with 51 others being reported in 17 other states.

By the end of the second week, the CDC had named the illness eosinophilia myalgia syndrome (EMS) and the U.S. Food and Drug Administration asked for a voluntary recall of L-Tryptophan tablets or capsules. But it took 287 cases in 37 states and one death for the FDA to act.

By that time, Drs. Ting and Voorhees had apologized for their initial reactions and their reluctance to talk to me.

Although the CDC now has a phone recording with a state-by-state breakdown of cases in the United States and territories, trying to get statistics or any other information from the CDC for the first few weeks of the story was a herculean task.

Dr. Edwin Kilbourne, chief of the CDC's Health Studies Branch, hung up on me during our first conversation and then refused to take or return any more of my calls until fairly recently. I finally enlisted the help of Stu Nagurka, an aide to New Mexico Representative Bill Richardson, who made daily calls to the CDC for me to get the updated numbers and whatever other information I needed.

Another CDC doctor called me a "pit bull" in my approach to the story. When I told her I took that as a compliment, she changed her mind and said I was more like "a little terrier—that kind that yaps at your ankles." This doctor recently called to congratulate me on winning the Pulitzer Prize.

For the first three weeks of the story, I worked between 12 and 15 hours most days and came in on weekends to stay on top of any developments. Observing my growing obsession with the story, a news photographer friend suggested *The Journal* and I were losing perspective—that we were exaggerating the importance of the story simply because we broke it. In fact, I took this comment to heart and suggested to my editors that we stop featuring the EMS stories on the front page.

As the number of cases increased, however, and reports of deaths started to come in, it became apparent to everyone that this was truly an important story. Even my already overworked colleagues at *Journal North,* who uncomplainingly covered my beats for nearly three months while I worked exclusively on the EMS story, shared the excitement of seeing a local story turn national and international, as well as the despair of learning about growing numbers of people who were sick or had died.

Presently, the CDC has reports of 21 deaths from EMS associated with the ingestion of L-Tryptophan out of nearly 1,500 cases nationwide. Cases have also been reported in Canada, Britain, France, Germany, Switzerland, Israel, North Yemen and Japan.

Researchers are still looking for the answer to this medical mystery. Some believe they may have found it in a possible contamination of the raw material for L-Tryptophan produced by one of the leading chemical companies in Japan.

But for those still suffering with EMS, about 85 percent of whom are women, learning the cause of their illness is only half the answer. The other half—and for them, probably the more important part— lies in learning more about EMS and whether they will ever be well again.

—Tamar Stieber
The Albuquerque Journal

THREE N.M. WOMEN CONTRACT UNUSUAL MEDICAL SYNDROME

ALL TOOK L-TRYPTOPHAN BUT DOCTORS SAY NO EVIDENCE IT CAUSED PROBLEM

TUESDAY, NOVEMBER 7, 1989

BY TAMAR STIEBER

SANTA FE—Physicians and medical researchers are investigating an unusual and potentially serious medical syndrome diagnosed in three northern New Mexico women within the past two months.

The women, two from Santa Fe and one from Los Alamos, have extremely high counts of a white blood cell called an eosinophil. The syndrome is known as eosinophilia.

One woman was still in the hospital Monday, where she has been treated for fluid on the lungs and in the abdomen, and for abnormal liver function, doctors said. The other two have been suffering intense and sometimes debilitating muscle and joint pain.

The only common thread doctors have found so far is that all three women have been taking a non-prescription dietary supplement, L-Tryptophan, but stress there is no evidence to indicate it caused the problem.

Eosinophilia, which in rare cases can result in heart failure, usually occurs as a result of bronchial asthma, allergies, drug reactions or parasitic infections such as trichinosis or amoebic dysentery.

Except when caused by asthma, the condition usually ceases within a few days or a week after the cause is eliminated. But doctors say they don't believe their patients, who range in age from 37 to 43, are suffering from any of these ailments.

The doctors describe their patients' reactions, which all started within the past two months, as a direct result of a tremendous increase in the number of eosinophils in their blood.

Like all white blood cells, eosinophils increase in number as needed to ward off infection. But the increase in the three women is extremely high, doctors say, and the cause is still a mystery.

Dr. Phillip Hertzman, a family practitioner with Los Alamos Medical Center, said that while normal levels of eosinophils generally range from one to five cells per cubic millimeter (or microliter) of blood, his patient has 10,000 eosinophils per cubic millimeter.

One of the Santa Fe patients also shows a level of 10,000 eosinophils while the other is in the 6,000 range, doctors said.

The eosinophil count rarely goes beyond 500 even when fighting off infection, Hertzman said.

"This is very unusual. I've never seen anybody with a count like that and I've been here for 13 years," he said. "Now we have three in a 30-mile radius."

Hertzman said he hasn't ruled out trichinosis, a parasite found in insufficiently cooked pork, in his patient. But he said he also is curious about L-Tryptophan, which doctors confirmed all three patients had been taking.

"I think the fact that we have three very unusual cases and all of them are on L-Tryptophan is very suspicious," said Hertzman. "But I don't know of any reason why L-Tryptophan per se would give someone eosinophilia."

Tryptophan is one of the essential amino acids that are the building blocks of proteins. Meats and dairy products are especially rich in tryptophan.

Recommended for sleep disorders, muscle tension and stress, L-Tryptophan is available in health food stores, drugstores and some supermarkets under many different brand names. The "L" indicates the tryptophan is a single molecule rather than a chain of molecules.

Dr. Kathryn Keith of the Women's Health Services Family Care and Counseling Center in Santa Fe confirmed her patient had taken L-Tryptophan but stressed that it was too early to determine if the supplement had anything to do with the symptoms of her patient and the other two women.

Dr. Mai Ting, director of Women's Health Services, called L-Tryptophan "a red herring."

"It's not just myself," Ting said. "I've spoken to other doctors in this town and in Albuquerque who feel the link between tryptophan and this particular situation is a red herring. A lot of people take tryptophan and nobody else has (reacted)."

Dr. Gerald Gleich, chair of the immunology department at the Mayo Medical School, Clinic and Foundation in Rochester, Minn., and a recognized authority on eosinophilia, said the clinic has been in contact with Hertzman, Keith and Dr. William Blevins.

Blevins is a Taos hematologist and oncologist whose Santa Fe patient is hospitalized because of her high eosinophil count. Gleich said he has seen only about 100 cases in his 24 years at the Mayo Clinic where the eosinophil counts were as high as the three cases in northern New Mexico.

However, the cause of most of the previous cases became apparent fairly early, he said.

Calling the triple occurrence of eosinophilia "pretty big league," Gleich said he, too, is suspicious about L-Tryptophan.

"Lightning can strike, but it doesn't strike twice," Gleich said in a telephone interview late last week. "It could be a red herring, but a red herring in three people? I'm not willing to buy that. I'm trained to look for unexpected associations. Once is chance, twice is kind of interesting, but three and I say full speed ahead" for an investigation.

"It's just a curious relationship," he said. "But it's too curious to be easily ignored."

Gerald Vince, district director for the Dallas office for the Food and Drug Administration, said L-Tryptophan does not need FDA approval.

"L-Tryptophan is an amino acid commonly used as a food supplement. There is no safety concern."

Carl Germano, a nutritionist for Country Life in Hauppauge, N.Y., which manufactures L-Tryptophan and other dietary supplements, also said he had never heard of this condition as a side effect.

He suggested that if a link were found between the high eosinophil count and L-Tryptophan, the fillers or binders in the capsules might be the villain rather than the tryptophan itself.

"You need a good detective for these cases. Modern medicine men are probably going to push that aside and neglect looking at their diet, which is important to explore," he said. "I strongly recommend they get a nutritionist on the case and see if there are comparisons with any other particular foods, other drugs or other items and how they are prepared."

Gleich said he has been in touch with the Centers for Disease Control in Atlanta, where he said one doctor told him he would notify the Food and Drug Administration about the possible link.

An FDA spokesman said Monday he had no information the agency had begun an investigation. Attempts to speak to a doctor at the CDC were unsuccessful.

Sixteen people died in 1986 as a result of a form of eosinophilia—hypereosinophilic syndrome—and 12 deaths were reported in 1987, said Sandy Smith, a spokeswoman for the National Center for Health Statistics in Washington, D.C.

Dr. Ron Voorhees, a medical investigator with the New Mexico Office of Epidemiology, acknowledged his office is investigating the cases but said L-Tryptophan is just one possible cause under consideration. He declined comment on others.

"This is a very unusual condition and we're trying to get a handle on it. We're looking at a lot of things," Voorhees said. "There could be an infection; it could be a substance in a medication; it could be a food allergy or it could be totally unrelated. All I really know is that three people have the condition around the same time."

Voorhees called it "unethical" for the Journal to publish speculation about L-Tryptophan's possible connection to the three cases, citing potential for public distress because of its widespread use.

Steve Blechman, vice president of research and development at Twin Laboratories in Ronkonkoma, N.Y.—a major manufacturer of vitamin and dietary supplements, including L-Tryptophan—said Voorhees contacted him about his company's product.

"He said it is highly unlikely there's an association between tryptophan and the women, but they're following up," Blechman said Monday. "As far as elevated white blood cells and eosinophilia, I've never heard of any association with tryptophan and this condition."

ILLNESS STRUCK 'HEALTHIEST WOMAN'

38-YEAR-OLD SAYS BODY SEEMED TO FALL APART

THURSDAY, NOVEMBER 9, 1989

BY TAMAR STIEBER

Judy Kody Paulsen was sick—and depressed.

She had been "the healthiest specimen of a 38-year-old woman you can find" until three months ago when her body suddenly seemed to fall apart.

After a battery of tests, Paulsen's doctors discovered she had a form of eosinophilia called hypereosinophilic syndrome—a rare and potentially serious condition characterized by an extremely high count of a white blood cell called an eosinophil.

Paulsen, an Albuquerque resident, thought she might be suffering from a pre-cancerous condition.

But Tuesday morning on the way to Albuquerque International Airport for a flight to the Mayo Clinic in Rochester, Minn., she received a fresh dose of hope.

Paulsen opened the Albuquerque Journal and noticed an article about three women with eosinophilia, all of whom had been taking an amino acid called L-Tryptophan. She began to read in earnest.

"I just about fainted," said Paulsen, who had been taking heavy doses of the dietary supplement for the past year and a half for premenstrual syndrome (PMS).

In a telephone interview Tuesday at the Salt Lake City airport while she waited for a connecting flight to Minneapolis, Paulsen recalled how her illness struck quickly and worsened steadily.

"Suddenly my muscles started aching," said Paulsen, a contact lens fitter for an ophthalmologist. "Then I had two acute episodes of severe, debilitating muscular problems. Then I woke up with a rash on my legs and I thought, 'Oh my gosh, I have Lyme disease.'"

Eosinophilia usually occurs as a result of bronchial asthma, allergies, drug reactions or parasitic infections such as trichinosis or amoebic dysentery. But test after test proved that Paulsen had none of those afflictions. And none of her doctors—including a rheumatologist, an internist, a pathologist and a dermatologist—could quite figure out why her eosinophil count was steadily increasing to over 40 percent.

Last month, her doctors got together and concluded she had a rare form of eosinophilia called eosinophilic perimyositis. They recommended she take high dosages of prednisone, a steroid used successfully to lower eosinophil counts. Last Friday, they agreed she should go to the Mayo Clinic to see a specialist in eosinophilic perimyositis.

Paulsen said she first heard about L-Tryptophan as a treatment for PMS in mid-1988, after reading a book that recommended higher-than-average amounts of the amino acid. Normally recommended in doses of 500 milligrams to 1,000 milligrams (one gram) per day, Paulsen was taking two grams of L-Tryptophan per day for the first 10 days of her menstrual cycle and three grams the rest of the month, as prescribed by the author of the book. At one point she was taking over four grams of L-Tryptophan per day. "That's a lot of anything," noted Paulsen, who has an interest in medicine and nutrition and has written a book on contact lenses.

Paulsen recalled that while she was taking the prednisone, she stopped taking L-Tryptophan. "And then I got better. But I saw no relationship. I just got tired of taking all those pills," she said. She attributed her improvement to the prednisone, even after she resumed taking the L-Tryptophan and had a relapse.

Although all of her medical records indicated she was on a steady program of L-Tryptophan, Paulsen said, understandably, none of her doctors made the association.

"Because they just couldn't understand how it could happen," she said. "Tryptophan is in so many other natural foods. People have been taking tryptophan as a food supplement for so many years."

Her internist, Dr. Avrum Organick, acknowledged that he never made the association. "I was familiar with it (L-Tryptophan) but it did not cause me to have any suspicion that the two were connected until I heard about it (this week)," he said.

Organick added that while he has recommended L-Tryptophan for sleep disorders, he's skeptical about using the amino acid for PMS. "That's like sending a boy to do a man's job," he said.

Paulsen is still at the Mayo Clinic and will consult today with one of the foremost authorities on eosinophilia in the United States, Dr. Gerald Gleich.

"Now we're at the base of hopefully finding the root of the problem," said Paulsen, who said until this week she had been in a state of depression. "We thought I had a pre-cancerous condition. My condition was steadily going downhill. I was losing weight. It had become so alarming," she said. "But now I'm in a state of euphoria because it may be as simple as getting rid of the tryptophan."

OTHER STATES REPORTING RARE SYNDROME CASES

FRIDAY, NOVEMBER 10, 1989

BY TAMAR STIEBER

SANTA FE—At least four people from out of state were added Thursday to the list of 21 New Mexicans suffering from a rare and potentially serious medical syndrome that may be linked to a dietary supplement.

The new cases of eosinophilia were reported as seven investigators from the Food and Drug Administration fanned across New Mexico from Los Alamos to Las Cruces collecting L-Tryptophan belonging to the patients.

Five new cases were reported in New Mexico Thursday, while the others were in Missouri, Arizona, Oregon and Mississippi.

In the five states, 20 of the patients had been taking L-Tryptophan, a non-prescription amino acid supplement, medical investigators confirmed. Most of the patients are women.

Doctors from the Mayo Clinic in Rochester, Minn., said a 41-year-old man from Kansas City, Mo., and a woman from Mississippi are being treated for eosinophilia—a condition characterized by extremely high levels of a white blood cell called an eosinophil. Both have been taking L-Tryptophan.

The New Mexico Office of Epidemiology confirmed another case, a man in Chinle, Ariz., who is believed to have been taking L-Tryptophan, said acting state epidemiologist Dr. Millicent Eidson.

Dr. LeRoy Gomez, director of the FDA office in Denver, said Oregon has reported two cases of eosinophilia but that he has only sketchy details. One, he said, apparently was linked to L-Tryptophan. He said he had no information about the other.

Gomez said he planned to contact the FDA in Seattle to begin an investigation in Oregon.

Besides the Arizona case, the New Mexico Office of Epidemiology received reports from three other states of eosinophilia cases that have been linked to the usage of L-Tryptophan, Eidson said. She refused to disclose which states or how many cases.

In New Mexico, the 21 cases have been reported since last week. At least 16 involved the use of L-Tryptophan, widely used for sleep disorders, premenstrual syndrome, muscle tension and stress.

Seven cases were in Albuquerque, nine in Santa Fe, two in Las Cruces and one each in Gallup, Corrales and Los Alamos.

Ten eosinophilia patients, including at least nine from New Mexico, have been hospitalized, Eidson said. One, a 51-year-old Gallup woman, is still in Presbyterian Hospital in Albuquerque.

The most common symptoms of eosinophilia seem to be severe, sometimes debilitating muscle pain and fatigue, doctors report. Patients have also complained of a variety of other symptoms including joint pain, pneumonia, abnormal liver function, rashes, blood in the urine and difficulty chewing.

Dr. Edwin Kilbourne, chief of the Health Studies Branch of the Division of Environmental Hazards and Health Effects at the Centers for Disease Control in Atlanta, said he had heard of only one out-of-state case and that he was "fuzzy" on the details.

"This is very interesting news indeed," Kilbourne said in a telephone interview Thursday night when asked about the two cases at the Mayo Clinic. "We had heard of it but we are not clear on all the details."

The out-of-state cases "raises the ante a bit," he added.

Gomez said four FDA investigators from Denver, two from Salt Lake City and another from Albuquerque will be working through the weekend collecting L-Tryptophan samples from eosinophilia patients and from stores in which the dietary supplement was purchased.

"A batch will be sent to Washington, D.C., tomorrow (Friday) for analysis," he said.

He added there are no plans at this time to order L-Tryptophan off store shelves across the nation.

"Right now, we're supporting the Department of Health in New Mexico," which asked for voluntary sales restrictions, he said. "We don't know if L-Tryptophan is responsible for the eosinophilia."

One physician from the Centers for Disease Control is also in New Mexico to work with the office of epidemiology in consulting with patients. The CDC's Kilbourne plans to arrive Monday.

While Kilbourne acknowledged the correlation between L-Tryptophan and the cluster of eosinophilia cases, he said all agencies are being very cautious about making a connection.

"The problem is an epidemic association (between L-Tryptophan and eosinophilia) and as far as I am aware it is not very solid," he said.

Dr. Irene Meissner, a neurologist at the Mayo Clinic treating the man from Kansas City, said her patient came to the clinic a few days ago because of his worsening clinical condition. She said she, too, believes it is premature to link L-Tryptophan to eosinophilia.

"The only thing we know for sure is that he is on tryptophan," said Meissner. She noted that, like all the New Mexican eosinophilic patients reported to the state epidemiology office, her patient has also suffered severe muscle pain. "But he's much iller than any of the patients (she's heard about)," Meissner said. The man is hospitalized.

Dr. Gerald Gleich, a recognized authority on eosinophilia and chair of the immunology department at the Mayo Clinic, said both the Kansas City man and the woman from Mississippi had been taking "considerable doses" of L-Tryptophan and that both are seriously ill. The physician treating the Mississippi woman did not return phone calls Thursday.

"The thing that's unusual is seeing so many patients with the same pattern. It's not like we haven't seen the likes of this before. What's different is there are so many at one time and they're all taking L-Tryptophan," Gleich said.

N.M. BANS SALE OR DISPLAY OF L-TRYPTOPHAN

TUESDAY, NOVEMBER 14, 1989

BY TAMAR STIEBER

SANTA FE—State health officials Monday banned the sale or display of a widely used dietary supplement that may be linked to an unusual and sometimes fatal blood disorder.

Dennis Boyd, secretary of the New Mexico Health and Environment Department, issued an order making it a misdemeanor, punishable by a $100 fine and/or six months in jail to sell or display L-Tryptophan.

The non-prescription amino acid has been used to relieve sleep disorders, premenstrual syndrome, muscle tension and stress.

L-Tryptophan has become a prime suspect in cases of eosinophilia reported since Oct. 31, when the New Mexico office of epidemiology learned that three women victims had taken the supplement.

New Mexico now has 30 reported cases and federal officials have tallied 81 reported cases in 18 states and Washington, D.C. It was not immediately known how many of the victims had taken L-Tryptophan.

The Food and Drug Administration issued a national warning Saturday advising consumers to stop using L-Tryptophan pending the results of an investigation into the possible link.

Sen. Pete Domenici, R-N.M., on Monday urged the FDA to issue a nationwide ban on L-Tryptophan sales.

Eosinophilia is characterized by a very high level of white blood cells called eosinophils. The most common symptoms include severe muscle pain, weakness, fever, joint pain, rashes, swelling and pneumonia. Doctors have been reporting a long list of other individual symptoms.

The National Center for Health Statistics in Washington, D.C., reported 16 deaths in 1986 and 12 in 1987 from a form of eosinophilia called hypereosinophilic syndrome.

The L-Tryptophan ban, announced at a news conference, is the

467

direct outcome of a case control study by the Health and Environment Department's office of epidemiology over the weekend.

Boyd said the study "confirms the link between L-Tryptophan and eosinophilia."

The department's Environmental Improvement Division last week asked retailers voluntarily to remove L-Tryptophan from store shelves.

"It doesn't seem anything but prudent to take the additional step," Boyd said. "We expect full compliance."

The Environmental Improvement Division will make spot checks, he said.

The federal Centers for Disease Control in Atlanta has received reports of 81 eosinophilia cases, said Stu Nagurka, press secretary for Rep. Bill Richardson, D-N.M.

Nagurka has been in contact with Dr. Edwin Kilbourne, chief of the Center's Health Studies Branch, to keep tabs on the increasing number of reports.

Nagurka said he didn't know how many of 81 people had taken L-Tryptophan but said, "I got the sense that it appears like most of them."

Dr. Millicent Eidson, an environmental epidemiologist for the state, said New Mexico now has at least 30 reported cases with half of them being hospitalized. At least 17 had taken L-Tryptophan, including 16 New Mexico women and a Chinle, Ariz., man who was treated in Gallup.

Speaking at the news conference, Eidson said New Mexico victims had taken 12 different brands of L-Tryptophan in doses ranging from one-half to three grams per day.

Besides New Mexico, states known to be reporting cases of eosinophilia are Texas, California, Missouri, Mississippi, Virginia, Minnesota and Oregon.

Nagurka said he did not have a breakdown on the latest group of reporting states but said Kilbourne "expressed thoughts that he wouldn't be surprised at some time to see cases from all 50 states."

Domenici, in a letter to FDA Commissioner Frank E. Young, urged the agency to issue a nationwide ban on L-Tryptophan.

"Given the high risk associated with L-Tryptophan, as detected by the New Mexico Health and Environment Department, I urge you to move quickly to consider temporarily halting sales of the drug (sic) nationwide," the senator wrote. "While most cases of the eosinophilia outbreak have occurred in New Mexico, I understand similar cases have arisen in other states."

Noting that Japan manufactures most of the L-Tryptophan sold in the United States, Domenici added: "If the problems are traced to that ingredient, the entire nation could be at risk."

Richard Ronk, deputy director of the FDA's Center for Food Safety and Applied Nutrition, said in a telephone interview the FDA has no plans at present to ask for a recall. He spoke generally and not in response to Domenici's letter.

The FDA is in the process of testing samples of the amino acid collected from patients in New Mexico.

"There are literally millions and millions of people who have eaten tryptophan products without any ill effects," he said. The mystery, he added, is why more people in New Mexico suffer from the condition than in any other state.

"This is still quite an open question," Ronk said. "It doesn't appear to be a bacteria and it doesn't appear to be a virus. Clearly it is far more than a coincidence. With that many cases of this, it is remarkable."

As of Monday, the FDA could confirm only that the samples of L-Tryptophan it had collected were between 98 percent and 102 percent pure. Those results can be plus or minus 4 percent.

Ronk, who said the next step is to test for contaminants, said his department has contacted the Japanese government to look at the manufacturing process, which is largely one of fermentation.

"We want to be sure there might not be some carryover of microbiological problem from the fermentation itself that might express an allergy in a person," he said. "Obviously, if tryptophan is involved, there are a number of people who seem much more sensitive to it than others."

Tryptophan is one of 20 naturally occurring amino acids, which form the building blocks of proteins. It is sold in health food stores, drug stores and some supermarkets as L-Tryptophan—or Levorotary-Tryptophan—which refers to its left-sided configuration, the only kind the body can metabolize.

FDA ASKS RECALL OF L-TRYPTOPHAN

SATURDAY, NOVEMBER 18, 1989

BY TAMAR STIEBER

The U.S. Food and Drug Administration Friday called for a national voluntary recall of all products in which L-Tryptophan is the major component because of its link to a nationwide outbreak of a potentially deadly blood disorder.

The recall followed a Friday morning meeting of the FDA's hazard assessment committee, said a high level FDA official who asked not to be named. The committee determined that L-Tryptophan, a non-prescription food supplement, is "a moderate to severe hazard," the official said.

A recall also means that manufacturers will have to buy back all the L-Tryptophan on health food, drug store and supermarket shelves, the source said.

"The actual effect is L-Tryptophan will come off the market and not come back on again until we can demonstrate it's OK. And, of course, it goes back to the manufacturers. They could lose it all," the source said.

Starting Monday, the 23 FDA field offices in the United States will mail letters to all manufacturers of these supplements in their jurisdictions asking them to recall all single-entity L-Tryptophan products, said FDA spokesman Chris Lecos. He said each manufacturer is expected to contact wholesalers, distributors and retailers to remove the products from the marketplace.

"The FDA is prepared to initiate seizure actions in the event its recall requests are not acted upon," Lecos said.

L-Tryptophan has been tied to a national outbreak of eosinophilia-myalgia syndrome (EMS), which was first reported by The Albuquerque Journal on Nov. 7. The outbreak began in New Mexico where three women who had been taking L-Tryptophan came down with the syndrome.

Since then, the Centers for Disease Control in Atlanta has reported 287 cases of EMS in 37 states and Washington, D.C. Most of these cases and a death in Oregon have been linked to L-Tryptophan. The

CDC is investigating three more deaths that may also be linked to the amino acid, Lecos said.

An FDA statement announcing the recall effort said there is a "strong, virtually unequivocal link between consumption of L-Tryptophan tablets or capsules and the syndrome," the Associated Press reported. However, the FDA said scientists investigating L-Tryptophan do not know why this is happening.

EMS is characterized by a high number of white blood cells called eosinophils, severe muscle pain and the absence of any other diseases normally associated with the condition.

"We think (the recall) is appropriate," said Dr. Ron Voorhees of the New Mexico Office of Epidemiology. "Given the seriousness of the illness and the strength of the association that we've shown and the studies done so far, I think it's very prudent."

The New Mexico office of epidemiology conducted a case control study last weekend that Dennis Boyd, secretary of the Health and Environment Department, said confirmed the link between L-Tryptophan and EMS.

"I think the FDA has done a wise thing for the American people. I think now they're doing their job," said Dr. Gerald Gleich, a recognized authority on eosinophilia and chairman of the immunology department of the Mayo Medical School, Clinic and Foundation in Rochester, Minn. Gleich had criticized the FDA for issuing only a warning on Nov. 11 instead of a nationwide ban of the supplement.

"I think at this point we have to assume in light of the almost crushing weight of evidence that there is a strong association. We have to accept that L-Tryptophan causes this (EMS), however obscure it turns out to be," he said.

MAKING THE CONNECTION

CHANCE HELPS DOCTORS BREAK EMS CASE

SUNDAY, NOVEMBER 19, 1989

BY TAMAR STIEBER

SANTA FE—Like most mysteries, it started small and grew.

In late October, three New Mexico doctors were trying to treat three northern New Mexico women—two in Santa Fe and one in Los Alamos—who were suffering incapacitating muscle pain. One nearly died, spending a month in the hospital with liver problems and fluid in her lungs and abdomen.

Since the Journal first reported Nov. 7 about those three cases of the mysterious illness, 37 states and the District of Columbia have discovered nearly 300 cases—most involving women—of what now has been diagnosed as eosinophilia-myalgia syndrome (EMS). In New Mexico, 19 EMS cases have been confirmed so far.

Friday night, after a week of pressure from state and federal health officials and lawmakers, the U.S. Food and Drug Administration issued a federal ban on L-Tryptophan, the over-the-counter food supplement now linked to EMS.

When the first three cases appeared in New Mexico, doctors were stumped.

The only common denominator appeared to be that the three New Mexico women showed an unusual and dangerously high level of white blood cells called eosinophils. Their doctors ruled out the usual causes of eosinophilia—bronchial asthma, allergies, drug reactions and parasitic infections. But they were at a loss about the cause of their patients' condition.

"The patient was in the hospital when I picked her up on Oct. 25," said Dr. William Blevins, a Taos hematologist/oncologist who was seeing the patients of a vacationing Santa Fe physician. "I had to review her chart and talk to her and explain that I didn't know why she had eosinophilia."

Still, Blevins was suspicious about two medications his patient was taking—one of which was L-Tryptophan.

L-Tryptophan has been used widely for more than a decade to remedy sleep disorders, premenstrual syndrome, muscle tension and stress—and more recently to help counteract the stimulant effect of psychotropic drugs and to ease withdrawal from alcohol or drugs. L-Tryptophan is the usable synthesized form of tryptophan, one of 20 naturally occurring amino acids that form the building blocks of proteins.

Dr. Phillip Hertzman of Los Alamos also was confounded by similar symptoms in a female patient from his family practice. Like Blevins' patient, the 43-year-old woman had an extremely high eosinophil count—more than 10,000 compared to a normal count of 0 to 500 eosinophils per cubic millimeter of blood.

She, too, had been taking L-Tryptophan.

But it took Dr. James W. Mayer, 43, a publicity-shy rheumatologist in Santa Fe, to make the connection.

Blevins and Hertzman independently referred their patients to Mayer in hopes he could find an answer for each patient's agonizing muscle pain.

Hertzman said, "I sent her to see Jim Mayer Oct. 26. That's when Jim said, 'You know, I have a similar patient in the hospital. You ought to talk to Dr. Blevins and see if there's a connection.' We talked and there really seemed to be a connection."

The Journal stumbled onto the mystery by accident.

A part-time Journal writer mentioned to a Journal editor that he had a friend under a doctor's care because of excruciating muscle pain. The friend had heard of another woman with the same condition. The cause at the time appeared to be unknown. The editor assigned a reporter to find the doctors and see if it might lead to a story.

Mayer reluctantly agreed to talk to The Journal about his role in the L-Tryptophan connection.

Carefully choosing his words, he acknowledged that he "found it of interest when both patients reported they had taken L-Tryptophan.

"It seemed reasonable to raise the possibility that L-Tryptophan might have a role in these problems," he said.

Then The Journal printed the story on its front page.

But not before Dr. Ron Voorhees of New Mexico Epidemiology said it would be "unethical" for The Journal to publish speculation about L-Tryptophan's connection to the three northern New Mexico cases.

Now, as reported cases continue to flood in from around the country, federal investigators continue to search for the explanation of the EMS–L-Tryptophan connection.

Despite the new name bestowed on it this week by the disease center, the syndrome may not be a new disease, say some doctors.

"From what I'm hearing around the country, there is some evidence coming in that this has been going on for a number of years—that other doctors had a few cases but could not find any common factors," said Dr. Millicent Eidson, an environmental epidemiologist with the New Mexico Health and Environment Department. "I've even heard of doctors that noted their patients were on L-Tryptophan but didn't think further of it. I think that probably happens a lot where someone thinks 'this probably isn't anything,' " she said.

"I wouldn't be surprised with this syndrome if there's a milder form of it, too, that's been around as long as the serious form. But we don't know how to define it," Eidson said.

Many doctors, especially in New Mexico, have agreed that it was pure chance that EMS was uncovered at this time, in this state—chance that three women within 30 miles should come down with the syndrome within weeks of each other; chance that two of them should go to the same rheumatologist.

"The press is why all of these cases have come to be so fast," Blevins said. "If it had not been printed in an article, hundreds of thousands of physicians wouldn't have read it."

And, he added, "If it would have gotten published in medical literature, it would have taken weeks and months.

"I think it was just very fortunate or chance or, who knows, maybe it was very spiritual that this all happened in the Santa Fe area. That for people's lives of suffering, there's a solution, an answer. People can get better."

Meanwhile, Blevins and Hertzman contacted Dr. Gerald Gleich, chairman of the department of immunology at the Mayo Medical School, Clinic and Foundation in Rochester, Minn. Gleich is a recognized authority on eosinophilia.

Gleich was interested immediately in the two cases. But it took a third New Mexico case—a Santa Fe woman in her 30s who also had used L-Tryptophan—to convince him that the tryptophan connection was no coincidence.

"Once is chance, twice is kind of interesting but three I say full speed ahead," said Gleich, who set the wheels in motion for what soon became a nationwide investigation.

First he notified the New Mexico Office of Epidemiology. Then he called the federal Centers for Disease Control in Atlanta, where doctors assured him they would contact the FDA to begin investigating L-Tryptophan.

RELAPSE A GRIM SPECTER IN L-TRYPTOPHAN PUZZLE

MONDAY, DECEMBER 11, 1989

BY TAMAR STIEBER

SANTA FE—Just a few months ago, Kathy King was playing in tennis tournaments, sailboarding, water skiing and running. Today, the 39-year-old Santa Fe woman is elated just to toss a Frisbee.

King, a graphic designer, spent a month in St. Vincent Hospital hovering between life and death. She was the first known victim of a nationwide outbreak of a rare and sometimes fatal blood disorder called eosinophilia myalgia syndrome (EMS).

Now King is home with her 6-year-old son and cherishing every day she's alive. She is relieved to know the cause of the mysterious condition that inflicted excruciating muscle pain upon her and at least 740 other people nationwide, including 22 New Mexicans. Many victims had to be hospitalized, and several died.

A 58-year-old woman from New York died from EMS—a rare blood disorder characterized by dangerously high levels of white blood cells called eosinophils—after it left her a paraplegic. Medical investigators are looking into three more deaths, including one in Minnesota and another in Oregon.

But the collective sigh of relief may have been premature after New Mexico doctors discovered a dietary supplement called L-Tryptophan was the probable cause of EMS. Many doctors are reporting their patients are having relapses long after they've stopped taking L-Tryptophan.

"That's what I was expecting," said King, who consented to an interview on condition her real name would not be used. But King has been lucky. Her condition has continued to improve.

□ □ □

King began taking L-Tryptophan in July for insomnia on the recommendation of a doctor. L-Tryptophan is the usable form of one of 20 naturally occurring essential amino acids that are the building blocks of proteins. The supplement, widely available for at least a decade in health food and drug stores, has been touted for years as an effective and safe treatment for insomnia, premenstrual syndrome and stress. The U.S. Food and Drug Administration sought a recall of L-Tryptophan Nov. 17.

"I'm not fooling myself about this. I was thinking there is probably a very good possibility I and other people may relapse," said King.

Not long after she started taking L-Tryptophan, King began to have mild, then debilitating muscle pain with accompanying soreness of her jaw, head and flesh. She wound up in the hospital with 38 pounds of extra fluid that prevented her lungs from expanding. The fluid spread to her stomach and into her lungs, and her liver was not functioning properly. By November, she had lost 30 percent of her muscle mass.

At the onset of her illness, doctors prescribed high doses—up to 90 milligrams—of a steroid called prednisone, which has helped bring eosinophil levels in the majority of EMS cases to near zero. King is down to 15 milligrams, has an almost normal eosinophil count. A normal count is between zero and 500, while some EMS patients have had counts up to 12,000. King also has regained some of her muscle strength—at least enough to flick her wrist for a Frisbee toss.

But she is discouraged by stories like that of Judy Kody Paulsen, a 38-year-old Albuquerque contact lens fitter who has EMS. Paulsen had been taking 80 milligrams of prednisone and suffered many of the medication's classic side effects—hot flashes, nervousness, moodiness, insomnia.

"It's the worst stuff I can possibly think of," said Paulsen, who stopped taking the steroid Nov. 27 on the advice of her doctor. Within days, she began to re-experience many of the symptoms she thought were gone. The muscle pain and weakness, the elevated eosinophil count that sent her to the Mayo Clinic in Rochester, Minn., last month to find out what she had—all returned with a vengeance.

Paulson first learned the cause of her symptoms in the Salt Lake City airport, on her way to the Mayo Clinic. She read in The Journal, which she had carried with her from Albuquerque, that at least two other women in New Mexico had similar symptoms that were probably related to L-Tryptophan. She had been taking the supplement since the middle of last year for premenstrual syndrome.

Relapse has tempered her initial euphoria at discovering the cause of her illness.

"This is so discouraging," Paulsen said last week, a day after she started a new daily regimen of 15 milligrams of prednisone. "I'm not looking forward to getting back on it. It makes me crazy."

But even with her relapse, Paulsen said she feels fortunate to have suffered a relatively mild case of EMS compared to King, for example, or to Joy Hunter, a 51-year-old Gallup woman who has been on morphine for a month-and-a-half for the pain caused by EMS.

"When I'm not on morphine, I roll on the bed. I burn with the sensations in my muscles. It feels like I've been burned and the burn is continuing," said Hunter, a registered nurse. "I can't tolerate this pain."

Only her strong faith in God and her belief that taking a life—even her own—is murder have kept Hunter from considering suicide. "I'm thinking (others) may think of doing something drastically physical to themselves."

Hunter started taking L-Tryptophan in July for symptoms similar to PMS, even though she already had gone through menopause. By late August or early September, she started feeling weak and achy. On Oct. 31, she was taken to Presbyterian Hospital in Albuquerque and put on a morphine drip almost immediately, along with high dosages of prednisone to lower her eosinophil count.

Since she left the hospital Nov. 18, Hunter's doctors cut her prednisone dosage from 100 milligrams to 20 milligrams. But, like Paulsen, she is feeling new pain in her muscles. "What do we do about it? Who really knows for sure?" said Hunter.

□ □ □

Dr. Gerald Gleich, head of the immunology department at the Mayo Medical School, Clinic and Foundation and an acknowledged authority on eosinophilia, agrees no one knows for sure the course of the disease, the best way to treat it or even why L-Tryptophan seems to stimulate the production of large numbers of eosinophils.

Gleich described eosinophils as "street people" that camp out on different tissues in the body—usually muscle, but also sometimes the nerves, fascia (the tissue surrounding the muscles) or the skin. The eosinophils deposit a residue of toxins on the tissue.

The resulting tissue damage may be permanent in some cases, said Gleich's colleague at the Mayo Clinic, Dr. Joseph Duffy, a rheumatologist who is also an expert on eosinophilia.

Duffy, who has been consulting on Paulsen's case, described a woman he examined Friday morning with body tissues that were "rock hard."

"It's hard to be certain she has any areas of normal skin. Her legs are like wood, her arms are like wood," Duffy said. "I've seen other people with this extent of muscle damage. How reversible it is, we don't know."

The woman had been taking L-Tryptophan since January and only stopped it last month. He has also seen cases where people who showed no adverse symptoms stopped taking L-Tryptophan and developed symptoms two weeks later.

Therefore, Duffy said, he is neither surprised nor alarmed that EMS patients are suffering relapses after reducing or eliminating the medication. In fact, he said, "Given the severity of the illness in some people, I would be amazed if it shut off in one month.

"People who are distressed by that I think are naive. Things don't turn around that fast."

Dr. Henry Falk, director of the environmental hazards division of the federal Centers for Disease Control in Atlanta, said he's only heard "anecdotally" that EMS patients have been having relapses after going off the steroid. Like Duffy, he is not surprised.

"We have been assuming from the beginning this is not something that goes away immediately when you stop taking L-Tryptophan," Falk said, referring to the CDC, the FDA and various other state and federal agencies that have been investigating the outbreak. "It's an ongoing problem for many patients. And it's the ongoing nature of this disease."

Duffy suggested several theories for relapses, including the possibility the body may never get rid of whatever is stimulating the production of eosinophils, or the body may be slow in flushing it out.

Or, he said, EMS symptoms may resurface when the prednisone— which acts as an eosinophil repressor—is withdrawn before tissue is fully healed. He also said if the eosinophilia-causing agent is still present when prednisone treatment is stopped, it may reactivate the syndrome.

Duffy pointed out that last year he cared for a patient who had had EMS symptoms since 1986. He only found out a few weeks ago she had been taking L-Tryptophan. Duffy said he didn't know how many other EMS cases might have existed before the national outbreak in November—or how many of them might be related to L-Tryptophan.

"I suspect maybe this is an iceberg of cases that is just beginning to surface," he said.

NOT A DROP TO DRINK

WASHINGTON (N.C.) DAILY NEWS

Betty Gray, 36, has worked as a reporter for the *Washington Daily News* for one year. Before that she owned a family insurance agency, a business she operated for 12 years. She is a native of Washington, N.C.

Mike Voss, 35, joined the *Daily News* in 1986 and is now the senior reporter at the paper. Besides his reporting duties at the *Daily News*, he has authored several plays and is editor of the weekly *West Craven Highlights*.

William J. Coughlin, 68, initiated, directed and edited the paper's coverage of the city's contaminated water supply. Before joining the paper 10 years ago as executive editor, he was a foreign correspondent, based in New Delhi, Saigon and Beirut, for the *Los Angeles Times*. He also served as Moscow and London bureau chief for *McGraw-Hill World News*.

THE BLOOD BROKERS

THE PHILADELPHIA INQUIRER

Gilbert M. Gaul, 38, has been writing about medical economics for *The Philadelphia Inquirer* since 1983. He previously worked as a reporter for the *Pottsville (Pa.) Republican*, *The Philadelphia Bulletin* and the *Lehighton* (Pa.) *Times-News.* In 1979, he was awarded the Pulitzer Prize for his reporting on how a group of businessmen with ties to organized crime bankrupted the Blue Coal Corporation.

EARTHQUAKE!
SAN JOSE MERCURY NEWS

San Jose Mercury News Staff.

ARSON FOR PROFIT
MINNEAPOLIS—ST. PAUL STAR TRIBUNE

Lou Kilzer, 39, joined the *Star Tribune* in 1987 as a special projects reporter. In 1986, his reporting about missing children for *The Denver Post* helped that paper win a Pulitzer Prize. He also worked as a reporter for the *Rocky Mountain News* in Denver and as editor of the *Triangle Review* in Fort Collins, Colorado, before coming to the *Star Tribune.*

Chris Ison, 32, was hired by the *Star Tribune* in 1986 as a St. Paul city government reporter. He spent the last year and a half working on the special project that centered on arson in St. Paul. Before joining the *Star Tribune* staff, Ison worked as a reporter for the *Duluth* (Minn.) *News-Tribune.*

TOM TOLES'S OUTRAGE

THE BUFFALO NEWS

Tom Toles, 38, a self-taught artist, has been *The Buffalo News*'s editorial cartoonist since 1982. That same year, he signed a contract with the Universal Press Syndicate, which distributes his work to 150 newspapers. He previously worked as an artist, graphics/design director, and editorial cartoonist for the *Buffalo Courier-Express*. He was a Pulitzer Prize finalist in 1985.

THE *EXXON VALDEZ* OIL SLICK

THE SEATTLE TIMES

Ross Anderson, 42, is chief political reporter for *The Seattle Times*. During 18 years with the paper, he has also served as Washington, D.C., correspondent, Sunday magazine staff writer and assistant city editor. He is currently on leave to write a book about Alaskan fishermen and the *Exxon Valdez* oil spill.

Bill Dietrich, 38, joined *The Times* in 1982 and has covered the environmental beat since returning from a Nieman fellowship at Harvard University in 1988. He previously worked at several Washington State newspapers, and he was the Washington, D.C., correspondent for the Gannett News Service.

Mary Ann Gwinn, 38, has worked for *The Times* for seven years, first as an environmental and news feature reporter and most recently as a feature writer for the Sunday magazine. Before joining *The Times*, she worked as a reporter and feature writer for the *Columbia* (Mo.) *Daily Tribune*.

Eric Nalder, 43, has been the chief investigative reporter for *The Times* since 1983. Before that he worked for more than seven years at the *Seattle Post-Intelligencer* as well as doing stints at the *Everett Herald* and at several weekly newspapers in Washington State. His articles for *The Times* have included an investigation of nuclear weapons plants operated by the U.S. Department of Energy.

TIANANMEN SQUARE

T H E   N E W   Y O R K   T I M E S

Nicholas D. Kristof, 30, became Beijing bureau chief for *The New York Times* in 1988. He joined the paper in 1984 as a financial reporter-trainee. He was made a domestic correspondent in Los Angeles in 1985 and a year later assigned to Hong Kong, where he worked as a correspondent until he was detached from his reporting duties to study Mandarin in Taiwan. He is married to Sheryl Wu-Dunn, with whom he shared the Pulitzer Prize.

Sheryl WuDunn, 30, has been writing from Beijing for *The Times* since March 1989. She previously has reported from Hong Kong for Reuters News Agency and the *South China Morning Post*. She also worked as a summer intern reporter at *The Wall Street Journal* and at the *Miami Herald*.

DESTRUCTION ALONG THE FAULT LINE

THE (OAKLAND) TRIBUNE

The (Oakland) *Tribune* Staff.

FACES OF DEMOCRATIC CHANGE

DETROIT FREE PRESS

David C. Turnley, 34, joined the *Detroit Free Press* in 1980. He is currently based in Paris. He has filed photographs for the *Free Press* from the Soviet Union, Africa, India, the Middle East, Europe and Asia. His photographs are distributed by the Black Star photo agency.

AMERICA'S ENDANGERED FARMLAND

THE POTTSTOWN (PA.) MERCURY

Thomas J. Hylton, 42, joined *The Pottstown* (Pa.) *Mercury* 19 years ago as a writer, and in 1986 he was named editorial editor. Besides his editorial duties, he has also been active in establishing nonprofit organizations that restore old buildings and plant and maintain trees in Pottstown. He has contributed articles to *The New York Times* and *The Washington Post*.

THE SOCIAL PROMISE OF ARCHITECTURE

SAN FRANCISCO CHRONICLE

Allan Temko, 66, architecture critic for the *San Francisco Chronicle*, joined the paper in 1961. Aside from his columns, he has written numerous books and has lectured about architecture at several universities. He is also an active participant in local and national environmental politics.

MURRAY'S LAWS OF SPORTS (AND LIFE)

LOS ANGELES TIMES

Jim Murray, 70, has been a sports columnist at the *Los Angeles Times* for 29 years. He began his journalism career in 1943 as a general assignment, police and federal beat reporter at the *New Haven Register*. A year later he moved to the *Los Angeles Examiner*. In 1948, he was hired by *Time* magazine as a Los Angeles correspondent. From 1959 until 1961, Murray was West Coast editor of *Sports Illustrated*, which he helped found. His writings have been collected in several books.

THE TRIUMPH OF ADAM AND MEGAN WALTER

COLORADO SPRINGS GAZETTE TELEGRAPH

Dave Curtin, 34, has been a police and general assignment reporter for the *Colorado Springs Gazette Telegraph* for two years. Before joining the paper, he worked in a variety of beats for the *Boulder Camera*, the *Greeley Tribune* and the *Durango Herald*, all in Colorado.

THE MAN FROM WALL STREET

THE WASHINGTON POST

Steve Coll, 31, was hired by *The Washington Post* as a staff writer in 1985. He served as New York financial correspondent for *The Post* from 1987 to 1989 and is currently a correspondent in India. Before joining *The Post,* he was a contributing editor for *California Magazine* and also wrote for other publications. He and David A. Vise are collaborating on a book about the S.E.C.

David A. Vise, 29, joined *The Washington Post* business staff in 1984. He specializes in Wall Street, the Securities and Exchange Commission and related matters. He received a master's degree in business administration from the Wharton School at the University of Pennsylvania and worked as an investment banker in the merger department at Goldman, Sachs & Company. He also previously worked as an intern reporter at *The Tennessean* in Nashville.

L-TRYPTOPHAN—A MEDICAL PUZZLE

THE ALBUQUERQUE JOURNAL

Tamar Stieber, 34, joined *The Albuquerque Journal* in May 1989 and was assigned to the Santa Fe bureau as a general assignment, special projects, medical and arts reporter. She previously covered the sheriff's department, medicine and the arts for the *Sonoma Index-Tribune* in northern California and was city hall reporter for the *Vallejo* (Calif.) *Times-Herald*.

ABOUT THE EDITOR

Kendall J. Wills is a free-lance journalist. A native of Milwaukee, he was previously assistant editor of the Op-Ed page of *The New York Times*. Mr. Wills earned a bachelor's degree at Columbia College and a master's degree from the School of International and Public Affairs at Columbia University.

"A Deathly Call of the Wild," by Mary Ann Gwinn, April 4, 1989. Reprinted with permission of *The Seattle Times*.

"Lessons Learned," by Bill Dietrich, September 24, 1989. Reprinted with permission of *The Seattle Times*.

Introductory essay on international reporting by Nicholas D. Kristof and Sheryl Wu-Dunn. Reprinted with permission of Nicholas D. Kristof and Sheryl WuDunn.

"Privately, More and More Chinese Say It's Past Time for Deng to Go," by Nicholas D. Kristof, April 17, 1989. Reprinted with permission of *The New York Times*.

"Biggest Beijing Crowds So Far Keep Troops from City Center; Party Reported in Bitter Fight," by Nicholas D. Kristof, May 21, 1989. Reprinted with permission of *The New York Times*.

"Facing the People, the Soldiers Fall Back," by Sheryl WuDunn, May 21, 1989. Reprinted with permission of *The New York Times*.

"Tide Turns Toward Chinese Hard-Liner," by Nicholas D. Kristof, May 26, 1989. Reprinted with permission of *The New York Times*.

"Troops Attack and Crush Beijing Protest; Thousands Fight Back, Scores Are Killed," by Nicholas D. Kristof, June 4, 1989. Reprinted with permission of *The New York Times*.

"In the Streets, Anguish, Fury and Tears," by Sheryl WuDunn, June 4, 1989. Reprinted with permission of *The New York Times*.

"Beijing Death Toll at Least 300; Army Tightens Control of City but Angry Resistance Goes On," by Nicholas D. Kristof, June 5, 1989. Reprinted with permission of *The New York Times*.

Introductory essay on spot news photography by Leroy Aarons and Tom Faupl. Reprinted with permission of *The* (Oakland) *Tribune*.

Eleven photographs by the photography staff of *The* (Oakland) *Tribune* reprinted with permission of *The* (Oakland) *Tribune*.

Pulitzer Prize nominating letter by Heath J. Meriwether, Executive Editor of the *Detroit Free Press*. Reprinted with permission of the *Detroit Free Press*.

Thirteen photographs by David C. Turnley in the *Detroit Free Press*. Reprinted with permission of the *Detroit Free Press*.

Introductory essay on editorial writing by Thomas J. Hylton. Reprinted with permission of Thomas J. Hylton.

"Bond Issue Is Essential to Protect Chester County's Future," by Thomas J. Hylton, October 23, 1989. Reprinted with permission of *The Pottstown* (Pa.) *Mercury*.

"Rampant Development May Doom Chester County's Farm Industry," by Thomas J. Hylton, October 23, 1989. Reprinted with permission of *The Pottstown Mercury*.

"Sprawling Growth Will Erode Chester County's Quality of Life," by Thomas J. Hylton, October 24, 1989. Reprinted with permission of *The Pottstown Mercury*.

"Suburbia Pays a Heavy Price for Neglecting Philadelphia," by Thomas J. Hylton, October 25, 1989. Reprinted with permission of *The Pottstown Mercury*.

"Southeast Pennsylvania Must Make Better Use of Its Land," by Thomas J. Hylton, October 26, 1989. Reprinted with permission of *The Pottstown Mercury*.

"Bond Issue Will Preserve Farmland and Open Space," by Thomas J. Hylton, October 27, 1989. Reprinted with permission of *The Pottstown Mercury*.

"Benefits of Open Space Bond Issue Far Outweigh Its Cost," by Thomas J. Hylton, October 28, 1989. Reprinted with permission of *The Pottstown Mercury*.

Introductory essay on medical reporting by Tamar Stieber. Reprinted with permission of Tamar Stieber.

"Three N.M. Women Contract Unusual Medical Syndrome," by Tamar Stieber, November 7, 1989. Reprinted with permission of *The Albuquerque Journal*.

"Illness Struck 'Healthiest Woman'," by Tamar Stieber, November 9, 1989. Reprinted with permission of *The Albuquerque Journal*.

"Other States Reporting Rare Syndrome Cases," by Tamar Stieber, November 10, 1989. Reprinted with permission of *The Albuquerque Journal*.

"N.M. Bans Sale or Display of L-Tryptophan," by Tamar Stieber, November 14, 1989. Reprinted with permission of *The Albuquerque Journal*.

"FDA Asks Recall of L-Tryptophan," by Tamar Stieber, November 18, 1989. Reprinted with permission of *The Albuquerque Journal*.

"Making the Connection," by Tamar Stieber, November 19, 1989. Reprinted with permission of *The Albuquerque Journal*.

"Relapse a Grim Specter in L-Tryptophan Puzzle," by Tamar Stieber, December 11, 1989. Reprinted with permission of *The Albuquerque Journal*.